Reinsurance Principles and Practices

Reinsurance Principles and Practices

Connor M. Harrison, CPCU, ARe, AU
Director of Curriculum
American Institute for CPCU/Insurance Institute of America

First Edition • Fourth Printing

American Institute for Chartered Property Casualty
Underwriters/Insurance Institute of America
720 Providence Road, Suite 100
Malvern, Pennsylvania 19355-3433

© 2004
American Institute for Chartered Property Casualty Underwriters/Insurance Institute of America

All rights reserved. This book or any part thereof may not be reproduced without the written permission of the copyright holder.

Unless otherwise apparent, examples used in AICPCU/IIA materials related to this course are based on hypothetical situations and are for educational purposes only. The characters, persons, products, services, and organizations described in these examples are fictional. Any similarity or resemblance to any other character, person, product, services, or organization is merely coincidental. AICPCU/IIA is not responsible for such coincidental or accidental resemblances.

This material may contain Internet Web site links external to AICPCU/IIA. AICPCU/IIA neither approves nor endorses any information, products, or services to which any external Web sites refer. Nor does AICPCU/IIA control these Web sites' content or the procedures for Web site content development.

AICPCU/IIA specifically disclaims any implied warranties of merchantability or fitness for a particular purpose. No warranty may be created or extended by sales representatives or written sales materials.

AICPCU/IIA materials related to this course are provided with the understanding that AICPCU/IIA is not engaged in rendering legal, accounting, or other professional service. Nor is AICPCU/IIA explicitly or implicitly stating that any of the processes, procedures, or policies described in the materials are the only appropriate ones to use. The advice and strategies contained herein may not be suitable for every situation.

Information which is copyrighted by and proprietary to Insurance Services Office, Inc. ("ISO Material") is included in this publication. Use of the ISO Material is limited to ISO Participating Insurers and their Authorized Representatives. Use by ISO Participating Insurers is limited to use in those jurisdictions for which the insurer has an appropriate participation with ISO. Use of the ISO Material by Authorized Representatives is limited to use solely on behalf of one or more ISO Participating Insurers.

First Edition • Fourth Printing • July 2007

Library of Congress Control Number: 2004108467
ISBN 978-0-89463-179-5

Foreword

The American Institute for Chartered Property Casualty Underwriters and the Insurance Institute of America (the Institutes) are independent, not-for-profit organizations committed to expanding the knowledge of professionals in risk management, insurance, financial services, and related fields through education and research.

In accordance with our belief that professionalism is grounded in education, experience, and ethical behavior, the Institutes provide a wide range of educational programs designed to meet the needs of individuals working in risk management and property-casualty insurance The American Institute offers the Chartered Property Casualty Underwriter (CPCU®) professional designation, designed to provide a broad understanding of the property-casualty insurance industry. CPCU students may select either a commercial or a personal risk management and insurance focus, depending on their professional needs.

The Insurance Institute of America (IIA) offers designations and certificate programs in a variety of disciplines, including the following:

- Claims
- Commercial underwriting
- Fidelity and surety bonding
- General insurance
- Insurance accounting and finance
- Insurance information technology
- Insurance production and agency management
- Insurance regulation and compliance
- Management
- Marine insurance
- Personal insurance
- Premium auditing
- Quality insurance services
- Reinsurance
- Risk management
- Surplus lines

You may choose to take a single course to fill a knowledge gap, complete a program leading to a designation, or take multiple courses and programs throughout your career. No matter which approach you choose, you will gain practical knowledge and skills that will contribute to your professional growth and enhance your education and qualifications in the expanding insurance market. In addition, many CPCU and IIA courses qualify for credits toward certain associate, bachelor's, and master's degrees at several prestigious colleges and universities, and all CPCU and IIA courses carry college credit recommendations from the American Council on Education.

The American Institute for CPCU was founded in 1942 through a collaborative effort between industry professionals and academics, led by faculty members at The Wharton School of the University of Pennsylvania. In 1953, the American Institute for CPCU merged with the Insurance Institute of America, which was founded in 1909 and which remains the oldest continuously functioning national organization offering educational programs for the property-casualty insurance business.

The Insurance Research Council (IRC), founded in 1977, helps the Institutes fulfill the research aspect of their mission. A division of the Institutes, the IRC is supported by industry members. This not-for-profit research organization examines public policy issues of interest to property-casualty insurers, insurance customers, and the general public. IRC research reports are distributed widely to insurance-related organizations, public policy authorities, and the media.

The Institutes strive to provide current, relevant educational programs in formats and delivery methods that meet the needs of insurance professionals and the organizations that employ them. Institute textbooks are an essential component of the education we provide. Each book is designed to clearly and concisely provide the practical knowledge and skills you need to enhance your job performance and career. The content is developed by the Institutes in collaboration with risk management and insurance professionals and members of the academic community. We welcome comments from our students and course leaders; your feedback helps us continue to improve the quality of our study materials.

Peter L. Miller, CPCU
President and CEO
American Institute for CPCU
Insurance Institute of America

Preface

Reinsurance Principles and Practices provides the reader with a comprehensive overview of reinsurance. It is written for students working toward the AICPCU/IIA's Associate in Reinsurance (ARe) designation.

The contents of *Reinsurance Principles and Practices* can be summarized as follows:

- Chapters 1, 2, and 3 provide an overview of reinsurance by describing reinsurance functions, types of reinsurance transactions, types of reinsurance, and the reinsurance placement process.
- Chapters 4 and 5 describe common clauses used in reinsurance agreements.
- Chapters 6 through 11 provide an in-depth discussion of the types of reinsurance introduced in Chapter 2. These types of reinsurance are quota share, surplus share, property per risk excess of loss, casualty excess of loss, catastrophe reinsurance, and aggregate excess of loss.
- Chapter 12 describes how reinsurers use audits of primary insurers to obtain a fuller understanding of their operations.
- Chapter 13 explains how state insurance regulation applies to and affects reinsurers.
- Chapter 14 provides an overview of the prescribed NAIC Annual Statement while focusing on those elements of an insurer's balance sheet and income statement that are affected by reinsurance transactions.
- Chapter 15 describes the methods that primary insurers and reinsurers use to estimate reserves. Reserves for losses and loss adjustment expense constitute the largest liability on insurers' balance sheets and one that is often underestimated.

Extensive sections from *Reinsurance Principles* and *Reinsurance Practices* were incorporated into this text. We are indebted to the following authors for these materials: Howard N. Anderson, CPCU, ARe, AIM; R. Michael Cass, CPCU, ARe, ARM; Michael W. Elliott, CPCU, ARe, AIAF; Peter R. Kensicki, DBA, CPCU, CLU; Gary S. Patrik, CPCU, FCAS; Robert C. Reinarz; and Bernard L. Webb, CPCU, FCAS, MAAA. Even more so, we are indebted to them because their ideas and contribution to the ARe program have influenced how we think about reinsurance.

Two individuals served as reviewers of the entire text, and their contributions appear throughout the text. The Institutes would like to thank the Transatlantic Reinsurance Company for allowing David T. Stewart, CPCU, ARe, RPLU, to serve as an overall reviewer for this text. David has served as an ARe course leader for the College of Insurance and St. John's University since the Institutes began offering the program. We have tried to incorporate David's rich teaching experience into the text. The Institutes would also like to thank the National Association of Insurance Commissioners for permitting Bryan J. Fuller, CPCU, ARe, to work extensively on this text. Bryan has shared his broad view of regulatory issues as they relate to reinsurance with us.

Many other individuals served as reviewers for selected chapters: Richard A. Banyard, CPCU, ARe; Edwin B. Barber, CPCU, ARe; Robb J. Canning, CPCU, ARe; Richard M. Carris, CPCU, CLU, ARe; George W. DeMenocal, CPCU, ARe; Michael W. Elliott, CPCU, ARe, AIAF; Bruce D. Evans, CPCU, ARe, ARM; Michael P. Holm, CPCU, ARe; Doris L. Hoopes, CPCU, ARe, ASLI; James P. Lynch, FCAS, MAAA; Deborah K. Ropelewski, CPCU, ARe, ARM; Jerome E. Tuttle, FCAS, CPCU, ARe; Paul Walther, CPCU, ARe; Richard G. Waterman, CPCU, ARe; and Earl L. Whitney, FSA.

For more information about the Institutes' programs, please call our Customer Support Department at (800) 644-2101, e-mail us at customersupport@cpcuiia.org, or visit our Web site at www.aicpcu.org.

Connor M. Harrison

Contents

1 Introduction to Reinsurance — 1.1
Reinsurance Defined — 1.3
Reinsurance Functions — 1.4
Reinsurance Transactions — 1.9
Reinsurance Sources — 1.13
Reinsurance Professional and Trade Associations — 1.15
Summary — 1.16

2 Types of Reinsurance and Reinsurance Program Design — 2.1
Pro Rata Reinsurance — 2.3
Excess of Loss Reinsurance — 2.10
Finite Risk Reinsurance — 2.20
Reinsurance Program Design — 2.21
Summary — 2.30

3 The Reinsurance Placement Process — 3.1
Reinsurance Marketing Systems — 3.3
Reinsurance Placement Process — 3.4
Reinsurance Placement Illustrations — 3.8
Summary — 3.19
Appendix — 3.21

4 Common Reinsurance Treaty Clauses, Part I — 4.1
Clauses Common to Most Reinsurance Treaties — 4.3
Interests and Liabilities Agreement — 4.27
Summary — 4.29

5 Common Reinsurance Treaty Clauses, Part II — 5.1
Other Common Treaty Clauses — 5.3
Ancillary Agreements — 5.16
Summary — 5.20

6 Quota Share Treaties — 6.1
Overview of Quota Share Treaties — 6.3
Common Clauses Modified for Use in Quota Share Treaties — 6.11
Clauses Designed or Adapted for Quota Share Treaties — 6.16
Quota Share Treaty Pricing — 6.22
Quota Share Profit-Sharing Ceding Commission Determination — 6.24
Quota Share Treaty Evaluation — 6.29
Summary — 6.31

7 Surplus Share Treaties — 7.1
Overview of Surplus Share Treaties — 7.3
Common Clauses Modified for Use in Surplus Share Treaties — 7.11
Clauses Designed or Adapted for Surplus Share Treaties — 7.18
Surplus Share Treaty Pricing — 7.22
Summary — 7.27

8 Property Per Risk Excess of Loss Treaties — 8.1
Overview of Property Per Risk Excess of Loss Treaties — 8.3
Clauses Designed or Adapted for Property Per Risk Excess of Loss Treaties — 8.6
Property Per Risk Excess of Loss Treaty Pricing — 8.16
Summary — 8.31

9 Casualty Excess of Loss Treaties 9.1
Overview of Casualty Excess of Loss Treaties 9.3
Common Clauses Modified for Use in Casualty Excess of Loss Treaties 9.5
Clauses Designed or Adapted for Casualty Excess of Loss Treaties 9.10
Casualty Excess of Loss Treaty Pricing 9.19
Summary 9.31

10 Catastrophe Reinsurance 10.1
Overview of Catastrophe Treaties 10.3
Clauses Designed or Adapted for Catastrophe Treaties 10.7
Catastrophe Modeling 10.15
Catastrophe Treaty Pricing 10.23
Alternatives to Traditional Catastrophe Reinsurance 10.30
Summary 10.31

11 Aggregate Excess of Loss Treaties 11.1
Overview of Aggregate Excess of Loss Treaties 11.3
Aggregate Excess of Loss Treaty Pricing 11.11
Summary 11.13

12 Reinsurance Audits 12.1
Overview of Reinsurance Audits 12.3
Authority to Conduct Audits 12.4
The Reinsurance Audit Process 12.4
Types of Reinsurance Audits 12.8
Managing General Agent Audits 12.15
Summary 12.17

13 Reinsurance Regulation 13.1
State Insurance Regulation 13.3
National Association of Insurance Commissioners (NAIC) 13.6
Regulatory Concerns About the Use of Reinsurance 13.10
Summary 13.19

14 Reinsurance Aspects of the NAIC Annual Statement 14.1
Balance Sheet With Supporting Exhibits and Schedules 14.3
Underwriting and Investment Exhibit 14.10
Schedule F 14.18
Schedule P 14.32
Summary 14.35

15 Reserves 15.1
Loss and Loss Adjustment Expense Reserves 15.3
Methods for Establishing Reserves 15.8
Salvage and Subrogation 15.23
Reserving Methods for Excess of Loss Reinsurers 15.24
Summary 15.27

Index 1

Chapter 1

Direct Your Learning

Introduction to Reinsurance

After learning the content of this chapter, you should be able to:

- Describe reinsurance and its six principal functions.
- Describe treaty reinsurance and facultative reinsurance.
- Describe the three sources of reinsurance.

OUTLINE

Reinsurance Defined

Reinsurance Functions

Reinsurance Transactions

Reinsurance Sources

Reinsurance Professional and Trade Associations

Summary

Develop Your Perspective

What are the main topics covered in the chapter?

Reinsurance is a means through which insurers can achieve their operational and financial objectives. This chapter describes the functions of reinsurance, types of reinsurance transactions, and reinsurance sources.

Identify why a primary insurer may want or need reinsurance.

- How could reinsurance address a primary insurer's needs?
- What are the types of reinsurance transactions?
- From which sources may a primary insurer purchase reinsurance?

Why is it important to learn about these topics?

This information provides you with the foundation you need to understand the significant role reinsurance performs in enabling an insurer to achieve its objectives.

Consider how reinsurance enables a primary insurer to achieve its business objectives.

- How could reinsurance help the primary insurer to stabilize its loss results?
- How could reinsurance help the primary insurer to avoid the financial consequences of a catastrophe loss?

How can you use what you will learn?

Review the objectives your company is trying achieve through its reinsurance agreements.

- Are your company's objectives being met through its reinsurance agreements?
- What sources of reinsurance does your company use to purchase reinsurance?

Chapter 1
Introduction to Reinsurance

How can a single insurer sell a $100 million commercial property policy and a $100 million commercial umbrella liability policy to the owners of a high-rise office building without the insurer jeopardizing its financial stability? How are insurers able to provide billions of dollars of property insurance in wind-prone Florida and earthquake-prone California? No insurer wants to place itself in a situation in which one fire, accident, or storm could wipe out its net worth. Additionally, no insurance regulator wants to allow an insurer to put itself in such a position. One method insurers use to protect themselves from the financial consequences of insuring others is reinsurance.

This chapter introduces reinsurance principles that are used throughout this text. The topics discussed in this chapter include reinsurance functions, reinsurance transactions, and reinsurance sources.

REINSURANCE DEFINED

Reinsurance is the transfer of insurance risk from one insurer to another through a contractual agreement under which one insurer (the **reinsurer**) agrees, in return for a **reinsurance premium**, to indemnify another insurer (the **primary insurer**) for some or all of the financial consequences of certain loss exposures covered by the primary insurer's policies.[1] Reinsurance is commonly referred to as "insurance for insurers."

This text uses the term primary insurer. However, the primary insurer may also be referred to as the ceding company, the cedent, the reinsured, or the direct insurer. An insurer can also be both a primary insurer and a reinsurer.

Insurance risk is uncertainty about the adequacy of insurance premiums to pay losses. The reinsurer typically does not assume all of the primary insurer's insurance risk. The reinsurance agreement usually requires the primary insurer to keep part of its original liability. The amount of insurance risk the primary insurer retains is called its **retention**. The retention can be expressed as a percentage of the original amount of insurance or as a dollar amount of loss. The reinsurance agreement does not alter the terms of the underlying (original) insurance policies or the primary insurer's obligations to honor them.

Reinsurance
The transfer of insurance risk from one insurer to another through a contractual agreement under which one insurer (the reinsurer) agrees, in return for a reinsurance premium, to indemnify another insurer (the primary insurer) for some or all of the financial consequences of certain loss exposures covered by the primary insurer's policies.

Reinsurer
The insurer that assumes all or part of the insurance risk from the primary insurer.

Reinsurance premium
The consideration paid by the primary insurer to the reinsurer for assuming some or all of the primary insurer's insurance risk.

Primary insurer
The insurer that transfers or cedes all or part of the insurance risk it has assumed to another insurer.

Insurance risk
Uncertainty about the adequacy of insurance premiums to pay losses.

Retention
The amount of insurance risk the primary insurer retains and that is not ceded to the reinsurer.

> **Risk**
>
> The Insurance Institute of America typically defines "risk" as uncertainty about the occurrence of a loss. However, risk has several other meanings that are useful in understanding reinsurance practices. In reinsurance, the term risk often refers to the subject of insurance, such as a building, a policy, a group of policies, or a class of business. Reinsurance practitioners use the term risk in this way and include it in common reinsurance clauses.

The reinsurance agreement specifies the terms under which the reinsurance is provided. For example, the reinsurance agreement may state that the reinsurer must pay a percentage of all the primary insurer's losses for loss exposures subject to the agreement or must reimburse the primary insurer for losses that exceed a specified amount. Additionally, the reinsurance agreement identifies the policy, group of policies, or other categories of insurance that are included in the agreement.

Reinsurers may transfer part of the liability they have accepted in reinsurance agreements to other reinsurers. Such an agreement is called a retrocession. Under a **retrocession**, one reinsurer (the **retrocedent**) transfers all or part of the reinsurance risk that it has assumed or will assume to another reinsurer (the **retrocessionaire**).

Retrocession is very similar to reinsurance except for the parties involved in the agreement. This text discusses reinsurance in the context of a primary insurer-reinsurer relationship, but this discussion applies equally to retrocessions.

Retrocession
A reinsurance agreement whereby one reinsurer (the retrocedent) transfers all or part of the reinsurance risk it has assumed or will assume to another reinsurer (the retrocessionaire).

Retrocedent
The reinsurer that transfers or cedes all or part of the insurance risk it has assumed to another reinsurer.

Retrocessionaire
The reinsurer that assumes all or part of the reinsurance risk accepted by another reinsurer.

REINSURANCE FUNCTIONS

Reinsurance performs six principal functions for primary insurers. A primary insurer may use several different reinsurance agreements to achieve these functions. This section discusses each function separately.

> **Six Principal Functions of Reinsurance**
> - Increase large line capacity
> - Provide catastrophe protection
> - Stabilize loss experience
> - Provide surplus relief
> - Facilitate withdrawal from a market segment
> - Provide underwriting guidance

Increase Large Line Capacity

One function of reinsurance is to increase large line capacity. The maximum amount of insurance or limit of liability that an insurer will accept on a single loss exposure is called the insurer's **line**. This line is influenced by the following:

- The maximum amount of insurance or limit of liability allowed by insurance regulations. Insurance regulations prohibit an insurer from retaining (after reinsurance, usually stated as net of reinsurance) more than 10 percent of its policyholders' surplus (net worth) on any one loss exposure.
- The size of a potential loss or losses that can safely be retained without impairing the insurer's earnings or policyholders' surplus.
- The specific characteristics of a particular loss exposure. For example, for some insurers, the line may vary depending on property attributes such as construction, occupancy, loss prevention features, and loss reduction features.
- The amount, types, and cost of available reinsurance.

Large line capacity is an insurer's ability to provide larger amounts of insurance for property loss exposures, or higher limits of liability for liability loss exposures, than it is otherwise willing to provide.

Reinsurers provide primary insurers with large line capacity by accepting liability for loss exposures that the primary insurer is unwilling or unable to retain. This function of reinsurance allows insurers with *limited* large line capacity to participate more fully in the insurance marketplace. For example, a primary insurer may want to compete for homeowner policies in markets in which the value of the homes exceeds the amount the primary insurer feels comfortable retaining. Reinsurance allows the primary insurer to increase its market share while limiting the financial consequences of potential losses.

Line
The maximum amount of insurance or limit of liability that an insurer will accept on a single loss exposure.

Large line capacity
An insurer's ability to provide larger amounts of insurance for property loss exposures, or higher limits of liability for liability loss exposures, than it is otherwise willing to provide.

Provide Catastrophe Protection

A second function of reinsurance is to provide catastrophe protection. Primary insurers use reinsurance to protect themselves from the financial consequences of a single catastrophic event causing multiple losses. Potential catastrophic perils include fire, windstorm (hurricane, tornado, and other wind damage), and earthquakes. Other catastrophes, such as industrial explosions, airplane crashes, or product recalls, could result in significant property and liability losses. Unless appropriate reinsurance is in place, catastrophes could greatly reduce insurer earnings or even threaten insurer solvency. Purchasing reinsurance for catastrophe protection is one way that primary insurers stabilize their loss experience, which is discussed next.

Stabilize Loss Experience

A third function of reinsurance is to stabilize loss experience. Loss experience typically fluctuates from year to year, creating variability in insurer financial results. Volatile loss experience may:

- Affect the stock value of a publicly traded insurer[2]
- Alter an insurer's financial rating by independent rating agencies
- Cause abrupt changes in the approaches taken in managing the underwriting, claim, and marketing departments
- Undermine the confidence of the sales force (especially independent agents who can place their customers with other insurers)
- Possibly lead to insolvency

Therefore, insurers prefer to have stable loss experience, and using reinsurance can help maintain stability. Reinsurance can be arranged to stabilize the loss experience of a type of insurance (for example, commercial auto), a class of business (for example, truckers), or all of the insurance that a primary insurer sells. A primary insurer can stabilize loss experience by obtaining reinsurance to do any, or all, of the following:

- Limit its liability for a single loss exposure
- Limit its liability for several loss exposures affected by a common event
- Limit its liability for loss exposures that aggregate claims over time

Stabilizing loss experience is a major function of reinsurance because it aids financial planning and supports growth. It also may encourage capital investment because investors are more likely to invest in companies with stable financial results. Exhibit 1-1 shows how reinsurance can stabilize a primary insurer's loss experience.

Provide Surplus Relief

Policyholders' surplus
An insurer's net worth as reported on the financial statement prescribed by state insurance regulators.

Net written premiums
Gross premiums charged to policyholders minus premiums paid to reinsurers plus reinsurance premiums assumed.

Capacity ratio
The ratio of net written premiums to policyholders' surplus.

A fourth function of reinsurance is to provide surplus relief. During periods of rapid growth, insurers may struggle to meet the policyholders' surplus requirements imposed by insurance regulators. **Policyholders' surplus** is an insurer's net worth as reported on the financial statement prescribed by state insurance regulators. The value of the policyholders' surplus is the amount by which assets exceed liabilities and it represents the financial resource the primary insurer can draw on to pay unexpected losses. Policyholders' surplus is also called surplus to policyholders or simply surplus. State insurance regulators expect an insurer's ratio of net written premiums to policyholders' surplus not to exceed 3 to 1 ($3 in net written premiums for every $1 in policyholders' surplus).[3] **Net written premiums** are the gross premiums charged to policyholders minus the premiums ceded to reinsurers plus reinsurance premiums assumed. The ratio of net written premiums to policyholders' surplus is called the **capacity ratio** (also called the leverage ratio).

EXHIBIT 1-1

Stabilization of Annual Loss Experience for a Primary Insurer With a $20 Million Retention

(1) Time Period (Year)	(2) Actual Losses ($000)	(3) Amount Reinsured ($000)	(4) Stabilized Loss Level ($000)
1	15,000	—	15,000
2	35,000	15,000	20,000
3	13,000	—	13,000
4	25,000	5,000	20,000
5	40,000	20,000	20,000
6	37,000	17,000	20,000
7	16,500	—	16,500
8	9,250	—	9,250
9	18,000	—	18,000
10	10,750	—	10,750
Total	$219,500	$57,000	$162,500

The total actual losses are $219.5 million, or an average of $21.95 million each time period. If a reinsurance agreement were in place to cap losses to $20 million, the primary insurer's loss experience would be limited to the amounts shown in the stabilized loss level column. The broken line that fluctuates dramatically in the graph below represents actual losses, the dotted line represents stabilized losses, and the horizontal line represents average losses.

Graph of Hypothetical Loss Data

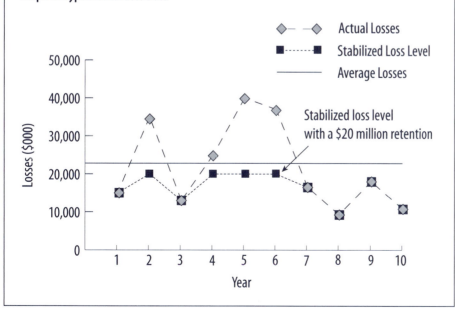

From an insurance regulator's perspective, if an insurer's capacity ratio reaches or exceeds 3 to 1, the insurer is selling more insurance than is prudent relative to the size of its net worth. Although the net written premiums should be sufficient to satisfy those liabilities, they may not be.

Insurers that are growing rapidly may have difficulty maintaining a desirable capacity ratio because of how they must account for their expenses to acquire new policies. State insurance regulation mandates that for accounting purposes, such expenses be recognized at the time a new policy is sold. Aggravating this situation is the requirement that insurers are required to recognize premiums as revenue only as they are earned over the policy's life. Immediately recognizing expenses combined with gradually recognizing revenue causes an insurer's policyholders' surplus to decrease and the capacity ratio to increase.

Some reinsurance agreements facilitate premium growth by allowing the primary insurer to deduct a ceding commission on loss exposures ceded to the reinsurer. The **ceding commission** is an amount paid by the reinsurer to the primary insurer to cover part or all of a primary insurer's policy acquisition expenses. The ceding commission immediately offsets the primary insurer's policy acquisition expenses for the reinsured policies and often includes a profit provision, or an additional commission, if the reinsurance ceded is profitable.

Ceding commission
An amount paid by the reinsurer to the primary insurer to cover part or all of the primary insurer's policy acquisition expenses.

This function of reinsurance is called **surplus relief** because the ceding commission replenishes the primary insurer's policyholders' surplus. Consequently, the surplus relief facilitates the primary insurer's premium growth and the increase in policyholders' surplus lowers its capacity ratio.

Surplus relief
A replenishment of policyholders' surplus provided by the ceding commission paid to the primary insurer by the reinsurer.

Facilitate Withdrawal From a Market Segment

A fifth function of reinsurance is to facilitate withdrawal from a market segment. A market segment may be a particular class of business, a geographic area, or a type of insurance. A primary insurer may want to withdraw from a market segment that is unprofitable, is undesirable, or does not fit into the primary insurer's strategic plan. When withdrawing from a market segment, the primary insurer has the following options:

- Stop selling new insurance policies and continue in-force insurance until all policies expire (often referred to as "run-off").
- Cancel all policies (if insurance regulations permit), and refund the unearned premiums to insureds.
- Withdraw from the market segment by purchasing portfolio reinsurance.

Portfolio reinsurance
A reinsurance agreement that reinsures the loss exposures of an entire type of insurance, class of business, or geographic area.

Portfolio reinsurance reinsures the loss exposures of an entire type of insurance, class of business, or geographic area. Such groupings of loss exposures are often called portfolios. Portfolio reinsurance is a way to facilitate withdrawal from a market segment, and is an exception to the general rule that reinsurers do not accept all of the liability for specified loss exposures of an insurer. In portfolio reinsurance, the reinsurer accepts all of the liability for certain loss exposures covered under the primary insurer's policies. However, the primary insurer must continue to fulfill its obligations to its insureds. For example, the primary insurer may decide to use portfolio reinsurance to withdraw from the errors and omissions insurance market. In this situation, the reinsurer typically agrees to indemnify the primary insurer for all losses incurred as of, and following, the date of the portfolio reinsurance agreement. However, the primary insurer continues to pay claims to (or on behalf of) its insureds who are covered by the underlying insurance.

Portfolio reinsurance can be expensive, particularly if the portfolio has been unprofitable and is expected to incur additional losses for the reinsurer. In many states, portfolio reinsurance must be approved by the state insurance department.

Sometimes a primary insurer wants to completely eliminate the liabilities it has assumed under the insurance policies it has issued. This can be accomplished through a novation. A **novation** is an agreement in which one insurer or reinsurer is substituted for another. A novation is not considered portfolio reinsurance because the substitute insurer assumes the direct obligations to insureds covered by the underlying insurance. Usually, either state insurance regulators' approval or the insured's approval is required to effect a novation.

Novation
An agreement under which one insurer or reinsurer is substituted for another.

Provide Underwriting Guidance

The sixth function of reinsurance is to provide underwriting guidance. Reinsurers work with a wide variety of insurers in many different circumstances. Consequently, reinsurers accumulate a great deal of underwriting expertise. A reinsurer's understanding of insurance operations and the insurance industry can assist other insurers, particularly inexperienced primary insurers entering into new markets and offering new products. For example, one medium-sized insurer reinsured 95 percent of its umbrella liability coverage over a period of years and relied heavily on the reinsurer for technical assistance in underwriting and pricing its policies. Without such technical assistance, certain primary insurers would find it difficult to generate underwriting profits from coverages with which they have limited expertise.

Reinsurers that provide underwriting assistance to primary insurers must respect the confidentiality of their clients' proprietary information. Reinsurers often learn about the primary insurer's marketing and underwriting strategies and should not reveal insurer-specific information to other parties.

REINSURANCE TRANSACTIONS

The two types of reinsurance transactions are treaty and facultative. In **treaty reinsurance**, the agreement covers an entire class or portfolio of loss exposures and provides that the primary insurer's individual loss exposures that fall within the treaty are automatically reinsured. Treaty reinsurance is

Treaty reinsurance
A reinsurance agreement that covers an entire class or portfolio of loss exposures and provides that the primary insurer's individual loss exposures that fall within the treaty are automatically reinsured.

also called obligatory reinsurance. The reinsurance agreement is typically called the treaty.

In **facultative reinsurance**, the reinsurer underwrites each loss exposure separately. The primary insurer chooses which loss exposures to submit to the reinsurer, and the reinsurer can accept or reject any loss exposures submitted. Facultative reinsurance is also called non-obligatory reinsurance. This section discusses each type of reinsurance transaction.

Facultative reinsurance
Reinsurance of individual loss exposures in which the primary insurer chooses which loss exposures to submit to the reinsurer, and the reinsurer can accept or reject any loss exposures submitted.

> **Two Types of Reinsurance Transactions**
> 1. Treaty
> 2. Facultative

Treaty Reinsurance

In treaty reinsurance, the reinsurer agrees in advance to reinsure all the loss exposures that fall within the treaty. Although some treaties allow the reinsurer limited discretion in reinsuring individual loss exposures, most treaties require that all loss exposures within the treaty's terms must be reinsured.

Primary insurers usually use treaty reinsurance as the foundation of their reinsurance programs. Treaty reinsurance provides primary insurers with the certainty needed to formulate underwriting policy and develop underwriting guidelines. Primary insurers work with reinsurance intermediaries (or with reinsurers directly) to develop comprehensive reinsurance programs that address the primary insurers' varied needs. The reinsurance programs that satisfy those needs often include several reinsurance agreements and the participation of several reinsurers.

Treaty reinsurance agreements are tailored to fit the primary insurer's individual requirements. The price and terms of each reinsurance treaty are individually negotiated.

Treaty reinsurance agreements are usually designed to address a primary insurer's need to reinsure many loss exposures over a period of time. Although the reinsurance agreement's term may be for only one year, the relationship between the primary insurer and the reinsurer often spans many years. A primary insurer's management usually finds that a long-term relationship with a reinsurer enables the primary insurer to be able to consistently fulfill its producers' requests to place insurance with them.

Most, but not all, treaty reinsurance agreements *require* the primary insurer to cede all eligible loss exposures to the reinsurer. Primary insurers usually make treaty reinsurance agreements so their underwriters do not have to exercise discretion in using reinsurance. If treaty reinsurance agreements permitted primary insurers to choose which loss exposures they ceded to the reinsurer, the reinsurer would be exposed to adverse selection. **Adverse selection** occurs when the primary insurer decides to reinsure those loss exposures that have an increased probability of loss because the retention of those loss exposures is undesirable.

Because treaty reinsurers are obligated to accept ceded loss exposures once the reinsurance agreement is in place, reinsurers usually want to know about the integrity and experience of the primary insurer's management and the degree to which the primary insurer's published underwriting guidelines represent its actual underwriting practices.

Facultative Reinsurance

In facultative reinsurance, the primary insurer negotiates a separate reinsurance agreement for each loss exposure that it wants to reinsure. The primary insurer is not obligated to purchase reinsurance, and the reinsurer is not obligated to reinsure loss exposures submitted to it. A facultative reinsurance agreement is written for a specified time period and cannot be cancelled by either party unless contractual obligations, such as payment of premiums, are not met.

The reinsurer issues a facultative certificate of insurance that is attached to the primary insurer's copy of the policy being reinsured. The **facultative certificate of reinsurance**, or simply facultative certificate, defines the terms of the facultative reinsurance coverage on a specific loss exposure.

Facultative reinsurance serves the following four functions:

1. Facultative reinsurance can provide large line capacity for loss exposures that exceed the limits of treaty reinsurance agreements.
2. Facultative reinsurance can reduce the primary insurer's exposure in a given geographic area. For example, a marine underwriter may be considering underwriting numerous shiploads of cargo that are stored in the same warehouse and that belong to different insureds. The underwriter could use facultative reinsurance for some of those loss exposures, thereby reducing the primary insurer's overall exposure to loss.
3. Facultative reinsurance can insure a loss exposure with atypical hazard characteristics and thereby maintain the favorable loss experience of the primary insurer's treaty reinsurance and any associated profit-sharing arrangements. Maintaining favorable treaty loss experience is important because the reinsurer has underwritten and priced the treaty with certain expectations. A loss exposure that is inconsistent with the primary insurer's typical portfolio of insurance policies may cause excessive losses and lead to the treaty's termination or a price increase.

   The treaty reinsurer is usually willing for the primary insurer to remove high-hazard loss exposures from the treaty by using facultative reinsurance. These facultative placements of atypical loss exposures also benefit the treaty reinsurer. For example, an insured under a commercial property policy may request coverage for an expensive fine arts collection that

Adverse selection
The decision to reinsure those loss exposures that have an increased probability of loss because the retention of those loss exposures is undesirable.

Facultative certificate of reinsurance
An agreement that defines the terms of the facultative reinsurance coverage on a specific loss exposure.

the primary insurer and its treaty reinsurer would not ordinarily want to cover. Facultative reinsurance of the fine arts collection would eliminate the underwriting concern by removing this loss exposure from the treaty. Often, the treaty reinsurer's own facultative reinsurance department provides this reinsurance. The facultative reinsurer knows that adverse selection occurs in facultative reinsurance. Consequently, the loss exposures submitted for reinsurance are likely to have an increased probability of loss. Therefore, facultative reinsurance is usually priced to reflect the likelihood of adverse selection.

4. Facultative reinsurance can insure particular classes of loss exposures that are excluded under treaty reinsurance.

Primary insurers purchase facultative reinsurance mainly to reinsure loss exposures that they do not typically insure or on exposures with high levels of underwriting risk. Consequently, primary insurers use facultative reinsurance for fewer of their loss exposures than they use treaty insurance. Primary insurers that find they are increasingly using facultative reinsurance may want to review the adequacy of their treaty reinsurance.

The expense of placing facultative reinsurance can be high for both the primary insurer and the reinsurer. In negotiating facultative reinsurance, the primary insurer must provide extensive information about each loss exposure. Consequently, administrative costs are relatively high because the primary insurer must devote a significant amount of time to complete each cession and to notify the reinsurer of any endorsement, loss notice, or policy cancellation. Likewise, the reinsurer must underwrite and price each facultative submission.

Hybrids of Treaty and Facultative Reinsurance

Reinsurers sometimes use hybrid agreements that have elements of both treaty and facultative reinsurance. The hybrid agreements usually describe how individual facultative reinsurance placements will be handled. For example, the agreement may specify the basic underwriting parameters of the loss exposures that will be ceded to the reinsurer as well as premium and loss allocation formulas. Although hybrid agreements may be used infrequently, they demonstrate the flexibility of the reinsurance market to satisfy the mutual needs of primary insurers and reinsurers. The two hybrid agreements briefly described next illustrate common reinsurance agreement variations.

- In a *facultative treaty,* the primary insurer and the reinsurer agree on how subsequent individual facultative submissions will be handled. A facultative treaty could be used when a class of business has insufficient loss exposures to justify treaty reinsurance, but has a sufficient number of loss exposures to determine the details of future individual placements.

- In a *facultative obligatory treaty,* although the primary insurer has the option of ceding loss exposures, the reinsurer is obligated to accept all loss exposures submitted to it. Facultative obligatory treaties are also called *semi-obligatory treaties.*

REINSURANCE SOURCES

Reinsurance can be purchased from three sources: professional reinsurers; reinsurance departments of primary insurers; and reinsurance pools, syndicates, and associations.

> **Three Sources of Reinsurance**
> 1. Professional reinsurers
> 2. Reinsurance departments of primary insurers
> 3. Reinsurance pools, syndicates, and associations

Professional Reinsurers

The first source for reinsurance is through professional reinsurers. A **professional reinsurer** is an insurer whose primary business purpose is serving other insurers' reinsurance needs. As do primary insurers, professional reinsurers interact with other insurers either directly or through intermediaries.

A reinsurer whose employees deal directly with primary insurers is called a **direct writing reinsurer**. These reinsurers do not necessarily obtain all of their business directly from primary insurers. Most direct writing reinsurers in the United States have broadened their marketing system by also soliciting reinsurance business through reinsurance intermediaries.

A **reinsurance intermediary** is a broker who negotiates reinsurance agreements between the primary insurer and one or more reinsurers. Reinsurance intermediaries work with primary insurers to develop reinsurance programs that are then placed with reinsurers. A reinsurance intermediary generally represents the primary insurer and receives a brokerage commission—almost always from the reinsurer—for placing the reinsurance and performing other necessary services. These services may include disbursing reinsurance premiums among participating reinsurers and collecting loss amounts owed to the insurer.

The variety of professional reinsurers leads to differences in how those reinsurers are used and what they can offer. However, the following are some broad generalizations about professional reinsurers.

- Primary insurers dealing with direct writing reinsurers often use fewer reinsurers in their reinsurance program.
- Reinsurance intermediaries often use more than one reinsurer to develop the reinsurance program for a primary insurer.
- Reinsurance intermediaries can often help secure high coverage limits and catastrophe coverage.
- Reinsurance intermediaries usually have access to various reinsurance solutions from both domestic and international markets.

Professional reinsurer
An insurer whose primary business purpose is serving other insurers' reinsurance needs.

Direct writing reinsurer
A professional reinsurer whose employees deal directly with primary insurers.

Reinsurance intermediary
A broker who negotiates reinsurance agreements between the primary insurer and one or more reinsurers.

- Reinsurance intermediaries can usually obtain reinsurance under favorable terms and at a competitive price because they can determine prevailing market conditions and work repeatedly in this market with many primary insurers.

Regardless of their approach to marketing reinsurance, professional reinsurers extensively evaluate the primary insurer before entering into a reinsurance agreement. A treaty reinsurer underwrites the primary insurer as well as the loss exposures being ceded. In evaluating the primary insurer, the reinsurer gathers information about the primary insurer's financial strength by analyzing the primary insurer's financial statements or by using information developed by a financial rating service. Other information about the primary insurer may be obtained from state insurance department bulletins and the trade press. Just as the reinsurer should evaluate the primary insurer, the primary insurer should evaluate the reinsurer's claim paying ability, reputation, and management competence before entering into the reinsurance agreement.

Reinsurers also consider the primary insurer's experience, reputation, and management. The reinsurer relies on the integrity of the primary insurer's management, and a relationship of trust must underlie any reinsurance agreement. Whether it involves a one-time facultative agreement or an ongoing treaty agreement, the relationship between the primary insurer and the reinsurer is considered to be one of "utmost good faith." This is because each party is obligated to and relies on the other for full disclosure of material facts about the subject of the agreement. It would be considered a breach of this duty of utmost good faith if the primary insurer withheld material facts relevant to the reinsurer's underwriting decision, intentionally underestimated prior losses, or failed to disclose hazardous conditions affecting loss exposures.

Reinsurance Departments of Primary Insurers

The second source for reinsurance is through the reinsurance departments of primary insurers. Some primary insurers also serve as reinsurers and provide treaty and facultative reinsurance. A primary insurer's reinsurance operations are usually separate from its primary insurance operations so that information from other insurers remains confidential.

A primary insurer may offer reinsurance to affiliated insurers, regardless of whether it offers reinsurance to unaffiliated insurers. Many primary insurers are groups of commonly owned insurance companies, and intragroup reinsurance agreements are used to balance the financial results of all insurers in the group. The use of intragroup reinsurance agreements does not preclude using professional reinsurers.

Reinsurance Pools, Syndicates, and Associations

Reinsurance pools, syndicates, and associations
Groups of insurers that share the loss exposures of the group, usually through reinsurance.

A third source for reinsurance is through **reinsurance pools, syndicates, and associations**, which are groups of insurers that share the loss exposures of the group, usually through reinsurance.

Some pools were formed by insurers whose reinsurance needs were not adequately met in the regular marketplace. Other reinsurance pools were formed to provide specialized insurance requiring underwriting and claim expertise that the individual insurers did not have. Reinsurance intermediaries have also formed reinsurance pools to provide reinsurance to their clients.

A reinsurance pool may offer reinsurance only to its member companies. Alternatively, it may also accept loss exposures from nonmember companies. Some reinsurance pools restrict their operations to narrowly defined classes of business while others reinsure most types of insurance.

REINSURANCE PROFESSIONAL AND TRADE ASSOCIATIONS

Unlike many primary insurers, reinsurers do not use service organizations such as the Insurance Services Office (ISO) and the American Association of Insurance Services (AAIS) to develop loss costs and draft contract wording. However, the reinsurance business has several associations that serve member companies and provide information to interested parties.

Intermediaries and Reinsurance Underwriters Association (IRU)

The Intermediaries and Reinsurance Underwriters Association (IRU) was founded in 1967 and comprises intermediaries and reinsurers that broker or assume non-life treaty reinsurance. IRU publishes the *Journal of Reinsurance*, which discusses concepts and research affecting the reinsurance market. IRU conducts claim seminars, sponsors an internship program for college students, and holds conferences for members.[4]

Brokers & Reinsurance Markets Association (BRMA)

The Brokers & Reinsurance Markets Association (BRMA) represents intermediaries and reinsurers that are predominately engaged in U.S. treaty reinsurance business obtained through reinsurance brokers. The organization is described as a forum for treaty reinsurance professionals. Through various member committees, BRMA seeks to identify and address industry-wide operational issues.

Of particular importance are BRMA's efforts in the area of reinsurance contract wording. The organization has compiled the *Contract Wording Reference Book*, which has become a benchmark for treaty reinsurance contracts. The BRMA *Contract Wording Reference Book* is available on its Web site.[5]

Reinsurance Association of America (RAA)

The Reinsurance Association of America (RAA) is a nonprofit trade association of professional reinsurers and intermediaries. All members are domestic U.S. companies or U.S. branches of international reinsurers. The association is headquartered in Washington, D.C.

The RAA engages in many activities, serving its members and providing information on reinsurance issues to interested parties outside the industry. In addition to member advocacy and lobbying at both the state and federal levels, the RAA analyzes aggregate data, and conducts seminars countrywide.[6]

SUMMARY

Reinsurance is the transfer of insurance risk from one insurer to another through a contractual agreement under which the reinsurer agrees, in return for a reinsurance premium, to indemnify the primary insurer for some or all of the financial consequences of certain loss exposures covered by the primary insurer's policies. Reinsurance performs six principal functions for primary insurers. These are:

1. *Increase large line capacity.* Allows the primary insurer to provide larger amounts of insurance than it would otherwise be willing or able to do.
2. *Provide catastrophe protection.* Protects the primary insurer from the financial consequences of a single catastrophic event that causes multiple losses.
3. *Stabilize loss experience.* Stabilizes the primary insurer's loss experience by limiting the primary insurer's liability for loss exposures.
4. *Provide surplus relief.* Replenishes policyholders' surplus.
5. *Facilitate withdrawal from a market segment.* Allows the primary insurer to use portfolio reinsurance to withdraw from a market segment without canceling all of the policies in that segment.
6. *Provide underwriting guidance.* Enables the primary insurer to benefit from the reinsurer's expertise, which is particularly useful to inexperienced primary insurers.

The two types of reinsurance transactions are:

1. Treaty
2. Facultative

Treaty reinsurance agreements provide coverage for an entire class or portfolio of loss exposures and involve an ongoing relationship between the primary insurer and the reinsurer. Treaty reinsurance agreements are usually obligatory; loss exposures must be ceded to and accepted by the reinsurer. Facultative reinsurance agreements insure individual loss exposures. Under a facultative agreement, the reinsurer is usually not obligated to accept the loss exposure submitted by the primary insurer.

Reinsurance is purchased through three sources:

1. Professional reinsurers
2. Reinsurance departments of primary insurers
3. Reinsurance pools, syndicates, and associations

A direct writing reinsurer deals directly with primary insurers. Alternatively, reinsurers may deal with primary insurers through reinsurance intermediaries. In either case, there must be a relationship of trust and utmost good faith between primary insurer and reinsurer.

Some primary insurers also serve as reinsurers, either only to affiliates, or to both affiliates and unaffiliated insurers.

Reinsurance pools, syndicates, and associations are groups of insurers that share the loss exposures of the group.

This chapter introduced reinsurance, its functions, and its sources. The next chapter discusses the different types of reinsurance agreements and how a primary insurer can establish a reinsurance program to meet its reinsurance needs.

CHAPTER NOTES

1. The Reinsurance Association of America (RAA), through its *Glossary of Terms*, has brought clarity to the use of many reinsurance terms. Many of the definitions of terms in this text were adapted from the RAA glossary. The Web site for the RAA is at http://www.raanet.org (accessed January 13, 2004).
2. Insurers that are publicly traded are usually referred to as "stock insurers" to differentiate them from "mutual insurers," which are owned by their policyholders.
3. Insurers writing more volatile types of insurance, such as medical malpractice, may strive to keep their ratio of net written premiums to policyholders' surplus at a ratio of 2 to 1 or less.
4. Intermediaries and Reinsurance Underwriters Association, http://www.irua.com (accessed January 13, 2004).
5. Brokers & Reinsurance Markets Association, http://www.brma.org (accessed January 13, 2004).
6. Reinsurance Association of America, http://www.reinsurance.org (accessed January 13, 2004).

Chapter 2

Direct Your Learning

OUTLINE

Pro Rata Reinsurance

Excess of Loss Reinsurance

Finite Risk Reinsurance

Reinsurance Program Design

Summary

Types of Reinsurance and Reinsurance Program Design

After learning the content of this chapter, you should be able to:

■ Describe the following types of pro rata reinsurance and their uses:
- Quota share reinsurance
- Surplus share reinsurance

■ Describe the following types of excess of loss reinsurance and their uses:
- Per risk excess of loss reinsurance
- Catastrophe excess of loss reinsurance
- Per policy excess of loss reinsurance
- Per occurrence excess of loss reinsurance
- Aggregate excess of loss reinsurance

■ Describe the characteristics of finite risk reinsurance.

■ Describe the factors affecting a primary insurer's reinsurance needs that should be considered in the design of a reinsurance program.

■ Describe factors considered in selecting retentions and reinsurance limits.

■ Given a case, identify the insurer's particular needs for reinsurance and recommend appropriate reinsurance agreements to address those needs.

Develop Your Perspective

What are the main topics covered in the chapter?

Reinsurance agreements can be categorized to reflect how they operate. This chapter describes the types of reinsurance agreements, their uses, and how they may be combined in a reinsurance program to satisfy an insurer's reinsurance needs.

Consider the different types of reinsurance agreements and how they can be used.

- What types of reinsurance are available to a primary insurer?
- What factors affect a primary insurer's need for reinsurance?
- What factors affect the amount of insurance risk that a primary insurer retains and the limits of its reinsurance agreements?

Why is it important to learn about these topics?

Most reinsurance agreements are negotiated to reflect the interests of the primary insurer and the reinsurer. Understanding the overall types of reinsurance will enable you to have a clearer understanding of how a particular agreement operates.

Evaluate a reinsurance agreement.

- Are you able to identify which type of reinsurance the agreement represents?

How can you use what you will learn?

Review the types of reinsurance agreements included in your company's reinsurance program.

- Are the types of reinsurance agreements used by your company consistent with its stated reinsurance needs?
- Does your company have a description of its reinsurance program that explains how its reinsurance agreements interrelate?

Chapter 2
Types of Reinsurance and Reinsurance Program Design

The first chapter discussed the two types of reinsurance transactions: treaty and facultative. Treaty and facultative reinsurance can also be subcategorized based on whether the liability for losses is shared proportionally (pro rata) or nonproportionally (excess of loss). Exhibit 2-1 shows the types of reinsurance and their relationships.

Reinsurance agreements are negotiated between a primary insurer and reinsurer. In many respects, each agreement is unique and its terms reflect the primary insurer's needs and the willingness of reinsurers in the marketplace to meet those needs. A primary insurer often uses several reinsurance agreements, which viewed together comprise the primary insurer's reinsurance program. Reinsurance program design is also introduced in this chapter. Subsequent chapters describe in greater depth the types of reinsurance introduced in this chapter.

PRO RATA REINSURANCE

Pro rata reinsurance is usually identified as one of two types: quota share or surplus share. The common characteristic of both types of **pro rata reinsurance** is that the primary insurer and the reinsurer proportionately share the amounts of insurance, policy premiums, and losses (including loss adjustment expenses). For example, if the primary insurer shares 60 percent of the liability for each loss exposure with the reinsurer, then the reinsurer would be entitled to 60 percent of the policy premiums and would be responsible for 60 percent of each loss.

Pro rata reinsurance
A type of reinsurance in which the primary insurer and reinsurer proportionately share the amounts of insurance, policy premiums, and losses (including loss adjustment expenses).

With pro rata reinsurance, the primary insurer cedes a portion of the original insurance premiums to the reinsurer as a reinsurance premium. The reinsurer usually pays the primary insurer a ceding commission for the loss exposures ceded. The ceding commission reimburses the primary insurer for policy acquisition expenses incurred when the underlying policies were sold. In addition to policy acquisition expenses, insurers incur **loss adjustment expenses**, which are the expenses required to settle claims. Loss adjustment expenses that can be related to a specific loss are usually shared proportionately by the primary insurer and the reinsurer.

Loss adjustment expenses
Expenses incurred by an insurer to settle claims.

EXHIBIT 2-1

Types of Reinsurance

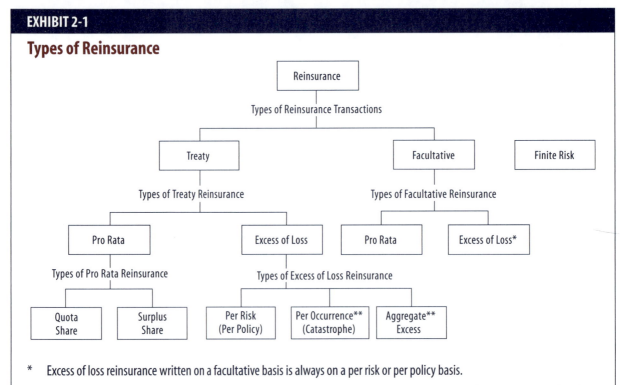

* Excess of loss reinsurance written on a facultative basis is always on a per risk or per policy basis.
** Per occurrence and aggregate excess of loss reinsurance relate to a type of insurance, a territory, or the primary insurer's entire portfolio of in-force loss exposures rather than to a specific policy or a specific loss exposure.

Flat commission
A ceding commission that is a fixed percentage of the ceded premiums.

Profit-sharing commission
A ceding commission that is contingent on the reinsurer realizing a predetermined percentage of excess profit on ceded loss exposures.

Sliding scale commission
A ceding commission based on a formula that adjusts the commission according to the profitability of the reinsurance agreement.

The amount of the ceding commission paid to the primary insurer is usually negotiated. The primary insurer remits the reinsurance premium to the reinsurer net of the ceding commission. The ceding commission is referred to as a **flat commission** when it is a fixed percentage of the ceded premium with no adjustment for the primary insurer's loss experience.

The reinsurance agreement may also include an additional commission, called a **profit-sharing commission** or profit commission, which is negotiated and paid to the primary insurer after the end of the treaty year if the reinsurer earns greater-than-expected profits on the reinsurance agreement. The profit-sharing commission percentage is predetermined and applied to the reinsurer's excess profits; that is, the profits remaining after losses, expenses, and the reinsurer's minimum margin for profit are deducted. Profit commission is also called contingent commission because its payment is contingent on the reinsurance agreement's profitability.

Sometimes, as an alternative to the flat commission and profit-sharing commission, the ceding commission initially paid to the primary insurer may be adjusted to reflect the actual profitability of the reinsurance agreement. This type of commission is called a **sliding scale commission** and is calculated based on a formula specified in the reinsurance agreement.

Quota Share Reinsurance

Quota share reinsurance is a type of pro rata reinsurance in which the primary insurer and the reinsurer share the amounts of insurance, policy premiums, and losses (including loss adjustment expenses) using a fixed percentage. For example, an insurer may arrange a reinsurance treaty in which it retains 45 percent of policy premiums, coverage limits, and losses while reinsuring the remaining amount. Because the reinsurer accepts 55 percent of the liability for each loss exposure subject to the treaty, this treaty would be called a "55 percent quota share treaty." Quota share reinsurance can be used with both property insurance and liability insurance but is more frequently used in property insurance.

Most reinsurance agreements specify a maximum dollar limit above which responsibility for additional coverage limits or losses reverts to the primary insurer (or is covered by another reinsurer). With a pro rata reinsurance agreement, that maximum dollar amount is stated in terms of the coverage limits of each policy subject to the treaty. For example, a primary insurer and a reinsurer may share amounts of insurance, policy premiums, and losses on a 45 percent and 55 percent basis respectively, subject to a $1 million maximum coverage amount for each policy.

In addition to a maximum coverage amount limitation, some pro rata reinsurance agreements include a per occurrence limit, which restricts the primary insurer's reinsurance recovery for losses originating from a single occurrence. This per occurrence limit may be stated as an aggregate dollar amount or as a loss ratio cap. **Loss ratio** is the ratio of incurred losses and loss adjustment expenses to earned premiums. The per occurrence limit diminishes the usefulness of pro rata reinsurance in protecting the primary insurer from the effects of catastrophic events. Primary insurers exposed to catastrophic losses usually include catastrophe excess of loss reinsurance, described later in this chapter, in their reinsurance programs.

Exhibit 2-2 shows how the amounts of insurance, policy premiums, and losses would be shared between a primary insurer and a reinsurer for three policies subject to their quota share treaty. These same examples are repeated in the discussion of surplus share reinsurance that follows so that a contrast can be drawn between these two types of pro rata reinsurance.

The following observations can be made about quota share reinsurance:

- As the retention and cession amounts are each a fixed percentage, the dollar amount of the retention and the dollar amount of the cession change as the amount of insurance changes. On policies with higher amounts of insurance, the primary insurer will have a higher dollar retention.
- Because the primary insurer cedes a fixed percentage under a quota share treaty, even policies with low amounts of insurance that the primary insurer could most likely safely retain are reinsured.

Quota share reinsurance
A type of pro rata reinsurance in which the primary insurer and the reinsurer share the amounts of insurance, policy premiums, and losses (including loss adjustment expenses) using a fixed percentage.

Loss ratio
The ratio of incurred losses and loss adjustment expenses to earned premiums.

EXHIBIT 2-2

Quota Share Reinsurance Example

Brookgreen Insurance Company has a quota share treaty with Cypress Reinsurer. The treaty has a $250,000 limit, a retention of 25 percent, and a cession of 75 percent. The following three policies are issued by Brookgreen Insurance Company and are subject to the pro rata treaty with Cypress Reinsurer.

- Policy A insures Building A for $25,000 for a premium of $400, with one loss of $8,000.
- Policy B insures Building B for $100,000 for a premium of $1,000, with one loss of $10,000.
- Policy C insures Building C for $150,000 for a premium of $1,500, with one loss of $60,000.

Division of Insurance, Premiums, and Losses Under Quota Share Treaty

	Brookgreen Insurance Retention (25%)	Cypress Reinsurance Cession (75%)	Total
Policy A			
Amounts of insurance	$6,250	$18,750	$25,000
Premiums	100	300	400
Losses	2,000	6,000	8,000
Policy B			
Amounts of insurance	$25,000	$75,000	$100,000
Premiums	250	750	1,000
Losses	2,500	7,500	10,000
Policy C			
Amounts of insurance	$37,500	$112,500	$150,000
Premiums	375	1,125	1,500
Losses	15,000	45,000	60,000

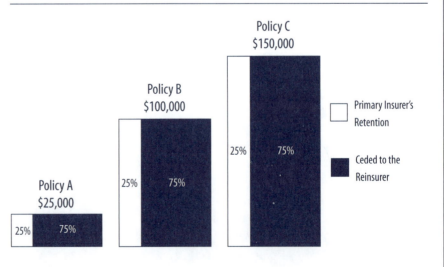

- Quota share treaties are straightforward to administer because of the fixed percentage used in sharing premiums and losses. The primary insurer can combine premium and loss amounts and quickly determine the amount owed to the reinsurer in premiums and the amount owed by the reinsurer in losses.
- Because the primary insurer and the reinsurer share liability for every loss exposure subject to a quota share treaty, the reinsurer is usually not subject to adverse selection. The loss ratio for the reinsurer is the same as that of the primary insurer for the ceded loss exposures.

One type of quota share treaty, called a **variable quota share treaty**, permits the cession percentage to vary based on specified predetermined criteria, such as the amount of insurance needed. A variable quota share treaty has the advantage of enabling the primary insurer to retain a larger proportion of the small loss exposures that are within its financial capability to absorb, while maintaining a safer and smaller retention on larger loss exposures.

Variable quota share treaty
A quota share reinsurance treaty in which the cession percentage retention varies based on specified predetermined criteria such as the amount of insurance needed.

Surplus Share Reinsurance

Surplus share reinsurance is a type of pro rata reinsurance in which the policies covered are those whose amount of insurance exceeds a stipulated dollar amount, or line. When the amount of insurance exceeds the line, the reinsurer assumes the surplus share of the amount of insurance (the difference between the amount of insurance and the primary insurer's line). Surplus share reinsurance is typically only used with property insurance.

Surplus share reinsurance
A type of pro rata reinsurance in which the policies covered are those whose amount of insurance exceeds a stipulated dollar amount, or line.

The primary insurer and the reinsurer share the policy premiums and losses proportionately. The primary insurer's share of the policy premiums and losses is that proportion that the line bears to the total amount of insurance (the line plus the amount of insurance ceded). The reinsurer's share of the premiums and losses is that proportion that the amount ceded bears to the total. For example, if the line is $50,000 and the amount ceded is $200,000, the primary insurer would receive 20 percent ($50,000 ÷ $250,000) of the policy premium and pay 20 percent of all losses, and the reinsurer would receive 80 percent ($200,000 ÷ $250,000) of the policy premium and pay 80 percent of all losses. Exhibit 2-3 shows how an insurer and a reinsurer would share policy premiums, coverage limits, and losses under a surplus share treaty for the same three policies shown in Exhibit 2-2.

The reinsurance limit—the total limit or capacity—of a surplus share treaty is expressed in multiples of the primary insurer's line. A primary insurer with a nine-line surplus share treaty has the capacity under the treaty to insure loss exposures with amounts of insurance that exceed its retention by a multiple of nine. For example, if the line is $300,000 for a nine-line surplus share treaty, the primary insurer has a total underwriting capacity of $3 million, calculated as the $300,000 line, plus nine multiplied by the $300,000 line. In addition to being expressed as a number of lines, the reinsurance limit of a surplus share treaty can also be expressed as an amount of insurance the reinsurer is willing to provide, such as $2.7 million in the preceding example ($300,000 multiplied by nine lines).

EXHIBIT 2-3

Surplus Share Reinsurance Example

Brookgreen Insurance Company has a surplus share treaty with Cypress Reinsurer and retains a line of $25,000. The treaty contains nine lines and provides for a maximum cession of $225,000. Therefore, the retention and reinsurance provide Brookgreen with the ability to issue policies with amounts of insurance as high as $250,000. The following three policies are issued by Brookgreen Insurance Company and are subject to the surplus share treaty with Cypress Reinsurer.

- Policy A insures Building A for $25,000 for a premium of $400, with one loss of $8,000.
- Policy B insures Building B for $100,000 for a premium of $1,000, with one loss of $10,000.
- Policy C insures Building C for $150,000 for a premium of $1,500, with one loss of $60,000.

Division of Insurance, Premiums, and Losses Under Surplus Share Treaty

	Brookgreen Insurance Retention	Cypress Reinsurance Cession	Total
Policy A			
Amounts of insurance	$25,000 (100%)	$0 (0%)	$25,000
Premiums	400	0	400
Losses	8,000	0	8,000
Policy B			
Amounts of insurance	$25,000 (25%)	$75,000 (75%)	$100,000
Premiums	250	750	1,000
Losses	2,500	7,500	10,000
Policy C			
Amounts of insurance	$25,000 (16.67%)	$125,000 (83.33%)	$150,000
Premiums	250	1,250	1,500
Losses	10,000	50,000	60,000

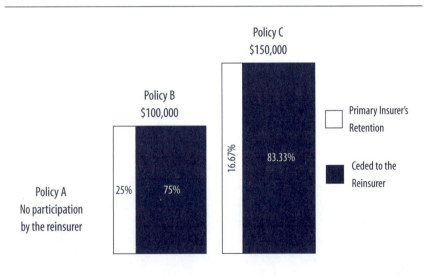

The following observations can be made about surplus share reinsurance:

- The surplus share treaty does not cover policies with amounts of insurance that are less than the primary insurer's line. Many primary insurers use surplus share reinsurance instead of quota share reinsurance so that they do not have to cede any part of the liability for loss exposures that can be safely retained.
- The amount of insurance for a large number of loss exposures may be too small to be ceded to the treaty but, in the aggregate, may cause the primary insurer to incur significant losses that are not reinsured. For example, many homeowners policies in the same region that do not exceed the primary insurer's line could incur extensive losses from a single occurrence, such as a hurricane.
- Because the percentage of policy premiums and losses varies for each loss exposure ceded, surplus share treaties are more costly to administer than quota share treaties. Primary insurers must keep records and, in many cases, periodically provide the reinsurer with a report, called a **bordereau**, that contains a detailed listing of premiums and losses reinsured under the treaty.
- Surplus share treaties usually provide surplus relief to the primary insurer because the reinsurer usually pays a reinsurance commission for those policies ceded. Because loss exposures with amounts of insurance that are less than the primary insurer's line are not reinsured, a surplus share treaty typically provides the primary insurer with less surplus relief than does a quota share treaty.

Bordereau
A report the primary insurer provides periodically to the reinsurer that contains a detailed listing of premiums and losses reinsured under the treaty.

Unlike the simplified example shown in Exhibit 2-3, many surplus share treaties allow the primary insurer to increase its line from a minimum amount to a maximum amount depending on the potential loss severity of the exposed limit. For example, Brookgreen Insurance Company's surplus share treaty may allow the company to increase its line on a "superior" loss exposure from $25,000 to $50,000. In this case, the nine-line surplus share treaty would give Brookgreen Insurance Company the large line capacity to insure loss exposures with amounts of insurance as large as $500,000; calculated as the $50,000 line, plus nine multiplied by the $50,000 line. The primary insurer's ability to vary its line also allows it to retain some loss exposures it may otherwise be required to cede. The flexibility provided by the reinsurer in the surplus share treaty is usually communicated to the primary insurer's underwriters through a line guide, or line authorization guide. The **line guide** provides the minimum and maximum line that the primary insurer can retain on a loss exposure.

Line guide
A document that provides the minimum and maximum line a primary insurer can retain on a loss exposure.

When the total underwriting capacity of the primary insurer's surplus share treaty is insufficient to meet its large line capacity needs, the primary insurer can arrange for additional surplus share reinsurance from another reinsurer. When a primary insurer arranges more than one surplus share treaty, the surplus share treaty that applies immediately above the primary insurer's line is referred to as the first surplus. Other surplus share treaties are referred to in the order that they provide additional large line capacity, such as second or third surplus treaties.

EXCESS OF LOSS REINSURANCE

> **Five Types of Excess of Loss Reinsurance**
> 1. Per risk excess of loss
> 2. Catastrophe excess of loss
> 3. Per policy excess of loss
> 4. Per occurrence excess of loss
> 5. Aggregate excess of loss

Excess of loss reinsurance
A type of reinsurance in which the primary insurer is indemnified for losses that exceed a specified dollar amount.

Excess of loss reinsurance, also called non-proportional reinsurance, is a type of reinsurance in which the primary insurer is indemnified for losses that exceed a specified dollar amount. There are five types of excess of loss reinsurance.

The different types of excess of loss reinsurance usually have a specific use. Per risk excess of loss reinsurance and catastrophe excess of loss reinsurance are generally used with property loss exposures. Per policy excess of loss reinsurance and per occurrence excess of loss reinsurance are generally used with liability loss exposures. Aggregate excess of loss reinsurance is used for both property and liability loss exposures.

The common characteristic of all types of excess of loss reinsurance is that the reinsurer responds to a loss only when the loss amount exceeds a specified dollar amount, known as the **attachment point**. The primary insurer fully retains losses that are less than the attachment point. The reinsurer sometimes requires the primary insurer to also retain responsibility for a percentage of the losses that exceed the attachment point. Excess of loss reinsurance can be visualized as a layer, or a series of layers, of reinsurance sitting on top of the primary insurer's retention. Exhibit 2-4 illustrates how excess of loss reinsurance can be layered.

Attachment point
The dollar amount above which the reinsurer responds to losses.

An excess of loss reinsurer's obligation to indemnify the primary insurer for losses depends on the amount of the loss and the layer of coverage that the reinsurer provides. The reinsurer providing the first layer of excess of loss reinsurance shown in Exhibit 2-4 would indemnify the primary insurer for losses that exceed $250,000 (the attachment point) up to total incurred losses of $500,000. This reinsurer describes its position in the primary insurer's excess of loss reinsurance program as being "$250,000 in excess of (denoted as 'xs') $250,000." The reinsurer in the second layer of the excess of loss reinsurance program would indemnify the primary insurer for losses that exceed $500,000 up to total incurred losses of $1 million, or "$500,000 xs $500,000." Losses that exceed the capacity of the primary insurer's excess of loss reinsurance remain the primary insurer's responsibility unless otherwise reinsured. In Exhibit 2-4, loss amounts in excess of $25 million are the primary insurer's responsibility.

EXHIBIT 2-4

How Excess of Loss Reinsurance Is Layered

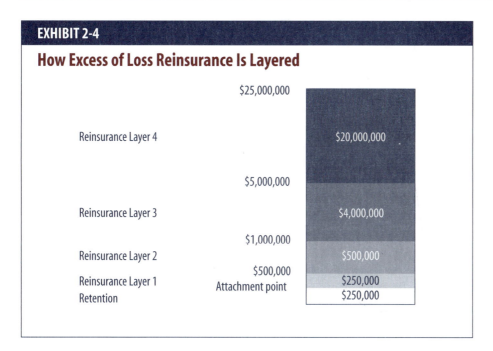

Unlike pro rata reinsurance, in which the reinsurance pricing follows that of the primary insurer's pricing, excess of loss reinsurance premiums are negotiated based on the likelihood that losses will exceed the attachment point. The reinsurance premium for excess of loss reinsurance is usually stated as a percentage (often called a rate) of the policy premium charged by the primary insurer (often called the **subject premium** or underlying premium). Therefore, unlike quota share and surplus share reinsurance, in which the reinsurer receives a proportional share of the underlying premium, the excess of loss reinsurer receives a nonproportional share of the premium.

Generally, reinsurers do not pay ceding commissions under excess of loss reinsurance agreements. However, the reinsurer may reward the primary insurer for favorable loss experience by paying a profit commission or by reducing the rate used in calculating the reinsurance premium.

The primary insurer's attachment point is usually set at a level so that claims that are frequent enough to be expected are retained. However, an excess of loss reinsurance agreement may have a low attachment point with the expectation that the primary insurer's volume of losses will be significant. A reinsurance agreement with a low attachment point is sometimes referred to as a **working cover**. A working cover enables the primary insurer to spread its losses over several years. The primary insurer and the reinsurer anticipate that profitable years will offset unprofitable ones. Primary insurers selling a type of insurance with which they have little expertise may choose to purchase a working cover until they better understand the frequency and severity of losses that the portfolio for that particular type of insurance produces. Reinsurers typically require a working cover to contain an occurrence limitation of two or three times the reinsurance limit. This requirement prevents the working cover from being exposed to catastrophic events such as an earthquake.

Subject premium
The premium the primary insurer charges on its underlying policies and to which a rate is applied to determine the reinsurance premium.

Working cover
An excess of loss reinsurance agreement with a low attachment point.

Co-participation provision
A provision in a reinsurance agreement that requires the primary insurer to retain a specified percentage of the losses that exceed its attachment point.

As previously mentioned, excess of loss reinsurance agreements sometimes contain a **co-participation provision** that requires the primary insurer to retain a specified percentage of the losses that exceed its attachment point. The purpose of this provision is to provide the primary insurer with a financial incentive to efficiently manage losses that exceed the attachment point. A co-participation provision is usually denoted by specifying a percentage before the position of its layer. For example, if the fourth layer in Exhibit 2-4 had a 5 percent co-participation provision, that layer would be specified as "95% of $20,000,000 xs $5,000,000."

In addition to indemnifying losses in a layer of coverage, the reinsurer's obligation may also extend to payment of loss adjustment expenses. Loss adjustment expenses are often a substantial insurer expense, especially for insurance for liability loss exposures. Therefore, excess of loss reinsurance agreements are usually very specific regarding how loss adjustment expenses attributable to specific losses are handled. In rare circumstances they may be excluded from the reinsurance agreement, but the following are the two most common approaches to handling loss adjustment expenses:

1. Prorate the loss adjustment expenses between the primary insurer and the reinsurer based on the same percentage share that each is responsible for the loss. This approach is commonly referred to as *pro rata in addition*.
2. Add the loss adjustment expenses to the amount of the loss when applying the attachment point of the excess of loss reinsurance agreement. This approach is commonly referred to as loss adjustment expense *included in the limit*.

If loss adjustment expenses are prorated, the primary insurer pays all of the loss adjustment expenses when the loss amount does not exceed the attachment point. If loss adjustment expenses are added to the loss amount, the reinsurer may have to pay a claim in which the loss amount alone does not exceed the attachment point. Primary insurers and reinsurers usually assess the potential for loss adjustment expenses independent of the actual loss potential when negotiating the excess of loss reinsurance agreement. Commonly, reinsurance agreements provide that loss adjustment expenses are prorated for property insurance and most types of liability insurance. However, excess of loss reinsurance covering liability insurance that usually involves substantial litigation often specifies that loss adjustment expenses are added to the amount of the loss when applying the attachment point. For instance, medical malpractice insurance often involves substantial loss adjustment expenses in the form of legal fees even if the claim can be settled with a nominal loss payment or no payment at all.

As outlined previously, there are five types of excess of loss reinsurance. This chapter now examines each of these individual types in greater detail.

Per Risk Excess of Loss Reinsurance

The first type of excess of loss reinsurance is per risk excess of loss reinsurance. **Per risk excess of loss reinsurance** covers property insurance and applies separately to *each loss* occurring to *each risk*. Per risk excess of loss is often referred to as property per risk excess of loss. The primary insurer usually determines what constitutes one risk (loss exposure). Exhibit 2-5 indicates how a reinsurer would respond if the primary insurer defined three separate buildings under a per risk excess of loss reinsurance agreement as three separate risks. In this example, a tornado damaged all three buildings in one occurrence. Because each building is a risk, the attachment point and reinsurance limit apply separately to each. The attachment point and reinsurance limit are stated as a dollar amount of loss.

Per risk excess of loss reinsurance
A type of excess of loss reinsurance that covers property insurance and that applies separately to *each loss* occurring to *each risk*.

EXHIBIT 2-5

Example of Per Risk Excess of Loss Reinsurance Applying $950,000 xs $50,000

Building Number	Loss Amount	Primary Insurer's Retention	Reinsurer's Payment
1	$ 500,000	$ 50,000	$ 450,000
2	350,000	50,000	300,000
3	700,000	50,000	650,000
Total	$1,550,000	$150,000	$1,400,000

Per occurrence limits are commonly included with per risk excess of loss reinsurance agreements. A per occurrence limit restricts the amount that the reinsurer pays as the result of a single occurrence affecting multiple risks. Had a per occurrence limit of $1 million been imposed in the example in Exhibit 2-5, the reinsurer would have been responsible for only $1 million of losses (instead of $1.4 million) because the three losses arose out of the same occurrence (the tornado). Catastrophe excess of loss reinsurance, discussed next, is usually purchased in conjunction with per risk excess of loss reinsurance to protect the primary insurer from one occurrence affecting multiple risks.

Catastrophe Excess of Loss Reinsurance

The second type of excess of loss reinsurance is catastrophe excess of loss reinsurance. **Catastrophe excess of loss reinsurance** protects the primary insurer from an accumulation of retained losses that arise from a single

Catastrophe excess of loss reinsurance
A type of excess of loss reinsurance that protects the primary insurer from an accumulation of retained losses that arise from a single catastrophic event.

catastrophic event. It may be purchased to protect the primary insurer and its reinsurers on a combined basis but is more frequently purchased to protect the primary insurer on a net basis after all other reinsurance recoveries are made. Examples of catastrophic events include tornadoes, hurricanes, and earthquakes. Such events, especially major hurricanes, can result in losses totaling billions of dollars.

As with per risk excess of loss reinsurance, the attachment point and reinsurance limit for catastrophe excess of loss reinsurance are stated as a dollar amount of loss. The attachment point is subject to negotiation, but it is usually set high enough so that it would be exceeded only if the aggregation of losses from a catastrophe would impair a primary insurer's policyholders' surplus. Additionally, losses exceeding the attachment point are usually subject to a co-participation provision.

Because the attachment point and reinsurance limit apply separately to each catastrophe occurring during a policy period, the catastrophe excess of loss reinsurance agreement defines the scope of a catastrophic occurrence through a loss occurrence clause (sometimes called an hours clause). The **loss occurrence clause** specifies a time period, in hours, during which the primary insurer's losses arising out of the same catastrophic occurrence can be aggregated and applied to the attachment point and reinsurance limits of the catastrophe excess of loss reinsurance agreement. Such clauses usually specify a time period of 72 consecutive hours (three days) for hurricane losses and 168 consecutive hours (seven days) for earthquake losses. When making a claim against the catastrophe excess of loss reinsurance agreement, the primary insurer can usually choose the date and time when the period of consecutive hours commences in order to maximize the amount of recovery under the agreement.

Loss occurrence clause
A reinsurance agreement clause that defines the scope of a catastrophic occurrence for the purposes of the agreement.

Exhibit 2-6 provides an example of the operation of a loss occurrence clause in a catastrophe excess of loss reinsurance agreement and shows how a primary insurer can select the period of coverage to its advantage. In this example, the primary insurer sustains $8 million in losses from a hurricane over a four-day period. The primary insurer has a $6 million xs $1 million catastrophe excess of loss reinsurance treaty with a loss occurrence clause that stipulates a period of seventy-two consecutive hours for a hurricane. In this simplified example, selecting the specific hour of the day that coverage begins is not an issue, and no co-participation provision applies. Given the distribution of losses over the four days, the primary insurer should elect to start the seventy-two-hour period on the second day to maximize its reinsurance recovery.

Payments from the reinsurer to the primary insurer for catastrophe losses reduce the reinsurance coverage limits available to respond to future losses. Catastrophe excess of loss reinsurance agreements often include a provision that requires the primary insurer to pay an additional premium to reinstate the limits of the agreement after a loss. This provision allows the reinsurer to obtain additional premiums and gives the primary insurer confidence that sufficient limits are available should another catastrophe occur during the reinsurance agreement's term.

EXHIBIT 2-6

Example of the Operation of a Loss Occurrence Clause in a Catastrophe Excess of Loss Reinsurance Agreement

Day	Losses	Period of Coverage Providing Maximum Recovery
1	$1,000,000	
2	1,000,000	
3	2,000,000	$7,000,000 (days 2–4)
4	4,000,000	
Total	$8,000,000	

The total losses that could potentially be applied to the reinsurance agreement are $7 million if the seventy-two-hour period starts on the second day, as opposed to $4 million if the period had started on the first day.

Primary insurers and their reinsurers usually do not anticipate that the catastrophe excess of loss reinsurance will be triggered every year. Catastrophe protection is purchased for the unlikely, but possible, event that may cause unstable operating results or that cannot be absorbed by the primary insurer's policyholders' surplus. A primary insurer's need for catastrophe reinsurance and the amount purchased depends on its catastrophe loss exposures.

Catastrophe Excess of Loss Reinsurance Example

Brookgreen Insurance Company (Brookgreen) decides to sell earthquake coverage in southern California but wants to limit its losses to approximately $1 million from any one earthquake. Brookgreen conducted a study and estimated that its maximum loss from any one earthquake, given its spread of earthquake loss exposures in southern California, would be $10 million. Brookgreen purchases catastrophe excess of loss reinsurance of 95% of $9,250,000 xs $750,000. If Brookgreen were to sustain a $10 million loss from an earthquake, it would retain $1,212,500 and the reinsurer would pay $8,787,500. These figures are calculated as follows:

Step 1—Determination of the loss amount exceeding the attachment point

Amount exceeding the attachment point = Amount of loss (subject to the reinsurance limit) − Retention

= $10,000,000 − $750,000
= $9,250,000.

Step 2—Determination of the co-participation

Amount of co-participation = Amount exceeding the attachment point × Co-participation percentage

= $9,250,000 × 0.05
= $462,500.

Continued on next page.

> **Step 3—Determination of the amount of loss owed by the reinsurer**
>
> Amount owed by = Amount exceeding − Amount of
> the reinsurer   the attachment point   co-participation
>
> = $9,250,000 − $462,500
> = $8,787,500.
>
> **Step 4—Determination of the amount retained by Brookgreen**
>
> Amount retained = Retention + Amount of
> by Brookgreen   co-participation
>
> = $750,000 + $462,500
> = $1,212,500.

Per Policy Excess of Loss Reinsurance

The third type of excess of loss reinsurance is per policy excess of loss reinsurance. **Per policy excess of loss reinsurance**, used primarily with liability insurance, applies the attachment point and the reinsurance limit separately to each insurance policy issued by the primary insurer regardless of the number of losses occurring under each policy. Exhibit 2-7 provides an example of how a reinsurer would respond under a $900,000 xs $100,000 per policy excess of loss treaty. In this example, three separate general liability policies issued by the same primary insurer incur losses from *separate events*.

Per policy excess of loss reinsurance
A type of excess of loss reinsurance that applies the attachment point and the reinsurance limit separately to each insurance policy issued by the primary insurer regardless of the number of losses occurring under each policy.

Per Occurrence Excess of Loss Reinsurance

The fourth type of excess of loss reinsurance is per occurrence excess of loss reinsurance. **Per occurrence excess of loss reinsurance** applies the attachment point and the reinsurance limit to the total losses arising *from a single event* affecting one or more of the primary insurer's policies. Per occurrence excess of loss reinsurance is usually used for liability insurance. Exhibit 2-8 provides an example of how a per occurrence excess of loss treaty applies to the three policies used in Exhibit 2-7. In Exhibit 2-8, a $100,000 attachment point applies to the total losses of the policies covering the same event, and there is a $4.9 million reinsurance limit. A per occurrence excess of loss treaty covering liability insurance usually has an attachment point that is less than the highest liability policy limit offered by the primary insurer.

Per occurrence excess of loss reinsurance
A type of excess of loss reinsurance that applies the attachment point and reinsurance limit to the total losses arising from a single event affecting one or more of the primary insurer's policies.

Clash Cover

Clash cover, a type of per occurrence excess of loss reinsurance for liability loss exposures, protects the primary insurer against aggregations of losses resulting from one occurrence that affects several insureds or several types of insurance. It can be provided for a combination of different types of liability insurance including auto liability, general liability, professional liability, and workers' compensation. Clash cover has an attachment point higher than any

Clash cover
A type of per occurrence excess of loss reinsurance for liability loss exposures that protects the primary insurer against aggregations of losses from one occurrence that affects several insureds or several types of insurance.

of the limits of the applicable underlying policies. The clash cover retention is not in addition to the retention of any other applicable per occurrence excess of loss reinsurance; it is net of those retentions.

For example, a primary insurer could issue a workers' compensation policy and a general liability policy with an each occurrence limit of $1 million. To obtain higher limits of coverage for an occurrence that may involve injury to both employees and nonemployees, a clash cover could be purchased in layers. If an explosion results in both workers' compensation and general liability claims, the primary insurer would be covered by the clash cover because the claims arise from a single occurrence (the explosion).

EXHIBIT 2-7

Example of Per Policy Excess of Loss Reinsurance Applying $900,000 xs $100,000

Primary Insurer has a $900,000 xs $100,000 per policy excess of loss treaty. The table below shows three policies for which Primary Insurer is indemnified by Reinsurer because the amount of loss arising out of each of the policies exceeds Primary Insurer's attachment point.

Policy	Loss Amount	Primary Insurer's Retention	Reinsurer's Payment
1	$ 300,000	$100,000	$ 200,000
2	500,000	100,000	400,000
3	600,000	100,000	500,000
Total	$1,400,000	$300,000	$1,100,000

EXHIBIT 2-8

Example of Per Occurrence Excess of Loss Reinsurance Applying $4,900,000 xs $100,000

Primary Insurer has a $4,900,000 xs $100,000 per occurrence excess of loss treaty. The table below shows how losses are accumulated to determine if the attachment point has been exceeded. Primary Insurer is indemnified by Reinsurer because the total amount of the loss arising out of all three policies exceeds Primary Insurer's attachment point.

Policy	Loss Amount		Primary Insurer's Retention		Reinsurer's Payment
1	$ 300,000				
2	500,000				
3	600,000				
Total	$1,400,000	=	$100,000	+	$1,300,000

As another example, Brookgreen Insurance Company (Brookgreen) insures the general liability loss exposure of six contractors working on a single job site. Each of the six contractors' policies has a limit of $1 million. Brookgreen has per occurrence excess of loss reinsurance of $3 million xs $250,000. Brookgreen also has a clash cover of $3 million xs $1 million. An explosion injures employees and nonemployees. The injured parties are awarded damages that total $6 million from the six contractors' policies. The losses from this single occurrence are paid as indicated in Exhibit 2-9.

EXHIBIT 2-9

Application of a Clash Cover to One Occurrence Involving Multiple Claims

Policy	Damages	Brookgreen Insurance Co. Retention	Per Occurrence Reinsurer	Clash Cover Reinsurer
1	$1,000,000	$ 250,000	$ 750,000	$ 0
2	1,000,000	—	1,000,000	0
3	1,000,000	—	1,000,000	0
4	1,000,000	750,000	250,000	0
5	1,000,000	—	Limit exhausted	1,000,000
6	1,000,000	—	—	1,000,000
Total	$6,000,000	$1,000,000	$3,000,000	$2,000,000

Brookgreen exhausted its per occurrence excess of loss reinsurance retention ($250,000) with payment of the $1 million loss from Policy 1. The per occurrence excess of loss reinsurer paid the remaining losses until the per occurrence limit of $3 million was exhausted. Brookgreen paid the remaining $750,000 under Policy 4 to fulfill its $1 million retention under the clash cover. The clash cover reinsurer then paid the remaining losses.

Both catastrophe excess of loss reinsurance (for property insurance) and clash cover (for liability insurance) are sometimes referred to as pure risk covers because they are expected to cover only rare events, not common claims covered by other excess of loss treaties.

Clash cover may be useful for types of liability insurance in which loss adjustment expenses are likely to be very high and the underlying per occurrence reinsurance limits include rather than pro rate these expenses. Examples include professional liability (such as medical malpractice, directors and officers liability, and accountants professional liability) and expenses associated with environmental claims (for example, asbestos and pollution liability). Primary insurers also use clash cover when they want protection from extra-contractual damages and excess of policy limits losses.

Extra-Contractual Damages

Extra-contractual damages are damages awarded to an insured as a result of an insurer improperly handling a claim. This improper behavior is known as bad faith, and it implies that the insurer has failed to deal fairly with the insured. Damages awarded to an insured for an insurer's bad faith in claim handling are usually not considered to be a loss covered by the underlying policy and therefore are usually not subject to indemnification by a reinsurer unless the reinsurance agreement specifically provides coverage.

> **Extra-contractual damages**
> Damages awarded to an insured as a result of an insurer improperly handling a claim.

Excess of Policy Limits Losses

An **excess of policy limits loss** results when an insured sues an insurer for failing to settle a claim within the insured's policy limits when the insurer had the opportunity to do so. Excess of policy limit losses are also extra-contractual obligations of the insurer, but are usually distinguished from extra-contractual damages by reinsurers because they are covered losses that, as a result of a mistake of the primary insurer, exceed policy limits. As with other extra-contractual obligations, the reinsurance agreement specifies whether excess of policy limit losses are subject to indemnification by the reinsurer.

> **Excess of policy limits loss**
> A loss that results when an insured sues an insurer for failing to settle a claim within the insured's policy limits when the insurer had the opportunity to do so.

Aggregate Excess of Loss Reinsurance

The fifth type of excess of loss reinsurance is aggregate excess of loss reinsurance. **Aggregate excess of loss reinsurance** covers aggregated losses that exceed the attachment point and that occur over a stated period, usually one year. Aggregate excess of loss reinsurance can be used for property or liability insurance. The attachment point in an aggregate excess of loss treaty can be stated as a dollar amount of loss or as a loss ratio. When the attachment point is stated as a loss ratio, the treaty is called stop loss reinsurance. With stop loss reinsurance, the primary insurer's retention may be a loss ratio of 90 percent, and the reinsurer would indemnify losses up to a loss ratio of 120 percent. The reinsurance agreement in this instance would specify the attachment point and reinsurance limit as "30% xs 90% loss ratio." The primary insurer retains responsibility for losses above a loss ratio of 120 percent.

> **Aggregate excess of loss reinsurance**
> A type of excess of loss reinsurance that covers aggregated losses that exceed the attachment point and that occur over a stated period, usually one year.

Aggregate excess of loss treaties are less common and can be more expensive than the other types of excess of loss reinsurance. When used, the treaty usually specifies an attachment point and reinsurance limit that does not result in the primary insurer earning a profit on the reinsured policies when the policies were unprofitable overall. Most aggregate excess of loss treaties also contain a co-participation provision of 5 to 10 percent to provide the primary insurer with an incentive to efficiently handle claims that exceed the attachment point.

> **Aggregate Excess of Loss Reinsurance Example**
>
> Brookgreen Insurance Company (Brookgreen) offers liability insurance to a tavern. This general liability policy has an each occurrence limit of $1 million and a general aggregate limit (capping the number of per occurrence dollars the insurer will pay during the policy period) of $2 million.
>
> Brookgreen purchases facultative per occurrence excess of loss reinsurance for this policy in excess of $500,000. This insurance protects Brookgreen against any loss above $500,000 but would not respond to any loss below $500,000. If the tavern suffered three separate losses of $450,000 each, Brookgreen would not recover from the reinsurer even though the total of all losses under the policy during the policy period exceeded $500,000.
>
> Because of concern about aggregation of losses from this and similar loss exposures, Brookgreen decides to purchase a $7 million xs $3 million aggregate excess of loss treaty that is applicable to all of its liability insurance. This treaty further stabilizes losses by indemnifying Brookgreen for accumulations of losses exceeding $3 million. For example, Brookgreen insures a cosmetics manufacturer whose wrinkle cream causes an increase in susceptibility to skin cancer. Brookgreen settles a class action suit brought by customers who used the product for $15 million. Brookgreen's net loss is $8 million (the $3 million retention plus $5 million loss amount that exceeds the $7 million limit).

Because of the stabilizing effect of aggregate excess of loss reinsurance on a primary insurer's loss ratio, it may be argued that it is the only type of reinsurance needed. However, aggregate excess of loss reinsurance has limited availability. When used, the aggregate excess of loss reinsurer usually expects to pay losses only after the primary insurer has been reimbursed under its other reinsurance agreements.

A catastrophe excess of loss reinsurance agreement, discussed previously, only protects against catastrophe losses (loss severity). An aggregate excess of loss reinsurance agreement provides the reinsured with broader protection because it includes catastrophes and unforeseen accumulations of non-catastrophic losses during a specified period (addressing both loss severity and loss frequency).

FINITE RISK REINSURANCE

An additional type of reinsurance is known as finite risk reinsurance. **Finite risk reinsurance** is a nontraditional type of reinsurance in which the reinsurer's liability is limited (or "finite") and anticipated investment income is expressly acknowledged as an underwriting component. Because this type of reinsurance transfers a limited amount of risk to the reinsurer with the objective of improving the primary insurer's financial result, it is often called financial reinsurance.

Finite risk reinsurance
A nontraditional type of reinsurance in which the reinsurer's liability is limited and anticipated investment income is expressly acknowledged as an underwriting component.

Finite risk reinsurance can be arranged to protect a primary insurer against a combination of a traditionally insurable loss exposure (for example, building loss caused by an explosion) and a traditionally uninsurable loss exposure (for example, possibility of loss due to economic variables such as product demand and market competition). Finite risk reinsurance can effectively handle extremely large and unusual loss exposures, such as catastrophic losses resulting from an oil-rig explosion or an earthquake.

A finite risk reinsurance agreement typically has a multi-year term—for example, three to five years—so it spreads risk as well as losses over several years, subject to an aggregate limit for the agreement's entire term. The primary insurer can rely on long-term protection, and the reinsurer can rely on a continual flow of premiums. Finite risk reinsurance provides the primary insurer with a predictable reinsurance cost over the coverage period. Consequently, both the primary insurer and the reinsurer tend to be flexible in negotiating pricing and terms.

Finite risk reinsurance premiums can be a substantial percentage— for example, 70 percent—of the reinsurance limit. This relationship between premium and reinsurance limit reduces the reinsurer's potential underwriting loss to a level that is much lower than the potential underwriting loss typically associated with traditional types of reinsurance.

Generally, finite risk reinsurance is designed to cover high severity losses. The reinsurer commonly shares profits with the primary insurer when it has favorable loss experience or has generated income by investing the prepaid premium. This profit-sharing income can compensate the primary insurer for the higher-than-usual premium for finite risk reinsurance. The reinsurer does not assess any additional premium even if its losses exceed the premium.

REINSURANCE PROGRAM DESIGN

A **reinsurance program** is the combination of reinsurance agreements that a primary insurer purchases to meet its reinsurance needs. Primary insurers work with reinsurers or reinsurance intermediaries to develop optimal reinsurance programs. This section discusses the factors that determine the primary insurer's reinsurance needs. It then discusses the considerations in setting retentions and limits for a reinsurance program.

Reinsurance program
The combination of reinsurance agreements that a primary insurer purchases to meet its reinsurance needs.

Factors Affecting Reinsurance Needs

Several factors determine the primary insurer's reinsurance needs. Among the factors to be considered are the following:

- Growth plans
- Types of insurance sold
- Geographic spread of loss exposures
- Insurer size

- Insurer structure
- Insurer financial strength
- Management's risk tolerance

These factors can interact to increase or decrease the primary insurer's need for reinsurance.

Growth Plans

A primary insurer that expects rapid premium growth is likely to need more reinsurance than a primary insurer that expects premium volume to remain stable or to shrink. This need for additional reinsurance arises for three reasons. First, and most important, rapid growth usually causes a drain on a primary insurer's policyholders' surplus. Pro rata reinsurance, because of the ceding commission paid by the reinsurer to the primary insurer, causes a replenishment of the primary insurer's policyholders' surplus.

Second, the loss ratio for a primary insurer's new business is likely to be less stable than the loss ratio for its established business, which has undergone renewal underwriting. This instability may be severe if the primary insurer is growing by selling types of insurance that it has not previously sold or by selling in markets in which it has no previous operating experience. For a rapidly growing primary insurer, new insurance sold may constitute a substantial part of total premium volume relative to renewals of existing policies. Consequently, the variability of the loss ratio on the new policies could cause some instability in the primary insurer's overall loss ratio. Reinsurance, while not abrogating the total loss amount, limits the amount of the loss sustained by the primary insurer to its retention amount.

Third, growth often entails expanding into markets with greater coverage requirements. To compete effectively in new markets, a primary insurer may have to offer coverage limits higher than those it was comfortable with in existing markets or insurance coverages it has not offered before. For example, a primary insurer may decide to enter the segment of the homeowners insurance market in which it must offer a personal umbrella with limits up to $2 million to match its competitors' products. Reinsurance enables primary insurers to provide larger amounts of coverage than they otherwise would be able to provide.

If a rapidly growing primary insurer only needs surplus relief, pro rata reinsurance is the appropriate choice. If loss ratio stability or large line capacity is the major concern, excess of loss reinsurance may be an appropriate choice to meet the primary insurer's need.

Types of Insurance Sold

The types of insurance that a primary insurer sells is a major determinant of its reinsurance needs. The insurance products offered by primary insurers vary in loss stability, which affects the primary insurer's ability to project loss experience. A reinsurance program must be tailored to the loss characteristics of the type of insurance that the primary insurer sells.

Primary insurers selling personal insurance generally need less reinsurance than those selling commercial insurance. Relative to commercial insurance loss exposures, personal insurance loss exposures need lower coverage limits. Additionally, personal insurance loss exposures are generally more homogeneous and subject to fewer severe hazards than are commercial insurance loss exposures. Because of the homogeneity among personal insurance loss exposures, the loss experience is usually more stable than that of commercial insurance loss exposures and therefore more predictable. Both personal and commercial insurance loss exposures are subject to catastrophic loss. Primary insurers usually address catastrophe reinsurance needs separately from reinsurance agreements designed to smooth loss experience fluctuations.

Some types of insurance require a greater commitment of policyholders' surplus (capital) than do others. State insurance regulators use a risk-based capital system to establish an insurer's minimum capital requirements. This system has several components, but it gives greatest weight to underwriting risk. **Underwriting risk** measures the loss volatility of the types of insurance sold by an insurer. According to calculations under the system, some types of insurance require the insurer to maintain more policyholders' surplus than do other types of insurance. For example, medical malpractice insurance is subject to severe losses that are difficult to forecast from past loss experience. A primary insurer selling medical malpractice insurance is therefore required to have sufficient policyholders' surplus to absorb unexpected fluctuations in losses. Primary insurers can reduce demands on their policyholders' surplus by using reinsurance that provides surplus relief.

Underwriting risk
A measure of the loss volatility of the types of insurance sold by an insurer.

The number of different types of insurance a primary insurer sells also affects its reinsurance needs. A primary insurer that sells most types of insurance is more diversified and therefore is likely to have a more stable loss ratio than a primary insurer that sells only a few types of insurance.

Geographic Spread of Loss Exposures

A wide geographic spread of a primary insurer's loss exposures may stabilize its loss ratio and minimize its reinsurance needs for several reasons. In property insurance, the geographic diversification of catastrophe loss exposures can stabilize loss ratios. While no part of the world is completely immune to natural catastrophes, the nature of catastrophe loss exposures differs by geographic area, and catastrophes seldom strike all geographic areas simultaneously. Consequently, if a property insurer's insured loss exposures are spread over a wide geographic area, poor loss experience in one area may be offset by good loss experience in another area in any given period.

Geographic diversification is an especially effective tool when property insurance is spread worldwide, but it can still be effective even if diversification is limited to the United States. For example, the West Coast is vulnerable to earthquakes, the South Atlantic and Gulf Coasts are vulnerable to hurricanes, and the middle of the country is vulnerable to tornadoes and earthquakes (such as in the New Madrid Earthquake Zone). However, these natural forces are not usually at their worst in all areas in the same year.

Primary insurers selling property insurance in a single geographic area are especially vulnerable to fluctuations caused by catastrophe losses and need reinsurance to cover such losses. When Hurricane Hugo struck South Carolina in 1989, it led to the insolvency of several local insurers, including some that had been in business for many years and that were considered financially strong before the hurricane. Hurricane Andrew, which struck Florida and Louisiana in 1992, also resulted in the insolvency of several property insurers. These insurers had concentrations of loss exposures in the hurricane area and inadequate reinsurance to cover their losses.

Geographic diversification can stabilize loss ratios for reasons other than limiting losses from natural catastrophe loss exposures. Insurance regulation, laws governing tort liability, law enforcement practices, and other factors affecting property or liability insurance losses vary by geographic area. Adverse changes in these factors in one geographic area may be offset by favorable developments in another if the loss exposures are spread geographically.

Insurer Size

Insurer size is also an important determinant of reinsurance needs. Typically, small primary insurers need proportionately more reinsurance than large primary insurers to stabilize loss ratios. According to the law of large numbers, actual losses tend to approach expected losses as the number of loss exposures increases. Therefore, the loss ratio of a large primary insurer is likely to be more stable than the loss ratio of a small one if the mix of business sold is identical. Large primary insurers therefore depend less on reinsurance for loss stabilization.

Insurer Structure

The legal form of a primary insurer may affect its reinsurance needs. Stock insurers have more access to capital markets than mutual and reciprocal insurers. Consequently, stock insurers may be willing to accept less stability in their loss ratios and depend on capital markets to replace the policyholders' surplus depleted by adverse loss fluctuations. However, this could be hazardous, because the providers of capital may not look favorably on an insurer that has just sustained heavy losses.

Insurer Financial Strength

A financially strong insurer needs less reinsurance than a weaker one for two reasons. First, it does not need surplus relief to increase its premium capacity. Second, it needs less reinsurance to stabilize its loss ratio. A stronger surplus position enables the primary insurer to absorb more adverse loss ratio variations. The resulting lower reinsurance costs are an added advantage for a financially strong primary insurer.

One aspect of evaluating an insurer's financial strength involves assessing the stability and liquidity of its invested assets. If a primary insurer plans to rely on its policyholders' surplus to absorb abnormal losses, that policyholders' surplus must be invested in assets that are readily marketable and not subject to wide fluctuations in market price. Otherwise, the primary insurer's financial resources may be insufficient to pay losses in a timely manner.

A primary insurer that holds large amounts of common stock in its investment portfolio needs to be more heavily reinsured than one that holds short-term bonds, because the common stock may be marketable only at a substantial loss in an unfavorable market. However, a large portfolio of long-term bonds could also sustain substantial market losses due to interest rate risk. A primary insurer that invests a large portion of its funds in wholly owned subsidiaries needs to have a substantial reinsurance program because the stock of subsidiaries is not generally marketable.

Management's Risk Tolerance

The primary insurer's senior management decides how much and what types of reinsurance to buy. Although statistical data and financial models may support the decision, the decision usually reflects the senior management's willingness to assume risk, that is, their risk tolerance. Senior management must be comfortable with the insurance risk assumed, particularly when setting retentions and changing the reinsurance program.

Senior management must be confident that other stakeholders are also comfortable with the adequacy of the primary insurer's reinsurance program. For example, the reinsurance program should reflect the risk tolerance of the board of directors, stockholders, or policyholders in a mutual company. Senior management must be sensitive to those stakeholders' attitudes.

The practical effect of any proposed reinsurance program changes on supervisors and underwriters must also be considered. For example, if treaty reinsurance is used to increase large line capacity, then individual underwriters must adjust to the higher amounts of insurance that the primary insurer can now safely offer. If the underwriters are not comfortable with the additional large line capacity available under the reinsurance treaty, they may continue to purchase facultative reinsurance when they do not need to. Those actions could negate the cost savings of the treaty.

Factors Affecting Retention Selection

Selecting the primary insurer's retention is an essential and sometimes complex step in designing a reinsurance program. Although the retention is based on the primary insurer's financial needs and the types of insurance that the primary insurer sells, it is also negotiable by the primary insurer and the reinsurer. Cost is always a factor in selecting a retention. The cost of a reinsurance treaty usually increases as the size of the retention decreases. Four factors to consider when selecting a retention are:

1. Maximum amount the primary insurer can retain
2. Maximum amount the primary insurer wants to retain

3. Minimum retention sought by the reinsurer
4. Co-participation provision

The first factor to consider in selecting a retention is the maximum amount that a primary insurer can retain. This amount is a function of two considerations: regulatory requirements and the primary insurer's financial strength. States impose limits, either by statute or by regulation, on an insurer's premium capacity and large line capacity.

State insurance regulations effectively limit premium capacity to three dollars of net written premiums for each dollar of policyholders' surplus. Large line capacity is limited by a statutory provision that an insurer cannot retain a net amount for a single loss exposure greater than 10 percent of its policyholders' surplus. These statutes and regulations determine the upper limits of the amount that an insurer can retain. Many conservative primary insurers prefer to retain significantly less than those limits, especially the statutory limit of 10 percent of policyholders' surplus.

Subject to the statutory and regulatory limits, a primary insurer's ability to retain loss exposures is also limited by its financial strength. An insurer should not retain loss exposures so large that the resulting losses can threaten its solvency under a worst-case scenario. Determining the loss size that could threaten the primary insurer's solvency involves some judgment. The primary insurer must consider not only the losses within the retention of the reinsurance agreement under consideration, but also the retentions of closely related reinsurance agreements. For example, in setting the retention of a property per risk excess of loss treaty, potential retained losses under the related catastrophe excess of loss treaty must be considered and vice versa.

The second factor to consider in selecting a retention is the maximum amount that the primary insurer wants to retain. The managers of many primary insurers are unwilling to accept possible maximum retentions. This unwillingness may be caused partly by the uncertainty of determining how much loss exposure can safely be assumed and partly by the conservatism of some managers.

In the case of publicly held stock insurance companies, market pressures may lead to retentions well below the maximum that the insurer could legally or financially bear. Investors favor insurers that report growing, or at least stable, earnings. A primary insurer that assumes large retentions under its reinsurance agreements risks alienating investors because its earnings are likely to vary widely from year to year.

The third factor to consider in selecting a retention is the minimum retention sought by the reinsurer. Reinsurers sometimes demand a minimum retention as a condition of providing reinsurance. This demand is especially likely for excess of loss treaties, particularly catastrophe treaties. The purpose of the minimum retention requirement is to encourage the primary insurer to implement sound loss control, underwriting, and loss adjustment practices. Occasionally, for profitable pro rata treaties, the reinsurer may seek a lower retention in order to participate more fully in the profitable business.

The fourth factor in selecting a retention is the co-participation provision. A co-participation provision requires the primary insurer to participate in losses beyond the retention for similar loss control, underwriting, and loss adjustment reasons previously described. Primary insurers should consider this potential co-participation when selecting their retentions.

Factors Affecting Reinsurance Limit Selection

Selecting treaty limits can be as complex as selecting retentions. The five factors to consider in selecting treaty limits vary by the kind of treaty involved. They are as follows:

1. Maximum policy limit
2. Extra-contractual obligations
3. Loss adjustment expenses
4. Clash cover
5. Catastrophe exposure

The first factor to consider in selecting reinsurance limits is the maximum policy limit sold by the primary insurer. It may seem that the limit for a treaty that applies separately to each policy should be set at the maximum policy limit sold by the primary insurer. This practice would ensure coverage for any loss incurred. However, this may not be the most economical way to provide full reinsurance coverage. For example, if a primary insurer has many policies outstanding with limits of $500,000 or less and relatively few with limits between $500,000 and $1 million, setting the treaty limit at $500,000 and relying on facultative reinsurance to provide the remaining protection on the few larger loss exposures may be more economical than setting the reinsurance treaty limit at $1 million.

The limit for a stop loss treaty is stated as a loss ratio. Ideally, the limit should be set at the highest loss ratio that the primary insurer is likely to reach. Cost may force the primary insurer to settle for a lower limit, even if the reinsurer is willing to provide a higher limit.

The second factor to consider in selecting reinsurance limits is the primary insurer's potential exposure to extra-contractual obligations. If a reinsurance treaty is to provide protection against extra-contractual obligations (extra-contractual damages and excess of policy limit losses), the reinsurance treaty limit should be substantially higher than the primary insurer's highest policy limit. Damages resulting from extra-contractual obligations may be several multiples of the highest coverage limit offered.

The third factor to consider in selecting reinsurance limits is the potential magnitude of loss adjustment expenses. Depending on the type of underlying policy, loss adjustment expenses can be a significant loss component in per risk and per occurrence excess of loss treaties. Because loss adjustment expenses are generally added to the amount of loss (not pro rated between the primary insurer and reinsurer), loss adjustment expenses should be considered when selecting retentions and reinsurance limits. A primary insurer selling medical malpractice insurance, which has significant loss adjustment expenses, may exhaust the coverage provided by a casualty per occurrence excess of loss treaty with the loss adjustment expenses alone and have no reinsurance available to provide loss indemnification. Consequently, the primary insurer must carefully consider reinsurance limits and add an additional layer of reinsurance to accommodate the loss adjustment expenses.

The fourth factor to consider in selecting reinsurance limits is the primary insurer's potential exposure to multiple policies responding to the same occurrence. Clash cover applies when claims from two or more policies arise as a result of the same occurrence. Clash cover limits should be set by considering the highest limits offered by the primary insurer and the perceived likelihood that multiple policies may be involved in a single occurrence.

The fifth factor to consider in selecting reinsurance limits is the primary insurer's potential exposure to catastrophe losses. Selecting the limit for a catastrophe treaty is a more complex task than selecting limits for per risk excess of loss treaties. Catastrophe losses involve an accumulation of losses arising from a single occurrence. The primary insurer's liability for such losses has no stated limit. The effective limit is set by the number and face amount of policies subject to losses by a single catastrophic occurrence that the primary insurer has in force in a geographic area. In the case of a hurricane, the area affected may cover hundreds of square miles.

Statistics on hurricanes have been collected for many years and show the paths that the hurricanes followed and the wind forces involved. If an insurer has data on the loss exposures that it has assumed in the storm area, it can estimate the storm losses from a hurricane of a given intensity that follows a specified path. Insurers can do similar analyses for flood and earthquake losses because severe losses from those causes are likely restricted to known flood zones and geological faults. Insurers can use computer programs that estimate catastrophe losses to help set treaty limits.

Case Studies in Reinsurance Program Design

The following case studies illustrate the application of reinsurance programs to specific situations. The programs outlined are realistic for the circumstances shown, but are not necessarily the only reinsurance options that are appropriate for the hypothetical insurers. Two caveats should be kept in mind when reading these cases. First, reinsurance program design is a function of conditions in the reinsurance market and who is developing the program. Second, reinsurance program design is usually based on an in-depth analysis of the primary insurer's historical loss experience, financial condition, and types of insurance, as well as such subjective factors as senior management's aversion to risk.

Ajax Insurance Company Case Study

Ajax Insurance Company (Ajax) sells personal insurance—personal auto and homeowners—in three contiguous states. In the past three years, Ajax has experienced profitable operations and growth in its written premiums. Because of its recent profitability and perceived opportunities in its existing markets, Ajax plans to expand its market share in the next twelve months by appointing additional agents.

Ajax has net written premiums of $30 million and policyholders' surplus of $10 million; a capacity ratio of 3 to 1. Ajax restricts the amount of homeowners property coverage it sells at any one location to $450,000, but its typical homeowners account has lower coverage limit needs. For homeowners liability coverage and personal auto liability coverage, Ajax sells amounts of insurance up to $300,000 per occurrence.

Based on its present operations and future plans, Ajax's reinsurance intermediary suggests a reinsurance program that will provide Ajax with the surplus relief that it needs to finance growth. The reinsurance intermediary also suggests that Ajax purchase a catastrophe excess of loss treaty to protect against the consequences of a catastrophic event. Additionally, the reinsurance intermediary recommends excess of loss reinsurance to stabilize liability losses.

For its property loss exposures, Ajax's reinsurance intermediary suggests a five-line surplus share treaty with a $25,000 minimum line that can be increased, based on the characteristics of the loss exposure, to a maximum line of $75,000. The recommended surplus share treaty would have a total underwriting capacity of $450,000 for superior loss exposures, calculated by multiplying the maximum line amount by five and adding Ajax's retention (line). The reinsurance intermediary believes that it can negotiate a 30 percent ceding commission, which should more than offset Ajax's policy acquisition expenses. This surplus share treaty should provide Ajax substantial surplus relief on the bulk of the loss exposures it insures. Additionally, this agreement would allow Ajax to insure accounts up to the maximum coverage limits that it wants to offer.

Ajax's reinsurance intermediary suggests a catastrophe excess of loss treaty that provides indemnification for losses that exceed $400,000 up to a maximum loss of $3 million with a 5 percent co-participation provision. The catastrophe excess of loss retention was selected by considering Ajax's policyholders' surplus. Based on the geographic concentration of its insured risks and its plans for expansion, Ajax projects that the worst catastrophic event would result in a maximum loss of $3 million. Ajax believes that such an event is extremely unlikely but would not want to lose much more than $500,000 in policyholders' surplus should the worst occur.

To provide stabilization, Ajax's reinsurance intermediary suggests a per occurrence excess of loss treaty with a $100,000 attachment point applying to the liability insurance it sells. The reinsurance intermediary is familiar with Ajax's past loss experience, as well as its competency in underwriting and claim handing. Ajax and the reinsurance intermediary do not anticipate that the reinsurer will participate in frequent losses at the level of this retention.

Medical Malpractice Insurance Company Case Study

Medical Malpractice Insurance Company (Med-Mal) sells only medical professional liability insurance for physicians and surgeons in a single state. Med-Mal insures physicians and surgeons statewide, but its policy portfolio is concentrated in the state's two largest cities. Its medical professional liability policy has a $1 million limit that applies on a per occurrence and an aggregate basis.

Med-Mal is concerned about an increase in successful lawsuits against physicians and surgeons in its state. One significant loss for another insurer operating in the state involved several surgeons who were insured under separate policies with the same insurer and who were successfully sued for injuries arising out of a common incident. Because of this loss and the unfavorable legal environment for medical malpractice insurance, Med-Mal is concerned about the possibility of an increase in the frequency and severity of future claims. Med-Mal also wants to avoid potential catastrophic occurrences in which multiple insureds, with multiple limits of liability, would be involved in the same occurrence.

Med-Mal's reinsurance intermediary recommends per occurrence excess of loss reinsurance of $750,000 xs $250,000 to limit the effect of any one claim. Med-Mal's reinsurer also recommends that the reinsurance program address the possibility that more than one insured could be sued as the result of a single occurrence and extra-contractual damages or excess policy limits judgments could be awarded. The reinsurer suggests clash cover with a $500,000 attachment point (applies to the retention after the per occurrence excess of loss treaty) to restrict the use of the clash cover to occurrences with more than one physician, and a $5 million limit to recognize the possibility of multiple insured doctors involved in a common incident and/or the awarding of damages (extra-contractual or excess of policy limits).

SUMMARY

Reinsurance agreements can be categorized as either pro rata (proportional) or excess of loss (nonproportional) reinsurance. Pro rata reinsurance involves the proportional sharing of amounts of insurance, policy premiums, and losses (including loss adjustment expenses) between the primary insurer and the reinsurer. Excess of loss reinsurance requires the reinsurer to indemnify the primary insurer for losses that exceed the primary insurer's retention. Pro rata reinsurance and excess of loss reinsurance are available on a facultative or treaty basis, and are used with both property and liability insurance. However, specific types of pro rata reinsurance and excess of loss reinsurance are usually used with either property or liability insurance.

Pro rata reinsurance has two types:

1. Quota share reinsurance
2. Surplus share reinsurance

With quota share reinsurance, the primary insurer and reinsurer share policy premiums, amounts of insurance, and losses using a fixed percentage. Surplus share reinsurance covers only those policies whose amount of insurance exceeds a stipulated dollar amount, or line. The primary insurer and the reinsurer then share policy premiums and losses proportionally according to the amount of the primary insurer's line and the total amount of insurance. Quota share reinsurance and surplus share reinsurance can be used for property or liability insurance. However, surplus share reinsurance is typically only used with property insurance.

Excess of loss reinsurance has five types:

1. Per risk excess of loss
2. Catastrophe excess of loss
3. Per policy excess of loss
4. Per occurrence excess of loss
5. Aggregate excess of loss

Per risk excess of loss and catastrophe excess of loss reinsurance are generally used with property insurance. Per policy excess of loss and per occurrence excess of loss reinsurance are generally used with liability insurance. Aggregate excess of loss reinsurance is usually used for property insurance but can be used for liability insurance as well. The distinguishing characteristic among these types of excess of loss reinsurance is how losses are treated (individually or cumulatively) in determining whether the attachment point has been exceeded.

Finite risk reinsurance is an additional, nontraditional type of reinsurance that can be arranged to protect a primary insurer against large and unusual loss exposures. Although finite risk reinsurance premiums are typically higher than for other forms of reinsurance, the finite risk reinsurer commonly shares profits with the primary insurer when it has favorable loss experience or has generated income by investing the prepaid premium.

Reinsurance program design is a process through which primary insurers analyze their reinsurance needs and develop an optimal reinsurance program. Reinsurance programs usually involve a combination of reinsurance agreements.

A primary insurer's reinsurance needs are determined by various factors, including:

- Growth plans
- Types of insurance sold
- Geographic spread of loss exposures
- Insurer size
- Insurer structure
- Insurer financial strength
- Management's risk tolerance

The retentions and reinsurance limits selected by the primary insurer affect the reinsurance program's usefulness as well as its cost. Factors to consider in selecting a retention include:

- Maximum amount the primary insurer can retain
- Maximum amount the primary insurer wants to retain
- Minimum retention sought by the reinsurer
- Co-participation provision

Factors to consider in selecting reinsurance limits include:

- Maximum policy limit
- Extra-contractual obligations
- Loss adjustment expenses
- Clash cover
- Catastrophe exposure

This chapter described the various types of reinsurance. The next chapter examines the marketing systems through which reinsurance is sold.

Chapter 3

Direct Your Learning

The Reinsurance Placement Process

After learning the content of this chapter, you should be able to:

- Describe the two reinsurance marketing systems.
- Describe the steps in the reinsurance placement process.
- Explain how a reinsurance placement operates for:
  - Facultative reinsurance placed through the direct writing marketing system
  - Treaty reinsurance placed through the broker marketing system

OUTLINE

Reinsurance Marketing Systems

Reinsurance Placement Process

Reinsurance Placement Illustrations

Summary

Appendix—Sample Documentation

Develop Your Perspective

What are the main topics covered in the chapter?

This chapter describes the two systems used to market reinsurance. It also describes the steps involved in the reinsurance placement process.

Identify how reinsurance is marketed.

- What marketing systems are available to a primary insurer that wants to purchase reinsurance?
- What steps are involved in the reinsurance placement process?

Why is it important to learn about these topics?

Awareness of the sources of reinsurance and the documentation involved in completing a reinsurance agreement will help you to understand the reinsurance placement process.

Consider how a primary insurer purchases reinsurance.

- What would a primary insurer consider when choosing a marketing system?
- What steps must a primary insurer follow when purchasing facultative reinsurance from a direct writing reinsurer?
- What steps must a primary insurer follow when purchasing treaty reinsurance using a reinsurance intermediary?

How can you use what you will learn?

Determine which reinsurance marketing system your company uses for its reinsurance needs.

- What characteristics of this reinsurance marketing system made it appealing to your company?
- What documents must your company provide in the reinsurance placement process?

Chapter 3
The Reinsurance Placement Process

This chapter begins by describing the two reinsurance marketing systems: the direct writing marketing system and the broker marketing system. It then discusses the reinsurance placement process, which involves the following three steps:

1. Select a reinsurance marketing system.
2. Develop a reinsurance agreement proposal.
3. Complete agreement documentation.

The chapter concludes by illustrating a facultative reinsurance placement through the direct writer marketing system and a treaty reinsurance placement through the broker marketing system.

REINSURANCE MARKETING SYSTEMS

Reinsurance is sold through two marketing systems: the direct writing marketing system and the broker marketing system. In the **direct writing marketing system**, reinsurers sell reinsurance to primary insurers without involving reinsurance intermediaries. Direct writing reinsurers employ their own sales force to solicit and negotiate the reinsurance agreement's terms. The sales force provides services such as:

- Reinsurance program design, including an actuarial evaluation of an appropriate retention for the primary insurer
- Advice on underwriting, accounting, and claim handling procedures and controls
- Reinsurance claim processing

Direct writing reinsurers generally have sufficient financial resources to provide sizable reinsurance programs. For example, one reinsurer may provide the entire reinsurance program for a primary insurer.

In the **broker marketing system,** a reinsurance intermediary brokers the reinsurance transaction between the primary insurer and reinsurer(s). Reinsurance intermediaries provide services such as:

- Examination of the worldwide reinsurance market to optimize the price, coverage, and financial security of the reinsurance

Direct writing marketing system
A reinsurance marketing system in which direct writing reinsurers sell reinsurance to primary insurers without involving reinsurance intermediaries.

Broker marketing system
A reinsurance marketing system in which a reinsurance intermediary brokers the reinsurance transaction between the primary insurer and reinsurer(s).

- Reinsurance program design, including an actuarial evaluation of an appropriate retention
- Assistance in negotiation of premiums and terms
- Advice on underwriting, accounting, and claim handling
- Reinsurance claim handling

Reinsurers pay the reinsurance intermediaries for their services through either a flat fee or a commission, called **brokerage.** The brokerage rates used to calculate the brokerage usually vary by type of reinsurance and premium amount. Reinsurance intermediaries establish an agency relationship with both the primary insurer and the reinsurer. As reinsurance intermediaries do not assume insurance risk, they do not need the same financial resources as direct writing reinsurers.

The number of reinsurers accepting reinsurance through reinsurance intermediaries is greater than the number acting as direct writing reinsurers. Some reinsurers operate in both the direct writing and broker marketing systems. Both systems are common in the United States. Internationally, the broker marketing system is more common.

Brokerage
Compensation in the form of a flat fee or a commission that is paid by the reinsurer to the reinsurance intermediary for services provided.

REINSURANCE PLACEMENT PROCESS

The reinsurance placement process involves three steps.

> **The Three Steps in the Reinsurance Placement Process**
> 1. Select a reinsurance marketing system.
> 2. Develop a reinsurance agreement proposal.
> 3. Complete agreement documentation.

Select a Reinsurance Marketing System

The first step in the reinsurance placement process is to select a reinsurance marketing system.

When choosing between a direct writing and a broker marketing system, a primary insurer should answer the following questions:

- Which reinsurance marketing system is consistent and compatible with the primary insurer's marketing system? That is, does the primary insurer sell insurance directly or through an intermediary? Does the primary insurer prefer a reinsurer that uses a marketing system similar to its own?
- Are a reinsurance intermediary's services needed? Is the primary insurer able and willing to allocate internal resources to find appropriate reinsurers and place reinsurance rather than to have a reinsurance intermediary perform those functions?

- Are the loss exposures to be reinsured highly specialized? Are there significant coverage needs that may require the participation of reinsurers that are domiciled outside the U.S. or are not licensed to sell insurance in the primary insurer's state?
- Are the knowledge and objectivity expected from a reinsurance intermediary worth the cost, as compared to the cost of using a direct writing reinsurer?
- Does the primary insurer already have a good business relationship with a direct writing reinsurer or reinsurance intermediary?

Answering those questions helps determine which marketing system better suits the primary insurer's needs.

Employees of direct writing reinsurers contact only those primary insurers viewed as compatible with the reinsurer's financial goals. By evaluating the primary insurer's financial information and by discussing financial information and goals with the primary insurer's management, direct writing reinsurers determine whether a mutually beneficial relationship is feasible. Because direct writing reinsurers assume some or all of the primary insurer's insurance risk, they carefully select which primary insurers will be contacted. In contrast, the reinsurance intermediary's role in the reinsurance placement process is to find reinsurers that are compatible with the primary insurer's goals.

Direct writing reinsurers emphasize efficiency in their relationship with the primary insurer. They deal directly with primary insurers in negotiating reinsurance agreement terms, handling reinsurance premiums, and processing reinsurance claims. This direct communication may be faster and less prone to misunderstandings than communication through a reinsurance intermediary. However, reinsurance intermediaries may secure better coverage and terms than primary insurers could on their own. Reinsurance intermediaries also distribute premiums and collect claim payments from the reinsurers involved in the reinsurance program. Primary insurers issue one check for premium payments and send one notice of loss or request for loss payments to the reinsurance intermediary.

Reinsurance relationships are established over long periods. A direct writing reinsurer or reinsurance intermediary may solicit a primary insurer's business for years before establishing a business relationship. The primary insurer's management must be comfortable with and have confidence in the reinsurer or the reinsurance intermediary before committing to a business relationship.

Develop a Reinsurance Agreement Proposal

The second step in the reinsurance placement process is to develop a reinsurance agreement proposal. Several tasks are necessary to determine the reinsurance agreement's final terms. These tasks differ for direct writing reinsurance agreements, reinsurance intermediary agreements, and agreements using both direct writing reinsurers and reinsurance intermediaries.

In the direct writing marketing system, all contact occurs between the primary insurer and the reinsurer. The primary insurer may initiate a reinsurance relationship with the reinsurer. Alternatively, if the primary insurer already has a relationship with a particular reinsurer, it may expand or change reinsurance programs already in place.

The primary insurer discusses its basic requirements and goals with the reinsurer. The reinsurer develops a proposal, usually in the form of a letter or memorandum, and submits it to the primary insurer. The reinsurer makes the proposal subject to acceptance by the primary insurer.

In the broker marketing system, the primary insurer is considered the reinsurance intermediary's client, so the reinsurance intermediary is expected to act in the primary insurer's interests when placing reinsurance. (The reinsurance intermediary also acts in the reinsurer's interests for certain purposes, such as collecting and disbursing reinsurance premiums.)

When purchasing reinsurance, the reinsurance intermediary works with the primary insurer to develop the proposal and performs the following tasks:

- Contacts prospective reinsurers
- Presents the proposal to prospective reinsurers
- Obtains quotes and acceptances
- Handles rejections and counteroffers
- Drafts the reinsurance agreement (in most cases)
- Facilitates the reinsurance agreement's documentation

In performing those tasks, the reinsurance intermediary makes the offer, on the primary insurer's behalf, to reinsurers that meet the primary insurer's requirements.

Before accepting the business, reinsurers may audit the primary insurer. The reinsurance intermediary coordinates those audits to minimize disruptions to the primary insurer's operations. Several reinsurance audits may be conducted simultaneously to minimize disruption to the primary insurer.

In the past, primary insurers worked with either a direct writing reinsurer or a reinsurance intermediary. However, because of the increased complexity of reinsurance, competition, and demands for more reinsurance than one reinsurer is willing to provide, the use of both direct writing reinsurers and reinsurance intermediaries has become more common.

The primary insurer may contact a direct writing reinsurer for a specific portion of its reinsurance program and a reinsurance intermediary for another portion. If the direct writing reinsurer cannot write the entire reinsurance program, it may contact another reinsurer rather than send the primary insurer to a reinsurance intermediary. In another case, the primary insurer may suggest that the direct writing reinsurer and reinsurance intermediary share a single reinsurance agreement.

If a reinsurance intermediary was initially involved in the reinsurance placement, the reinsurance intermediary may approach the direct writing reinsurer about the primary insurer's reinsurance program if additional reinsurance coverage is needed or if the primary insurer has a specialized need and the direct writing reinsurer has the required expertise. The direct writing reinsurer may recognize the reinsurance intermediary relationship, or it may function independently. Many direct writing reinsurers have established internal departments to work with reinsurance intermediaries in an attempt to access additional business opportunities.

Those complex relationships involving direct writing reinsurers and reinsurance intermediaries can complicate preagreement negotiations. Therefore, primary insurers, reinsurers, and reinsurance intermediaries must take precautions to prevent misunderstandings by documenting the liabilities assumed by each party to the agreement.

Complete Agreement Documentation

The third step in the reinsurance placement process is to complete agreement documentation. Both preagreement and final agreement documentation are an integral part of any reinsurance placement.

Preagreement documentation is used for the following purposes:

- Establishing underwriting intent
- Providing necessary information
- Meeting regulatory requirements

Preagreement negotiations create the spirit of the agreement. A complete and concise record of negotiations ensures that all parties understand the agreement's intent. The preagreement documentation also serves as a record of why and how the underwriting decision was made.

Reinsurers need certain underwriting information to decide whether to accept or reject a proposal. The documentation prepared during preagreement negotiations contains information that is used in the formal proposal and the final agreement. That information should be as accurate and complete as possible.

Two types of preagreement documentation are required by state insurance statutes. The first type is the broker of record letter. When a reinsurance intermediary places reinsurance on a primary insurer's behalf, the reinsurance intermediary must have written authorization from the primary insurer to negotiate the agreement. A broker of record letter provides that authorization and protects reinsurers from assuming insurance through a reinsurance intermediary who does not have authority from the primary insurer. A broker of record letter also protects primary insurers by clarifying their relationship with the reinsurance intermediary.

The second type of preagreement documentation required by state insurance statutes is the premium and loss account. Reinsurance intermediaries are required to maintain at least one premium and loss account, which separates their own funds from those of primary insurers and reinsurers. Premiums and claim payments of multiple primary insurers or reinsurers can be in the same account if the records clearly identify for whom the funds are held. This recordkeeping requirement prevents offsetting the funds paid to one insurer with funds paid by another insurer.

Considerable time may elapse between negotiations and the final agreement. Consequently, primary insurers, reinsurance intermediaries, and reinsurers often use the preagreement documentation to guide premium cessions and loss payments before the final agreement is signed. This practice works because reinsurers that agree to the reinsurance agreement's terms are bound by those terms even if the agreement has not been signed.

However, state insurance regulators prefer that primary insurers have final agreements rather than preagreement documentation to guide their actions. One accounting rule developed by the National Association of Insurance Commissioners (NAIC) requires that reinsurance agreements be signed no later than nine months after the effective date in order for the agreement to receive reinsurance accounting treatment. This accounting rule, often referred to as the nine-month rule, encourages contract delivery.

Preagreement documentation can also help resolve issues even after the final agreement is signed. Disputes in reinsurance agreements generally are resolved through arbitration. Reinsurance arbitrators are not precluded from referring to the preagreement documentation to ascertain the intentions of the parties and using that information to resolve the dispute. However, preagreement documentation has only limited use in litigated reinsurance issues because, in the United States, the final agreement is considered to supercede all preagreement negotiation and documentation.

REINSURANCE PLACEMENT ILLUSTRATIONS

This section illustrates the reinsurance placement process. Using both facultative and treaty placement examples, the differences in agreement documentation for those types of reinsurance are highlighted.

For simplicity, these illustrations are for facultative reinsurance placed through a direct writing reinsurer and treaty reinsurance placed through a reinsurance intermediary. However, both facultative and treaty reinsurance can be placed either through a direct writing reinsurer or a reinsurance intermediary.

Facultative Reinsurance Placed Through the Direct Writing Marketing System

Often, the primary insurer's underwriter will not commit to selling an underlying insurance policy until the reinsurance terms are finalized.

Consequently, because facultative reinsurance terms often determine the underlying policy's coverage and price, the facultative reinsurance agreement is usually finalized quickly.

Common preagreement and final documentation in a facultative reinsurance placement includes the following:

- Proposal
- Clearance and underwriting
- Authorization
- Confirmation
- Reinsurance binder
- Policy documentation
- Facultative reinsurance certificate

Proposal

The primary insurer submits a proposal directly to the reinsurer. The proposal, also called a submission, contains sufficient underwriting information for the reinsurer to make an initial judgment about whether the proposed reinsurance fits the reinsurer's underwriting guidelines. The proposal also outlines the essential terms to be included in the final agreement.

Clearance and Underwriting

After the proposal is received, the reinsurer can use a clearance process to gather information about both the primary insurer and the underlying insured. The clearance process can answer the following questions:

- Is the reinsurer already providing reinsurance coverage for the insured represented in the submission?
- Is another underwriter employed by the same reinsurer also evaluating the same proposal?
- Has the reinsurer provided reinsurance for the same loss exposure before, and if so, what was the reinsurer's previous underwriting experience?

The clearance process can help to prevent situations in which the reinsurer accepts more than the maximum amount of reinsurance it wants to provide on any one loss exposure. Acceptance of too much reinsurance coverage on a loss exposure is called overlining.

After the clearance process is completed, the reinsurance underwriter determines what additional information is required. Property facultative reinsurance underwriters and primary insurance underwriters require much of the same information, including details about construction, occupancy, protection, and external exposures (these categories of information are often referred to by the acronym COPE). Additionally, both property and casualty facultative reinsurance underwriters need to know the premium quoted by the primary insurer for the loss exposure, the type of reinsurance sought (pro rata or excess of loss), and the amount of facultative reinsurance coverage requested. The reinsurer may also request that the primary insurer provide additional information on the loss exposure, such as loss control and financial information.

Using that information and a facultative reinsurance worksheet, the facultative reinsurance underwriter analyzes the loss exposure to determine whether it meets the reinsurer's underwriting criteria. The facultative reinsurance underwriter considers the following questions in performing that analysis:

- Is this the type of loss exposure that the reinsurer wants to reinsure, and has it been priced to stand a reasonable chance of earning an underwriting profit?
- If the loss exposure is unacceptable, could a specific change make the loss exposure acceptable?
- Is this type of loss exposure excluded from the reinsurer's retrocession arrangements, if any?
- How much expertise do the primary insurer's underwriters have with this type of loss exposure?
- Is the amount of reinsurance coverage requested for the loss exposure within the reinsurer's capacity?
- Is more information required before an underwriting decision can be made? If so, what is required?

Exhibits 3A-1 and 3A-2 in this chapter's Appendix show a sample casualty facultative reinsurance worksheet and an underwriting record that a facultative reinsurance underwriter may use.

If the facultative reinsurance underwriter decides that the loss exposure is acceptable, the next step is to price the reinsurance. Underwriters generally make pricing decisions based on their knowledge of the individual loss exposure being submitted and their experience with similar loss exposures. In addition, facultative reinsurers usually have established procedures that their underwriters follow so that the facultative pricing is within a range acceptable to the reinsurer, competitive with other reinsurers, and consistent with other submissions with similar hazard characteristics.

Using their pricing procedures, facultative reinsurers attempt to determine the extent to which their assumed liability will be subject to losses from the underlying policy and what they think is a fair price for that exposure to loss. This is known as exposure rating. Similar approaches to pricing are used for both casualty facultative reinsurance and property facultative reinsurance. However, there are differences in approach for each type.

When pricing casualty facultative reinsurance, underwriters often rely on increased limit factor tables developed by insurance advisory organizations such as the Insurance Services Office (ISO). Increased limit factor tables are tables used by primary insurers to price layers of underlying coverage in excess of the primary insurer's base limit. For example, a primary insurer's base limit for general liability policies may be $100,000 per occurrence and $200,000 aggregate (denoted $100/$200) but those amounts of insurance can be increased in increments (for example, $200/$200, $100/$300, $1,000/$3,000, and so forth) by application of an increased limit factor to the premium developed for the base limit. Likewise, casualty facultative reinsurance underwriters can use increased limit factor tables as guidance to price the liability they have assumed. The advantage of using increased limit factor tables is that they are actuarially developed and based on considerable industry-wide or company loss data, thereby making them a sound approach to reinsurance pricing.

In contrast, property facultative reinsurance underwriters rely more extensively on the hazard characteristics of the loss exposure in pricing than do casualty facultative reinsurance underwriters. They do this because there are more tangible attributes of the loss exposures that can be evaluated by the underwriter with property insurance than with casualty insurance.

Property facultative reinsurance underwriters often refer to the Lloyd's of London property first loss scale or to computerized analytical tools in pricing. **Lloyd's property first loss scale** functions similarly to increased limit factor tables by providing an approach to allocate premium between a primary and an excess layer. Although not actuarially based, the Lloyd's property first loss scale has been used extensively for many years and has proved to be a reliable pricing tool. ISO has developed PSOLD (Commercial Property Size-of-Loss Database) that is designed to aid reinsurers in pricing excess layers of property coverage. The PSOLD product is backed by an extensive aggregate loss history and provides the reinsurance underwriter with flexibility in choosing the data to consider in pricing.

Lloyd's property first loss scale
A scale used to allocate premium between a primary and an excess layer.

Exposure rating, using the approaches described, is often the first step in facultative reinsurance pricing. Reinsurance underwriters then usually modify the pricing derived from their pricing procedure to reflect loss adjustment expenses, profits and contingencies, unique characteristics of the loss exposure, the effect of inflation, potential investment income, and the competitiveness of the current facultative reinsurance marketplace.

Authorization

If the loss exposure is acceptable, the facultative reinsurance underwriter communicates the authorization to the primary insurer, quoting the reinsurance premium and reinsurance coverage terms. An **authorization** is the reinsurer's offer to reinsure the loss exposure at a certain premium and under specific terms and conditions. It is not a guarantee that a reinsurance certificate will be issued. Additional loss exposure information and the final policy provisions must meet the reinsurer's underwriting criteria. Authorizations are usually valid for a period that may range from one to sixty days depending on the effective date and nature of the loss exposure. This period allows the primary insurer's underwriter to negotiate with the original insured or make a determination as to whether the reinsurance should be purchased. Exhibit 3A-3 in this chapter's Appendix shows a sample facultative reinsurance authorization.

Authorization
The reinsurer's offer to reinsure the loss exposure at a certain premium and under specific terms and conditions.

Confirmation

Confirmation
The primary insurer's acceptance of the facultative reinsurer's authorization.

To accept the authorization, the primary insurer typically informs the reinsurer immediately and sends a formal **confirmation** after the underlying policy is issued. The confirmation serves as notice to the reinsurer that the underlying policy has been accepted or bound by the primary insurer. It outlines the terms, conditions, and premium of the underlying policy. The primary insurer also provides any additional information about the loss exposure that was requested by the reinsurer.

Reinsurance Binder

Binder
Temporary written agreement issued by the facultative reinsurer stating that the reinsurer accepts the loss exposure subject to satisfactory review of the underlying policy.

Until a facultative reinsurance certificate is issued to officially confirm the reinsurance transaction, a binder is issued, which serves as evidence of facultative reinsurance coverage. The reinsurance **binder** is the temporary written agreement issued by the facultative reinsurer stating that the reinsurer accepts the loss exposure subject to satisfactory review of the underlying policy. A binder describes the loss exposure and summarizes the facultative agreement.

Exhibit 3A-4 in this chapter's Appendix shows a sample facultative reinsurance binder.

Policy Documentation

The primary insurer sends a copy of the underlying policy to the reinsurer. If the underlying policy uses a standard coverage form developed by an insurance advisory organization such as ISO or the American Association of Insurance Services (AAIS), the primary insurer sends only the declarations page and any applicable endorsements to the reinsurer. If the underlying policy uses coverages developed by the primary insurer, or if it contains unusual coverages or provisions, the primary insurer sends a copy of the entire underlying policy to the reinsurer.

Facultative Reinsurance Certificate

After the reinsurer receives the primary insurer's documentation, the reinsurer issues a facultative reinsurance certificate that is attached to the primary insurer's copy of the underlying policy. The certificate is usually a short document (often one page) with the coverage and premium provisions on the front and the operating provisions on the back. The certificate identifies the underlying insured, the primary insurer, and the underlying insurance policy to which the reinsurance applies. Like the primary insurer's underlying insurance policy, the facultative reinsurance certificate is the final legal contract that specifies all the reinsurance terms, conditions, exclusions, and ceding commission (if applicable).

Exhibits 3A-5 and 3A-6 in this chapter's Appendix show the declarations and general conditions, respectively, for a sample facultative reinsurance certificate. The general conditions contain many clauses that are similar to those contained in a reinsurance treaty, such as those concerning retention and limit, definitions, premium taxes, insolvency, and offset.

A facultative reinsurance certificate can be either a pro rata or an excess of loss certificate. A pro rata facultative reinsurance certificate states the facultative limit as either a percentage or a dollar amount. For example, a quota share facultative reinsurance certificate could state the limit as "20% of $1,000,000" or "$200,000 part of $1,000,000." Both statements indicate that the reinsurer has accepted 20 percent of the $1 million original coverage limit. The pro rata facultative reinsurance certificate also shows the primary insurer's retention because the primary insurer can have more than one pro rata certificate on the same loss exposure. For example, the primary insurer may retain 50 percent of $1 million and purchase two separate facultative quota share reinsurance certificates, one for 20 percent and one for 30 percent. Both reinsurers would want to know how much of the original loss exposure the primary insurer is retaining net.

An excess of loss facultative reinsurance certificate states the certificate limit as a dollar amount in excess of the primary insurer's retention, such as "$250,000 xs $750,000." This means that the reinsurer has accepted $250,000 of a $1 million loss exposure and that the primary insurer has retained $750,000. If the reinsurance is in excess of other reinsurance, the other reinsurers are identified in the certificate.

Treaty Reinsurance Placed Through the Broker Marketing System

The documentation for purchasing treaty reinsurance through a reinsurance intermediary is similar to that for facultative reinsurance. In addition to the broker of record letter and the premium and loss account required by state insurance statutes, the documentation includes the following:

- Proposal
- Clearance and underwriting
- Authorization
- Treaty documentation

Treaty documentation differs from facultative documentation because treaties cover many loss exposures rather than only one.

Proposal

Reinsurance proposals contain a significant amount of underwriting information about the primary insurer and the loss exposures insured. Because the reinsurance intermediary's proposal specifies the proposed treaty terms applicable until the treaty is finalized, the proposal must provide enough information for the parties to proceed with the reinsurance transaction.

As a minimum, the proposal's underwriting section should contain the following seven categories of information:

1. Types and number of underlying policies issued, including limits profiles and geographic distribution of loss exposures
2. Past and projected premium base of the loss exposures that will be covered by the reinsurance agreement, as well as historical rate change information for the underlying loss exposures
3. Loss history of the policies subject to the treaty
4. Primary insurer's management philosophy
5. Primary insurer's financial information, such as audited financial statements and financial rating service information (such as that provided by A.M. Best Company or Standard & Poor's)
6. Primary insurer's operating systems and procedures
7. Results of on-site reviews of the primary insurer's operations

The first type of information that the underwriting section of a proposal should contain is a description of the types and number of underlying policies issued and the percentage of premiums for each type of policy. Exhibit 3-1 illustrates this part of the proposal for the Kalmia Insurance Company.

EXHIBIT 3-1

Homeowners Policies Issued by Kalmia Insurance Company

Policy Type	Percentage of HO Premiums	Number of Policies
HO-2	1%	100
HO-3	75%	5,357
HO-4	14%	2,800
HO-6	7%	700
HO-8	3%	500

Limits profiles summarize coverage limits and corresponding premiums for the loss exposures subject to the treaty. A typical limits profile categorizes the primary insurer's policies into ranges to help the reinsurer understand the loss exposures subject to the treaty. Exhibit 3-2 illustrates a limits profile for the Kalmia Insurance Company's homeowners business.

This description of the types of loss exposures should also indicate where the loss exposures are located and how much insurance coverage is being provided in each geographic area. Although this geographic distribution information is crucial for property catastrophe coverages, it can also be useful in evaluating casualty treaties. Some jurisdictions are known for consistently high jury awards in liability cases, so the casualty treaty underwriter should recognize how much insurance is issued in those jurisdictions. Exhibit 3-3 illustrates a geographic distribution of in-force property insurance policies. Based on this information, the property treaty underwriter could evaluate coastal wind or hail loss exposures.

EXHIBIT 3-2
Limits Profile—Kalmia Insurance Company Homeowners Business

Property Limits[1]	Average Limits ($)	Number of Policies	Average Premiums ($)	Total Estimated Premiums ($)
$0–$25,000	17,350	1,102	289	318,478
$25,001–$50,000	45,750	1,496	317	474,232
$50,001–$100,000	77,400	809	356	288,004
$100,001–$150,000	133,900	803	423	339,669
$150,001–$200,000	184,225	1,691	489	826,899
$200,001–$250,000	231,025	1,708	514	877,912
$250,001–$300,000	267,845	1,044	556	580,464
$300,001 and over	348,000	804	617	496,068
Total		9,457		$4,201,726

[1]Coverage A—Dwelling Limit

EXHIBIT 3-3
Geographic Distribution of In-Force Property Insurance Policies Issued by Kalmia Insurance Company

Geographic Area	Number of Policies	Percentage of Premiums
Alabama	1,322	13.9%
Georgia	2,272	24.0%
Florida		
Dade County	3,222	34.2%
Broward County	2,641	27.9%
Total	5,863	62.1%
Geographic Total	9,457	100.0%

The second type of information that the underwriting section of a proposal should contain is the past and projected premium base of the loss exposures that will be covered by the treaty and the rate changes associated with the underlying exposures. The premiums shown should be annotated to explain if they are written or earned, if they are past or projected or both, and the extent to which the proposal's premium base is representative of the treaty's loss exposures.

Some insurance policies, such as homeowners and businessowners policies, provide both property and liability coverage under one premium. When the reinsurance agreement covers only the property or liability insurance element, the appropriate premium must be extracted to create a rating base for the treaty. For example, 85 percent of the total homeowners premiums may be included as the subject premium for a property treaty.

The third type of information that the underwriting section of a proposal should contain is the loss history of the policies subject to the treaty. A comprehensive loss history is fundamental for estimating future experience. The number of years of loss history that should be provided depends on the type of insurance policies being reinsured and the stability of the loss ratio these policies produce.

Property insurance claims are usually reported soon after the loss occurrence. Property claims are usually settled quickly although issues about the damaged property's value might delay settlement. Business income losses are categorized as property losses but take longer to settle than most other types of property claims because the policyholders' losses occur over time. Reinsurers usually request three to five years of loss history for property insurance.

Liability insurance claims typically take longer to settle than property claims. Unlike property claims, liability claims are not necessarily reported immediately because injuries and damages often take time to manifest and it may be months or years before the injured party seeks a remedy. Reinsurers may require ten or more years of loss history for liability insurance. Because a liability claim's ultimate value may not be known for many years after the occurrence of the event causing the loss, insurers and reinsurers use loss reserve analysis techniques to evaluate the adequacy of loss reserves.

The loss history should list *all* claims for the policies subject to the treaty even if the claim does not affect the treaty under consideration. Complete past loss data are important because the reinsurer will want to consider the effect of inflation on the amount of future claims of a similar nature. The loss history also indicates whether the loss amounts shown are net of reinsurance or whether they are gross amounts of loss with no reduction for reinsurance recoveries (called ground-up losses). The loss information should include the following:

- Date of loss
- Date loss notice was received
- Amounts paid and amounts outstanding as loss reserves along with the amount of insurance of the policy affected by the claim
- Significant loss reserve changes
- Date(s) of loss payments

- Current status of each claim: whether open (claims with future payments expected) or closed (settled claims)
- Any multiple claims against the same policy limit

The fourth type of information that the underwriting section of the proposal should contain is the primary insurer's management philosophy. This allows the primary insurer to explain various facets of its operations to potential reinsurers, including its management's risk tolerance, insurance markets in which it competes, and its pricing policies and philosophies. This information also often includes management's future plans, the background of key members of the primary insurer's management team, and a summary of the primary insurer's support staff.

Reinsurance underwriters look for stable and consistent management practices that lead to predictable results. If the primary insurer is inclined to change reinsurers, production sources, or types of insurance sold, such changes may reduce the stability necessary to build a long-term reinsurance relationship.

The fifth type of information that the underwriting section of the proposal should contain is the primary insurer's financial information. Reinsurers usually expect the last several years of the primary insurer's financial statements developed for shareholders and regulators. Treaty underwriters may also require the primary insurer to submit the quarterly versions of these statements since the last year-end report was filed. Finally, reinsurers consult financial rating services, such as A.M. Best and Standard and Poor's, for a third-party analysis of the primary insurer's financial condition and future prospects.

The sixth type of information that the underwriting section of the proposal should contain is the primary insurer's operating systems and procedures. Primary insurers' systems and procedures are usually described in their operating manuals. Underwriting guides, line guides, and claim department manuals are typically the most useful. Underwriting guides indicate the types of insurance sold by the primary insurer and its underwriting and rating procedures. Line guides indicate the primary insurer's retention on each class of loss exposure ceded under the treaty. Claim department manuals indicate procedures for handling claims and setting reserves.

The seventh type of information that the underwriting section of the proposal should contain is the results of on-site reviews of the primary insurer's operations. Reinsurance underwriters can develop a more comprehensive understanding of the primary insurer's management, staff, and operations by reviewing operating manuals in conjunction with on-site visits to the primary insurer. Visits may occur at any time before or after the reinsurer offers an authorization on the treaty.

On-site reviews may reveal that the underwriting staff is too small or inexperienced to manage the type of insurance considered, or may reveal aggressive underwriting techniques that emphasize production over control and quality. Claim reviews may expose consistent underreserving that creates inaccuracies in long-term operating results. A claim review may also expose stair-stepping of reserves, meaning that individual reserves are increased incrementally rather than being adequately reserved at the outset, a sign that the claim department may generally be failing to accurately estimate claims' ultimate value.

Clearance and Underwriting

Reinsurance underwriters must fully understand the treaty's proposed terms and suggest alternatives if necessary to make the treaty acceptable. Therefore, underwriters should evaluate the following terms of a reinsurance treaty.

Pricing. The most frequently negotiated treaty term is its price. Pro rata treaty pricing is a function of the reinsurance commission paid by the reinsurer to the primary insurer. A primary insurer receiving a commission that is greater than its original acquisition expenses may consider pro rata less expensive, because the difference (often called override) may reduce overall expenses or losses under the agreement. Therefore, the profitability of the reinsurance treaty depends on the profitability of the underlying policies and the reinsurance commission. Excess of loss treaty pricing is based on reinsurance rates that are applied to the subject premium. The treaty proposal often contains suggested commission levels (pro rata treaties) or reinsurance rates (excess of loss treaties).

Treaty commencement and termination. The treaty proposal typically indicates the beginning and ending date of the reinsurance coverage. Some treaties provide coverage on a continuous basis, which means that the treaty continues until cancelled. Other treaties provide coverage on a term basis, which means the treaty will expire on a particular date. The commencement and termination provision of a treaty usually indicates whether it is written on a losses-occurring basis (includes losses on underlying policies in effect as of the treaty's inception date as well as newly issued or renewed underlying policies) or on a policies-attaching basis (includes only those losses for underlying policies sold or renewed after the treaty's inception date).

Cancellation. In continuous treaties, cancellation terms should indicate when a cancellation takes effect and what advance notice is required. The cancellation terms should also indicate whether cancellation will occur on a cut-off basis (terminates the reinsurer's responsibility for losses with the treaty's expiration date) or a run-off basis (continues the reinsurer's responsibility for losses until the expiration of the underlying policy), or whether the selection of cut-off or run-off is the primary insurer's option.

Exclusions. Treaties contain exclusions, as do the underlying policies that they reinsure. Treaties usually exclude high hazard loss exposures and causes of loss typically not covered by reinsurance. By excluding specific loss exposures, treaty exclusion provisions establish the parameters for the types of loss exposures the primary insurer can reinsure. As with other treaty terms, treaty exclusions can be negotiated, and they should be negotiated if they appear to overly restrict the primary insurer's marketing strategy.

Authorization

Often, the reinsurance intermediary first offers the reinsurance proposal to a lead reinsurer. A **lead reinsurer** negotiates the treaty terms and generally assumes a significant share of the treaty's liability. If the lead reinsurer accepts the proposal, the lead reinsurer then quotes the rates and other reinsurance terms. After the primary insurer accepts the lead reinsurer's terms, the proposal is presented to additional reinsurers. Additional reinsurers that accept the proposal are known as following reinsurers. **Following reinsurers** take a percentage of the treaty's liability on the same terms and conditions as the lead reinsurer.

Lead reinsurer
The reinsurer that negotiates the treaty terms and that generally assumes a significant share of the treaty's liability.

Following reinsurers
Reinsurers that take a percentage of the treaty's liability on the same terms and conditions as the lead reinsurer.

The treaty underwriter's authorization indicates the amount of reinsurance (usually expressed as a percentage of the underlying amount of insurance) that the reinsurer is willing to reinsure. Each reinsurer's participation percentage may be the same in the final treaty as it appears in the authorization, but not always. If a treaty is undersubscribed (has an insufficient number of participating reinsurers to provide the necessary reinsurance) or oversubscribed (has more participating reinsurers than needed to provide the necessary reinsurance), reinsurers usually adjust their participation percentages.

The reinsurer can initially communicate the authorization by telephone, followed by a written confirmation. The confirmation letter is not usually executed until the final percentage participation has been determined. This eliminates the need to reissue the confirmation letter if the participation changes. Most treaty authorizations do not contain the time limitations typical of facultative reinsurance because often many reinsurers are involved and the underlying policies to be reinsured are not awaiting reinsurance in order that the underlying policy can be issued. Exhibit 3A-7 in this chapter's Appendix contains a sample treaty confirmation letter and confirmation signing page.

Treaty Documentation

Formal treaty documentation includes the confirmation letter, interests and liabilities agreement, and treaty clauses. A subsequent chapter addresses the interests and liabilities agreement and treaty clauses.

The reinsurance intermediary and reinsurers should have an originally signed confirmation letter in their treaty files. The primary insurer receives a copy of the signed confirmation letter from the reinsurance intermediary to complete the placement process.

SUMMARY

Reinsurance is sold through two marketing systems: the direct writing marketing system and the broker marketing system. In the direct writing marketing system, a direct writing reinsurer deals directly with the primary insurer. In the broker marketing system, a reinsurance intermediary deals directly with the reinsurer on the primary insurer's behalf.

The reinsurance placement process involves the following three steps:

1. Select a reinsurance marketing system.
2. Develop a reinsurance agreement proposal.
3. Complete agreement documentation.

Selecting a reinsurance marketing system involves weighing several considerations. With both marketing systems, emphasis is placed on developing long-term relationships that will prove to be beneficial and profitable to both the primary insurer and reinsurer. Development of a reinsurance proposal involves assessing the primary insurer's reinsurance needs and the reinsurance market resources that can satisfy them. The approach taken to developing a reinsurance proposal differs somewhat between direct writing reinsurers and broker market reinsurers that receive business through reinsurance intermediaries. Completion of agreement documentation involves reducing the negotiations into writing. Precontract documentation is useful in guiding the reinsurance transaction until the final agreement is executed and may be an aid in resolving disputes.

This chapter concludes with illustrations of reinsurance placements. For simplicity, these illustrations are for facultative reinsurance placed through a direct writing reinsurer and treaty reinsurance placed through a reinsurance intermediary.

Facultative reinsurance placement through a direct writing reinsurer includes a proposal, clearance process and underwriting, authorization, confirmation, reinsurance binder, policy documentation, and facultative reinsurance certificate.

The documentation for purchasing treaty reinsurance through a reinsurance intermediary is similar to that for facultative reinsurance and includes a proposal, clearance process and underwriting, authorization, and treaty documentation.

The next chapter examines some of the common clauses found in reinsurance treaties and discusses the interests and liabilities agreement used when there is more than one participating reinsurer.

Appendix
Sample Documentation

This appendix contains examples of documents that may be used in the reinsurance placement process.

EXHIBIT 3A-1

Casualty Facultative Reinsurance Worksheet

☐ UMBRELLA ☐ X/S UMB ☐ BUFFER ☐ EXCESS ☐ HOME OFFICE REFERRAL

BRANCH

UNDERWRITER

NAME AND ADDRESS OF RISK

DATE RECEIVED

CEDING CO. POLICY LIMIT   PRODUCER #/PRODUCER & ADDRESS/CLIENT CONTACT

MAX. LIMIT TO BE PURCHASED BY RISK: CEDING CO./CO. #   SUBMISSION: PHONE   MAIL   OTHER

DESCRIPTION OF OPERATIONS

PRIMARY OPERATION   PAYROLL   AREA   SALES/RECEIPTS

U/W's EVALUATION

HAZARD RATING (LMH) — CATASTROPHE POTENTIAL — PRIMARY/LEAD PROGRAMS — SPECIFIC vs CLASS

TYPE:
- AL
- GL Operations ( )
- Premises ( )
- Products ( )
- Comp. Ops. ( )
- EL ( )
- OVERALL

U/L CONSIDERATIONS

(✔ FOR YES)	EXP	COV	(✔ FOR YES)	EXP	COV	AUTOS	#	$	=$	%L = I = LH =
COMPREHENSIVE AL			AIRCRAFT			PPT				
COMPREHENSIVE GL			LANDING FACILITY			PU/VAN/LT				
ISO Y/N FORM:			WATERCRAFT			MED TRK				
PAST AS CLAIMS MADE			MARINE FACILITY							
GENERAL AGGREGATE			RAILROAD							
PER: LOC/PROJECT			WC EL			HVY TRK				
PERSONAL INJURY			OD							
BLANKET CONTRACTUAL			FELA							
PRODUCTS/COMP. OPS.			ADMIRALTY			TRACTORS				
CCC REAL PROPERTY			BROAD AS PRIMARY							
CCC PERSONAL PROPERTY			NON-CONCURRENT DATES							
BROAD FORM PD			CLAIMS MADE			TRAILERS				
XCU/DEZ			RETRO DATE			BUSES				
LIQUOR LIAB.			DISCOVERY PERIOD							
INCID. MEDICAL MALP.			LASER ENDT							
PROF. LIAB./E&O										
ADVERTISER'S LIAB.										
FOREIGN LIAB. (GL/AL)										

LOSSES

PAST 5 YEARS   VALUATION DATE: O/S CLM SERVICE Y/N   EXPIRING PROGRAM: (LEAD/EXCESS)
1ST $ BASIS Y/N   AGG X/S $100,000 Y/N   OCC X/S $10,000 Y/N
YEAR:

The Reinsurance Placement Process 3.23

U/L CARRIERS & EFF. DATES	COVERAGE	U/L LIMITS	U/L PREMIUM	EXP MOD	MANUAL PREMIUM	X/S FACT	X/S PREMIUM	JUDG FACT	SUGGESTED PREMIUM
	AUTO								
	PREMISES								
	OPERATIONS								
	PROD COMP OPS								
	EL								

	FF	X		ATTACH:		LAYER	TOTAL	RATE
CONFIRMING CONDITIONS				SCHOOL DISTRICT LIMITATION ENDT	**EXCESS LAYER PRICING**	FIRST 1MM		
			AUTO LIAB	CONTRACTOR'S LIMITATION ENDT		1MM X/S 1MM		
			AIRCRAFT LIAB	MUNICIPALITY AMENDATORY ENDT		1MM X/S 2MM		
			ASSUMED PRODUCTS	FINANCIAL INSTITUTION ENDT		1MM X/S 3MM		
			ASBESTOS ABSOLUTE	OIL INDUSTRY LIMITATION & JOINT VENTURE ENDT		1MM X/S 4MM		
			POLLUTION ABSOLUTE	INSURANCE COMPANY AS NAMED INSURED ENDT		TOTAL 5MM		
			CONTRACTUAL	PARTNERSHIP AS NAMED INSURED ENDT				
			PERSONAL INJURY	INDIVIDUAL AS NAMED INSURED ENDT		5MM X/S 5MM		
			DISCRIMINATION	CROSS SUITS LIMITATION ENDT		5MM X/S 10MM		
			CCC REAL PROPERTY			5MM X/S 15MM		
			CCC PERS PROPERTY			5MM X/S 20MM		
			ERISA	SUBJECT TO: – CIRCLE APPLICABLE –				
			FIDUCIARY LIAB	(APPLICATION, 10K, INSPECTION REPORT,				
			EMPLOYERS LIAB/W.O.D.	PRODUCT BROCHURES, PRICING OF X/S LAYERS,				
			X/S WORK COMP.	COPY OF LEAD/FORM WE FOLLOW,				
			DIRECTORS & OFFICERS	ACCEPTABLE UL CARRIERS/TERMS)–				
			WATERCRAFT					
			PRODUCTS/COMP OPS					
			PROF LIAB:					
				RESERVE CERTIFICATE #:		RATE PER _____		
				QUOTE OPTIONS:				

REMARKS/NOTES: (FINAL LEAD QUOTE/CLIENTS LEAD/ALTERNATIVES OFFERED)

EXHIBIT 3A-2
Underwriting Record

RISK CLEARANCE

FRC RECORD ID#:

RISK IS
☐ CLEAR   ☐ NOT CLEAR   ☐ DETAILS ATTACHED

OPERATOR'S INITIALS   DATE   TYPE
                               NEW/RENEWAL

COVERAGE

LIMITS

REMARKS (U/W, TYPE OF OPERATION, ETC.)

INTER-BRANCH COMMENTS

GENERAL PROCESSING INFORMATION

OWNERSHIP CODE	INDUSTRY CODE	TYPE OF COVERAGE EXCESS/OTHER
LAYER POSITION	QUOTE/BINDER TEXT ID	
COVERAGE FORM	CERT TEXT ID	
DIARY REASON (OPT)	DATE	

☐ QUOTE: GOOD FOR _____ DAYS / UNTIL RENEWAL OR ___/___/___ (U/W   DATE:)

☐ BINDER: EFFECTIVE ___/___/___ FOR _____ DAYS   (U/W   DATE:)

☐ CERTIFICATE: TERM   ☐ ANNUAL   ☐ OTHER _____ TO _____ (U/W   DATE:)

CEDING COMPANY POLICY LIMIT   ☐ $_____,000,000/$_____,000,000   ☐ $_____,000 SIR

☐

CEDING COMPANY RETENTION   ☐   _____%

☐   _____% OF THE 1ST $_____,000/$_____,000 PLUS   _____% OF $_____,000/$_____,000 X/S $_____,000/$_____,000

☐

LIMITS   ☐   _____%

☐   _____% OF THE 1ST $_____,000/$_____,000 PLUS   _____% OF $_____,000/$_____,000 X/S $_____,000/$_____,000

☐

PREMIUM OUR SHARE	COMMISSION	RATE OF:	PER:
$	NET/GROSS @ %	$	
MINIMUM	DEPOSIT	INSTALLMENTS	
$	$		

PROGRESSING NOTES: ☐ ORDER REPORT: ☐ D&B
                                                                        ☐ OTHER
                                                      ☐ RETROCESSIONAL FACILITIES, IF APPLICABLE

TWO HEADS	CM APPROVAL	HO REFERRAL	HO CONFIRMATION DATE	FCH PAGE #

CERTIFICATE CODING – PREMIUM DISTRIBUTION				U/W SIGNOFF		DATE:	
LINE OF BUSINESS		BI (07)	PD (46)	CSL (13)			
SUBLINE				1ST LAYER	2ND LAYER	3RD LAYER	
	CODE	ATTACHMENT PT ↓ %	ATTACHMENT PT ↓ %	ATTACHMENT PT ↓ %	ATTACHMENT PT ↓ %	ATTACHMENT PT ↓ %	
AUTO (COMML)	005						
AUTO – NO FAULT	(40)						
M & C (OPERATIONS)	065						
OL & T (PREMISES)	080						
PRODUCTS/COMP OPS	085						
EMPLOYER'S LIAB.	040						
CONTRACTUAL	025						
LIQUOR LAW	060						
O & CP	075						
RAILROAD PROT	100						
WORK COMP	120						
AUTO (PERSONAL)	010						
COMP PERS LIAB	020						
DIC	030						
D & O	035						
EIL							
E & O	050						
MED MALPR	07035						
PROD INTEG IMP	090						
PRODUCTS RECALL	095						
RETROACTIVE							
REVIEW/REMARKS							

EXHIBIT 3A-3

Facultative Reinsurance Authorization

Reinsurance Company

Casualty Facultative Reinsurance Quotation

JUNE 11, 2004

JOHN DOE
SISTERDALE INSURANCE COMPANY
123 STREET
SOMECITY, PA 19355

INSURED:	ABC COMPANY	REFERENCE NO:	999998 – 2004
CITY, STATE:	SOMECITY, PA	EFFECTIVE DATE:	05/01/04 – 05/01/05

DEAR JOHN:

WE HEREBY OFFER OUR REINSURANCE QUOTATION AS FOLLOWS:

ITEM 1 – TYPE OF INSURANCE
BODILY INJURY AND PROPERTY DAMAGE LIABILITY OTHER THAN AUTOMOBILE

ITEM 2 – POLICY LIMITS
$2,000,000 EACH OCCURRENCE / $2,000,000 GENERAL AGGREGATE / $2,000,000 PRODUCTS & COMPLETED OPERATIONS AGGREGATE

ITEM 3 – COMPANY RETENTION
A. 100% OF THE FIRST $1,000,000 CSL EACH OCCURRENCE / $2,000,000 GENERAL AGGREGATE / $2,000,000 PRODUCTS & COMPLETED OPERATIONS AGGREGATE
B. NIL OF THE NEXT $1,000,000 CSL EACH OCCURRENCE / NIL GENERAL AGGREGATE / NIL PRODUCTS & COMPLETED OPERATIONS AGGREGATE

ITEM 4 – REINSURANCE ACCEPTED
A. NIL OF THE FIRST $1,000,000 CSL EACH OCCURRENCE / $2,000,000 GENERAL AGGREGATE / $2,000,000 PRODUCTS & COMPLETED OPERATIONS AGGREGATE
B. 100% OF THE NEXT $1,000,000 CSL EACH OCCURRENCE / NIL GENERAL AGGREGATE / NIL PRODUCTS & COMPLETED OPERATIONS AGGREGATE

ITEM 5 – BASIS OF REINSURANCE
EXCESS OF LOSS

PREMIUM
$60,800,000 GROSS ESTIMATED PREMIUM

ESTIMATED EXPOSURE AMOUNT
1,000,000

CEDING COMMISSION
25.00%

REINSURANCE RATE
$60.8 PER $1,000 RECEIPTS

COMMENTS

THE ABOVE REINSURANCE QUOTATION IS VALID FOR ONLY 60 DAYS FROM THE DATE OF THIS LETTER. PLEASE NOTIFY US PRIOR TO THE INCEPTION DATE OF THE POLICY TO BIND COVERAGE. ANNUAL PREMIUM IS SUBJECT TO A MINIMUM OF *100%* OF THE DEPOSIT PREMIUM.
ISSUING COMPANY: IIA CASUALTY COMPANY

RESPECTFULLY YOURS,

	ISSUING BRANCH	CORPORATE OFFICE
	500 STREET	200 STREET
	SOMECITY, PA 19355	SOMECITY, PA 19355
	800-555-1000	800-555-1001
JANE SMITH	FAX 555-555-1111	FAX 555-555-1100

EXHIBIT 3A-4

Facultative Reinsurance Binder

Reinsurance Company

Casualty Facultative Reinsurance Quotation

AUGUST 11, 2004

JOHN DOE
SISTERDALE INSURANCE COMPANY
123 STREET
SOMECITY, PA 19355

INSURED:	ABC COMPANY	REFERENCE NO:	999998 – 2004
CITY, STATE:	SOMECITY, PA	EFFECTIVE DATE:	06/16/04 – 06/16/05

DEAR JOHN:

WE HEREBY OFFER OUR REINSURANCE QUOTATION AS FOLLOWS:

ITEM 1 – TYPE OF INSURANCE
UMBRELLA LIABILITY

ITEM 2 – POLICY LIMITS
$23,000,000 EACH OCCURRENCE / $23,000,000 AGGREGATE WHERE APPLICABLE, EXCESS $2,000,000 EACH OCCURRENCE / $4,000,000 GENERAL AGGREGATE / $4,000,000 PRODUCTS & COMPLETED OPERATIONS AGGREGATE, EXCESS UNDERLYING

ITEM 3 – COMPANY RETENTION
$18,000,000 PART OF $23,000,000 CSL

ITEM 4 – REINSURANCE ACCEPTED
$5,000,000 PART OF $23,000,000 CSL

ITEM 5 – BASIS OF REINSURANCE
CONTRIBUTING EXCESS

PREMIUM
$24,867,000 GROSS ESTIMATED PREMIUM

CEDING COMMISSION
27.50%

ESTIMATED EXPOSURE AMOUNT
$5,000,000.00

REINSURANCE RATE
$4.97 PER $1,000 SALES

COMMENTS
PLEASE EXCLUDE POLLUTION, ASBESTOS, ALL CCC.

PLEASE FORWARD A COPY OF THE COMPANY POLICY WITHIN 90 DAYS OF BINDING. UPON RECEIPT OF YOUR POLICY, A CASUALTY REINSURANCE CERTIFICATE WILL BE ISSUED. ANNUAL PREMIUM IS SUBJECT TO A MINIMUM OF *100%* OF THE DEPOSIT PREMIUM. ISSUING COMPANY: IIA CASUALTY COMPANY.

RESPECTFULLY YOURS,

ISSUING BRANCH
500 STREET
SOMECITY, PA 19355
800-555-1000
FAX 555-555-1111

CORPORATE OFFICE
200 STREET
SOMECITY, PA 19355
800-555-1001
FAX 555-555-1100

JANE SMITH

EXHIBIT 3A-5

Facultative Reinsurance Certificate—Declarations

Reinsurance Company

Certificate of Casualty Facultative Reinsurance Quotation

JOHN DOE
SISTERDALE INSURANCE COMPANY
123 STREET
SOMECITY, PA 19355

ISSUING BRANCH
500 STREET
SOMECITY, PA 19355
800-555-1000
FAX 555-555-1111

CORPORATE OFFICE
200 STREET
SOMECITY, PA 19355
800-555-1001
FAX 555-555-1100

INSURED:	ABC COMPANY	REFERENCE NO:	999998 – 2004
CITY, STATE:	SOMECITY, PA	EFFECTIVE DATE:	01/01/04 – 01/01/05

CLIENT POLICY NO(S): 9999-9999-TEA   CLIENT POLICY TERM: 01/01/04 – 01/01/05

ITEM 1 – TYPE OF INSURANCE
AUTOMOBILE BODILY INJURY AND PROPERTY DAMAGE LIABILITY EXCLUDING NO-FAULT BENEFITS

ITEM 2 – POLICY LIMITS
BI & PD $1,000,000 CSL EACH ACCIDENT

ITEM 3 – COMPANY RETENTION
A. 100% OF THE FIRST $250,000 CSL EACH ACCIDENT
B. NIL OF THE NEXT $750,000 CSL EACH ACCIDENT

ITEM 4 – REINSURANCE ACCEPTED
A. NIL OF THE FIRST $250,000 CSL EACH ACCIDENT
B. 100% OF THE NEXT $750,000 CSL EACH ACCIDENT

ITEM 5 – BASIS OF REINSURANCE
EXCESS OF LOSS

PREMIUM
$41,000.00 NET ESTIMATED PREMIUM

CEDING COMMISSION
NIL

ESTIMATED EXPOSURE AMOUNT
$20,200,000

REINSURANCE RATE
$202.97 PER UNIT

COMMENTS

ANNUAL PREMIUM IS SUBJECT TO A MINIMUM OF 100% OF THE DEPOSIT PREMIUM

IIA CASUALTY COMPANY

February 11, 2004

JANE SMITH

Authorized Signature

EXHIBIT 3A-6

Facultative Reinsurance Certificate—General Conditions

IIA CASUALTY COMPANY

Reinsuring Agreements and Conditions

In consideration of the payment of the premium, and subject to the terms, conditions and limit(s) of liability set forth herein and in the Declarations and any endorsements made a part hereof, IIA Casualty Company (herein called the "Reinsurer") does hereby reinsure the ceding company named in the Declarations (herein called the "Company") in respect of the Company's policy(ies) set forth in the Declarations as follows:

A. **Retention and Limit.** The Company shall retain for its own account or for that of its treaty reinsurers, if applicable, the liability specified in the Declarations, Item 3. The Reinsurer shall indemnify the Company against losses or damages the Company is legally obligated to pay under the policy or policies reinsured, subject to the limits and coverage set out in Item 4 of the Declarations. The liability of the Reinsurer shall follow that of the Company, subject to all terms, conditions and limits of the Company's policy or policies except where this Certificate specifically provides otherwise, or where the reinsurance is non-concurrent.

B. **Term.** The certificate period shall be as specified in the Declarations at 12:01 a.m. as to both dates at the place specified in the Company's policy(ies).

C. **Inspection and Information.** The Company shall make available for inspection, and place at the disposal of the Reinsurer at all reasonable times, all records of the Company relating to this Certificate or claims in connection therewith. The Company shall furnish the Reinsurer with a copy of all policies, all endorsements and material underwriting information and agrees to notify the Reinsurer promptly of all changes that in any manner affect this Certificate.

D. **Claims and Losses.** The Company shall notify the Reinsurer promptly of any occurrence or claim and any subsequent developments pertaining thereto which in the Company's estimate of the value of injuries or damages sought, without regard to liability, might result in judgment in an amount sufficient to involve this Certificate. The Company shall also notify the Reinsurer promptly of any occurrence or claim in respect of which the Company has created a loss reserve equal to or greater than fifty (50) percent of the Company's retention specified in Item 3 of the Declarations; or, if this reinsurance applies on a contributing excess basis, when notice of claim is received by the Company. While the Reinsurer does not undertake to investigate or defend claims or suits, it shall nevertheless have the right and be given the opportunity, with full cooperation of the Company, to associate counsel at its own expense and to join with the Company and its representatives in the defense and control of any claim, suit or proceeding involving this Certificate.

All loss settlements made by the Company, provided they are within the terms, conditions and limit(s) of this Certificate, shall be binding on the Reinsurer. Upon receipt of an acceptable proof of loss, the Reinsurer shall promptly pay its proportion of such loss as set forth in the Declarations.

E. **Adjustment Expense.** The Reinsurer shall pay its proportion of expenses which are within the terms of the Company's policy(ies) (other than office expenses and/or payment to any salaried employee) incurred by the Company in the investigation and settlement of claims or suits and its proportion of court costs and interest on any judgment or award, in the ratio that the Reinsurer's loss payment bears to the Company's gross loss payment. If there is no loss payment, the Reinsurer shall pay a proportion of such expenses only in respect of business accepted on a Contributing Excess basis and then only in the percentage stated in Item 4 of the Declarations in the first layer of participation.

F. **Definitions.** As used in this Certificate, the terms below shall have the following meaning:
   1. Excess of Loss – The limit of liability of the Reinsurer, as stated in Item 4 of the Declarations, applies only to that portion of loss settlement within the policy limits in excess of the applicable retention of the Company, as stated in Item 3 of the Declarations.
   2. Contributing Excess – The Company's policy applies in excess of other valid insurance, reinsurance or a self-insured retention and the limit of liability of the Reinsurer applies proportionally to all loss settlements within the policy limits in the percentage set forth in Item 4 of the Declarations.
   3. Non-concurrent – The reinsurance provided does not apply to any hazards or risks of loss or damage covered under the Company's policy other than those specifically set forth in the Declarations. The retention of the Company and liability of the Reinsurer shall be determined as though the Company's policy applied only to the hazards or risks of loss or damage specifically described in the Declarations.

G. **Rights.** This Agreement is solely between the Company and the Reinsurer and performance of the obligations of each party under this Agreement shall be rendered solely to the other party. In no event shall anyone other than the Company or, in the event of the Company's insolvency, its liquidator, have any rights under this Certificate.

H. **Salvage and Subrogation.** The Company shall pay or credit the Reinsurer with the Reinsurer's portion of any recovery obtained from the salvage or subrogation. Adjustment expense for recoveries shall be deducted from the amount recovered. If the reinsurance is on an Excess basis, recoveries shall be distributed to the parties in an order inverse to that in which their liabilities accrued.

I. **Premium Taxes.** The Company will be liable for all taxes on premiums ceded to the Reinsurer under this Certificate.

J. **Insolvency.** In the event of the insolvency of the Company, the reinsurance provided by this Certificate shall be payable by the Reinsurer on the basis of the liability of the Company under the policy or policies reinsured without diminution because of such insolvency directly to the Company or its receiver, liquidator or statutory successor.

Continued on next page.

The Reinsurer shall be given written notice of the pendency of each claim against the company on any policy reinsured hereunder within a reasonable time after such claim is filed in the insolvency proceedings. The Reinsurer shall have the right to investigate each such claim and interpose at its own expense in the proceeding where such claim is to be adjudicated any defenses which it may deem available to the Company or its receiver, liquidator or statutory successor. The expense thus incurred by the Reinsurer shall be chargeable, subject to court approval, against the Insolvent Company as part of the expense of liquidation to the extent of a proportionate share of the benefit, which may accrue to the Company solely as the result of the defense undertaken by the Reinsurer.

K. **Offset.** The Reinsurer may offset any balance, whether on account of premiums, commissions, claims, losses, adjustment expense, salvage or any other amount due from one party to the other under this Certificate or under any other agreement entered into between the Company and the Reinsurer, whether acting as assuming reinsurer or as a ceding company.

L. **Exclusions.** Regardless of the terms and conditions of the Company's policy(ies), this Certificate shall not apply to:
   1. Nuclear incident as provided in the Standard Nuclear Incident Exclusion clause Liability Reinsurance; or,
   2. War as provided in the standard War Exclusion clauses; or
   3. Fiduciary liability in connection with the Employee Retirement Income Security Act of 1974 and as it may be amended.

M. **Arbitration.** As a condition precedent to any right of action hereunder, any dispute arising out of the interpretation, performance or breach of this Certificate, including the formation or validity thereof, shall be submitted for decision to a panel of three arbitrators. Notice requesting arbitration will be in writing and sent certified or registered mail, return receipt requested.

One arbitrator shall be chosen by each party and the two arbitrators shall, before instituting the hearing, choose an impartial third arbitrator who shall preside at the hearing. If either party fails to appoint its arbitrator within 30 days after being requested to do so by the other party, the later, after 10 days notice by certified or registered mail of its intention to do so, may appoint the second arbitrator.

If the two arbitrators are unable to agree upon the third arbitrator within 30 days of their appointment, the third arbitrator shall be selected from a list of six individuals (three named by each arbitrator) by a judge of the federal district court having jurisdiction over the geographical area in which the arbitration is to take place, or if the federal court declines to act, the state court having general jurisdiction in such area.

All arbitrators shall be disinterested active or former executive officers of insurance or reinsurance companies or Underwriters at Lloyd's London.

Within 30 days after notice of appointment of all arbitrators, the panel shall meet and determine timely periods for briefs, discovery procedures and schedules for hearings.

The panel shall be relieved of all judicial formality and shall not be bound by the strict rules of procedure and evidence. The decision of any two arbitrators when rendered in writing shall be final and binding.

The panel shall make its decision considering the custom and practice of the applicable insurance and reinsurance business as promptly as possible following the termination of the hearings. Judgment upon the award may be entered in any court having jurisdiction thereof. Each party shall bear the expense of its own arbitrator and shall jointly and equally bear with the other party the cost of the third arbitrator. The remaining costs of the arbitration shall be allocated by the panel. The panel may, at its discretion, award such further costs and expenses as it considers appropriate, including attorney fees, to the extent permitted by law.

N. **Cancellation.** Should the Company's policy(ies) be canceled, this Certificate shall terminate automatically at the same time and date. This Certificate may also be canceled by the Company upon not less than 30 days prior written notice, stating when this reinsurance shall terminate. This Certificate may also be canceled by the Reinsurer upon prior written notice to the Company, stating when this reinsurance shall terminate. The date of such termination shall be either:
   1. The date written notice is mailed plus the number of days required to cancel the Company's policy(ies) plus 15 days, but in no event exceeding 75 days in all; or,
   2. In the event of cancellation for non-payment of premium, the date written notice is mailed plus 15 days.

Proof of mailing shall be deemed proof of notice, and calculation of the earned premium shall follow the Company's calculation in the use of short rate or pro rata tables.

O. **Changes.** The terms of this Certificate shall not be waived or changed except by endorsement executed by a duly authorized representative of the Reinsurer.

IN WITNESS THEREOF, IIA Casualty Company has caused this Certificate of Reinsurance to be signed by its duly authorized officers at Somecity, Pennsylvania. The same shall not be binding upon the Reinsurer unless countersigned by an authorized representative of the Reinsurer.

Corporate Secretary

Chief Executive Officer
IIA Reinsurance

EXHIBIT 3A-7

Treaty Confirmation Letter and Confirmation Signing Page

Reinsurance Services

111 Any Street, Any Town, Any State 11111
Phone 800-555-1212 Facsimile 800-555-1213

January _____, ____

Ms. Susan P. Jones, CPCU
Vice President—Underwriting
XYZ Reinsurance Company
Anywhere, USA

    ABC Insurance Company
    Excess Catastrophe Reinsurance Contract
    Effective: January 1, _____
    Reinsurance Confirmation

As previously communicated via our January _____, _____ facsimile, we are pleased to formally confirm your participation on the captioned Contract. Your final line(s) are detailed in the attached Reinsurance Confirmation Signing Page.

The final terms and conditions are summarized in the enclosed Reinsurance Confirmation slip that follows our earlier correspondence. Please review the attached material at your earliest opportunity and advise if you have any questions or comments.

Subject to your approval, and in accordance with New York Regulation 98, please sign and return a copy of the Reinsurance Confirmation Signing Page as evidence of your agreement to accept this reinsurance.

Formal documentation will be drafted and forwarded to reinsurers following ABC's review and approval. In the interim, please let us know if we can be of any assistance. We appreciate your continued support of this reinsurance program.

    Sincerely,

    Dean Haddy, ARe
    Senior Reinsurance Analyst

Continued on next page.

Confirmation Signing Page

Reinsurance Services
111 Any Street
Any Town, Any State 11111

Telephone (800) 555-1212
Facsimile (800) 555-1213

Company: ABC Insurance Company
Contract: Excess Catastrophe Reinsurance Contract
Reinsurer: XYZ Reinsurance Company

On the basis of the terms outlined in Reinsurance Confirmation dated January _____, _____, the undersigned reinsurer confirms its agreement to accept a share(s) in the Contract(s) listed below, effective January 1, _____:

	Coverage Percent	Limit	Retention	Your Participation Percent	Your Dollar Line	Your Reference No.
1st XS Cat	100.0%	$4,000,000	$1,000,000	3.0%	$120,000	
2nd XS Cat	100.0%	$5,000,000	$5,000,000	2.0%	$100,000	

Revisions/Remarks: _____

Signed: _____
XYZ Reinsurance Company

Date: _____

Please sign and return one copy.

Chapter 4

Your Learning

Common Reinsurance Treaty Clauses, Part I

After learning the content of this chapter, you should be able to:

- Explain the purpose and operation of each of the following reinsurance treaty clauses:
  - Preamble
  - Affiliated companies clause
  - Reinsuring clause
  - Definitions clause
  - Access to records clause
  - Service of suit clause
  - Federal excise tax clause
  - Currency clause
  - Governing law clause
  - Exclusion clauses
  - Arbitration clause
  - Insolvency clause
  - Offset clause
  - Intermediary clause
  - Unauthorized reinsurance clause
  - Errors and omissions clause
- Explain the purpose and operation of the interests and liabilities agreement that may be attached to a reinsurance treaty.

OUTLINE

Clauses Common to Most Reinsurance Treaties

Interests and Liabilities Agreement

Summary

Develop Your Perspective

What are the main topics covered in the chapter?

Although each reinsurance treaty is unique, there are some clauses that are common to most treaties. This chapter explains the purpose of those common clauses, as well as the interests and liabilities agreement that may be attached to a treaty with multiple participating reinsurers.

Identify the clauses that are common to most reinsurance treaties.

- What is the purpose of each of those common clauses?

Why is it important to learn about these topics?

Understanding how common clauses operate is essential to understanding the rights and duties of the parties to the reinsurance treaty.

Examine a reinsurance treaty.

- Which of the clauses in the reinsurance treaty are considered to be common clauses?
- Which of the common clauses discussed in this chapter are not present in the reinsurance treaty?

How can you use what you will learn?

Analyze one of your company's reinsurance treaties.

- How do the clauses in your company's reinsurance treaty differ from those presented in this chapter?
- If different clauses were used, do they expand or limit the rights and duties of the parties?

Chapter 4
Common Reinsurance Treaty Clauses, Part I

Reinsurance agreements are usually broad in scope and contain wording to cover many different situations. Each reinsurance agreement's wording is unique because it states the intent of the parties to that particular agreement. However, some clauses are common to most reinsurance agreements. Because the wording contained in common clauses varies, understanding them is essential to understanding the rights and duties of the parties to the reinsurance agreement. This chapter discusses those common clauses, as well as the interests and liabilities agreement, which is a separate agreement that is used when there is more than one participating reinsurer.

Although most of the common clauses can be used both for facultative and treaty reinsurance, this chapter discusses the clauses in a treaty context.

CLAUSES COMMON TO MOST REINSURANCE TREATIES

Reinsurance practitioners have developed common clauses that can be used in most reinsurance treaties. Some of those common clauses are necessary for the treaty to function and are contained in almost every treaty. In addition, some clauses are required under state regulation.

The purpose and provisions of the following common clauses are described in this chapter:

- Preamble
- Affiliated companies clause
- Reinsuring clause
- Definitions clause
- Access to records clause
- Service of suit clause
- Federal excise tax clause
- Currency clause
- Governing law clause

- Exclusion clauses
- Arbitration clause
- Insolvency clause
- Offset clause
- Intermediary clause
- Unauthorized reinsurance clause
- Errors and omissions clause

Preamble

Preamble
The introduction to a reinsurance treaty that identifies the parties to the treaty.

The **preamble** is the introduction to a reinsurance treaty that identifies the parties to the treaty. The primary insurer is usually designated as the "Company" or the "Reinsured." Exhibit 4-1 shows an example of a preamble for a property quota share treaty.

EXHIBIT 4-1

Preamble

PROPERTY QUOTA SHARE
REINSURANCE AGREEMENT
NUMBER 01234
entered into by and between
HILL COUNTRY FIRE AND MARINE INSURANCE COMPANY
Des Moines, Iowa
(hereinafter referred to as the "Company")
and
Delmar Reinsurance Company
Wilmington, Del.
(hereinafter referred to as the "Reinsurer")

Affiliated Companies Clause

Affiliated companies clause
A reinsurance treaty clause that broadens the treaty's scope to include the primary insurer's affiliated companies.

The **affiliated companies clause** states that the primary insurer specified in the preamble includes the primary insurer's affiliated companies. The purpose of the affiliated companies clause is to broaden the reinsurers liability by including losses suffered by the primary insurer's affiliated companies.

Some versions of the affiliated companies clause require that the reinsurer receive notification of the addition of newly affiliated companies. If notificationn is required, and if the reinsurer is not willing to extend the agreement to the newly affiliated company, the primary insurer is usually given a specified period, such as forty-five days, to make other reinsurance arrangements for that affiliate.

Exhibit 4-2 shows an example of an affiliated companies clause that requires notice to and approval of the reinsurer when adding an affiliated company. This example names the "first named affiliated company" as the agent for communication between the "Company" and the "Reinsurer."

EXHIBIT 4-2

Affiliated Companies Clause

2 C

AFFILIATED COMPANIES

Whenever the word "Company" is used in this Contract, such term shall be held to include any or all of the affiliated companies which are or may hereafter be under common control, provided that notice be given to the Reinsurer of any such newly affiliated companies which may hereafter come under common control as soon as practicable with full particulars as to how such affiliation is likely to affect this Contract. In the event of either party maintaining that such affiliation calls for alteration in existing terms, and an agreement for alteration not being arrived at, then the business of such newly affiliated company is covered at existing terms only for a period of forty-five (45) days after notice by either party that it does not wish to cover such business.

The first named affiliated company hereunder shall be deemed to be the agent of the Company.

The retention of the Company and the liability of the Reinsurer and all other benefits accruing to the Company as provided in this Contract or any amendments hereto, shall apply to the affiliated companies comprising the Company as a group and not separately to each of the affiliated companies.

Source: Brokers & Reinsurance Markets Association (BRMA), http://www.brma.org/download/bcwrb002.doc (accessed January 23, 2004).

Reinsuring Clause

The **reinsuring clause** (sometimes called the business reinsured clause or business covered clause) establishes the obligatory nature of the cessions under the treaty and describes the type of reinsurance provided. It may also contain the following:

- Definition of policies
- Insurance policies covered
- Basis of attachment for policies

Reinsuring clause
A reinsurance treaty clause that establishes the obligatory nature of the cessions under the treaty and describes the type of reinsurance provided.

Definition of Policies

A standard reinsuring clause defines policies as "policies, contracts, and binders of insurance." The reinsuring clause may have a provision specifying that policies sold on an installment premium basis, reporting form basis, or on a continuous basis are to be considered renewed as of the end of the annual period beginning with the policy's inception date. Sometimes the definition provision includes reinsurance assumed by the primary insurer, which means that the treaty is a retrocession as well. The sample reinsuring clause in Exhibit 4-3 includes reinsurance in the definition of policies.

EXHIBIT 4-3

Reinsuring Clause

44 D

REINSURING CLAUSE

By this Contract the Company obligates itself to cede to the Reinsurer and the Reinsurer obligates itself to accept _____% quota share reinsurance of the Company's gross liability under policies, contracts and binders of insurance or reinsurance (hereinafter called "policies") in force at and becoming effective at and after *(hour) (date) (year),* including renewals, and classified by the Company as _____.

The liability of the Reinsurer with respect to each cession hereunder shall commence obligatorily and simultaneously with that of the Company, subject to the terms, conditions and limitations hereinafter set forth.

Source: BRMA, http://www.brma.org/download/bcwrb044.doc (accessed January 23, 2004).

Insurance Policies Covered

The provision that describes the insurance policies covered by a reinsuring clause can be specific or general. For example, the reinsuring clause may name a particular type of insurance or may describe the loss exposures covered as all policies underwritten by a particular department of the primary insurer. Examples of how insurance policies can be identified in a reinsuring clause include the following:

- Homeowners
- Commercial property and multi-peril, inland marine, and dwelling fire business
- Property business
- Insurance policies underwritten by the primary insurer's commercial casualty department
- Insurance policies sold by Washington General Agency, Seattle, Washington, for and on behalf of the Company

Generally, the broader the reinsuring clause, the more exclusions are necessary to indicate precisely what is covered. For example, the reinsuring clause may indicate that the treaty covers all policies originating from the property department of the primary insurer. However, the reinsurer may intend to exclude a specific type of property insurance, such as boiler and machinery.

Basis of Attachment for Policies

This provision of a reinsuring clause identifies which of the primary insurer's policies, according to their effective dates, are covered by the treaty. The two common bases of reinsurance treaty attachment are risks attaching and losses occurring.

- The **risks attaching basis** covers policies issued or renewed by the primary insurer on or after the reinsurance treaty's effective date.
- The **losses occurring basis** covers the unearned portion of policies in force as well as policies issued or renewed by the primary insurer on or after the reinsurance treaty's effective date.

When a reinsurer accepts liability on a risks attaching basis, it becomes responsible only for losses under policies issued or renewed on or after the treaty's effective date. Primary insurers should realize that claims may be presented after the treaty's inception date for losses that occurred before the inception date. These losses are not covered by the new treaty. The previous treaty may cover those losses (run-off); but if it does not, a coverage gap exists in the primary insurer's reinsurance program. The risks attaching basis can be modified to include in-force, new, and renewed policies as an alternative, with reinsurers collecting an appropriate premium for this exposure. Another alternative would be to use a losses occurring basis.

When a reinsurer assumes liability on a losses occurring basis, it becomes responsible for all losses occurring on or after the reinsurance treaty's inception date, regardless of when the underlying policy was issued. The losses occurring basis may be used if the primary insurer has an expiring reinsurance treaty on a cut-off basis in order to prevent a gap in reinsurance coverage. The sample reinsuring clause in Exhibit 4-3 illustrates an obligatory cession and assumption on a losses occurring basis.

Two other bases of reinsurance treaty attachment exist that are more limited in scope and, consequently, used less frequently. These limited bases of attachment are policies issued and in-force policies.

- The **policies issued basis** covers only new policies issued on or after the reinsurance treaty's effective date.
- The **in-force policies basis** covers only the unearned portion of in-force policies.

Reinsurers may want to use the policies issued basis when the primary insurer has significantly changed its underwriting guidelines to correct unfavorable loss experience. The treaty would cover newly issued policies, but the existing policies with poor loss experience would not be covered.

Risks attaching basis
A reinsurance attachment basis that covers policies issued or renewed by the primary insurer on or after the reinsurance treaty's effective date.

Losses occurring basis
A reinsurance attachment basis that covers the unearned portion of policies in force as well as policies issued or renewed by the primary insurer on or after the reinsurance treaty's effective date.

Policies issued basis
A reinsurance attachment basis that covers only new policies issued on or after the reinsurance treaty's effective date.

In-force policies basis
A reinsurance attachment basis that covers only the unearned portion of in-force policies.

Primary insurers may want to use the in-force policies basis to run-off existing policies. Because no new policies are being sold, the in-force policies basis would provide all the coverage needed.

Primary insurers' accounting systems may dictate which attachment basis can be used. For example, if a primary insurer's accounting system is not capable of separating earned and unearned premium on a risks attaching basis, the primary insurer would need to use another basis, such as the losses occurring basis.

Definitions Clause

Definitions clause
A reinsurance treaty clause that defines the terms used in the treaty.

The **definitions clause** defines the terms used in the treaty. The purpose of a separate definitions clause is to make locating the definitions easy. However, some reinsurance treaty drafters prefer to define a term when it first appears in the treaty. For example, risk may be defined in the reinsuring clause, and net loss may be defined in the treaty's losses section. Ultimately it is a matter of individual preference.

Even if a definitions clause is used, some terms may still be defined as they are used in other clauses. For example, net profit may be defined in an exclusion clause, rather than in the definitions clause. Exhibit 4-4 shows an example of a simple definitions clause.

EXHIBIT 4-4

Definitions Clause

A. The term "Policy" as used in this Agreement shall mean any binder, policy, or contract of insurance or reinsurance issued, accepted, or held covered provisionally or otherwise, by or on behalf of the Company.

B. The term "Casualty Business" as used in this Agreement shall mean all insurances and reinsurances written by the Company and classified by the Company as Casualty.

Access to Records Clause

Access to records clause
A reinsurance treaty clause that gives the reinsurer the contractual right to inspect all of the primary insurer's records that pertain to the coverage provided by the treaty.

The **access to records clause** gives the reinsurer the contractual right to inspect all of the primary insurer's records that pertain to the coverage provided by the reinsurance treaty. This right is essential for conducting underwriting, claims, and transactional audits of the primary insurer. It is also important to the reinsurer because in a dispute it protects the reinsurer against attempts by the primary insurer to withhold information. A sample access to records clause is shown in Exhibit 4-5. The provisions of this clause answer the following questions.

...he sample access to records clause in ...or its designated representatives" are ...ccess to records clause only specified ... interpreted to mean the employees ...ed by the reinsurer to inspect the primary insurer's records on its behalf.

What is the scope of the investigation of records? The reinsurer's right of access is limited to records that relate to the reinsurance provided by the treaty. For example, a reinsurer could not assert a right to access records on a type of insurance that the treaty does not cover.

What material must be made available for review? Generally, *all* of the primary insurer's records that pertain in any way to the treaty must be made available. For these purposes, records include accounting, underwriting, and claim information on any media, including computer records. The types of documents or records are usually not listed because that may limit the primary insurer's disclosure obligation to those documents or records specifically named.

Where must the records be made available for review? Although the clause may not specify the location, generally the reinsurer must go to where the records are normally located. An exception is when the records are in long-term storage. Under such circumstances, the reinsurer can expect the primary insurer to bring the records out of storage and make them available for review at the business office responsible for maintaining those records.

When must access be made available? The sample clause in Exhibit 4-5 specifies "all reasonable times," a phrase that is undefined. Generally, "all reasonable times" means during the primary insurer's normal business hours.

Is there a time limitation to access? The reinsurer usually has the right to access the primary insurer's records even after the treaty has been terminated. For example, environmental claims often involve the research of old policies and treaties.

EXHIBIT 4-5

Access to Records Clause

1 B

ACCESS TO RECORDS

The Reinsurer or its designated representatives shall have free access to the books and records of the Company on matters relating to this reinsurance at all reasonable times for the purpose of obtaining information concerning this Contract or the subject matter hereof.

Source: BRMA, http://www.brma.org/download/bcwrb001.doc (accessed January 23, 2004).

Service of Suit Clause

Service of suit clause
A reinsurance treaty clause that allows the primary insurer to seek a legal remedy from a court in a convenient jurisdiction when the treaty involves an international reinsurer that is not licensed or otherwise authorized to sell reinsurance in the United States. It also allows the reinsurer to commence suit in any court in the U.S. that has jurisdiction.

The **service of suit clause** allows the primary insurer to seek a legal remedy from a court in a convenient jurisdiction when the reinsurance treaty involves an international reinsurer that is not licensed or otherwise authorized to sell reinsurance in the United States. It also allows the reinsurer to commence a suit in any court of its choosing in the U.S. that has jurisdiction. Reinsurance is a worldwide business and it is common for international reinsurers to participate in large U.S. reinsurance programs. Without the service of suit clause, the primary insurer would be forced to bring suit or respond to suits in the reinsurer's country and under that country's laws if a contract dispute could not be resolved amicably among the parties to the treaty.

The service of suit clause designates an agent for service of process. Usually, the agent is a law firm that represents alien reinsurers. However, the agent could be an individual or the insurance commissioner in the primary insurer's state of domicile if that state's statutes require such a designation.

Finally, the service of suit clause requires the reinsurer to abide by the final court decision, allowing, however, for an appeal.[1]

Exhibit 4-6 shows an example of a service of suit clause. A statement at the beginning of the sample clause in Exhibit 4-6 specifies that the clause applies only to alien or unauthorized reinsurers. This enables the clause to be used in all reinsurance treaties, regardless of whether any party is an alien or unauthorized reinsurer.

EXHIBIT 4-6

Service of Suit Clause

49 A

SERVICE OF SUIT

(This Article only applies to reinsurers domiciled outside of the United States and/or unauthorized in any state, territory, or district of the United States having jurisdiction over the Company).

It is agreed that in the event of the failure of the Reinsurer hereon to pay any amount claimed to be due hereunder, the Reinsurer hereon, at the request of the Company, will submit to the jurisdiction of a court of competent jurisdiction within the United States. Nothing in this Article constitutes or should be understood to constitute a waiver of the Reinsurer's rights to commence an action in any court of competent jurisdiction in the United States, to remove an action to a United States District Court, or to seek a transfer of a case to another court as permitted by the laws of the United States or of any state in the United States. It is further agreed that service of process in such suit may be made upon _(Name and Address)_, and that in any suit instituted, the Reinsurer will abide by the final decision of such court or of any appellate court in the event of an appeal.

> The above-named are authorized and directed to accept service of process on behalf of the Reinsurer in any such suit and/or upon the request of the Company to give a written undertaking to the Company that they will enter a general appearance upon the Reinsurer's behalf in the event such a suit shall be instituted.
>
> Further, pursuant to any statute of any state, territory or district of the United States which makes provision therefore, the Reinsurer hereon hereby designates the Superintendent, Commissioner or Director of Insurance or other officer specified for that purpose in the statute, or his successor or successors in office, as its true and lawful attorney upon whom may be served any lawful process in any action, suit or proceeding instituted by or on behalf of the Company or any beneficiary hereunder arising out of this Contract of reinsurance, and hereby designates the above-named as the person to whom the said officer is authorized to mail such process or a true copy thereof.

Source: BRMA, http://www.brma.org/download/bcwrb049.doc (accessed March 29, 2004).

Federal Excise Tax Clause

The **federal excise tax clause** states that the primary insurer is responsible for administering and remitting the federal excise tax levied against alien reinsurers party to the reinsurance treaty. Federal excise tax is imposed on insurance and reinsurance policies issued by alien insurers. Reinsurance premiums are taxed at a rate of 1 percent on the gross amount ceded without reduction for ceding commissions received on reinsurance ceded.

The federal excise tax is owed when the reinsurance premium payment is made to an alien reinsurer. The primary insurer also becomes liable for the federal excise tax when payments are made to a nonresident agent, solicitor, or reinsurance intermediary, or when funds are transferred to any bank, trust fund, or similar recipient designated by the alien insurer.

The federal excise tax clause also states that the primary insurer is responsible for recovering any overpayment of federal excise tax on the reinsurer's behalf.

Transactions with alien reinsurers may be exempt from U.S. federal excise tax. Alien reinsurers whose premiums are subject to U.S. income tax are generally exempt from federal excise tax. A few countries have trade agreements with the U.S. that exempt reinsurers in both countries from paying federal excise taxes. The most notable examples are Germany, Great Britain, and Bermuda. If the reinsurer is exempt from federal excise tax, there is no need to include a federal excise tax clause in the reinsurance agreement.

Exhibit 4-7 shows an example of a federal excise tax clause.

Federal excise tax clause
A reinsurance treaty clause that states that the primary insurer is responsible for administering and remitting the federal excise tax levied against alien reinsurers party to the treaty.

> **EXHIBIT 4-7**
>
> ### Federal Excise Tax Clause
>
> 17 B
>
> FEDERAL EXCISE TAX
>
> (Applicable to those reinsurers, excepting Underwriters at Lloyd's London and other reinsurers exempt from Federal Excise Tax, who are domiciled outside the United States of America.)
>
> A. The reinsurer has agreed to allow for the purpose of paying the Federal Excise Tax (one percent) of the premium payable hereon to the extent such premium is subject to the Federal Excise Tax.
>
> B. In the event of any return of premium becoming due hereunder the Reinsurer will deduct the aforesaid percentage from the return premium payable hereon and the Company or its agent should take steps to recover the tax from the United States Government.

Source: BRMA, http://www.brma.org/download/bcwrb017.doc (accessed January 23, 2004).

Currency Clause

The **currency clause** specifies the following:

- The base currency (such as U.S. dollars) used in the treaty
- The basis of any conversion to the base currency

Frequently, the currency clause requires reporting in original currencies (those currencies that appear on the underlying policies) and converting those currencies at the prevailing exchange rates on the date that balances are entered on the primary insurer's books.

The sample currency clause shown in Exhibit 4-8 specifies U.S. dollars as the base currency.

Currency clause
A reinsurance treaty clause that specifies the base currency for the treaty and the basis of any conversion to the base currency.

> **EXHIBIT 4-8**
>
> ### Currency Clause
>
> 12 A
>
> CURRENCY
>
> Whenever the word "Dollars" or the "$" sign appears in this Contract, they shall be construed to mean United States Dollars and all transactions under this Contract shall be in United States Dollars.
>
> Amounts paid or received by the Company in any other currency shall be converted to United States Dollars at the rate of exchange at the date such transaction is entered on the books of the Company.

Source: BRMA, http://www.brma.org/download/bcwrb012.doc (accessed January 23, 2004).

Governing Law Clause

The **governing law clause** specifies which law governs the reinsurance treaty. Without such a clause, the law of any alien reinsurer's domicile would likely prevail in the event of a dispute with the alien reinsurer.

Exhibit 4-9 shows an example of a governing law clause.

Governing law clause
A reinsurance treaty clause that specifies which law governs the treaty.

EXHIBIT 4-9

Governing Law Clause

71 A

GOVERNING LAW

This Contract shall be governed as to performance, administration and interpretation by the laws of the State of _____, exclusive of the rules with respect to conflicts of law, except as to rules with respect to credit for reinsurance in which case the applicable rules of all states shall apply.

Source: BRMA, http://www.brma.org/download/bcwrb071.doc (accessed January 23, 2004).

Exclusion Clauses

Virtually all reinsurance treaties contain exclusions that limit the treaty's coverage. Each treaty reflects the specific intentions of the parties, so no standard list of exclusions exists. Also, no standard exclusion wordings exist, although the Lloyd's of London Non-Marine Association (NMA) has developed some exclusion wordings that are widely used.

Exclusion clauses usually apply to the following:

- High-hazard loss exposures
- Causes of loss or losses that are not customarily covered by reinsurance treaties

Examples of high-hazard loss exposures include loss exposures covered by boiler and machinery policies or by policies for businesses that transport and dispose of radioactive waste. Examples of excluded causes of loss are nuclear incidents, pollution, war, or insolvency fund assessments. Some exclusions are specific to a particular type of reinsurance. For example, a casualty treaty may specifically exclude burglary and theft coverage. Exclusions that are specific to a particular type of treaty are discussed in subsequent chapters. In some cases, reinsurers depend on the exclusions contained in the primary insurers' policies rather than using reinsurance treaty exclusions.

This section discusses the following types of exclusion clauses:

- Nuclear incident
- Pollution
- War risks
- Terrorism
- Insolvency fund

Nuclear Incident Exclusion Clause

Most worldwide primary insurers and reinsurers participate in nuclear reinsurance pools. Because of that participation, reinsurers avoid accumulating additional nuclear loss exposures through treaties with primary insurers. Therefore, a **nuclear incident exclusion clause** in a treaty excludes nuclear loss exposures, except for specific incidental loss exposures such as the nuclear hazards common to the radiological services of hospitals.

Nuclear incident exclusion clause
A reinsurance treaty clause that excludes nuclear loss exposures, except for specific incidental loss exposures.

Nuclear incident exclusion clauses vary by type of insurance and by territory. Exhibit 4-10 shows an excerpt from a sample nuclear incident exclusion clause that could be attached to a U.S. property treaty covering boiler and machinery loss exposures located in the U.S. The sample clause in Exhibit 4-10 applies to "any loss or liability" resulting from the primary insurer's participation in nuclear reinsurance pool. It also excludes the primary insurer's losses or liability (as an insurer or reinsurer) from the types of loss exposures that a nuclear reinsurance pool normally insures.

EXHIBIT 4-10

Nuclear Incident Exclusion Clause (Excerpt)

35 E

NUCLEAR INCIDENT EXCLUSION CLAUSE PHYSICAL DAMAGE AND LIABILITY
(BOILER AND MACHINERY POLICIES) – REINSURANCE – U.S.A.

(1) This reinsurance does not cover any loss or liability accruing to the Reassured as a member of, or subscriber to, any association of insurers or reinsurers formed for the purpose of covering nuclear energy risks or as a direct or indirect reinsurer of any such member, subscriber or association.

(2) Without in any way restricting the operation of paragraph (1) of this Clause it is understood and agreed that for all purposes of this reinsurance all original Boiler and Machinery Insurance or Reinsurance contracts of the Reassured shall be deemed to include the following provisions of this paragraph;

This Policy does not apply to "loss," whether it be direct or indirect, proximate or remote

(a) from an Accident caused directly or indirectly by nuclear reaction, nuclear radiation or radioactive contamination, all whether controlled or uncontrolled; or

(b) from nuclear reaction, nuclear radiation or radioactive contamination, all whether controlled or uncontrolled, caused directly or indirectly by, contributed to or aggravated by an Accident.

(3) However, it is agreed that loss arising out of the use of Radioactive Isotopes in any form is not hereby excluded from reinsurance protection.

Source: BRMA, http://www.brma.org/download/bcwrb035.doc (accessed January 23, 2004).

Pollution Exclusion Clause

A **pollution exclusion clause** excludes loss or damage resulting from pollution. A variety of pollution exclusion clauses are currently in use. Usually, the pollution exclusion clause is tailored to the type of loss exposure—property or liability—underlying the reinsurance treaty. Reinsurers typically do not want to provide pollution coverage in treaties except under very narrowly defined circumstances. In some cases, a reinsurer will ask a primary insurer to warrant that they will use the standard Insurance Services Office (ISO) pollution exclusion clause in the underlying general liability policies. Exhibit 4-11 shows an example of a broad pollution exclusion clause relating to loss exposures insured through underlying general liability policies.

Pollution exclusion clause
A reinsurance treaty clause that excludes loss or damage resulting from pollution.

EXHIBIT 4-11

Pollution Exclusion Clause

39C

POLLUTION EXCLUSION CLAUSE – GENERAL LIABILITY – REINSURANCE

A. This reinsurance excludes all loss and/or liability accruing to the reinsured company as a result of:

1. bodily injury or property damage arising out of the actual, alleged or threatened discharge, dispersal, release or escape of pollutants:

    a. at or from premises owned, rented or occupied by a named insured;

    b. at or from any site or location used by or for a named insured or others for the handling, storage, disposal, processing or treatment of waste;

    c. which are at any time transported, handled, stored, treated, disposed of, or processed as waste by or for a named insured or any person or organization for whom a named insured may be legally responsible; or

    d. at or from any site or location on which a named insured or any contractors or subcontractors working directly or indirectly on behalf of a named insured are performing operations:

        (i) if the pollutants are brought on or to the site or location in connection with such operations; or

        (ii) if the operations are to test for, monitor, clean up, remove, contain, treat, detoxify or neutralize the pollutants;

2. any governmental direction or request that a named insured test for, monitor, clean up, remove, contain, treat, detoxify or neutralize pollutants.

B. Subparagraphs A(1)(a) and A(1)(d)(i) above do not apply to bodily injury or property damage caused by heat, smoke or fumes from a hostile fire.

C. "Hostile fire" means a fire which becomes uncontrollable or breaks out from where it was intended to be.

D. "Pollutants" means any solid, liquid, gaseous or thermal irritant or contaminant, including smoke, vapor, soot, fumes, acids, alkalis, chemicals and waste. Waste includes material to be recycled, reconditioned or reclaimed.

Source: BRMA, http://www.brma.org/download/bcwrb039.doc (accessed January 23, 2004).

War Risk Exclusion Clause

War risk exclusion clause
A reinsurance treaty clause that excludes loss or damage resulting from organized war or warlike activities.

The **war risk exclusion clause** excludes loss or damage resulting from organized war or warlike activities. The clause typically contains two notable provisions:

1. The exclusion does not apply to loss exposures located in the U.S. if the primary insurer's policy includes a standard war risk exclusion clause.
2. The exclusion does not apply to losses from general riots, strikes, and civil commotion.

The clause has a limited effect on reinsurance for the majority of U.S. primary insurers because their policies already exclude war risks in most cases. Exhibit 4-12 shows an example of a war risk exclusion clause.

EXHIBIT 4-12

War Risk Exclusion Clause

56 B

WAR RISK EXCLUSION CLAUSE (REINSURANCE)

As regards interests which at time of loss or damage are on shore, no liability shall attach hereto in respect of any loss or damage which is occasioned by war, invasion, hostilities, acts of foreign enemies, civil war, rebellion, insurrection, military or usurped power, or martial law or confiscation by order of any government or public authority.

This War Exclusion Clause shall not, however, apply to interests which at time of loss or damage are within the territorial limits of the United States of America (comprising the fifty States of the Union and the District of Columbia, its territories and possessions, including the Panama Canal Zone and the Commonwealth of Puerto Rico and including Bridges between the United States of America and Mexico provided they are under United States ownership), Canada, St. Pierre and Miquelon, provided such interests are insured under original policies, endorsements or binders containing a standard war or hostilities or warlike operations exclusion clause.

Nevertheless, this clause shall not be construed to apply to loss or damage occasioned by riots, strikes, civil commotion, vandalism, malicious damage, including acts committed by agents of any government, party or faction engaged in war, hostilities or other warlike operation, provided such agents are acting secretly and not in connection with any operations of military or naval armed forces in the country where the interests insured are situated.

Source: BRMA, http://www.brma.org/download/bcwrb056.doc (accessed January 23, 2004).

Terrorism Exclusion Clause

Terrorism exclusion clause
A reinsurance treaty clause excludes loss or damage resulting from acts of terrorism.

A **terrorism exclusion clause** excludes loss or damage resulting from acts of terrorism. Many reinsurers began adding terrorism exclusion clauses to reinsurance treaties after the terrorist attacks of September 11, 2001. Primary insurers and reinsurers were obligated to cover most of the losses resulting from the attacks, which were unprecedented in terms of the loss of life, personal injury, and property damage. Because of the unpredictability and potential extent of future terrorism losses, most reinsurers determined terrorism to be an uninsurable cause of loss. Exhibit 4-13 shows an example of a terrorism exclusion clause.

> **EXHIBIT 4-13**
>
> **Terrorism Exclusion Clause**
>
> 56 F
>
> TERRORISM EXCLUSION ENDORSEMENT (Reinsurance)
>
> Notwithstanding any provision to the contrary within this reinsurance or any endorsement thereto it is agreed that this reinsurance excludes loss, damage, cost or expense of whatsoever nature directly or indirectly caused by, resulting from or in connection with any act of terrorism regardless of any other cause or event contributing concurrently or in any other sequence to the loss.
>
> For the purpose of this endorsement an act of terrorism means an act, including but not limited to the use of force or violence and/or the threat thereof, of any person or group(s) of persons, whether acting alone or on behalf of or in connection with any organisation(s) or government(s), committed for political, religious, ideological or similar purposes including the intention to influence any government and/or to put the public, or any section of the public, in fear.
>
> This endorsement also excludes loss, damage, cost or expense of whatsoever nature directly or indirectly caused by, resulting from or in connection with any action taken in controlling, preventing, suppressing or in any way relating to any act of terrorism.
>
> If the Reinsurers allege that by reason of this exclusion, any loss, damage, cost or expense is not covered by this reinsurance the burden of proving the contrary shall be upon the Reassured.
>
> In the event any portion of this endorsement is found to be invalid or unenforceable, the remainder shall remain in full force and effect.

Source: BRMA, http://www.brma.org/download/bcwrb056.doc (accessed January 23, 2004).

In November 2002, the Terrorism Risk Insurance Act of 2002 (TRIA) was signed into law. TRIA requires all *commercial* property and casualty insurers that are "licensed or admitted to engage in the business of providing primary or excess insurance in any State" to make terrorism insurance coverage available to their policyholders. Terrorism exclusion clauses contained in commercial property and casualty policies in force when TRIA was enacted are now void to the extent that they exclude "acts of terrorism" as defined by TRIA. The goal of the Act is to provide primary insurers and reinsurers with time to develop marketplace capacity for terrorism loss exposures so that a permanent governmental terrorism insurance mechanism is unnecessary. The terrorism reinsurance coverage provided under the Act began to phase out in 2004 and terminates on December 31, 2005. It is hoped that prior to the Act's termination, primary insurers and reinsurers should have developed an acceptable stand-alone terrorism coverage that can be offered to commercial insureds.

Insolvency Fund Exclusion Clause

Insolvency fund exclusion clause
A reinsurance treaty clause that states that reinsurers will not indemnify primary insurers for any assessments that the primary insurers must pay to state guaranty funds because of another primary insurer's insolvency.

State guaranty funds
Nonprofit, unincorporated associations established in all states to pay the outstanding claims of insolvent primary insurers.

Virtually all reinsurance treaties contain an **insolvency fund exclusion clause** stating that reinsurers will not indemnify primary insurers for any assessments that the primary insurers must pay to state guaranty funds because of another primary insurer's insolvency. **State guaranty funds** are nonprofit, unincorporated associations established in all states to pay the outstanding claims of insolvent primary insurers. All insurers selling types of insurance covered by the guaranty fund are automatically association members. The sample insolvency fund exclusion clause in Exhibit 4-14 includes a broad definition of "insolvency fund" to provide maximum protection for the reinsurer.

EXHIBIT 4-14

Insolvency Fund Exclusion Clause

20 A

INSOLVENCY FUND EXCLUSION

It is agreed that this Contract excludes all liability of the Company arising by contract, operation of law, or otherwise, from its participation or membership, whether voluntary or involuntary, in an insolvency fund. "Insolvency Fund" includes any guaranty fund, insolvency fund, plan, pool, association, fund or other arrangement, howsoever denominated, established or governed, which provides for any assessment of or payment or assumption by the Company of part or all of any claim, debt, charge, fee, or other obligation of an insurer, or its successors or assigns, which has been declared by any competent authority to be insolvent, or which is otherwise deemed unable to meet any claim, debt, charge, fee or other obligation in whole or in part.

Source: BRMA, http://www.brma.org/download/bcwrb020.doc (accessed January 23, 2004).

Arbitration Clause

Arbitration clause
A reinsurance treaty clause that states that an arbitration process will be used to resolve disputes between the parties to the treaty.

The **arbitration clause** states that an arbitration process will be used to resolve disputes between the parties to the reinsurance treaty. Arbitration is typically conducted by a panel of disinterested third parties who are familiar with insurance and reinsurance business practices. Exhibit 4-15 shows one example of an arbitration clause, but many versions of arbitration clauses are in use. The following items are specifically addressed in the sample arbitration clause in Exhibit 4-15.

EXHIBIT 4-15

Arbitration Clause

6 L

ARBITRATION

As a condition precedent to any right of action hereunder, any dispute arising out of the interpretation, performance or breach of this Contract, including the formation or validity thereof, shall be submitted for decision to a panel of three arbitrators. Notice requesting arbitration will be in writing and sent certified or registered mail, return receipt requested.

One arbitrator shall be chosen by each party and the two arbitrators shall, before instituting the hearing, choose an impartial third arbitrator who shall preside at the hearing. If either party fails to appoint its arbitrator within _____ days after being requested to do so by the other party, the latter, after _____ days notice by certified or registered mail of its intention to do so, may appoint the second arbitrator.

If the two arbitrators are unable to agree upon the third arbitrator within _____ days of their appointment, the third arbitrator shall be selected from a list of six individuals (three named by each arbitrator) by a judge of the federal district court having jurisdiction over the geographical area in which the arbitration is to take place, or if the federal court declines to act, the state court having general jurisdiction in such area.

All arbitrators shall be disinterested active or former executive officers of insurance or reinsurance companies or Underwriters at Lloyd's, London.

Within _____ days after notice of appointment of all arbitrators, the panel shall meet and determine timely periods for briefs, discovery procedures and schedules for hearings.

The panel shall be relieved of all judicial formality and shall not be bound by the strict rules of procedure and evidence. Unless the panel agrees otherwise, arbitration shall take place in _____(City, State)_____, but the venue may be changed when deemed by the panel to be in the best interest of the arbitration proceeding. Insofar as the arbitration panel looks to substantive law, it shall consider the law of the State of _____. The decision of any two arbitrators when rendered in writing shall be final and binding. The panel is empowered to grant interim relief as it may deem appropriate.

The panel shall interpret this Contract as an honorable engagement rather than as merely a legal obligation and shall make its decision considering the custom and practice of the applicable insurance and reinsurance business as promptly as possible following the termination of the hearings. Judgment upon the award may be entered in any court having jurisdiction thereof.

Each party shall bear the expense of its own arbitrator and shall jointly and equally bear with the other party the cost of the third arbitrator. The remaining costs of the arbitration shall be allocated by the panel. The panel may, at its discretion, award such further costs and expenses as it considers appropriate, including but not limited to attorneys fees, to the extent permitted by law.

Source: BRMA, http://www.brma.org/download/bcwrb006.doc (accessed January 23, 2004).

Arbitration required. The parties must use an arbitration panel as described in the arbitration clause if they are unable to settle a dispute. In Exhibit 4-15, the sample clause's stipulation "As a condition precedent to any right of action hereunder…" means that before either party can take legal action, the dispute must be arbitrated. Insurers have made many unsuccessful attempts to circumvent the provisions of an arbitration clause. For example, insurers have claimed the following:

- The treaty has expired.
- The clause applies to disputes arising out of transactions under the treaty, not to disputes over the treaty wording itself.
- The clause does not apply to denials of coverage under the treaty.
- The clause handles disputes over business practice, not fraud.

These and similar arguments have not been successful.

Time limits. A goal of arbitration is to resolve the dispute quickly. Consequently, the arbitration clause specifies that arbitrators must be appointed within a specified time limit, usually thirty days. The parties then have a prescribed time within which to present their cases to the arbitration panel. The panel has the authority to approve time extensions to allow all material and witnesses' statements to be presented.

Arbitrators' qualifications. The arbitrators must be active or retired executives of insurers or reinsurers. In the sample clause in Exhibit 4-15, the term "executive" is undefined and in practice is interpreted to mean a senior officer, a vice president, or someone with a high rank. The reasons why arbitrators must be executives include the following:

- Usually, a person has not actively participated in reinsurance treaty negotiations and practices until reaching a senior officer level.
- An executive has a broad enough background in insurance practices to consider both sides of a dispute.

Additionally, the arbitrators must be disinterested in the arbitration proceedings. Arbitrators usually indicate any involvement they had or have with either of the parties to the arbitration, particularly having served as an appointed arbitrator in a previous arbitration. This minimizes concerns about future legal challenges due to conflicts of interest.

Rules of procedure and evidence. In the sample clause in Exhibit 4-15, the arbitrators are "relieved of all judicial formality and shall not be bound by the strict rules of procedure and evidence." This is a shortened reference to older terminology that stated that the panel should make its decision based on insurance and reinsurance custom and usage. The instruction reflects the fact that arbitrators are not jurists, they are laypersons who are specialists in the subject giving rise to the dispute. Arbitrators should use their best judgment to determine the agreement's original intent and rule accordingly. It is not desirable for the arbitration decision to be contrary to the parties' intent because of a legal technicality.

The decision. The sample clause in Exhibit 4-15 provides that the decision of any two arbitrators is binding on both parties, and any court having jurisdiction can enter the judgment. The arbitration panel does not have the power to enforce its decision. Therefore, if one party does not comply with the decision, the other party must seek enforcement through the civil justice system.

Insolvency Clause

The **insolvency clause** states that the reinsurer agrees to pay its reinsurance obligations under the reinsurance treaty if the primary insurer becomes insolvent, whether or not the primary insurer has paid its obligations to the underlying policyholders. This clause is required in most states and ensures that reinsurers pay the state insurance department liquidator the same amount that they would otherwise have paid had the primary insurer been solvent. Exhibit 4-16 shows an example of an insolvency clause.

> **Insolvency clause**
> A reinsurance agreement clause that states that the reinsurer agrees to pay its reinsurance obligations if the primary insurer becomes insolvent, whether or not the primary insurer has paid its obligations to the underlying policyholders.

EXHIBIT 4-16

Insolvency Clause

19 F

INSOLVENCY

In the event of the insolvency of the Company, this reinsurance shall be payable directly to the Company, or to its liquidator, receiver, conservator or statutory successor on the basis of the liability of the Company without diminution because of the insolvency of the Company or because the liquidator, receiver, conservator or statutory successor of the Company has failed to pay all or a portion of any claim. It is agreed, however, that the liquidator, receiver, conservator or statutory successor of the Company shall give written notice to the Reinsurer of the pendency of a claim against the Company indicating the policy insured which claim would involve a possible liability on the part of the Reinsurer within a reasonable time after such claim is filed in the conservation or liquidation proceeding or in the receivership, and that during the pendency of such claim, the Reinsurer may investigate such claim and interpose, at its own expense, in the proceeding where such claim is to be adjudicated, any defense or defenses that it may deem available to the Company or its liquidator, receiver, conservator or statutory successor. The expense thus incurred by the Reinsurer shall be chargeable, subject to the approval of the court, against the Company as part of the expense of conservation or liquidation to the extent of a pro rata share of the benefit which may accrue to the Company solely as a result of the defense undertaken by the Reinsurer.

Where two or more reinsurers are involved in the same claim and a majority in interest elect to interpose defense to such claim, the expense shall be apportioned in accordance with the terms of this Contract as though such expense had been incurred by the insolvent Company.

Should the Company go into liquidation or should a receiver be appointed, all amounts due either Company or Reinsurer, whether by reason of premium, losses, or otherwise under this Contract or any other contract heretofore or hereafter entered between the parties (whether such contract is all assumed or ceded), shall be subject to the right of offset at any time and from time to time, and upon the exercise of the same, only the net balance shall be due.

Source: BRMA, http://www.brma.org/download/bcwrb019.doc (accessed January 23, 2004).

The following items are specifically addressed in the sample insolvency clause in Exhibit 4-16:

Without diminution. The sample clause states that the reinsurer must pay claims allowed against the insolvent primary insurer "without diminution." In other words, the reinsurer must pay the full value of claims under the treaty.

The liquidator of an insolvent primary insurer will demand full payment from a reinsurer despite the primary insurer's inability to pay all or part of an underlying claim. For example, suppose that a primary insurer (now insolvent) had an adjusted loss before insolvency of $350,000, but the loss was not paid to the claimant. The liquidator paid the claimant $262,500, or 75 percent of the loss. The primary insurer had excess of loss reinsurance for $400,000 xs $100,000. Payment without diminution required that the excess of loss reinsurer pay $250,000 ($350,000 less the $100,000 retention) rather than $162,500 ($262,500 less the $100,000 retention). The net effect in this example was that the reinsurer paid the bulk of the loss, thereby preserving primary insurer funds to satisfy other claimants and creditors. Exhibit 4-17 illustrates the effect of the insolvency clause in this example.

EXHIBIT 4-17

Effect of Insolvency Clause

	Primary Insurer Non Insolvent	Primary Insurer Insolvent	
		Without Insolvency Clause	With Insolvency Clause
Loss payable	$350,000	$262,500	$262,500
Reinsurer	250,000	162,500	250,000
Primary insurer/Liquidator	100,000 (retention)	100,000 (retention)	12,500

Notice requirements. The liquidator must notify the reinsurer of a pending claim so that the reinsurer has sufficient time to investigate the claim and decide whether to participate in the liquidator's defense of the claim. Without sufficient notice, the reinsurer may find out too late that its position is prejudiced regarding the claim.

Right to investigate and to defend. The reinsurer has the right to participate at its own expense in a claim's defense. The claim section of reinsurance treaties covering third-party insurance normally specifies this right. Even though the right is rarely included in first-party treaties, the reinsurer may become involved in the defense of first-party claims with the primary insurer's consent. This provision of the insolvency clause reaffirms a reinsurer's rights under a treaty covering third-party business and extends these rights to a treaty covering first-party insurance.

This defense provision is important because the reinsurer must pay without diminution. To protect its own interests by ensuring that a reasonable claim value is established and that reasonable defenses are pursued, the reinsurer may choose to incur the extra costs to investigate and defend claims.

Reimbursable expenses. With court approval, the reinsurer's expenses to investigate and settle a claim can be wholly or partially reimbursable by the insolvent primary insurer. The amount is limited to the proportionate share of the benefit that accrues to the primary insurer. If there is no reduction in the full value of the claim because of the reinsurer's efforts, no benefit was realized, and therefore no expenses are reimbursed. When two or more reinsurers are involved and a majority interest elects to investigate and defend a claim, the expenses are apportioned according to the treaty's terms as if the insolvent primary insurer had incurred them.

Reinsurance proceeds payable. According to the sample insolvency clause in Exhibit 4-16, the reinsurer pays claim amounts to the liquidator. However, many claimants of insolvent primary insurers seek payment directly from reinsurers because payments may be made more quickly, and payments may be for a larger sum than the liquidator would pay.

Depending on the primary insurer's state of domicile, the insolvency clause can contain exceptions allowing the reinsurer to pay someone other than the liquidator. An exception applies when the treaty specifically provides for payment to another payee (with a cut-through endorsement). However, the liquidator may not want such an arrangement because it does not allow the liquidator to control the funds paid by the reinsurer.

The insolvency clause may not require the liquidator or court to approve the reinsurer's direct payment to an insolvent primary insurer's claimant. However, it is prudent for a reinsurer to seek such approval. Without approval, the reinsurer could find that it is still required to pay the full amount of the reinsurance recoverable to the liquidator, even though it paid the claim in full directly to the underlying insured on behalf of the insolvent primary insurer.

Offset Clause

The **offset clause** allows the primary insurer and the reinsurer to offset balances due to each other. For example, if the primary insurer owes $125,000 in reinsurance premium and the reinsurer owes the primary insurer $75,000 for a claim, then the primary insurer can send the net balance of $50,000 to the reinsurer. Likewise, if a reinsurer owes more in claims than the primary insurer owes in premium, the reinsurer can send the net claim balance to the primary insurer.

Offsets can apply to premium and losses between the same parties within a single treaty (narrow offset) or across multiple treaties (broad offset). For example, a broad offset would allow the primary insurer and reinsurer to consider all balances due to one another from all their reinsurance treaties together in determining the net amount owed. The sample clause shown in Exhibit 4-18 allows broad offset.

Offset clause
A reinsurance treaty clause that allows the primary insurer and the reinsurer to offset balances due to each other.

> **EXHIBIT 4-18**
>
> **Offset Clause**
>
> 36 B
>
> OFFSET
>
> The Company and Reinsurer may offset any balance or amount due from one party to the other under this Contract or any other contract heretofore or hereafter entered into between the Company and the Reinsurer, whether acting as assuming reinsurer or ceding company. However, in the event of the insolvency of any party hereto, offset shall only be allowed in accordance with applicable law.

Source: BRMA, http://www.brma.org/download/bcwrb036.doc (accessed January 23, 2004).

Intermediary Clause

State insurance regulators require that an intermediary clause be included whenever a reinsurance intermediary is involved in a reinsurance transaction. The **intermediary clause** requires the reinsurer to accept financial responsibility (the credit risk) for funds transferred from the primary insurer to the reinsurer through a reinsurance intermediary. The NAIC *Financial Condition Examiners Handbook* requires such wording for insurers to take credit for reinsurance on their financial statements.[2]

The intermediary clause identifies the reinsurance intermediary by name and states that all communications must be channeled through the reinsurance intermediary. Communications can include notices, statements, premium, return premium, commissions, taxes, losses, loss adjustment expenses, salvages, and loss settlements. It is common for the primary insurer to have direct contact with the reinsurer without the reinsurance intermediary actively participating in the dialogue. However, the reinsurance intermediary should be kept fully informed of the details of such communication.

The intermediary clause further states that payments made by the primary insurer to the reinsurance intermediary constitute payment to the reinsurer. However, payments made by the reinsurer to the reinsurance intermediary constitute payment to the primary insurer *only to the extent to which they are actually received by the primary insurer*. For most purposes, the reinsurance intermediary is the primary insurer's agent, not the reinsurer's agent. However, the intermediary clause requires the reinsurer to take the credit risk if the reinsurance intermediary becomes insolvent, which, for this purpose, makes the reinsurance intermediary the reinsurer's agent. Exhibit 4-19 shows an example of an intermediary clause.

Intermediary clause
A reinsurance treaty clause required by state insurance regulation that requires the reinsurer to accept financial responsibility (the credit risk) for funds transferred from the primary insurer to the reinsurer through a reinsurance intermediary.

EXHIBIT 4-19

Intermediary Clause

23 A

INTERMEDIARY

___(Intermediary Name)___ is hereby recognized as the Intermediary negotiating this Contract for all business hereunder. All communications (including but not limited to notices, statements, premium, return premium, commissions, taxes, losses, loss adjustment expense, salvages and loss settlements) relating thereto shall be transmitted to the Company or the Reinsurer through ___(Intermediary Name and Address)___. Payments by the Company to the Intermediary shall be deemed to constitute payment to the Reinsurer. Payments by the Reinsurer to the Intermediary shall be deemed to constitute payment to the Company only to the extent that such payments are actually received by the Company.

Source: BRMA, http://www.brma.org/download/bcwrb023.doc (accessed January 23, 2004).

Unauthorized Reinsurance Clause

The **unauthorized reinsurance clause** specifies those requirements that an unauthorized reinsurer must satisfy in order for the transaction to receive favorable accounting treatment as a reinsurance transaction.

State insurance regulators require the inclusion of the unauthorized reinsurance clause in reinsurance treaties with unauthorized reinsurers because of the effect that uncollectable reinsurance has had on the solvency of primary insurers. Because unauthorized reinsurers are not licensed to operate in the primary insurer's state of domicile, state insurance regulators have no direct regulatory authority over them. The unauthorized reinsurance clause, and the state insurance regulations supporting it, give state insurance regulators some indirect control over unauthorized reinsurers.

The unauthorized reinsurance clause requires primary insurers to withhold reinsurance premium owed to unauthorized reinsurers until the reinsurer's obligations for outstanding losses and loss adjustment expenses (including incurred but not reported loss reserves) are either satisfied or extinguished. As an alternative to totally funding these obligations through a separate reserve on its books, the primary insurer can obtain a letter of credit from the reinsurer or other proof of collateral acceptable to state insurance regulators. An excerpt from a sample unauthorized reinsurance clause is shown in Exhibit 4-20.

Unauthorized reinsurance clause
A reinsurance treaty clause required by state insurance regulation that specifies those requirements that an unauthorized reinsurer must satisfy in order for the transaction to receive favorable accounting treatment as a reinsurance transaction.

> **EXHIBIT 4-20**
>
> ## Unauthorized Reinsurance Clause (Excerpt)
>
> 55 A
>
> UNAUTHORIZED REINSURANCE
>
> (Applies only to a Reinsurer who does not qualify for full credit with any insurance regulatory authority having jurisdiction over the Company's reserves.)
>
> As regards policies or bonds issued by the Company coming within the scope of this Contract, the Company agrees that when it shall file with the insurance regulatory authority or set up on its books reserves for unearned premium and losses covered hereunder which it shall be required by law to set up, it will forward to the Reinsurer a statement showing the proportion of such reserves which is applicable to the Reinsurer. The Reinsurer hereby agrees to fund such reserves in respect of unearned premium, known outstanding losses that have been reported to the Reinsurer and allocated loss adjustment expense relating thereto, losses and allocated loss adjustment expense paid by the Company but not recovered from the Reinsurer, plus reserves for losses incurred but not reported, as shown in the statement prepared by the Company (hereinafter referred to as "Reinsurer's Obligations") by funds withheld, cash advances or a Letter of Credit. The Reinsurer shall have the option of determining the method of funding provided it is acceptable to the insurance regulatory authorities having jurisdiction over the Company's reserves.
>
> When funding by a Letter of Credit, the Reinsurer agrees to apply for and secure timely delivery to the Company of a clean, irrevocable and unconditional Letter of Credit issued by a bank and containing provisions acceptable to the insurance regulatory authorities having jurisdiction over the Company's reserves in an amount equal to the Reinsurer's proportion of said reserves. Such Letter of Credit shall be issued for a period of not less than one year, and shall be automatically extended for one year from its date of expiration or any future expiration date unless thirty (30) days (sixty (60) days where required by insurance regulatory authorities) prior to any expiration date the issuing bank shall notify the Company by certified or registered mail that the issuing bank elects not to consider the Letter of Credit extended for any additional period.
>
> The Reinsurer and Company agree that the Letters of Credit provided by the Reinsurer pursuant to the provisions of this Contract may be drawn upon at any time, notwithstanding any other provision of this Contract, and be utilized by the Company or any successor, by operation of law, of the Company including, without limitation, any liquidator, rehabilitator, receiver or conservator of the Company for the following purposes, unless otherwise provided for in a separate Trust Agreement:
>
> (a) to reimburse the Company for the Reinsurer's Obligations, the payment of which is due under the terms of this Contract and which has not been otherwise paid;
>
> (b) to make refund of any sum which is in excess of the actual amount required to pay the Reinsurer's Obligations under this Contract;
>
> (c) to fund an account with the Company for the Reinsurer's Obligations. Such cash deposit shall be held in an interest bearing account separate from the Company's other assets, and interest thereon not in excess of the prime rate shall accrue to the benefit of the Reinsurer;
>
> (d) to pay the Reinsurer's share of any other amounts the Company claims are due under this Contract.

Source: BRMA, http://www.brma.org/download/bcwrb055.doc (accessed January 23, 2004).

Errors and Omissions Clause

The **errors and omissions (E&O) clause** states that neither party is relieved from its obligations under the reinsurance treaty because of an inadvertent error or omission. Mistakes, such as failing to cede loss exposures that should have been ceded or ceding loss exposures that do not fall within the reinsurance treaty's scope, are not a basis to void the treaty as long as these mistakes are corrected when discovered. Because of the volume of transactions that are typical of most reinsurance treaties, it is anticipated that clerical errors will occur. The E&O clause prevents these clerical errors from affecting the operation of the treaty. Exhibit 4-21 shows an example of an E&O clause.

Errors and omissions (E&O) clause
A reinsurance treaty clause that states that neither party is relieved from its obligations under the treaty because of an inadvertent error or omission.

EXHIBIT 4-21

Errors and Omissions Clause

14 C

ERRORS AND OMISSIONS

Any inadvertent delay, omission or error shall not be held to relieve either party hereto from any liability which would attach to it hereunder if such delay, omission or error had not been made, provided such omission or error is rectified upon discovery.

Source: BRMA, http://www.brma.org/download/bcwrb014.doc (accessed January 23, 2004).

INTERESTS AND LIABILITIES AGREEMENT

The **interests and liabilities agreement**, also known as ILA, is not a reinsurance treaty clause but is a separate agreement, attached to and forming part of a reinsurance treaty in which multiple reinsurers participate, that controls the participation and liability of each participating reinsurer. In particular, the interests and liabilities agreement does the following:

- Identifies the treaty to which it applies
- Identifies the parties to the treaty
- States the percentage participation of individual reinsurers
- Establishes that several, not joint, liability applies to each reinsurer
- States an effective date
- Provides for proper execution by authorized officers of the primary insurer and each reinsurer

The interests and liabilities agreement controls each reinsurer's liability under the multi-party reinsurance treaty in two ways. First, it specifies a percentage of participation for the reinsurer. Second, it specifies that the reinsurer's participation is *several* not *joint* with the other reinsurers participating in the reinsurance treaty. **Several liability** means that each reinsurer is responsible only for the part of the total obligation that represents its participation. **Joint liability** means the reinsurers share responsibility for the entire

Interests and liabilities agreement
A separate agreement, attached to and forming part of a reinsurance treaty, that controls the participation and liability of each reinsurer participating in the reinsurance treaty.

Several liability
Liability of a party for only the part of the total obligation that represents its participation.

Joint liability
Liability of two or more parties in which they share responsibility for the entire obligation.

obligation. For example, if one reinsurer fails to meet its obligation, the other reinsurers assume that delinquent reinsurer's responsibility to indemnify the primary insurer. Some reinsurance treaties with multiple reinsurers address the issue of several versus joint liability in the arbitration clause.

When multiple reinsurers are not involved in a reinsurance treaty, the interests and liabilities agreement is not needed. However, many reinsurance treaties, particularly those placed by reinsurance intermediaries, involve participation by multiple reinsurers. Those reinsurers who want to participate to a limited extent in large treaties can do so with certainty about their obligations because of the inclusion of the interests and liabilities agreement. Exhibit 4-22 shows an example of an interests and liabilities agreement.

EXHIBIT 4-22

Interests and Liabilities Agreement

21 A

INTERESTS AND LIABILITIES AGREEMENT

to

(insert the title of heading of the

Reinsurance Contract which is the subject of the ILA

e.g. "First Catastrophe Excess Reinsurance Contract")

_____

(hereinafter referred to as the "Contract")

between

(insert the name(s) of the Company(ies)

(hereinafter referred to individually

or collectively as the "Company")

and

(insert the name of the Reinsurer)

(hereinafter referred to as the "Subscribing Reinsurer")

Under the terms of the Contract, which is attached to this Agreement, the Subscribing Reinsurer agrees to participate in a _____% share of the interests and liabilities of the Reinsurer(s) described in the Contract. The participation of the Subscribing Reinsurer shall be several and not joint with any other reinsurers participating in the Contract.

This Agreement shall become effective _____ and shall expire _____ .

> Signed in _(duplicate, triplicate, or whatever is appropriate)_
> in _(City, State)_ this day of _(month) (year)_ .
> _(Subscribing Reinsurer)_
> By_____
> Title_____
> Signed in _(duplicate, triplicate, or whatever is appropriate)_
> in _(City, State)_ , this day of _(month) (year)_ .
> _(Company)_
> By_____
> Title_____

Source: BRMA, http://www.brma.org/download/bcwrb021.doc (accessed January 23, 2004).

SUMMARY

Each reinsurance treaty's wording is unique because it states the intent of the parties to that particular treaty. However, some clauses are common to most reinsurance treaties. Understanding these common clauses is essential to understanding the rights and duties of the parties to the treaty.

The following clauses are common to most reinsurance treaties:

- *Preamble.* The preamble is the introduction to a reinsurance treaty that identifies the parties to the treaty.
- *Affiliated companies clause.* The affiliated companies clause broadens the reinsurance treaty's scope to include the primary insurer's affiliated companies.
- *Reinsuring clause.* The reinsuring clause establishes the obligatory nature of the cessions under the treaty and describes the type of reinsurance provided.
- *Definitions clause.* The definitions clause defines the terms used in the reinsurance treaty.
- *Access to records clause.* The access to records clause establishes the reinsurer's right to inspect all of the primary insurer's records that pertain to the coverage provided by the reinsurance treaty.
- *Service of suit clause.* The service of suit clause allows the primary insurer to seek a legal remedy from a court in a convenient jurisdiction when the reinsurance treaty involves an unauthorized or alien reinsurer. It also allows the reinsurer to commence suit in any court in the U.S. that has jurisdiction.

- *Federal excise tax clause.* The federal excise tax clause states that the primary insurer is responsible for administering and remitting the federal excise tax levied against alien reinsurers party to the reinsurance treaty.
- *Currency clause.* The currency clause specifies the base currency for the reinsurance treaty and the basis of any conversion to the base currency.
- *Governing law clause.* The governing law clause specifies which law governs the reinsurance treaty
- *Exclusion clauses.* The exclusion clauses limit the coverage of the reinsurance treaty.
- *Arbitration clause.* The arbitration clause states that an arbitration process will be used to resolve disputes between the parties to the reinsurance treaty.
- *Insolvency clause.* The insolvency clause states that the reinsurer agrees to pay its reinsurance obligations if the primary insurer becomes insolvent, whether or not the primary insurer has paid its obligations to the underlying policyholders.
- *Offset clause.* The offset clause allows the primary insurer and the reinsurer to offset balances due to each other.
- *Intermediary clause.* The intermediary clause requires the reinsurer to accept financial responsibility (the credit risk) for funds transferred from the primary insurer to the reinsurer through a reinsurance intermediary.
- *Unauthorized reinsurance clause.* The unauthorized reinsurance clause specifies the requirements that an unauthorized reinsurer must satisfy in order for the transaction to receive favorable accounting treatment as a reinsurance transaction.
- *Errors and omissions clause.* The errors and omissions clause states that neither party is relieved from its obligations under the treaty because of an inadvertent error or omission.

The insolvency clause, intermediary clause, and unauthorized reinsurance clause are required by most state insurance regulators.

The interests and liabilities agreement (ILA) is a separate agreement, attached to and forming part of a reinsurance treaty, that controls the participation and liability of each reinsurer participating in the reinsurance treaty. ILAs are common when multiple reinsurers participate in a treaty.

The next chapter continues the examination of common clauses by discussing clauses that vary by type of reinsurance or provide specialized coverage. It also discusses ancillary agreements that clarify reinsurance treaty terms.

CHAPTER NOTES

1. The National Association of Insurance Commissioners (NAIC) Reinsurance Task Force has established an Enforceability of Foreign Judgments Subgroup to determine what difficulties can occur in collecting from alien jurisdictions. Particular difficulties have been experienced concerning default judgments, arbitral awards, and punitive damages. For example, Germany does not recognize punitive damage awards from U.S. courts.
2. NAIC, *Financial Condition Examiners Handbook* (1995), Rule E, "General Rules for Allowance of Reinsurance Credits," pp. 5–9. Problems have arisen in some states whose statutes do not address the NAIC Financial Examiners Handbook.

Chapter 5

Direct Your Learning

Common Reinsurance Treaty Clauses, Part II

After learning the content of this chapter, you should be able to:

- Explain the purpose and operation of each of the following reinsurance treaty clauses:
  - Commencement and termination clause
  - Reports and remittances clause
  - Excess of policy limits clause
  - Extra-contractual obligations clause
  - Territory clause
  - Self-insured obligations clause
- Explain the purpose and operation of each of the following ancillary agreements:
  - Special acceptance
  - Cut-through endorsement
  - Guarantee endorsement
  - Indemnity agreement

OUTLINE

Other Common Treaty Clauses

Ancillary Agreements

Summary

Develop Your Perspective

What are the main topics covered in the chapter?

Reinsurance treaties often include common clauses that vary based on the type of reinsurance used or that provide specialized coverage. This chapter explains the purpose and operation of these additional common clauses and ancillary agreements.

Identify specialized common clauses and ancillary agreements.

- What is the purpose of these common clauses?
- What is the purpose of ancillary agreements to the treaty?

Why is it important to learn about these topics?

Understanding how common clauses and ancillary agreements operate is essential to understanding the rights and duties of the parties to the reinsurance treaty.

Examine a reinsurance treaty.

- Which of the clauses in the treaty are common clauses that vary by type of reinsurance or that address a special need?
- Are there any ancillary agreements to the treaty?

How can you use what you will learn?

Review one of your company's reinsurance treaties.

- How do the clauses in your company's reinsurance treaty differ from those presented in this chapter?
- If different clauses were used, do they expand or limit the coverage provided by the reinsurance agreement?

Chapter 5
Common Reinsurance Treaty Clauses, Part II

As described in the previous chapter, reinsurance agreements usually contain many common clauses because most reinsurance agreements address many of the same types of issues. This chapter continues the discussion of common clauses by presenting clauses that vary by type of reinsurance or that provide specialized coverage. Although the titles of these clauses are commonly used, their provisions may vary significantly among reinsurance agreements, depending on the needs of the parties to the agreement. The last part of this chapter discusses ancillary agreements that provide additional coverages or clarify reinsurance agreement terms. Although most of these types of clauses or agreements can be used both for facultative and treaty reinsurance, this chapter discusses the clauses in a treaty context.

OTHER COMMON TREATY CLAUSES

The following common clauses vary by type of reinsurance:

- Commencement and termination clause
- Reports and remittances clause

Common clauses that provide specialized coverage include the following:

- Excess of policy limits clause
- Extra-contractual obligations clause
- Territory clause
- Self-insured obligations clause

Commencement and Termination Clause

The **commencement and termination clause** states the reinsurance treaty's duration and the circumstances that would trigger its termination. In many treaties, this clause may also specify the basis of attachment discussed in the previous chapter. Clearly specifying the beginning and end of the reinsurance relationship is critical in determining the loss exposures covered by the treaty. For example, a primary insurer may determine that the terms

Commencement and termination clause
A reinsurance treaty clause that states the treaty's duration and the circumstances that would trigger the treaty's termination.

of the commencement and termination clause in its reinsurance treaty do not encompass certain of its loss exposures so that alternative reinsurance arrangements must be made.

Two important elements of the commencement and termination clause are the normal term of the treaty and the circumstances under which it can be canceled.

Normal Term

The commencement and termination clause specifies the date and time that coverage begins and ends. However, commencement and termination can also be addressed in two separate clauses: effective time and termination.

Effective time. The effective time for commencement of coverage is usually 12:01 AM standard time. Under pro rata or excess of loss property treaties, standard time pertains to the time zone at the location of the loss exposure. Under casualty excess of loss treaties, standard time pertains to the time zone at the mailing address of the named insured shown in the declarations page in the original policy. Under clash cover (liability insurance) and catastrophe treaties (property insurance), standard time pertains to the time zone at the primary insurer's home office. The time of termination is usually 12:01 AM standard time, with the time zone applying in the same manner as for commencement. To be clear, treaties should specify exactly what time and time zone apply.

Continuous contract
A reinsurance treaty that remains in effect until canceled by one of the parties to the treaty.

Termination. A **continuous contract** is a reinsurance treaty that remains in effect until canceled by one of the parties to the treaty. Wording in the termination clause may state, "This contract shall continue in force until terminated." Termination of a continuous contract usually requires ninety days' notice, and termination can occur (1) at any time, (2) quarterly, (3) semiannually, or (4) annually. The primary insurer and reinsurer generally negotiate the length of the notice period.

Term contract
A reinsurance treaty that terminates on a specific date.

A **term contract** is a reinsurance treaty that terminates on a specific date. Wording in the termination clause may state, "This agreement shall remain in effect from 01/01/2003 until 01/01/2004." Generally, a term contract does not terminate until the expiration date, except by mutual agreement of the parties. Term contracts usually do not provide run-off of existing policies and the primary insurer will typically want to purchase coverage for any in-force loss exposures at the expiration date of the treaty.

Run-off basis
A reinsurance treaty provision that allows all policies in force at the date of termination to be covered under the treaty until they expire.

Treaties that are on a risks attaching basis usually provide for termination on either a run-off or a cut-off basis. The **run-off basis** allows all policies in force at the date of termination to be covered under the treaty until they expire. The reinsurer retains the unearned premium represented by in-force policies, and remains liable for covered losses under those policies until the expiration of the primary insurance policies plus any additional time specified in endorsements made to those policies.

The **cut-off basis** allows the reinsurer's responsibility for losses occurring under the primary insurance policies to end at the treaty's termination date. Unearned premiums held by the reinsurer for in-force policies are returned to the primary insurer. The primary insurer has no reinsurance protection for new losses arising from these policies and the primary insurer's balance sheet must be adjusted to reflect the additional liability for the unearned premiums and any associated loss reserves. Exhibit 5-1 shows an example of a continuous contract commencement and termination clause with the primary insurer's option of run-off or cut-off liability at termination.

Cut-off basis
A reinsurance treaty provision that allows the reinsurer's responsibility for losses occurring under the primary insurance policies to end at the treaty's termination date.

EXHIBIT 5-1

Commencement and Termination Clause

57 A

COMMENCEMENT AND TERMINATION

This Contract shall incept at 12:01 A.M. Local Standard Time _(month), (day), (year)_ at the location of the risk and shall remain in force for an indefinite period, but either party shall have the right to cancel as of _(month), (day), (year)_ or any _(month, day)_ thereafter by giving at least _____ days prior written notice by certified or registered mail.

In the event either party cancels in accordance with the paragraph above, the Reinsurer shall participate in all policies ceded within the terms of this Contract written or renewed by the Company after receipt of notice of cancellation but prior to termination.

In the event of the termination of this Contract, at the Company's option:

A. The Reinsurer shall remain liable for all cessions in force at termination of this Contract; however, the liability of the Reinsurer shall cease with respect to losses occurring subsequent to the first anniversary, natural expiration or cancellation of each policy ceded, but not to extend beyond 12 months after such termination; or

B. The Reinsurer shall be relieved of all liability hereunder for losses occurring subsequent to termination of this Contract.

The Reinsurer shall refund to the Company the unearned reinsurance premium applicable to the unexpired liability (calculated on a pro rata basis), less the commission allowed by the Reinsurer thereon at conclusion of the runoff if option a) above is elected, or at termination if option b) above is elected. The Reinsurer will continue to be liable for its proportionate share of the outstanding losses (reported or unreported) on policies ceded hereunder with a date of loss prior to the conclusion of the runoff, or termination, as the case may be.

Source: Brokers & Reinsurance Markets Association (BRMA), http://www.brma.org/download/bcwrb057.doc (accessed January 26, 2004).

Cancellation Circumstances

A reinsurance treaty can be canceled by any of the following:

- Formal notice of cancellation
- Mutual consent
- Liquidation of either party
- Sudden death provision
- Special termination clause
- Nonpayment of balances

Formal notice of cancellation. The commencement and termination clause usually requires ninety days for formal notice of cancellation. The clause specifies a mailing method, such as certified mail or registered mail, to avoid confusion about when notice was mailed. Although not specified in the treaty, customary practice accepts the actual mailing (appropriately postmarked) on or before the notice date as constructive receipt of the notice by the other party. That practice precludes the performance of a third party (such as the Postal Service) from affecting compliance with contractual provisions.

Mutual consent. Reinsurance treaties can be canceled by the contracting parties' mutual consent. The parties can agree to cancel the treaty effective immediately or on some other date. For example, cancellation by mutual consent can arise when the primary insurer sells fewer policies than it or the reinsurer had anticipated and the reinsurance treaty is not needed or not cost effective to continue. Under such circumstances, mutual termination of the reinsurance treaty serves the interests of both the primary insurer and the reinsurer. Cancellation by mutual consent does not require any specific wording because any contract can be canceled by mutual consent.

Liquidation of either party. Although the commencement and termination clause may not specifically address liquidation, usually neither party objects to cancellation when one party's business is terminated. Many states have a statute requiring cancellation in the event of liquidation.

Sudden death provision. The commencement and termination clause may include a sudden death provision. Sudden death provisions allow one party, usually the reinsurer, to cancel the reinsurance treaty on a cut-off basis if specific events occur. A sudden death provision may be included in reinsurance treaties with primary insurers that are newly formed, have limited written premium, or have limited financial resources. The following are reasons for immediate termination often included in sudden death provisions:

- Change in the primary insurer's ownership, management, or control
- Reduction in the primary insurer's paid-in capital or policyholders' surplus
- Insolvency of the primary insurer
- Reduction of the primary insurer's net retention

Reinsurers often want the option to cancel the reinsurance treaty if the management of the primary insurer changes after commencement because primary insurer management is an important underwriting characteristic. For example, the new management may choose a different underwriting direction that will involve the cession of loss exposures not anticipated when the reinsurance treaty was negotiated. While difficult to quantify, reinsurers want business relationships with primary insurers in which they have confidence. The sudden death provision gives the reinsurer the opportunity to review the primary insurer's new management and cancel the reinsurance treaty if considered appropriate.

Reinsurers usually avoid financially impaired primary insurers. The reduction in a primary insurer's financial rating that typically accompanies a financial impairment often limits the primary insurer's marketing access to quality insureds. Also, financially impaired primary insurers are usually unable to remit reinsurance premium due to the reinsurer on a timely basis, if at all. The sudden death provision could specify either a reduction in paid-in capital or a reduction of policyholders' surplus as the type of financial impairment that would allow the reinsurer to cancel the reinsurance treaty.

Reinsurers typically want to cancel the reinsurance treaty immediately if the primary insurer becomes insolvent. State insurance regulators' initial response to solvency concerns is to stop the primary insurer from issuing new policies. This regulatory response usually makes the reinsurance treaty inoperative. As consequence of the primary insurer's insolvency, many key employees of the primary insurer often leave that employment for other opportunities, thereby depriving the primary insurer of personnel resources the reinsurer considered important when negotiating the reinsurance treaty. The sudden death provision gives the reinsurer a convenient contractual means to terminate the treaty regardless of regulatory action.

Reinsurers usually want the option to cancel the reinsurance treaty if it is discovered that the primary insurer has reduced its net retention through another reinsurance agreement. Reinsurers want the primary insurer to have a significant financial stake in the profitability of the reinsured policies. A reduction in the primary insurer's net retention implies the primary insurer anticipates that the ceded loss exposures will be unprofitable. The sudden death provision gives the reinsurer the right to cancel the reinsurance treaty if the primary insurer's net retention is reduced. Exhibit 5-2 shows an example of a sudden death provision.

> **EXHIBIT 5-2**
>
> ### Sudden Death Provision
>
> The Reinsurer (and the Company) shall also have the option to terminate this Agreement in whole or in part for the reasons set forth below:
>
> 1. The sale, merger, or acquisition of the Company by or with any other party or the sale or change in controlling interest of the Company so as to produce a loss in control over conduct of the business by the current owners and/or management, except any change of control or ownership within any insurance holding company system that effects no change in ultimate controlling party.
>
> 2. A reduction of the paid-in capital of the Company for any reason whatsoever.
>
> 3. The appointment of a receiver, administrator, trustee, or conservator for the Company or the commencement of any liquidation, rearrangement, or bankruptcy proceeding against the Company.
>
> 4. Should the Company at any time reinsure its minimum or net retention on any class of business to which this Agreement applies.
>
> The Company shall immediately notify the Reinsurer in writing, giving details to the extent of its knowledge thereof, of the particulars of any of the events set forth in subparagraphs 1, 2, 3, or 4. The Reinsurer may commence termination proceedings within thirty days of the receipt of such notice, by sending to the Company by registered mail to its principal office, notice stating the time and date when termination shall be effective (not less than thirty days after the date of mailing such notice). If the Company fails to immediately notify the Reinsurer of any of the aforementioned events, the Reinsurer may commence such termination at any time after it has acquired knowledge of any such event. Upon termination of this Agreement for any of the reasons set forth in subparagraphs 1, 2, 3, or 4 above, the Reinsurer shall not be liable for claims or losses resulting from occurrences taking place after the effective time and date of termination. (In such an event, the Reinsurer shall return to the Company the reinsurance premium unearned, calculated on the monthly pro rata basis, less the commission previously allowed thereon, and less any other amounts due from the Company to the Reinsurer.)

Special termination clause. Special termination clauses operate similarly to sudden death provisions except that either the reinsurer or the primary insurer has the option of terminating the reinsurance treaty if specific criteria are met. Exhibit 5-3 shows an example of a special termination clause.

Nonpayment of balances. The nonpayment of balances provision provides the reinsurer with a contractual right to cancel the reinsurance treaty on a cut-off basis if the primary insurer fails to pay balances owed to the reinsurer in a timely fashion.

A reinsurer may insist this provision be included in reinsurance treaties with primary insurers that have had a history of being slow to pay balances owed to reinsurers. Exhibit 5-4 shows an example of a nonpayment of balances provision.

EXHIBIT 5-3

Special Termination Clause

63 A

SPECIAL TERMINATION

Either the Company or the Reinsurer may terminate this Contract at any time by the giving of _____ days notice in writing to the other party upon the happening of any one of the following circumstances:

(a) A State Insurance Department or other legal authority orders the other party to cease writing business, or

(b) One party has become insolvent or has been placed into liquidation or receivership (whether voluntary or involuntary), or there has been instituted against it proceedings for the appointment of a receiver, liquidator, rehabilitator, conservator, or trustee in bankruptcy, or other agent known by whatever name, to take possession of its assets or control of its operations, or

(c) One party's policyholders' surplus has been reduced by whichever is greater, either 50% of the amount of surplus at the inception of this Contract or 50% of the amount at the latest anniversary, or has lost any part of, or has reduced its paid-up capital, or

(d) One party has become merged with, acquired or controlled by any company, corporation, or individual(s) not controlling the party's operations previously, or

(e) One party has reinsured its entire liability under this Contract without the terminating party's prior written consent.

In the event of such termination, the liability of the Reinsurer shall be terminated in accordance with the termination provisions of this Contract.

However, if the terminating party is the Company, the Company shall have the right, by the giving of prior written notice, to relieve the Reinsurer of liability for losses occurring subsequent to the date of termination of this Contract. In such event, the Reinsurer shall return the unearned portion of any premiums paid hereunder and the minimum premium provisions, if any, shall be waived.

Source: BRMA, http://www.brma.org/download/bcwrb063.doc (accessed January 26, 2004).

EXHIBIT 5-4

Nonpayment of Balances

Notwithstanding any other provisions set forth in this Agreement, if any amount payable by the Company to the Reinsurer becomes overdue, the Reinsurer may terminate this Agreement at any time in its entirety, by sending the Company by registered mail, or certified mail to its principal office, notice stating the time and date when, not less than thirty days after the date of mailing of such notice, termination shall be effective. Failure on the part of the Reinsurer to exercise this right of termination shall not serve to waive the enforcement of this right for cause thereafter.

Upon termination, the Reinsurer shall not be liable for any claims or losses resulting from occurrences taking place after the effective time and date of termination. The Reinsurer shall return to the Company the reinsurance premium unearned, calculated on a monthly pro rata basis, less any commission previously allowed thereon, and less any other amounts due from the Company to the Reinsurer.

Reports and Remittances Clause

Reports and remittances clause
A reinsurance treaty clause that requires the primary insurer to submit information to the reinsurer so that net balances owed to each party can be calculated and remitted and financial statements can be completed.

The **reports and remittances clause** requires the primary insurer to submit information to the reinsurer so that net balances owed to each party can be calculated and remitted and financial statements can be completed. The reports and remittances clause used in pro rata reinsurance typically requires the reporting of more information than the one used in excess of loss reinsurance. Exhibit 5-5 shows an example of a reports and remittances clause used in pro rata reinsurance. It is appropriate for a treaty on a written premium basis in which the remitting time is different from the reporting time. Exhibit 5-6 shows an example of a reports and remittances clause for excess of loss reinsurance.

EXHIBIT 5-5

Reports and Remittances Clause—Pro Rata Reinsurance

45 C

REPORTS AND REMITTANCES

Within _____ days after the close of each _____, the Company will furnish the Reinsurer with a report summarizing the written premium ceded less return premium and commission, losses paid, loss adjustment expense paid, monies recovered, and net balance due either party. In addition, the Company will furnish the Reinsurer a _____ statement showing the unearned premium, the total reserves for outstanding losses including loss adjustment expense, a breakdown by American Insurance Association catastrophic code numbers for paid and outstanding catastrophe losses and loss adjustment expense, and such other information as may be required by the Reinsurer for completion of its NAIC annual statements.

> The net balance will be paid within _____ days after the close of the respective _____. Should payment due from the Reinsurer exceed as respects any one loss, the Company may give the Reinsurer notice of payment made or its intention to make payment on a certain date. If the Company has paid the loss, payment will be made by the Reinsurer immediately. If the Company intends to pay the loss by a certain date and has submitted a satisfactory proof of loss or similar document, payment will be due from the Reinsurer twenty-four (24) hours prior to that date, provided the Reinsurer has a period of five (5) working days after receipt of said notice to dispatch the payment. Cash loss amounts specifically remitted by the Reinsurer as set forth herein will be credited to its next _____ account.

Source: BRMA, http://www.brma.org/download/bcwrb045.doc (accessed January 26, 2004).

EXHIBIT 5-6

Reports and Remittances Clause—Excess of Loss Reinsurance

Within 45 days after the close of each calendar quarter, the Company shall furnish to the Reinsurer a statement of the premium calculation, calculated according to Article _____. Balances are due and payable with the premium calculation. The Company shall furnish all necessary statistics to allow the Reinsurer to prepare its statutory report.

Excess of Policy Limits Clause

The **excess of policy limits (XPL) clause** requires the reinsurer to indemnify the primary insurer for losses in excess of policy limits. Losses in excess of policy limits are the damages awarded against the primary insurer in favor of the insured because of the primary insurer's failure to settle a third-party claim against the insured by reason of bad faith, fraud, or gross negligence. The damages are for losses that would have been covered under the policy had the policy limits been higher. The excess of policy limits clause is usually used in reinsurance treaties covering liability loss exposures, and those property loss exposures that have bailee liability exposures. Excess of policy limit clauses may limit the scope of the reinsurance coverage provided by specifically stating that only compensatory and not punitive damages are covered.

An excess of policy limits clause usually provides that the original loss and the loss in excess of policy limits constitute one loss. An excess of policy limits clause's inclusion usually does not change the reinsurance treaty limits. However, some pro rata treaties anticipate that higher than normal limits will be needed for losses in excess of policy limits and increase the treaty limits for these losses. For example, a pro rata reinsurance treaty may have a limit of

Excess of policy limits (XPL) clause
A reinsurance treaty clause that requires the reinsurer to indemnify the primary insurer for damages awarded against the primary insurer in favor of the insured because of the primary insurer's failure to settle a third-party claim against the insured by reason of bad faith, fraud, or gross negligence.

$1 million and provide for losses in excess of policy limits up to "one additional limit" or $2 million total; a 100 percent increase (subject to a co-participation provision).

Excess of policy limit clauses usually include a co-participation provision that applies to the losses in excess of policy limits. Reinsurers that include a co-participation clause often also specify that the primary insurer's co-participation percentage cannot be reduced by other reinsurance unless the reinsurance is with an affiliated company of the primary insurer.

Loss adjustment expenses, often a considerable sum in claims involving excess of policy limits damages, are usually shared between the primary insurer and the reinsurer in the same proportion in which they share the loss. If the primary insurer has any other insurance or reinsurance that applies, those recoveries reduce the loss applicable to the treaty. Exhibit 5-7 shows an example of an excess of policy limits clause for use in a pro rata reinsurance treaty in which the percentage of coverage and limit provided for excess of policy limits coverage are specified elsewhere in the treaty.

EXHIBIT 5-7

Excess of Policy Limits Clause

15 B

EXCESS OF ORIGINAL POLICY LIMITS

This Contract shall protect the Company, within the limits hereof, in connection with loss in excess of the limit of its original policy, such loss in excess of the limit having been incurred because of failure by it to settle within the policy limit or by reason of alleged or actual negligence, fraud, or bad faith in rejecting an offer of settlement or in the preparation of the defense or in the trial of any action against its insured or reinsured or in the preparation or prosecution of an appeal consequent upon such action.

However, this Article shall not apply where the loss has been incurred due to fraud by a member of the Board of Directors or a corporate officer of the Company acting individually or collectively or in collusion with any individual or corporation or any other organization or party involved in the presentation, defense or settlement of any claim covered hereunder.

For the purpose of this Article, the word "loss" shall mean any amounts for which the Company would have been contractually liable to pay had it not been for the limit of the original policy.

Source: BRMA, http://www.brma.org/download/bcwrb015.doc (accessed January 26, 2004).

Extra-Contractual Obligations Clause

The **extra-contractual obligations (ECO) clause** requires the reinsurer to indemnify the primary insurer for losses involving extra-contractual damages. Extra-contractual damages are damages awarded against the primary insurer in favor of the insured because of the primary insurer's bad faith, fraud, or gross negligence in handling a claim. The damages are for losses that go beyond the scope of the underlying policy coverage. The extra-contractual obligations clause is used in reinsurance agreements covering either property or liability loss exposures.

The extra-contractual obligations clause has many of the same provisions as the excess of policy limits clause. For example, both clauses provide for a sharing of losses and expenses between the reinsurer and the primary insurer, specify whether the coverage limit of the treaty increases for these claims, and require that other insurance or reinsurance applicable to the claim serves to reduce the net loss before the application of the treaty. While the provisions may be similar, the extra-contractual obligations clause may have a higher co-participation percentage so that the primary insurer has a greater share of these losses, and the reinsurer may be unwilling to increase the treaty limit for these losses. Exhibit 5-8 compares the coverage provided by extra-contractual obligations and excess of policy limits clauses. Exhibit 5-9 shows an example of an extra-contractual obligations clause designed for use in a pro rata reinsurance treaty in which the percentage of coverage and limit provided for extra-contractual obligations are specified elsewhere in the treaty.

Extra-contractual obligations (ECO) clause
A reinsurance treaty clause that requires the reinsurer to indemnify the primary insurer for extra-contractual damages awarded against the primary insurer in favor of the insured because of the primary insurer's bad faith, fraud, or gross negligence in handling a claim.

EXHIBIT 5-8

Comparison of Excess of Policy Limits and Extra-Contractual Obligations Clauses

	XPL	ECO
Allegations by the Plaintiff	Primary insurer's bad faith, fraud, or gross negligence in handling a third-party claim against the insured	Primary insurer's bad faith, fraud, or gross negligence in handling the insured's claim
Relationship of Damages to Policy Coverage	Would be covered by the policy if the policy limit was higher	Go beyond policy coverage
Type of Coverage Typically Used With	Liability insurance and property insurance with bailee liability loss exposures	Property or liability insurance

> **EXHIBIT 5-9**
>
> **Extra-Contractual Obligations Clause**
>
> 16 B
>
> EXTRA CONTRACTUAL OBLIGATIONS
>
> This Contract shall protect the Company for any Extra Contractual Obligations within the limits hereof. The term "Extra Contractual Obligations" is defined as those liabilities not covered under any other provision of this Contract and which arise from the handling of any claim on business covered hereunder, such liabilities arising because of, but not limited to, the following: failure by the Company to settle within the policy limit, or by reason of alleged or actual negligence, fraud, or bad faith in rejecting an offer of settlement or in the preparation of the defense or in the trial of any action against its insured or reinsured or in the preparation or prosecution of an appeal consequent upon such action.
>
> The date on which any Extra Contractual Obligation is incurred by the Company shall be deemed, in all circumstances, to be the date of the original disaster and/or casualty.
>
> However, this Article shall not apply where the loss has been incurred due to fraud by a member of the Board of Directors or a corporate officer of the Company acting individually or collectively or in collusion with any individual or corporation or any other organization or party involved in the presentation, defense or settlement of any claim covered hereunder.

Source: BRMA, http://www.brma.org/download/bcwrb016.doc (accessed January 26, 2004).

Territory Clause

Territory clause
A reinsurance treaty clause that defines the geographic area within which loss exposures must be located to be covered by the treaty.

The **territory clause** defines the geographic area within which loss exposures must be located to be covered by the reinsurance treaty. Through the territory clause, the reinsurer manages the geographic spread of its loss exposures and ensures that the primary insurer is operating in mutually agreed-on areas. For example, a primary insurer may operate in only one state and the territory clause would limit the treaty's applicability to policies sold in that state. Subsequent expansion for this primary insurer into other states is a reinsurance underwriting issue that would require reinsurer approval before the treaty is modified.

Exhibit 5-10 shows an example of a territory clause.

> **EXHIBIT 5-10**
>
> **Territory Clause**
>
> 51 B
>
> TERRITORY
>
> This Contract shall apply to risks located in the United States of America, its territories, its possessions, the Commonwealth of Puerto Rico, the District of Columbia, and incidental foreign exposures.

Source: BRMA, http://www.brma.org/download/bcwrb051.doc (accessed January 26, 2004).

Self-Insured Obligations Clause

The **self-insured obligations clause** extends the reinsurance treaty to include policies issued by the primary insurer that provide coverage for its own loss exposures. This clause is needed because a primary insurer's insurance contracts with itself are legally unenforceable, and would not otherwise create an indemnification obligation for the reinsurer. The self-insured obligations clause enables the primary insurer to reinsure its own loss exposures as though they were for an unaffiliated insured.

Reinsurers are usually willing to add the self-insured obligations clause to maintain goodwill with the primary insurer, but with specific conditions. Those conditions may include the following:

- The reinsurer must be notified, or even approve, of these agreements. However, some self-insured obligation clauses provide for automatic approval without notification.
- The primary insurer must charge itself the same premium that it would charge unaffiliated insureds.
- The primary insurer's payment of a claim to itself creates a legally binding payment for the purposes of the reinsurance treaty even though such action has no true legal status outside the reinsurance treaty.

Additionally, reinsurers often require that primary insurers document their intention to insure their own exposures either through an actual policy or internal memorandum. Exhibit 5-11 shows an example of a self-insured obligations clause.

Self-insured obligations clause
A reinsurance treaty clause that extends the treaty to include policies issued by the primary insurer that provide coverage for its own loss exposures.

EXHIBIT 5-11

Self-Insured Obligations Clause

48 D

SELF-INSURED OBLIGATIONS

As respects all business the subject matter hereof, this Contract shall cover self-insured obligations of the Company assumed by it as a self-insurer including self-insured obligations in excess of any valid and collectible insurance available to the Company to the same extent as if all types of insurance covered by this Contract were afforded under the broadest forms of policies issued by the Company, provided such self-insured obligations are within the scope of underwriting criteria furnished by the Company to the Reinsurer.

For the purpose of this Contract "self-insured obligations" are defined as insurable exposures of the Company on which the Company has issued an actual policy subject to the provisions stipulated in the first paragraph of this Article.

An insurance or reinsurance wherein the Company hereby reinsured and/or its affiliated and/or subsidiary companies are named as the Insured or Reinsured party, either alone or jointly with

Continued on next page.

> some other party, shall be deemed to be an insurance or reinsurance coming within the scope of this Contract, notwithstanding that no legal liability may arise in respect thereof by reason of the fact that the Company hereby reinsured and/or its affiliated and/or subsidiary companies are named as the Insured or Reinsured party or one of the Insured or Reinsured parties.

Source: BRMA, http://www.brma.org/download/bcwrb048.doc (accessed January 26, 2004).

ANCILLARY AGREEMENTS

Reinsurers may use ancillary agreements to provide additional coverages to primary insurers or to add endorsements to clarify reinsurance treaty terms. Ancillary agreements include special acceptance, cut-through endorsement, guarantee endorsement, and indemnity agreement.

Types of Ancillary Agreements
- Special acceptance
- Cut-through endorsement
- Guarantee endorsement
- Indemnity agreement

Special Acceptance

Special acceptance
An ancillary agreement that provides a means to extend the reinsurance treaty to include loss exposures that would otherwise be excluded.

The **special acceptance** is an ancillary agreement that provides a means to extend the reinsurance treaty to include loss exposures that would otherwise be excluded. The agreement is needed in reinsurance treaties involving several reinsurers where securing an exception to the reinsurance treaty exclusions would be difficult to administer.

Special acceptance agreements often specify that the lead reinsurer approves the special acceptances on behalf of all the reinsurers involved in the treaty. Exhibit 5-12 shows an example of a special acceptance clause. Exhibit 5-13 shows an example of a special acceptance letter by a lead reinsurer.

Not all reinsurance treaties involving multiple reinsurers include a special acceptance clause. Many reinsurers do not want to rely on the lead reinsurer for those decisions and prefer that the primary insurer submit special acceptances to all reinsurers for approval.

> **EXHIBIT 5-12**
>
> **Special Acceptance Clause**
>
> Liability of the Company under policies excluded hereunder, may, upon special acceptance by the Lead Reinsurer, be covered by this Agreement and shall be subject to the terms hereof except as such terms shall be modified by such acceptance.

> **EXHIBIT 5-13**
>
> **Special Acceptance Letter**
>
> May 18, 2004
>
> Ms. Audrey Amann
> Commercial Lines Department
> Crowley Fire and Marine Insurance Companies
> 123 XYZ Lane
> West Chester, Pennsylvania 19382
>
> Re: KENCO Enterprises
> Policy Number: 33.140124
>
> Dear Ms. Amann,
>
> This will acknowledge your letter of April 29, 2004, enclosing a copy of the captioned policy.
>
> For the purposes of this policy only, the reinsurance limit under the reinsurance treaty between our companies applicable to the Employers Liability Stopgap coverage is increased to the extent necessary to complete a policy limit for such coverage of $1,000,000 each occurrence for the policy period from March 1, 2004, to March 1, 2005.
>
> This acceptance applies only to the current policy and its present provisions, and any changes or renewal should be brought to our attention for further consideration.
>
> An extra copy of this letter is enclosed for your use as a reminder of the special handling required on this policy.
>
> Sincerely,
>
> Richard Balaban, CPCU, ARe
>
> Senior Vice President

Cut-Through Endorsement

A **cut-through endorsement** gives the insured a direct cause of action against the reinsurer for the reinsured amount of a loss if the primary insurer becomes insolvent. The insured is not a party to the reinsurance treaty and without the endorsement has no right to recover directly from the reinsurer. Normally, the insured needs no such right because the solvent primary insurer fulfills its obligations under the original policy and is indemnified by the reinsurer to the

Cut-through endorsement
An endorsement attached to an insurance policy that gives the insured a direct cause of action against the reinsurer for the reinsured amount of a loss if the primary insurer becomes insolvent.

extent specified in the reinsurance treaty. However, the liquidator of an insolvent primary insurer is not able to treat insurance claimants any differently than any other creditor of the primary insurer in satisfying unmet obligations. The cut-through endorsement provides the insured with direct rights against the reinsurer, bypassing the primary insurer's insolvency proceeding.

A cut-through endorsement is usually requested when the primary insurer does not satisfy the financial standards established by the insured's lender. The endorsement can take many forms depending on the needs of the parties and the applicable state law. Typically, the cut-through endorsement states that reinsurance proceeds will be paid directly to the payee in the event that the primary insurer is unable to pay a loss. The payee may be the insured, the lender, or both. The reinsurer will respond to the insured and lender, as their interests may appear, up to the limit of the reinsurance treaty. A cut-through clause may be added to the reinsurance agreement to allow the primary insurer to issue cut-through endorsements when required.

The insolvent primary insurer's liquidator sometimes contests the enforcement of the cut-through endorsement because it reduces available funds that can be directed to other creditors. The insolvency clause reinforces this argument in that it specifies that the reinsurance will be paid to the liquidator "without diminution." In this case, reinsurers may be required to pay a claim twice—once on behalf of the insured under the terms of the cut-through endorsement, and again to the liquidator of the insolvent primary insurer.

Reinsurers may also prefer to avoid cut-through endorsements because of the administrative expenses in tracking them and the potential third-party liability. Because the cut-through endorsement is only attached to policies when requested, the primary insurer and reinsurer must keep records of the endorsed policies. In reinsurance treaties involving more than one reinsurer, all of the reinsurers must subscribe to an indemnity agreement with the reinsurer who issues the cut-through endorsement. Indemnity agreements are discussed later in this chapter. Exhibit 5-14 shows an example of a cut-through endorsement.

EXHIBIT 5-14

Cut-Through Endorsement

In the event of the temporary or permanent discontinuance of business by the Company, or if the Company be adjudged insolvent, or if the Company shall fail to pay any loss under said policy or policies within the time provided in said policy or policies, then the insured or insureds under said policy or policies shall have the right to bring an action hereon against the Reinsurer in the state of the Reinsurer's domicile to recover that portion of the loss sustained by such insured or insureds, and for which the Company would be liable under the terms and provisions of said policy or policies, that exceeds the primary liability retained by the Company hereunder and that is assumed by the Reinsurer hereunder.

Guarantee Endorsement

A **guarantee endorsement** applies to policies covering mortgaged property and is similar to a cut-through endorsement. Whereas a cut-through endorsement allows the insured to recover the reinsured amount of a loss direct from the reinsurer, a guarantee endorsement allows the insured to recover the entire covered loss from the reinsurer, regardless of how much of that loss was reinsured.

A *guarantee bond* is used in Texas because guarantee endorsements are not approved for use in Texas. A guarantee bond must conform to the Texas Department of Insurance requirements.

> **Guarantee endorsement**
> An endorsement attached to an insurance policy covering mortgaged property that gives the insured a direct cause of action against the reinsurer for the entire covered amount of a loss if the primary insurer becomes insolvent.

Indemnity Agreement

Only one reinsurer is the named guarantor under guarantee endorsements or cut-through endorsements. However, frequently several reinsurers participate in one treaty. Under such circumstances, the co-reinsurers execute an **indemnity agreement** (sometimes called a hold-harmless agreement) that provides that the co-reinsurers will pay their proportionate share of the liabilities assumed under the cut-through endorsement or guarantee endorsement to the issuing reinsurer.

The key provisions of the indemnity agreement are that (1) the co-reinsurer will pay its proportionate share of the loss and associated loss adjustment expenses (the proportionate share is defined as the same share that the co-reinsurer has in the treaty) and (2) the issuing reinsurer is not required to issue assumption of liability agreements and can cancel any outstanding agreements at any time. The latter provision ensures that the co-reinsurers clearly understand the issuing reinsurer's rights and obligations. Exhibit 5-15 shows an example of an indemnity agreement.

> **Indemnity agreement**
> An ancillary agreement among co-reinsurers to a reinsurance treaty, that provides that they will pay their proportionate share of the liabilities assumed under a cut-through endorsement or guarantee endorsement to the issuing reinsurer.

EXHIBIT 5-15

Indemnity Agreement

(Assumption of Liability Agreements—Other Participating Reinsurers)

Participating Reinsurer

Policy Issuing Company

This Agreement between Excellent Reinsurance Company, 123 William Street, New York, New York 10038 (hereinafter referred to as the "Indemnitee") and the Participating Reinsurer designated above (hereinafter referred to as the "Indemnitor") is entered into for the benefit of the Indemnitee for the reasons stated in the following recitals:

SECTION ONE—RECITALS

(a) The Policy Issuing Company designated above has requested the Indemnitee issue Reinsurance Endorsements, Indemnification Agreements and Guarantee Endorsements

Continued on next page.

(hereinafter referred to as "Assumption of Liability Agreements") for the benefit of the mortgagees under which the Indemnitee may, in the event of the insolvency of the Policy Issuing Company, become directly obligated to the mortgagees for the payment of certain losses to real property under the insurance policies issued to said mortgagees; and

(b) The Indemnitor has a reinsurance agreement with the Policy Issuing Company covering a proportion of the risk of loss under said policies; and

(c) The Indemnitee, as a condition precedent to the issuance of Assumption of Liability Agreements, requires other participating reinsurers to assume a proportion of risk under said Assumption of Liability Agreements.

SECTION TWO—INDEMNIFICATION

In consideration of the Indemnitee issuing said Assumption of Liability Agreements, the Indemnitor agrees that in the event the Indemnitee is required to pay any loss directly to any Mortgagee, the Indemnitor shall pay the Indemnitee:

(a) The same proportionate share of the loss paid by the Indemnitee as the Indemnitor has in the above referenced reinsurance agreement; and

(b) The same proportionate share of any necessary expenses, attorney's fees or costs incurred in the performance of such Assumption of Liability Agreements.

SECTION THREE—OBLIGATION OF INDEMNITEE

This Agreement shall not in any way be construed to require the Indemnitee to issue Assumption of Liability Agreements, or to deprive the Indemnitee of any right to cancel such Agreements at any time it might desire.

SECTION FOUR—BINDING EFFECT OF AGREEMENT

This Agreement shall be binding upon and inure to the benefit of the parties, their successors and assigns.

IN WITNESS whereof, the parties hereto have executed this Agreement on this the _____ day of _____, 20_____.

Company: Excellent Reins. Co.

By:_____   By: _____

SUMMARY

This chapter continued the discussion of common treaty clauses by describing clauses that vary by type of reinsurance or provide specialized coverage. It also discussed ancillary agreements.

Clauses that vary by type of reinsurance include:

- *Commencement and termination clause.* The commencement and termination clause states the treaty's duration and the circumstances that would trigger the treaty's termination.

- *Reports and remittances clause.* The reports and remittances clause requires the primary insurer to submit information to the reinsurer so that net balances owed to each party can be calculated and remitted and financial statements can be completed.

Clauses that provide specialized coverage include:

- *Excess of policy limits (XPL) clause.* The excess of policy limits clause requires the reinsurer to indemnify the primary insurer for damages awarded against the primary insurer in favor of the insured because of the primary insurer's failure to settle a third-party claim against the insured by reason of bad faith, fraud, or gross negligence.
- *Extra-contractual obligations (ECO) clause.* The extra-contractual obligations clause requires the reinsurer to indemnify the primary insurer for extra-contractual damages awarded against the primary insurer in favor of the insured because of the primary insurer's bad faith, fraud, or gross negligence in handling a claim.
- *Territory clause.* The territory clause defines the geographic area within which loss exposures must be located to be covered by the treaty.
- *Self-insured obligations clause.* The self-insured obligations clause extends the treaty to include policies issued by the primary insurer that provide coverage for its own loss exposures.

Ancillary agreements include:

- *Special acceptance.* A special acceptance provides a means to extend the reinsurance treaty to include loss exposures that would otherwise be excluded.
- *Cut-through endorsement.* A cut-through endorsement gives the insured a direct cause of action against the reinsurer for the reinsured amount of a loss if the primary insurer becomes insolvent.
- *Guarantee endorsement.* A guarantee endorsement is attached to an insurance policy covering a mortgaged property and gives the insured a direct cause of action against the reinsurer for the entire covered amount of a loss if the primary insurer becomes insolvent.
- *Indemnity agreement.* An indemnity agreement is an agreement among co-reinsurers that provides that they will pay their proportionate share of the liabilities assumed under a cut-through endorsement or guarantee endorsement to the issuing reinsurer.

Chapter 6

Direct Your Learning

Quota Share Treaties

After learning the content of this chapter, you should be able to:

- Explain the purpose and operation of quota share treaties and how quota share treaties are used in a primary insurer's reinsurance program.
- Explain the functions performed by quota share treaties and how quota share treaties are used in a primary insurer's reinsurance program.
- Explain the purpose and operation of common clauses that are modified for use in quota share treaties.
- Explain the purpose and operation of clauses designed or adapted for quota share treaties.
- Describe the components that are reflected in quota share treaty pricing.
- Calculate the profit-sharing ceding commission for a quota share treaty.
- Evaluate the effectiveness of a quota share treaty.

OUTLINE

Overview of Quota Share Treaties

Common Clauses Modified for Use in Quota Share Treaties

Clauses Designed or Adapted for Quota Share Treaties

Quota Share Treaty Pricing

Quota Share Profit-Sharing

Ceding Commission Determination

Quota Share Treaty Evaluation

Summary

Develop Your Perspective

What are the main topics covered in the chapter?

This chapter describes the operation, common clauses, and pricing of quota share treaties.

Identify the purpose and operation of quota share reinsurance.

- What functions does a quota share treaty serve for a primary insurer?
- What components are reflected in quota share treaty pricing?

Why is it important to learn about these topics?

Quota share treaties are the most effective form of reinsurance in providing surplus relief and are a versatile means to address other primary insurer reinsurance needs. The ability to understand, analyze, and evaluate quota share treaties is important to enable you to determine whether quota share treaties help your company or client-insurer achieve its objectives.

Examine a quota share treaty.

- How are common clauses modified for use in quota share treaties?
- What clauses are designed specifically for quota share treaties and how do they operate?

How can you use what you will learn?

Evaluate one of your company's or client insurer's quota share reinsurance treaties.

- Does this quota share treaty address your company's or client-insurer's needs?
- Does this quota share treaty have the financial and operational effects desired by your company or client-insurer?

Chapter 6
Quota Share Treaties

Pro rata reinsurance is the oldest type of reinsurance and quota share is the simplest type of pro rata reinsurance. Surplus share reinsurance, discussed in the next chapter, is a more sophisticated adaptation of quota share reinsurance. Because quota share reinsurance involves a simple sharing arrangement between the primary insurer and the reinsurer, it is used to address a variety of reinsurance needs for primary insurers.

This chapter explains the following:

- How quota share treaties operate
- How common clauses are modified for use in quota share treaties
- How clauses designed or adapted for quota share treaties operate
- How quota share treaties are priced
- How the profit-sharing ceding commission paid to the primary insurer is determined
- How quota share treaties are evaluated

OVERVIEW OF QUOTA SHARE TREATIES

Quota share reinsurance is a type of pro rata reinsurance in which the primary insurer and reinsurer share the amounts of insurance, policy premiums, and losses using a fixed percentage. Quota share reinsurance can be provided on a facultative basis (the reinsurance of individual loss exposures) or on a treaty basis (an ongoing arrangement in which categories of loss exposures meeting prescribed criteria are reinsured). This chapter describes quota share reinsurance in a treaty context. Quota share treaties can be used for property or liability insurance, but property quota share treaties are much more common. This section expands the overview of quota share reinsurance provided in a previous chapter.

A quota share treaty's operation is straightforward. During the reinsurance negotiation process, the primary insurer and the reinsurer determine the following:

- Types of insurance or other specified categories of loss exposures to which the quota share treaty will apply
- Quota share percentage
- Treaty limit
- Ceding commission

For example, a small primary insurer may plan to expand from selling only personal auto insurance to selling homeowners insurance. This primary insurer may be able to negotiate an 80 percent quota share treaty subject to maximum policy limits of $300,000 for the homeowners insurance it expects to sell. This means that the primary insurer retains 20 percent of the amounts of insurance, policy premiums, and losses for all policies covered by the treaty, and the reinsurer assumes the balance. In addition, this means that the highest amount of insurance for any underlying policy that can be completely addressed by the treaty is $300,000. Exhibit 6-1 shows an example of an 80 percent quota share treaty and how the amounts of insurance, policy premiums, and losses are shared between the primary insurer and the reinsurer.

EXHIBIT 6-1

80 Percent Quota Share Treaty

	Primary Insurer 20% Retention	Reinsurer 80% Cession	Total
Policy A			
Amount of Insurance	$10,000	$40,000	$50,000
Amount of Premium	500	2,000	2,500
Amount of Loss	300	1,200	1,500
Policy B			
Amount of Insurance	$40,000	$160,000	$200,000
Amount of Premium	800	3,200	4,000
Amount of Loss	14,000	56,000	70,000
Policy C			
Amount of Insurance	$60,000	$240,000	$300,000
Amount of Premium	1,800	7,200	9,000
Amount of Loss	55,000	220,000	275,000

In the previous example, loss exposures with amounts of insurance greater than $300,000 would be included in the treaty but only up to the reinsurance limit. Amounts exceeding the limit can be handled either by another reinsurance treaty arranged by the primary insurer or by a facultative reinsurance agreement for that particular loss exposure. Alternatively, the primary insurer can either retain the amounts of insurance greater than the limit or decline to insure those loss exposures that exceed the limit.

The ceding commission that the reinsurer pays to the primary insurer reimburses the primary insurer for policy acquisition expenses. Pro rata treaties sometimes include a commission greater than the primary insurer's expense so that effectively the primary insurer can share in the profits earned by the reinsurer on the ceded loss exposures. This additional commission is referred to as a profit-sharing commission and it is contingent on the ceded insurance's profitability. The ceding commission, netted from the reinsurance premium, provides the surplus relief sought by many primary insurers when choosing pro rata reinsurance as a means of transferring insurance risk.

The fixed percentage sharing arrangement of premiums and losses applies to all loss exposures included for coverage under the terms of the quota share treaty, which means that both the primary insurer and the reinsurer will have the same loss ratio on the ceded loss exposures. Because the primary insurer and reinsurer share the same underwriting results, quota share treaties often create a closer working relationship between the primary insurer and the reinsurer than that found with other types of reinsurance agreements. Using Policy A from Exhibit 6-1, Exhibit 6-2 shows that the loss ratio—losses divided by premiums—is the same for both the primary insurer and the reinsurer.

EXHIBIT 6-2

Comparison of the Loss Ratios of the Parties to a Quota Share Treaty

	Primary Insurer 20% Retention	Reinsurer 80% Cession	Total
Policy A			
Amount of Insurance	$10,000	$40,000	$50,000
Amount of Premium	500	2,000	2,500
Amount of Loss	300	1,200	1,500
Loss Ratio	60%	60%	60%

Under a quota share treaty, all losses, regardless of size, are reimbursed by the reinsurer based on the cession percentage. For example, even a $1,000 claim for the theft of the policyholder's engagement ring against a $300,000 homeowners policy would be shared with the reinsurer based on the cession percentage.

The primary insurer's and the reinsurer's potential liabilities increase as the amounts of insurance and loss exposures subject to the quota share treaty increase. Therefore, the primary insurer and the reinsurer should consider the average amounts of insurance needed and the number of loss exposures covered when establishing the treaty. For example, consider a quota share treaty with a 20 percent retention. At the time the treaty was purchased, it covered a small portfolio of homeowners policies with an average amount insured of $100,000. However, the portfolio now contains 5,000 policies in the same geographic area with average amounts insured of $200,000. Conceivably, a single catastrophe could cause a total loss to all 5,000 homes insured, resulting in a $200 million retention for the primary insurer and an $800 million liability for the reinsurer.

To address the situation just described, some reinsurers have required that pro rata reinsurance treaties include a per occurrence limit that applies to combined losses originating from a single occurrence. The per occurrence limit diminishes the usefulness of the pro rata reinsurance in protecting the primary insurer from the financial effects of catastrophic events. Reinsurers often use per occurrence limits as a defensive measure until they can better determine what their catastrophic loss exposure is and price it accordingly. For example, following Hurricane Andrew in 1992, many reinsurers required that a per occurrence limit be included in new and renewed pro rata reinsurance treaties. However, the reinsurers removed many of these limits once they obtained information on the primary insurers' catastrophe exposures.

Because quota share treaties apply to all loss exposures subject to the treaty, regardless of the amounts of insurance needed, small loss exposures that the primary insurer could safely retain are reinsured. Participation in these small and usually profitable loss exposures is one of the advantages for the reinsurer of quota share treaties. From the primary insurer's perspective, the unnecessary reinsurance of small loss exposures is a disadvantage of quota share treaties and a reason to consider using surplus share reinsurance or variable quota share reinsurance.

Variable quota share reinsurance is a form of quota share reinsurance in which the primary insurer's retention and the cession to the reinsurer vary by the amount of insurance needed for the loss exposure or some other criterion. Primary insurers can apply a lower quota share cession percentage for loss exposures needing lower amounts of insurance and a higher quota share cession percentage for loss exposures needing higher amounts of insurance. Variable quota share treaties address primary insurers' concerns that quota share reinsurance forces them to unnecessarily cede larger amounts on profitable loss exposures. Although the cession percentage in a variable quota share treaty changes with each loss exposure's attributes, the cession percentages are established when the treaty is negotiated, as is the cession percentage used in a standard quota share treaty. Exhibit 6-3 shows how the cession percentages in a variable quota share treaty may change based on the amounts of insurance needed for each loss exposure ceded. For example, a loss exposure with an $80,000 amount of insurance needed would be subject to an 80 percent cession.

EXHIBIT 6-3

Variable Quota Share Treaty Cession Percentages

Amount of Insurance	Cession Percentage	Maximum Cession
$0–$25,000	20%	$5,000
$25,001–$50,000	60%	$30,000
$50,001–$75,000	75%	$56,250
$75,001–$100,000	80%	$80,000

Exhibit 6-4 shows the effect on the ceded premium of a variable quota share treaty compared to an 80 percent standard quota share treaty for the same subject premium and using the variable quota share cession percentages shown in Exhibit 6-3. In the example in Exhibit 6-4, the variable quota share treaty yields a much smaller total ceded premium than the standard quota share treaty because of the primary insurer's large premium volume sold in lower amounts (or limits) of insurance.

EXHIBIT 6-4

Comparison of Standard Quota Share and Variable Quota Share Treaties

Amount of Insurance	Written Premium	Standard Quota Share		Variable Quota Share	
		Cession Percentage	Ceded Premium	Cession Percentage	Ceded Premium
$0–$25,000	$ 7,500,000	80%	$ 6,000,000	20%	$1,500,000
$25,001–$50,000	5,300,000	80%	4,240,000	60%	3,180,000
$50,001–$75,000	1,035,000	80%	828,000	75%	776,250
$75,001–$100,000	465,000	80%	372,000	80%	372,000
Totals	$14,300,000		$11,440,000		$5,828,250

A primary insurer's use of a variable quota share treaty usually results in a smaller cession of total premium than would be the case under a standard quota share treaty. As a consequence of the smaller total premium cession, a variable quota share treaty will usually provide less surplus relief than a comparable standard quota share treaty. Because the cession percentage must be determined for each loss exposure, a variable quota share treaty involves more administrative expense than a standard quota share treaty.

Although the loss ratio is the same for the primary insurer and the reinsurer in a standard quota share treaty, this may not be the case with a variable quota share treaty. In Exhibit 6-4, variable quota share treaty policies with low amounts of insurance and a smaller cession percentage may have a lower loss ratio than policies with higher amounts of insurance and a larger cession percentage. In this example, the reinsurer may reassess its participation and attempt to negotiate greater participation in the primary insurer's more profitable insurance policies.

Functions of Quota Share Treaties

Quota share treaties serve the following five functions for the primary insurer:

1. Increase large line capacity
2. Provide catastrophe protection
3. Provide surplus relief
4. Facilitate withdrawal from a market segment
5. Provide underwriting guidance

Although quota share treaties serve all of these functions, some functions are better served than others and some would be better served by other types of reinsurance.

Increase Large Line Capacity

Quota share reinsurance is reasonably effective in providing the primary insurer with increased large line capacity, depending on the cession percentage in the quota share treaty. For example, quota share reinsurance may enable a small primary insurer to compete for homeowners business with amounts of insurance that are greater than its policyholders' surplus could otherwise support. However, quota share reinsurance is less effective in increasing large line capacity than other forms of reinsurance because the primary insurer's liability increases as the amounts of insurance increase.

Provide Catastrophe Protection

Quota share treaties provide the primary insurer with some catastrophe protection, although these treaties are usually not purchased primarily to fulfill that function. A quota share reinsurer pays its share of each loss incurred under the quota share treaty whether it resulted from a catastrophe or from several different events. As discussed previously, some pro rata reinsurance treaties contain a per occurrence cap on the reinsurer's liability for catastrophic losses. Even those quota share treaties that include a per occurrence limit provide some, albeit limited, catastrophe protection. Primary insurers that insure loss exposures likely to be affected by catastrophes usually purchase catastrophe reinsurance (to be discussed in a later chapter), which is designed and priced to serve this function. A primary insurer's quota share treaty may expressly exclude catastrophe losses in recognition of a separate catastrophe reinsurance agreement.

Some primary insurers use reciprocal quota share treaties with other primary insurers to minimize their concentration of loss exposures in a single geographic area and thereby reduce their catastrophe loss exposures. For example, a primary insurer writing homeowners insurance in a limited geographic area, such as Alabama, Georgia, and Florida, may enter into a quota share treaty with a primary insurer operating in another U.S. region. This quota share treaty would enable each insurer to geographically diversify its loss exposures.

Provide Surplus Relief

Quota share is the most effective type of reinsurance that a primary insurer can use to obtain surplus relief. Quota share treaties allow the primary insurer to cede a large amount of premium to reduce its net written premiums and to receive a ceding commission to increase its policyholders' surplus. The effect of a quota share reinsurance transaction serves to improve the primary insurer's financial strength. For rapidly growing primary insurers that are depleting their policyholders' surplus more rapidly than they are earning profit, quota share reinsurance provides the financing they need to support further growth. Primary insurers become less dependent on quota share reinsurance as they increase their policyholders' surplus through profitable operations.

Facilitate Withdrawal From a Market Segment

A primary insurer may decide that an existing type of insurance or geographic area (market segment) no longer fits its long-term business strategy. To withdraw from a market segment, a primary insurer may transfer its entire liability to a reinsurer. The primary insurer can effectively eliminate the financial consequences of the unwanted loss exposures from its operating results by purchasing a 100 percent quota share treaty (portfolio reinsurance). Reinsurers would consider a 100 percent quota share treaty if it offered an opportunity for profit or positive cash flow. Because portfolio reinsurance transactions often reflect a significant shift in a primary insurer's business strategy, some states require that these transactions be reviewed and approved by insurance regulators before they are executed.

Provide Underwriting Guidance

Primary insurers starting to sell a new insurance product or entering a new territory often rely on the expertise of a reinsurer in making fundamental decisions about underwriting standards, coverage forms, and pricing. Reinsurers generally welcome these opportunities to provide advice because they have the chance to influence the types of loss exposures that will be reinsured. Reinsurers providing reinsurance on a quota share basis are more likely to be involved in primary insurer underwriting policy decisions about the ceded loss exposures because the primary insurer and the reinsurer loss ratios are the same.

Quota Share Treaties as Part of a Reinsurance Program

Primary insurers will often use quota share treaties when they begin selling a new insurance product, enter a new territory, or need surplus relief. In developing a reinsurance program, a primary insurer and its reinsurer must determine how the quota share treaty fits into the overall program. Usually, a primary insurer does not rely on a quota share treaty alone but combines it with surplus share treaties, excess of loss treaties, or facultative reinsurance. The reinsurance program design must consider the order in which the primary insurer's treaties will respond to losses. The three categories that describe the order of treaty application are:

1. Gross account basis
2. Net of pro rata basis
3. Net of all reinsurance basis

A quota share treaty that applies on a **gross account basis** reimburses the primary insurer for covered losses before other pro rata reinsurance treaties apply.

A quota share treaty on a **net of pro rata** basis applies after other applicable pro rata reinsurance recoveries apply. For example, the primary insurer may have a surplus share reinsurance treaty that applies to the same loss exposures as, and would respond before, the primary insurer's net of pro rata quota share treaty.

A quota share treaty on a **net of all reinsurance basis** applies after all other applicable reinsurance recoveries apply, whether that reinsurance is pro rata or excess of loss. For example, a primary insurer may have a property per risk excess of loss treaty and a property quota share treaty on the same loss exposure. If the property quota share treaty is on a net of all reinsurance basis, the property per risk excess of loss treaty would reduce the loss before the property quota share treaty is applied.

Quota share treaties may also be used by a captive insurer. A **captive insurer** (or captive) is a subsidiary formed to insure the loss exposures of its parent company or companies and affiliates. A captive insurer could offer insurance directly to its owner, but to do so it must satisfy state insurance licensing requirements. Instead, many captive insurers use the services of a fronting company. A **fronting company** is a licensed insurer that issues insurance policies with the intention of using reinsurance to transfer the loss exposures to a captive insurer, reinsurer, or unauthorized insurer. A 100 percent quota share treaty is often used to transfer the liability assumed by the fronting company to the captive insurer. The captive insurer can reduce its liability through a retrocession agreement.

Gross account basis
A basis of treaty application in which the treaty reimburses the primary insurer for covered losses before other pro rata reinsurance treaties apply.

Net of pro rata basis
A basis of treaty application in which the treaty recoveries apply to losses after other pro rata reinsurance recoveries apply.

Net of all reinsurance basis
A basis of treaty application in which the treaty recoveries apply to losses after all other reinsurance recoveries apply.

Captive insurer
A subsidiary formed to insure the loss exposures of its parent company or companies and affiliates.

Fronting company
A licensed insurer that issues insurance policies with the intention of using reinsurance to transfer the loss exposures to a captive insurer, reinsurer, or unauthorized insurer.

EXHIBIT 6-5

Quota Share Treaty as Part of a Reinsurance Program

$3,000,000 xs $1,000,000

Retention

70% Quota Share
$1,000,000 Maximum Policy Limit

☐ Retention
■ Quota Share Treaty
☐ Excess of Loss Treaty

Exhibit 6-5 illustrates how a quota share treaty and excess of loss treaty may be arranged for a reinsurance program.

COMMON CLAUSES MODIFIED FOR USE IN QUOTA SHARE TREATIES

Some common clauses are modified for use in quota share treaties. Those clauses include:

- Reinsuring clause
- Definitions clause
- Commencement and termination clause
- Reports and remittances clause

Reinsuring Clause

The reinsuring clause specifies the quota share percentage assumed by the reinsurer and states whether the quota share cession is obligatory. It also describes the policies covered and states the basis of attachment, in other words, whether it applies to in-force policies, newly issued policies, renewed policies, or all three. The sample reinsuring clause shown in Exhibit 6-6 states that coverage is provided for losses for in-force policies issued prior to the inception of the quota share treaty and new policies issued on or after the inception date of the treaty.

EXHIBIT 6-6

Reinsuring Clause

44 C

REINSURING CLAUSE

By this Contract the Company obligates itself to cede to the Reinsurer and the Reinsurer obligates itself to accept _____ % quota share reinsurance of the Company's net liability under policies, contracts and binders of insurance or reinsurance (hereinafter called "policies") in force at and becoming effective at and after _(hour)_ _(date)_ _(year)_, including renewals, and classified by the Company as _____.

"Net liability" as used herein is defined as the Company's gross liability remaining after cessions, if any, to _____.

The liability of the Reinsurer with respect to each cession hereunder shall commence obligatorily and simultaneously with that of the Company, subject to the terms, conditions and limitations hereinafter set forth.

Source: Brokers & Reinsurance Markets Association (BRMA), http://www.brma.org/download/bcwrb044.doc (accessed January 29, 2004).

The reinsuring clause establishes that the reinsurer's obligation to the primary insurer begins at exactly the same time as the primary insurer's obligation to the insured begins. When the primary insurer underwriter agrees to issue a policy, the reinsurer automatically assumes its proportional liability for the loss exposure covered by the underlying policy.

Definitions Clause

The terms defined in the definitions clause vary by quota share treaty depending on the needs and concerns of the parties. For example, the treaty may define "net retained insurance liability" to clarify whether the treaty applies on a gross account or net basis. A quota share treaty may contain a specific definition for "occurrence" if the treaty has an occurrence limit. Exhibit 6-7 shows an example of a definitions clause.

EXHIBIT 6-7

Definitions Clause

The term "net retained insurance liability" as used herein means the remaining portion of the Company's gross liability on each risk reinsured under this Agreement after deducting recoveries from all reinsurance, other than the reinsurance provided hereunder and other than the reinsurance provided in Article XIV.

The term "net premiums written" as used herein means gross premiums and additional premiums less return premiums and less premiums ceded on all other reinsurance, other than the reinsurance provided in Article XIV.

The term "occurrence" as used herein means each occurrence, disaster, or casualty or series of occurrences, disasters, or casualties arising out of one event.

Commencement and Termination Clause

The commencement and termination clause defines the term of the quota share treaty and the circumstances that would trigger its termination. In most cases, the quota share treaty's effective date is the first day of a month or a calendar quarter, and the effective time is 12:01 AM standard time at the location of the loss exposure for property treaties and at the insured's mailing address for casualty treaties.

The commencement and termination clause clearly states the termination provisions. Most quota share treaties provide coverage for losses from policies that were subject to the treaty after the termination date (run-off basis). For example, the sample commencement and termination clause shown in Exhibit 6-8 obligates the reinsurer to pay losses until the first anniversary or natural expiration or cancellation of each policy, up to a maximum of twelve months after the treaty's termination.

Reinsurers prefer a treaty written with a provision that permits immediate termination (cut-off basis) if cancellation is because of poor loss experience. The unearned premium reserve is returned, and the reinsurer is not responsible for losses occurring after the termination date. In this situation, the primary insurer must retain the liability transferred back from the reinsurer, purchase other reinsurance, or cancel the underlying policies. For these reasons, the primary insurer usually prefers not to have this type of cancellation provision included in the treaty. Most insurance policies are issued for a one-year term. Consequently, no unearned premiums would remain more than twelve months after the treaty's termination. However, if policies are issued for more than one year, such as a builders' risk policy, the treaty must contain provisions either to extend the reinsurer's liability to cover the total run-off or to return the balance of the unearned premium reserve to the primary insurer.

EXHIBIT 6-8

Commencement and Termination Clause

57 B

COMMENCEMENT AND TERMINATION CLAUSE

This Contract shall incept at 12:01 A.M. Local Standard Time *(month, day, year)* at the location of the risk and shall remain in force for an indefinite period, but either party shall have the right to cancel as of *(month, day, year)* or any *(month, day)* thereafter by giving at least _____ days prior written notice by certified or registered mail.

In the event either party cancels in accordance with the paragraph above, the Reinsurer shall participate in all policies ceded within the terms of this Contract written or renewed by the Company after receipt of notice of cancellation but prior to termination, and shall remain liable for all cessions in force at termination of this Contract; however, the liability of the Reinsurer shall cease with respect to losses occurring subsequent to the first anniversary, natural expiration or cancellation of each policy ceded, but not to extend beyond 12 months after such termination.

The Reinsurer shall refund to the Company the unearned reinsurance premium applicable to the unexpired liability (calculated on a pro rata basis), less the commission allowed by the Reinsurer thereon at conclusion of the runoff. The Reinsurer will continue to be liable for its proportionate share of the outstanding losses (reported or unreported) on policies ceded hereunder with a date of loss prior to the conclusion of the runoff.

Source: BRMA, http://www.brma.org/download/bcwrb057.doc (accessed January 29, 2004).

Reports and Remittances Clause

The reports and remittances clause requires the primary insurer to submit information to the reinsurer so that net balances owed to each party can be calculated and remitted and so that financial statements can be completed. This information includes premiums, claims, unearned premiums, and outstanding losses. The primary insurer and reinsurer agree on the reporting format that the primary insurer will use. Traditionally, information on the loss exposures that are subject to the treaty are reported on a bordereau.

The reports and remittances clause may specify the following conditions:

- The primary insurer must maintain adequate records regarding the liabilities ceded and report cessions periodically in the designated format.
- The primary insurer and reinsurer must pay balances within a specified period.
- The primary insurer must report large individual losses and can request that the reinsurer pay its share of such losses immediately.
- The primary insurer must provide information regarding catastrophe losses.

The primary insurer's records must be adequate to report all of the necessary data on the policies covered by the quota share treaty. Reporting can be monthly, quarterly, semiannually, or annually. The reinsurer monitors the reporting to determine how the treaty is performing. The reporting format is important to the reinsurer because the format can make it easier to prepare loss development reports and to complete financial statements.

The payment period for balances can be negotiated. The period is seldom less than thirty days or greater than ninety days. The number of days depends on when the primary insurer receives payments from its policyholders and the degree of competition among reinsurers. For example, if the primary insurer usually receives premium payments from policyholders forty-five days after issuing policies, the primary insurer's cash flow would be reduced if payments were due to the reinsurer in thirty days. Primary insurers also want to hold premiums as long as possible to earn investment income on them. If reinsurers are in a highly competitive market, they will be more likely to extend the payment period in order to attract business.

Cash call
A reinsurance treaty provision that permits the primary insurer to obtain payment from the reinsurer for certain losses without having to wait until the next payment period.

The primary insurer may not want to delay recovery of the reinsurer's share of a loss until the next payment period. Therefore, the reports and remittances clause may have a **cash call** provision stating that the primary insurer can obtain payment from the reinsurer for certain losses without that delay should those losses exceed a certain agreed dollar amount (typically a large amount). An unusually large loss may create cash flow problems for the primary insurer, leading it to request a cash call. If the primary insurer is ceding the anticipated volume of loss exposures to the quota share treaty, the reinsurer usually has adequate cash flow to pay its share of large losses without waiting for the next payment period.

The dollar amount of a loss that qualifies under the cash call provision varies by the primary insurer's size and the treaty's terms. Because the reinsurer is asked to pay the loss immediately, the reinsurer can offset its payment with any balance overdue from the primary insurer. The amount received through the cash call provision is then deducted from the losses figure in the next report. The sample reports and remittances clause shown in Exhibit 6-9 specifies the size of the loss that will trigger the cash call provision. Other treaties may include those specifications in a separate cash call clause.

Finally, the reports and remittances clause requires the primary insurer to provide catastrophe information to the reinsurer so that the reinsurer can prepare for unusually large loss payments and can report those losses under the reinsurer's own catastrophe retrocessions.

EXHIBIT 6-9

Reports and Remittances Clause

45 D

REPORTS AND REMITTANCES

Within _____ days after the close of each _____, the Company will furnish the Reinsurer with a report summarizing the written premium ceded less return premium and commission, losses paid, loss adjustment expense paid, monies recovered, and net balance due either party. In addition, the Company will furnish the Reinsurer a _____ statement showing the unearned premium, the total reserves for outstanding losses including loss adjustment expense, a breakdown by American Insurance Association catastrophic code numbers for paid and outstanding catastrophe losses and loss adjustment expense, and such other information as may be required by the Reinsurer for completion of its NAIC annual statements.

Amounts due the Reinsurer will be remitted with the report _____. Amounts due the Company will be remitted within _____ days following receipt of the report. Should payment due from the Reinsurer exceed _____ as respects any one loss, the Company may give the Reinsurer notice of payment made or its intention to make payment on a certain date. If the Company has paid the loss, payment will be made by the Reinsurer immediately. If the Company intends to pay the loss by a certain date and has submitted a satisfactory proof of loss or similar document, payment will be due from the Reinsurer twenty-four (24) hours prior to that date, provided the Reinsurer has a period of five (5) working days after receipt of said notice to dispatch the payment. Cash loss amounts specifically remitted by the Reinsurer as set forth herein will be credited to its next _____ account.

Source: BRMA, http://www.brma.org/download/bcwrb045.doc (accessed January 29, 2004).

CLAUSES DESIGNED OR ADAPTED FOR QUOTA SHARE TREATIES

The previous section described common clauses that are modified for use in quota share treaties. This section describes clauses that were designed or adapted specifically for use in quota share treaties and that enable the agreement to operate as such. These clauses include:

- Retention and limits clause
- Reinsurance premium clause
- Sliding scale commission clause
- Portfolio transfer clause
- Losses, loss adjustment expenses, and salvages clause
- Outside reinsurance clause
- Warranties clause
- Original conditions clause

Retention and Limits Clause

Retention and limits clause
A reinsurance treaty clause that specifies the primary insurer's minimum net retention and the maximum amount of insurance that the primary insurer can cede to the reinsurer.

The **retention and limits clause** specifies the primary insurer's minimum net retention and the maximum amount of insurance that the primary insurer can cede to the reinsurer under the quota share treaty. If the primary insurer uses the quota share treaty on a net of pro rata basis or on a net of all reinsurance basis, the clause may state the treaty's maximum limit as a percentage of the primary insurer's net retention after deduction of other reinsurance. The sample retention and limits clause shown in Exhibit 6-10 includes that wording.

EXHIBIT 6-10

Retention and Limits Clause

The liability of the Reinsurer shall not exceed $ 240,000 on any one risk (i.e., 80 % of $ 300,000). The Company shall be the sole judge of what constitutes one risk; provided, however, any non-fire resistive building and its contents shall never be considered as constituting more than one risk. As respects dwelling properties insured under Homeowners, Farmowners and Ranchowners policies, the dwelling building, contents therein, outbuildings and extra living expense shall be considered as constituting one risk.

The Company shall retain net for its own account, subject to the reinsurance provided in Article XIV, the remaining 20 % of its net retained insurance liability on each risk reinsured under this Agreement.

Reinsurance Premium Clause

The **reinsurance premium clause** specifies how the subject premium is determined and when the primary insurer must pay the reinsurer its share of the unearned premium. If the quota share treaty covers the property loss exposure of package policies in which one indivisible premium applies to both property and liability coverages, the reinsurance premium clause specifies the percentage of the indivisible premium that represents the property loss exposure. The reinsurance premium clause determines the basis for calculating ceding commissions. Exhibit 6-11 shows an example of a reinsurance premium clause.

Reinsurance premium clause
A reinsurance treaty clause that specifies how the subject premium is determined and when the primary insurer must pay the reinsurer its share of the unearned premium.

EXHIBIT 6-11

Reinsurance Premium Clause

42 A

REINSURANCE PREMIUM

The Company will cede to the Reinsurer its proportionate share of the unearned premium on the business in force at the inception of this Contract for the business described herein. Additionally, the Company will cede to the Reinsurer its proportionate share of the net subject written premium on all policies written or renewed with an effective date on or after the inception of this Contract.

"Net subject written premium" as used in this Contract will mean the gross written premium of the Company for the classes of business reinsured hereunder, plus additions, less return premium for cancellations and reductions, and less premium for reinsurance that inures to the benefit of this Contract.

Source: BRMA, http://www.brma.org/download/bcwrb042.doc (accessed January 29, 2004).

Sliding Scale Commission Clause

The **sliding scale commission clause** specifies how the primary insurer and reinsurer will share profits from the underlying insurance covered by the treaty. Sliding scale commission is calculated retrospectively by adjusting the ceding commission percentage based on the actual loss ratio of the ceded loss exposures. Sliding scale commissions are commonly used in quota share treaties and some surplus share treaties. A provisional ceding commission is paid during the reinsurance treaty's term and is usually an amount close to the actual acquisition costs incurred by the primary insurer at the expected loss ratio for the reinsured policies. For each percentage point reduction in the actual loss ratio during a specified experience period, the ceding commission percentage may increase, up to a specified maximum percentage. Similarly, for each percentage point incurred above the expected loss ratio the ceding commission percentage may decrease, but not below a specified

Sliding scale commission clause
A reinsurance treaty clause that specifies how the primary insurer and reinsurer will share profits from the underlying insurance covered by the treaty.

minimum percentage. If the treaty has limited historical loss experience or is subject to catastrophe loss exposures, the sliding scale commission clause may contain a provision that carries forward losses to the next experience period. Exhibit 6-12 shows an example of how a sliding scale commission may be applied.

EXHIBIT 6-12

Sliding Scale Commission Example

Boerner Insurance Company (Boerner) has a quota share treaty with a sliding scale commission clause with a 35 percent provisional ceding commission and a 60 percent expected loss ratio. In the sliding scale shown below, commission scale "slides up" 1 percent for each 1 percent reduction in Boerner's loss ratio. For example, at the end of the treaty period Boerner might have developed a 55 percent loss ratio and have been rewarded with a 5 percent increase over the 35 percent provisional ceding commission.

Actual Loss Ratio	Ceding Commission Rate
60% or more	35%
59%	36%
58%	37%
57%	38%
56%	39%
55%	40%
54%	41%
53%	42%
52%	43%
51%	44%
50%	45%
Less than 50%	46%

Sliding scale commission clauses are usually used in quota share treaties in which the loss ratio is relatively stable, such as property insurance. These clauses can also be used in surplus share treaties, but the potential for large losses under surplus share treaties usually negates the potential profit sharing, so profit-sharing ceding commissions, discussed later in this chapter, are used instead.

Generally, the reinsurer is responsible for calculating the sliding scale commissions. However, who performs the calculations can be negotiated. Direct writing reinsurers typically prefer to do their own calculations.

Portfolio Transfer Clause

The **portfolio transfer clause** specifies how the unearned premium reserve is transferred, the payment terms, and the reinsurer's obligation for losses. If one reinsurer is simply replacing another reinsurer on the same treaty, the unearned premium reserve is transferred from the outgoing reinsurer to the incoming reinsurer. The sample portfolio transfer clause shown in Exhibit 6-13 states that the primary insurer must pay the unearned premium reserve to the incoming reinsurer within sixty days of the treaty's inception.

Payment terms under a portfolio transfer clause are important because the incoming reinsurer is responsible for paying losses on the in-force policies and should have funds to pay those losses as quickly as possible. Sometimes primary insurers have difficulty recovering unearned premium reserves from terminating reinsurers. Consequently, the primary insurer may want to delay paying the unearned premium reserve to the incoming reinsurer. However, under the portfolio transfer clause the primary insurer is contractually obliged to remit the unearned premium reserve to the incoming reinsurer within a specified time.

Portfolio transfer clause
A reinsurance treaty clause that specifies how the unearned premium reserve is transferred, the payment terms, and the reinsurer's obligation for losses.

EXHIBIT 6-13

Portfolio Transfer Clause

Within 60 days after the inception of this Agreement, the Company shall remit to the Reinsurer the unearned premium reserve on business ceded hereunder that was in force at the inception of this Agreement. The Reinsurer will allow a commission on the premium ceded at the rate provided herein. In consideration of the premium so transferred, and subject to the terms and conditions of this Agreement, the Reinsurer will accept liability for its share of losses which occur on or after the inception date.

Losses, Loss Adjustment Expenses, and Salvages Clause

The **losses, loss adjustment expenses, and salvages clause** of a quota share treaty states that the primary insurer has the full authority to settle claims for the loss exposures ceded under the treaty. The clause also states that the reinsurer is responsible only for its proportion of the losses and loss adjustment expenses. Because the reinsurer shares in the losses, the reinsurer is entitled to its pro rata share of salvages, discounts, and other recoveries that reduce the amount of the loss. Exhibit 6-14 shows an example of a losses, loss adjustment expenses, and salvages clause.

Losses, loss adjustment expenses, and salvages clause
A reinsurance treaty clause that gives the primary insurer the authority to settle claims, and that provides for the sharing of losses, loss adjustment expenses, and salvages between the primary insurer and the reinsurer.

> **EXHIBIT 6-14**
>
> ### Losses, Loss Adjustment Expenses, and Salvages Clause
>
> The Company shall settle all loss claims under its policies, and the Reinsurer shall pay to the Company its pro rata share of such loss claims as payable by the Company.
>
> The Reinsurer shall also bear its pro rata share of expenses incurred by the Company in the investigation, adjustment and litigation of all claims under its policies, including the pro rata share of salaries and expenses of staff adjusters as allocated to the claim, but excluding the office expenses of the Company and the salaries and expenses of its other employees. Such expenses shall be in addition to the limits set forth in Article V.
>
> The Reinsurer shall benefit pro rata in all salvage, discounts and other recoveries.

Outside Reinsurance Clause

With quota share treaties, primary insurers must cede, and reinsurers must accept, the types of loss exposures identified in the reinsuring clause. Occasionally, the primary insurer wants to insure a loss exposure but does not want to expose it to the treaty. Additionally, state law, policyholder requirements, or the amount of insurance needed may require separate reinsurance agreements. However, if the primary insurer reinsures such loss exposures outside the treaty through a facultative agreement, the treaty's obligatory nature may appear to be violated. The **outside reinsurance clause** allows the primary insurer to secure other reinsurance in certain circumstances. A sample outside reinsurance clause is shown in Exhibit 6-15.

Outside reinsurance clause
A reinsurance treaty clause that allows the primary insurer to cede certain loss exposures outside the existing treaty.

> **EXHIBIT 6-15**
>
> ### Outside Reinsurance Clause
>
> It is understood and agreed that outside reinsurance placed by the Company for the following purposes shall not be deemed to be in violation of the obligatory provisions of this Agreement:
>
> A. For the benefit of the Reinsurer hereunder; or
>
> B. In compliance with any state law, or at the direction of an insurance department; or
>
> C. For the purpose of meeting conditions imposed by the insured or by a mortgagee having an interest in the property insured; or
>
> D. On any risk where, in the opinion of the Company, the ultimate amount of reinsurance required will exceed the respective amount of reinsurance which may be ceded hereunder.

Warranties Clause

The **warranties clause** specifies conditions with which the primary insurer must comply to ensure coverage under the quota share treaty. For example, the sample warranties clause in Exhibit 6-16 specifies that the Insurance Services Office (ISO) Seepage and Pollution Exclusion Clause must be attached to all policies subject to the reinsurance agreement. Warranted conditions are those for which the primary insurer's lack of compliance voids reinsurance coverage for losses, and they are used when the reinsurer wants to ensure absolute compliance. Primary insurer underwriters should have a thorough understanding of treaty terms and conditions so that compliance is complete.

Warranties clause
A reinsurance treaty clause that specifies conditions with which the primary insurer must comply to ensure coverage under the treaty.

EXHIBIT 6-16

Warranties Clause

The Company warrants that all business subject to this Agreement contains the full Insurance Services Office's Seepage and Pollution Exclusion Clause or so deemed, wherever legal and applicable.

Original Conditions Clause

The **original conditions clause** establishes that the liability assumed by the reinsurer under the reinsurance treaty is on the same basis (rates, terms, and conditions) as the underlying coverage provided by the primary insurer.

The original conditions clause states that the reinsurer's share of the underlying premium, net of ceding commission, will not be reduced by dividends (if any) paid by the primary insurer to the underlying insured. Many primary insurers have dividend plans that enable policyholders to share in their profits when losses are better than expected. However, the reinsurance premium is based on the total amount of subject premium. A sample original conditions clause is shown in Exhibit 6-17.

Original conditions clause
A reinsurance treaty clause that establishes that the liability assumed by the reinsurer under the reinsurance treaty is on the same basis (rates, terms, and conditions) as the underlying coverage provided by the primary insurer.

EXHIBIT 6-17

Original Conditions Clause

All amounts ceded hereunder shall be subject to the same rates, clauses, conditions, waivers, and to the same modifications and alterations as the respective policies of the Company. The Reinsurer shall be credited with its exact proportion of the original premiums less commission hereon received by the Company, prior to disbursement of any dividends.

QUOTA SHARE TREATY PRICING

This ceding commission is the key pricing variable under quota share treaties. The amount of ceding commission the reinsurer is willing to pay to the primary insurer is affected by the following five considerations:

1. Primary insurer's retention
2. Reinsurance treaty's limit
3. Primary insurer's policy acquisition expenses
4. Primary insurer's expected loss ratio on the portfolio included, as well as its underwriting ability and rate adequacy
5. Competition in the reinsurance marketplace

The first consideration that affects the ceding commission is the primary insurer's retention. The primary insurer sets a retention for a quota share treaty based on its management's attitude towards risk, its size, its financial needs, and the geographic spread of the loss exposures it cedes to the treaty.

If the primary insurer's management is unwilling to retain a significant amount of underwriting risk, that primary insurer will want a low retention. The primary insurer's size also influences the retention amount. Regulatory and statutory requirements may prevent a primary insurer from retaining as much underwriting risk as it would like.

In consideration of its financial needs, a primary insurer selects a retention based on its estimate of the amount of surplus relief that it will need. To estimate needed surplus relief, the primary insurer must estimate its expected written premiums for the coming year and its expected policyholders' surplus at the end of the year. For example, a primary insurer may estimate that at year-end its written premiums will be $25 million and its policyholders' surplus will be $5 million. This primary insurer's capacity ratio at year-end would be 5 to 1 ($25 million ÷ $5 million = 5), exceeding the acceptable limit (3 to 1) for this ratio. A 40 percent quota share treaty would strengthen the primary insurer's capacity ratio because 40 percent or $10 million of written premiums would be paid to the reinsurer. This would reduce the primary insurer's net written premiums to $15 million and therefore reduce its capacity ratio to 3 to 1. Additionally, the ceding commission paid by the reinsurer will increase the primary insurer's policyholders' surplus and further strengthen the capacity ratio. In practice, most primary insurers would choose to cede enough written premiums to bring the capacity ratio below 3 to 1.

The primary insurer also bases a quota share treaty retention on the geographic spread of the loss exposure ceded to the treaty. The geographic retention depends on the following:

- Concentration of loss exposures in a geographic area
- Susceptibility of the area to catastrophes
- Cost of catastrophe protection

A primary insurer may decide that a concentration of loss exposures of $50 million in an area prone to hurricane damage is more than it wants to retain. A quota share treaty would be one way to reduce that concentration. For example, a 40 percent quota share treaty would reduce the primary insurer's liability to $30 million. If $30 million was still more than the primary insurer wanted to retain, the primary insurer could decide to purchase catastrophe excess of loss reinsurance or increase the cession to the quota share treaty. That decision would depend on the cost of the catastrophe excess of loss reinsurance compared to the cost of a larger cession to the quota share treaty.

A reinsurer may agree to whatever retention the primary insurer selects. However, to encourage good underwriting practices on the part of the primary insurer, the reinsurer usually requires that the primary insurer retain a reasonable proportion of the loss exposures. To evaluate the primary insurer's retention, the reinsurer will request information on the insurance policies the primary insurer has already sold, underwriting guidelines, acceptable amounts of insurance, claim history on the loss exposures subject to the treaty, and hazardous classes of business insured.

The second consideration affecting the ceding commission is the reinsurance treaty's limit. The reinsurer protects itself by imposing a maximum limit on the amount of insurance the primary insurer can cede. That maximum limit affects the amount of premium ceded and therefore the amount of ceding commission the reinsurer is willing to pay. Generally, the more premium subject to the treaty, the greater the ceding commission percentage. If the treaty covers two or more types of insurance, the maximum limit may be different for each type. A quota share treaty may include a per occurrence limit to restrict the accumulation of losses from a single event. Including a per occurrence limit usually results in higher ceding commission than would be paid had the limit not been included.

The third consideration affecting the ceding commission is the primary insurer's policy acquisition expenses. The ceding commission is normally established as an amount that equals the primary insurer's policy acquisition expenses so that the reinsurer is paying its proportionate share of the cost of selling the underlying insurance policies.

The fourth consideration affecting the ceding commission is the primary insurer's expected loss ratio, as well as its underwriting ability and rate adequacy. The reinsurer studies the primary insurer's underwriting ability and rate adequacy to see how they compare with those of other primary insurers selling the same type of insurance. If the primary insurer's rates are inadequate, the amount of premium ceded to the quota share treaty will be inadequate, and the reinsurer will want to reduce the ceding commission. If the primary insurer's underwriters are failing to exercise sound underwriting practices, the liability accepted by the primary insurer will be greater than anticipated by the rates charged.

The reinsurer examines the primary insurer's past loss experience to identify trends that may project the results for the coming year. Insurer pricing often appears adequate in the short term, but it may prove to be inadequate in the long term when all of the primary insurer's losses are known. Therefore, reinsurers often rely on the primary insurer's past loss experience to gauge its underwriting ability. One source for historical loss experience is Schedule P of the primary insurer's NAIC Annual Statement. Schedule P data may need to be adjusted if the primary insurer's reinsurance program has changed significantly. The data may also need to be adjusted for changes in economic cycles, random fluctuations, and changes in procedures or claim-reserving philosophy.

In addition to analyzing loss reserves, the reinsurer may analyze paid claims. Using paid claims data, the reinsurer can avoid problems resulting from changes in claim-handling procedures and claim-reserving philosophy that might have contributed to over- or under-reserving. Even if reserving problems are not suspected, reported and paid claims data provide useful information because those data add to the total amount of information available about the primary insurer.

Based on the analysis of premium and losses, a reinsurer can estimate the primary insurer's expected loss ratio on the loss exposures subject to the treaty. The reinsurer may then increase or decrease the ceding commission offered, or agree to a sliding scale commission rather than a flat commission, based on the treaty's estimated profitability.

The fifth consideration affecting the ceding commission is the competition in the reinsurance marketplace. After evaluating all other factors, the amount of the ceding commission (or type of ceding commission) may be a matter of offering terms that the primary insurer will accept. When the reinsurance market is competitive, reinsurers are willing to offer higher ceding commission than they would when the market is less competitive. Ceding commission amounts that are higher than the primary insurer's actual acquisition expenses are called an override. Reinsurers should consider the override when evaluating the profitability of the quota share treaty.

QUOTA SHARE PROFIT-SHARING CEDING COMMISSION DETERMINATION

The following example illustrates how a reinsurer can use estimated premium and costs to determine a profit-sharing ceding commission for a quota share treaty.

Assume the following background information:

- A primary insurer plans to purchase a 40 percent quota share treaty covering its retained losses on an excess of loss treaty.
- The primary insurer wants a flat ceding commission of 20 percent for its policy acquisition expenses.

- The reinsurer is willing to reward the primary insurer for favorable underwriting performance through a profit-sharing commission, which is paid in addition to the flat ceding commission.
- The estimated subject premium is $6,300,000.
- The reinsurer's costs and minimum profit comprise 7 percent of the reinsurance premium.
- The underlying policies covered by the quota share treaty have an insignificant catastrophe loss exposure.
- The primary insurer's past premium and losses, based on data from Schedule P of its NAIC Annual Statement, are shown in Exhibit 6-18. The notes below the figures explain the adjustments made to the primary insurer's original Schedule P figures.

The reinsurer determines the profit-sharing commission percentage in three steps:

Step 1: Estimate the quota share reinsurance premium.

Step 2: Subtract reinsurer and primary insurer costs.

Step 3: Determine a percentage for the profit-sharing commission.

EXHIBIT 6-18

Primary Insurer's Past Premium and Losses

(1) Historical Accident Year	(2) Losses Including Loss Adj. Exp.	(3) Earned Premium
1	$3,803,595	$5,763,023
2	4,073,302	6,266,619
3	3,659,134	5,808,149
4	4,149,709	6,193,595
5	4,007,660	6,261,969

Notes

- The losses in Column (2) are net of recoveries from excess of loss reinsurance, so these losses are representative of the losses to which this quota share treaty will be subject. The losses are also trended and developed to estimate their final settlement values in current dollars.

- The earned premiums in Column (3) are net of premiums for excess of loss reinsurance, so these premiums are representative of the premiums that will be subject to this quota share treaty. They are also adjusted for the primary insurer's insurance rate change history to restate the historical premium using current insurance rates. After this adjustment, premium is usually called on level, which means that all the premiums are stated at current levels.

- Premiums and losses were adjusted to reflect changes over the years in the retention for the excess of loss reinsurance program.

Step 1: Estimate the Quota Share Reinsurance Premium

The estimated quota share reinsurance premium is the estimated subject premium multiplied by the quota share percentage. Using the background information, the reinsurer calculates the estimated quota share reinsurance premium as follows:

$$\text{Estimated quota share reinsurance premium} = \text{Estimated subject premium} \times \text{Quota share percentage}$$
$$= \$6{,}300{,}000 \times 40$$
$$= \$2{,}520{,}000.$$

Step 2: Subtract Reinsurer and Primary Insurer Costs

The reinsurer must subtract its costs and minimum profit, the flat ceding commission required by the primary insurer, and estimated average losses and loss adjustment expenses from the estimated quota share reinsurance premium.

A reinsurer's costs incurred in providing a pro rata treaty include overhead and brokerage paid to a reinsurance intermediary (when applicable). These costs may be reduced by an investment income offset. Investment income can be generated because the reinsurer receives the premium provided by the quota share treaty before it must pay losses to the primary insurer. The reinsurer bases the size of the investment income offset on the amount of investment income that it expects to earn on the premium. Not all reinsurers explicitly provide for investment income offset. In addition to its expenses associated with the treaty, the reinsurer must determine its minimum profit. Assume the reinsurer determines that its costs and minimum profit percentage is the sum of the following elements:

Overhead	4.5%
Brokerage	1.0%
Investment income offset	(3.5%)
Minimum profit percentage	5.0%
Reinsurer's costs and minimum profit percentage	7.0%

The reinsurer's costs and minimum profit are then calculated as follows:

$$\text{Reinsurer's costs and minimum profit} = \text{Reinsurer's costs and minimum profit percentage} \times \text{Estimated quota share reinsurance premium}$$
$$= 0.07 \times \$2{,}520{,}000$$
$$= \$176{,}400.$$

According to the background information, the flat ceding commission percentage required by the primary insurer is 20 percent of the estimated quota share reinsurance premium.

$$\text{Flat ceding commission} = \text{Flat ceding commission percentage} \times \text{Estimated quota share reinsurance premium}$$

$$= 0.20 \times \$2{,}520{,}000$$

$$= \$504{,}000.$$

To estimate losses and loss adjustment expenses, the reinsurer first estimates a loss ratio for the coming treaty year and then applies it to the treaty's subject premium. Past loss and premium information can be used to estimate a loss ratio, as shown in Exhibit 6-19. This estimate assumes that the primary insurer's historical losses are representative of what the losses will be for the coming treaty year.

EXHIBIT 6-19
Calculation of Historical Loss Ratios for a Primary Insurer

(1) Historical Accident Year	(2) Losses and Loss Adj. Exp.	(3) Earned Premiums	(4) (2) ÷ (3) Loss Ratio
1	$3,803,595	$5,763,023	0.66
2	4,073,302	6,266,619	0.65
3	3,659,134	5,808,149	0.63
4	4,149,709	6,193,595	0.67
5	4,007,660	6,261,969	0.64
			Average = 0.65

For each year, the reinsurer calculates a loss ratio by dividing losses and loss adjustment expenses by earned premiums, as shown in Column (4) of Exhibit 6-19. The reinsurer averages the resulting loss ratios to project the loss ratio that will occur in the coming treaty year, as shown on the bottom line of Exhibit 6-19. This projected loss ratio is 65 percent. If the historical loss ratios show an upward or downward trend, the reinsurer should project the loss ratio based on the trend rather than on the average.

The reinsurer can now estimate its average losses and loss adjustment expenses under the quota share treaty by multiplying the estimated quota share reinsurance premium by the projected loss ratio.

$$\text{Estimated average treaty losses and loss adjustment expense} = \text{Estimated quota share reinsurance premium} \times \text{Projected loss ratio}$$

$$= \$2{,}520{,}000 \times 0.65$$

$$= \$1{,}638{,}000.$$

The reinsurer calculates the estimated amount of premium available for profit sharing by subtracting reinsurer's costs and minimum profit, the flat ceding commission paid to the primary insurer, and the estimated average losses and loss adjustment expenses from the estimated quota share premium, as shown below.

Estimated quota share premium	$2,520,000
Reinsurer's costs and minimum profit (7%)	(176,400)
Flat ceding commission to primary insurer (20%)	(504,000)
Estimated average losses and loss adjustment expense (65%)	(1,638,000)
Estimated amount of premium available for profit sharing	$ 201,600

Step 3: Determine a Percentage for the Profit-Sharing Commission

Before determining a percentage for the profit-sharing commission, the reinsurer must examine the volatility of the primary insurer's losses because actual losses could be higher or lower than the estimated average losses. In this example, the primary insurer's loss ratio has been stable over the past few years at 63 to 67 percent. Because the underlying insurance appears to be sold at a profit with little catastrophe loss exposure, the reinsurer may quote a 50 percent profit-sharing commission so that both parties equally enjoy any additional profits realized. The estimated profit-sharing commission amount is calculated as follows:

$$\text{Estimated profit-sharing commission} = \text{Profit-sharing commission percentage} \times \text{Estimated amount of premium available for profit sharing}$$

$$= 0.50 \times \$201{,}600$$

$$= \$100{,}800.$$

In summary, the reinsurer quotes the primary insurer a 50 percent profit-sharing rate in addition to the flat ceding commission. The profit-sharing commission percentage is applied to the amount of premium remaining after the reinsurer's costs and minimum profit, the flat ceding commission, and estimated average losses and loss adjustment expenses are subtracted. In the above example, the reinsurer estimates a profit-sharing commission of $100,800, a flat ceding commission of $504,000, and average losses and loss adjustment expenses of $1,638,000. If the reinsurer provides the quota share treaty, those figures will be adjusted at the end of the treaty year based on actual premium and losses. For example, if actual losses are lower than the estimated average losses, the amount of profit sharing would increase. If actual losses are higher than the estimated average loss, the profit sharing would decrease until the amount available for profit sharing is zero. At that point, no profit-sharing commission is paid. If the calculation generates a loss, some reinsurance treaties require the loss to be carried forward into the calculation of the reinsurance profit-sharing formula for subsequent treaty years.

QUOTA SHARE TREATY EVALUATION

Primary insurers and reinsurers should monitor and evaluate existing quota share treaties as a part of reinsurance program design. This section illustrates how the performance of a quota share treaty can be evaluated.

Assume that the existing quota share treaty covers property insurance policies and is structured as illustrated in Exhibit 6-20.

EXHIBIT 6-20

Existing Property Quota Share Reinsurance Treaty

Quota Share Structure:

25% Quota share applying on a net of all reinsurance basis

Sliding Scale Commission:

35% Provisional commission

30% Minimum commission

55% Specified loss ratio

Commission slides 0.5% inversely for each 1% the loss ratio differs from 55%

Historical Experience:

Subject written premiums	$44,000,000
Subject earned premiums	$40,000,000
Subject incurred losses including a sufficient provision for IBNR	$26,400,000

Current Evaluation

From the information in Exhibit 6-20, the following calculations can be made concerning the existing quota share treaty:

The subject loss ratio is the subject incurred losses divided by the subject earned premiums.

$$\text{Subject loss ratio} = \text{Subject incurred losses} \div \text{Subject earned premiums}$$
$$= \$26{,}400{,}000 \div \$40{,}000{,}000$$
$$= 0.66.$$

The ceding commission is the provisional commission plus one-half of the difference between the specified loss ratio and the subject loss ratio.

$$\text{Ceding commission} = \text{Provisional commission} + [0.5 \times (\text{Specified loss ratio} - \text{Subject loss ratio})]$$
$$= 0.35 + [0.5 \times (0.55 - 0.66)]$$
$$= 0.295.$$

The commission adjustment compares the ceding commission to the stated minimum commission. In this case, the ceding commission is less than the stated minimum commission, so the stated minimum commission of 30 percent applies.

Ceded written premiums are calculated by multiplying the quota share percentage by the subject written premiums.

$$\text{Ceded written premiums} = \text{Quota share percentage} \times \text{Subject written premiums}$$
$$= 0.25 \times \$44{,}000{,}000$$
$$= \$11{,}000{,}000.$$

Ceded earned premiums are calculated by multiplying the quota share percentage by the subject earned premiums.

$$\text{Ceded earned premiums} = \text{Quota share percentage} \times \text{Subject earned premiums}$$
$$= 0.25 \times \$40{,}000{,}000$$
$$= \$10{,}000{,}000.$$

The ceded incurred loss is the subject loss ratio multiplied by the ceded earned premiums.

$$\text{Ceded incurred losses} = \text{Subject loss ratio} \times \text{Ceded earned premiums}$$
$$= 0.66 \times \$10{,}000{,}000$$
$$= \$6{,}600{,}000.$$

Those calculations can be used for a historical evaluation of the quota share treaty.

Historical Evaluation

To evaluate the quota share treaty's performance, the reinsurer considers the long-term profit margin. The reinsurer's desired profit margin should reflect the surplus relief effect that the quota share treaty provides to the primary insurer, the historical underwriting profit margin, and investment income. The following examples continue to use the figures contained in, or derived from, Exhibit 6-20.

Surplus Relief Effect

Ceded unearned premiums are calculated by subtracting the ceded earned premiums from the ceded written premiums.

$$\text{Ceded unearned premiums} = \text{Ceded written premiums} - \text{Ceded earned premiums}$$
$$= \$11{,}000{,}000 - \$10{,}000{,}000$$
$$= \$1{,}000{,}000.$$

The reinsurer pays the primary insurer a provisional commission of 35 percent of the ceded written premiums. However, $1 million of that premium is unearned. The surplus relief effect experienced by the primary insurer is the provisional commission multiplied by the ceded unearned premiums.

$$\text{Surplus relief effect} = \text{Provisional commission} \times \text{Ceded unearned premiums}$$
$$= 0.35 \times \$1{,}000{,}000$$
$$= \$350{,}000.$$

Underwriting Profit Margin

The reinsurer's underwriting profit margin is calculated as follows:

$$\text{Reinsurer's underwriting profit margin} = \left[\text{Ceded earned premiums} - \text{Commissions} - \text{Expenses} - \text{Losses}\right] \div \text{Ceded earned premiums.}$$

The reinsurer can account for its commissions and expenses by adding an expense loading to the ceding commission and applying the combined percentage to the ceded earned premiums. Assume in this case that the general expense loading is 6 percent. The reinsurer then evaluates the past experience on the treaty using the following formula:

$$\text{Reinsurer's underwriting profit margin} = \left[\text{Ceded earned premiums} - \left(\left(\text{Ceded commission} + \text{General expense loading}\right) \times \text{Ceded earned premiums}\right) - \text{Ceded incurred losses}\right] \div \text{Ceded earned premiums}$$

$$= [\$10{,}000{,}000 - ((0.30 + 0.06) \times \$10{,}000{,}000) - \$6{,}600{,}000] \div \$10{,}000{,}000$$

$$= [\$10{,}000{,}000 - \$3{,}600{,}000 - \$6{,}600{,}000] \div \$10{,}000{,}000$$

$$= -\$200{,}000 \div \$10{,}000{,}000$$

$$= -0.02.$$

The reinsurer's underwriting profit margin is compared to the profit margin that the reinsurer desires, the surplus relief effect, and the amount of underwriting risk transferred. If the reinsurer's anticipated profit margin is 10 percent, the –2 percent actual profit margin (a loss) may prompt the reinsurer not to renew the quota share treaty. Alternatively, the reinsurer may reduce the minimum sliding scale commission or change to a flat ceding commission.

Investment Income

The reinsurer can estimate the investment income that it expects to earn on this treaty. Reinsurance treaties generate investment income for the reinsurer because the premium net of expenses can be invested until claims are paid. Property claims generally settle rather quickly, so investment income will likely not be significant. However, liability claims often take years to settle and the reinsurer may earn substantial investment income before losses are paid.

SUMMARY

Quota share reinsurance, a form of pro rata reinsurance, involves the sharing of amounts of insurance, policy premiums, and losses using a fixed percentage. Quota share reinsurance can be provided on a facultative or treaty basis. This chapter describes quota share reinsurance in a treaty context. A variation of standard quota share reinsurance is variable quota share reinsurance, in which the predetermined percentage used to share amounts of insurance, policy premium, and losses varies based on the amount of insurance needed for the loss exposure or some other criterion.

Quota share treaties serve the following five functions:

1. Increase large line capacity
2. Provide catastrophe protection
3. Facilitate withdrawal from a market segment
4. Provide surplus relief
5. Provide underwriting guidance

The extent to which a quota share treaty fulfills these functions depends on the premium and losses of the subject business, as well as the terms of the quota share treaty. Quota share treaties can apply before other pro rata reinsurance treaties (gross account basis), after other pro rata reinsurance (net of pro rata basis), or after all other reinsurance (net of all reinsurance basis). The order of indemnification affects the financial benefit the quota share treaty provides to the primary insurer.

Some common clauses are modified for use in quota share treaties. These clauses include:

- Reinsuring clause
- Definitions clause
- Commencement and termination clause
- Reports and remittances clause

Other clauses are designed or adapted for quota share treaties. These clauses include:

- *Retention and limits clause.* The retention and limits clause specifies the primary insurer's minimum net retention and the maximum amount of insurance that the primary insurer can cede to the reinsurer.
- *Reinsurance premium clause.* The reinsurance premium clause specifies how the subject premium is determined and when the primary insurer must pay the reinsurer its share of the unearned premiums.
- *Sliding scale commission clause.* The sliding scale commission clause specifies how the primary insurer and reinsurer will share profits from the underlying insurance covered by the treaty.
- *Portfolio transfer clause.* The portfolio transfer clause specifies how the unearned premium reserve is transferred, the payment terms, and the reinsurer's obligation for losses.
- *Losses, loss adjustment expenses, and salvages clause.* The losses, loss adjustment expenses, and salvages clause gives the primary insurer the authority to settle claims and provides for the sharing of losses, loss adjustment expenses, and salvages between the primary insurer and the reinsurer.
- *Outside reinsurance clause.* The outside reinsurance clause allows the primary insurer to cede certain loss exposures outside the existing treaty.

- *Warranties clause.* The warranties clause specifies conditions with which the primary insurer must comply to ensure coverage under the treaty.
- *Original conditions clause.* The original conditions clause establishes that the liability assumed by the reinsurer under the reinsurance agreement is on the same basis (rates, terms, and conditions) as the underlying coverage provided by the primary insurer.

Because premium, limits, and losses are shared proportionately, the key pricing variable under quota share treaties is the ceding commission paid by the reinsurer to the primary insurer. The amount of ceding commission the reinsurer is willing to pay the primary insurer is affected by the following five considerations:

1. Primary insurer's retention
2. Reinsurance treaty's limit
3. Primary insurer's policy acquisition expenses
4. Primary insurer's expected loss ratio on the portfolio included, as well as its underwriting ability and rate adequacy
5. Competition in the reinsurance marketplace

Primary insurers and reinsurers should monitor and evaluate the performance of existing quota share treaties as part of reinsurance program design. To evaluate a treaty's performance, the reinsurer considers the long-term profit margin, which should reflect the surplus relief effect for the primary insurer, the historical underwriting profit margin, and investment income.

Quota share reinsurance is the simplest type of pro rata reinsurance. The next chapter discusses surplus share reinsurance, which is a more sophisticated adaptation of quota share reinsurance.

Chapter 7

Direct Your Learning

Surplus Share Treaties

After learning the content of this chapter, you should be able to:

- Explain the purpose and operation of surplus share treaties.
- Explain the functions performed by surplus share treaties and how surplus share treaties are used in a primary insurer's reinsurance program.
- Explain the purpose and operation of common clauses that are modified for use in surplus share treaties.
- Explain the purpose and operation of clauses designed or adapted for surplus share treaties.
- Explain how limits profiles are used to analyze the composition of the insurance policies that the primary insurer wants to reinsure.
- Explain how primary insurers use line guides to control retentions in surplus share treaties.

OUTLINE

Overview of Surplus Share Treaties

Common Clauses Modified for Use in Surplus Share Treaties

Clauses Designed or Adapted for Surplus Share Treaties

Surplus Share Treaty Pricing

Summary

Develop Your Perspective

What are the main topics covered in the chapter?

This chapter describes the purpose, operation, contractual clauses, and pricing of surplus share treaties.

Identify the purpose and operation of surplus share reinsurance.

- What functions does a surplus share treaty serve for a primary insurer?
- How does the line guide assist the primary insurer underwriter in selecting an appropriate retention?

Why is it important to learn about these topics?

Surplus share treaties are used to provide primary insurers with large line capacity, loss stabilization, and surplus relief. The ability to understand, analyze, and evaluate surplus share treaties is important to enable you to determine whether they are helping your company or client-insurer achieve its objectives.

Review a surplus share treaty.

- How are common clauses modified for use in surplus share treaties?
- What clauses are designed or adapted for surplus share treaties and how do they operate?

How can you use what you will learn?

Evaluate one of your company's or client-insurer's surplus share treaties.

- Does this surplus share treaty address your company's or client-insurer's needs?
- Does this surplus share treaty provide the large line capacity, loss stabilization, and surplus relief needed by your company or client-insurer?

Chapter 7
Surplus Share Treaties

Surplus share reinsurance is a type of pro rata reinsurance and can be used to address the needs of primary insurers insuring large, complex property loss exposures. This chapter explains the following:

- How surplus share treaties operate
- How primary insurers use surplus share treaties to meet their reinsurance needs
- How surplus share treaties fit into a reinsurance program
- How common clauses modified for use in surplus share treaties operate
- How clauses designed specifically for surplus share treaties operate
- How surplus share treaties are priced

OVERVIEW OF SURPLUS SHARE TREATIES

Under a surplus share treaty, the primary insurer determines what loss exposures are subject to the treaty and what percentage share it will retain in respect of each ceded loss exposure. By obtaining reinsurance for only the surplus share of an underlying policy's coverage limit, the primary insurer restricts its liability to the same coverage limit amount for similar categories of loss exposures. This section expands the overview of surplus share reinsurance provided in a previous chapter.

As with quota share reinsurance, the primary insurer and the reinsurer party to a surplus share treaty share in the underlying policy premium and losses for each loss exposure on a percentage basis. Unlike quota share reinsurance, the percentage used to share policy premium and losses varies for each loss exposure subject to a surplus share treaty. The percentage is determined by the ratio of the ceded loss exposure's coverage limit to the amount of the primary insurer's retention, as Exhibit 7-1 illustrates.

Surplus share reinsurance addresses two disadvantages that primary insurers encounter with quota share reinsurance. The first disadvantage is that in quota share reinsurance, every loss exposure, regardless of coverage limit, is subject to cession, even those loss exposures that the primary insurer could safely retain in their entirety.

EXHIBIT 7-1

Illustration of a Surplus Share Treaty With a Minimum Line of $100,000

	Underlying Insurance Policies			
	1	2	3	4
Underlying Policy Limit	$75,000	$200,000	$300,000	$600,000
Line (per Line Guide)	$100,000	$100,000	$100,000	$100,000
Primary Insurer's Retention	$75,000	$100,000	$100,000	$100,000
Percentage of Policy Premium and Losses Retained by Primary Insurer (Retention ÷ Policy Limit)	100%	50%	33%*	17%*
Percentage of Policy Premium and Losses Ceded to Surplus Share Reinsurer	0%	50%	67%*	83%*

*Rounded

In contrast, surplus share reinsurance applies only to those loss exposures with coverage limits that exceed the primary insurer's line. Therefore, loss exposures with coverage limits below the primary insurer's line are not reinsured even though they are in the category of loss exposure that would otherwise be subject to the surplus share treaty. For example, see policy 1 in Exhibit 7-1.

The line used to establish the applicability of a surplus share treaty should not be confused with the attachment point used in excess of loss reinsurance. The primary insurer's line establishes the threshold that determines whether the surplus share treaty applies to an individual loss exposure, whereas the attachment point establishes the dollar amount above which the reinsurer responds to losses.

As with quota share treaties, surplus share treaties share all losses from the first dollar (ground-up losses), regardless of the loss amount. For example, a primary insurer would be indemnified by its reinsurer for the reinsurer's proportionate share of a $1,000 loss although the primary insurer's line for this loss exposure is $100,000.

The second disadvantage of quota share reinsurance is that the primary insurer's retention is a fixed percentage and therefore the dollar amount of retention increases as the coverage limit needed increases. In contrast, the line in a surplus share treaty is a specified dollar amount; therefore, the primary insurer's retention does not necessarily increase as the coverage limit needed increases. Unlike quota share reinsurance, in which the percentage of sharing is the same for all loss exposures subject to the treaty (with variable quota share being an exception), a surplus share treaty is usually supported by a line guide that permits the primary insurer to vary the dollar amount of the line depending on each loss exposure's loss severity potential. For example, a simplified line guide may specify a $100,000 line for buildings that do not have automatic sprinkler systems and a $300,000 line for those that do. The primary insurer can justify this larger line because buildings with automatic sprinkler systems generally experience fewer severe losses.

Exhibit 7-2 illustrates a surplus share treaty supported by a simplified line guide and provides three cases that demonstrate the discretion afforded the primary insurer's underwriters in establishing the line for a specific loss exposure. In these cases, the primary insurer's underwriter categorizes insurance applicants as high, average, or low quality based on the simplified line guide. A more detailed discussion of line guides is presented later in this chapter.

EXHIBIT 7-2

Illustration of a Surplus Share Treaty Supported by a Simplified Line Guide

Insurer:	Primary Insurer
Reinsurer:	Reinsurance Company
Type of Reinsurance:	Surplus Share Treaty
Causes of Loss:	Broad Form Causes of Loss
Lines:	Class A (highest quality) $150,000
	Class B (average quality) $100,000
	Class C (lowest quality) $50,000
Limits:	Five lines but no more than $250,000 on any one loss exposure
	Minimum line of $50,000
Special Conditions:	The primary insurer may bypass the treaty or limit the reinsurer's liability if the loss potential warrants such action.

Case 1 – The insurance applicant, the owner of a plumbing supply business, requests coverage for $250,000 of business personal property contained in a leased fire-resistive building. The business personal property consists primarily of plumbing supplies, equipment, and tools. The building is located in a small industrial park that has adequate fire protection.

Because of this loss exposure's positive loss characteristics, the primary insurer's underwriter categorizes it as Class A. The underwriter sets the maximum line for this loss exposure at $150,000 as suggested by the line guide.

Case 2 – The insurance applicant owns a $300,000, two-story building that has a multiple occupancy use. The building's first floor is used as a retail tobacco shop, and the second floor has two residential apartments. The building is thirty years old and is joisted-masonry construction (masonry walls with wood joists). The building is located in an urban shopping district, and the

Continued on next page.

> neighboring properties are of similar construction and use. The fire protection applicable to the property is classified as below average because of the community's outdated firefighting equipment.
>
> The primary insurer's underwriter considers this loss exposure to be of average quality and classifies it as Class B. The underwriter establishes the line for this loss exposure at $50,000, which is half the suggested line but satisfies the minimum line.
>
> Case 3 – The insurance applicant owns a fifteen-unit wood-frame motel valued at $100,000 that is located in a rural area with limited public fire protection. The applicant also owns a nearby manufacturing plant that is already insured by the primary insurer.
>
> The primary insurer's underwriter recognizes this loss exposure as unacceptable because of its wood-frame construction and limited public fire protection. Rather than decline the loss exposure, the underwriter agrees to insure (and price) property insurance on the motel if facultative reinsurance can be obtained. In this case, the primary insurer chooses to use its discretion to bypass the surplus share treaty so that adverse loss results from this loss exposure cannot affect the profitability (and future pricing) of the treaty.

Surplus share reinsurance is often written in layers. The surplus share treaty that provides the first layer of reinsurance after the primary insurer's retention is called a first surplus treaty. The first surplus treaty could apply over other reinsurance, such as a quota share treaty or a facultative excess of loss agreement. A second, third, and even a further surplus treaty may handle loss exposures with even greater coverage limit needs and provide the primary insurer with additional large line capacity. Reinsurance coverage provided by higher layers is used only when an individual loss exposure is greater than the preceding layer or layers plus the primary insurer's retention.

Exhibit 7-3 illustrates a reinsurance program that includes three surplus share treaties (each with three lines) and that provides the primary insurer with the capacity to insure loss exposures requiring coverage limits up to $500,000. These three surplus share treaties operate together to share premium and losses in the same manner as a reinsurance program with a nine-line first surplus treaty. Exhibit 7-3 also shows how the coverage limit needs of a $450,000 loss exposure would be addressed by the three surplus share treaties.

Exhibit 7-4 shows how a $10,000 loss for a $450,000 policy would be shared in the reinsurance program set out in Exhibit 7-3. Any loss sustained by this $450,000 loss exposure would be shared using the same percentages as those shown in Exhibit 7-4.

The policy premium for the $450,000 loss exposure is also shared using the percentages in Exhibit 7-4. However, each reinsurer's share of the premium is then reduced by a predetermined percentage and the excess is paid to the primary insurer as a ceding commission. For simplicity, a 40 percent ceding commission is used for each layer in Exhibit 7-5. However, a lower ceding commission percentage is typically negotiated for higher surplus share layers.

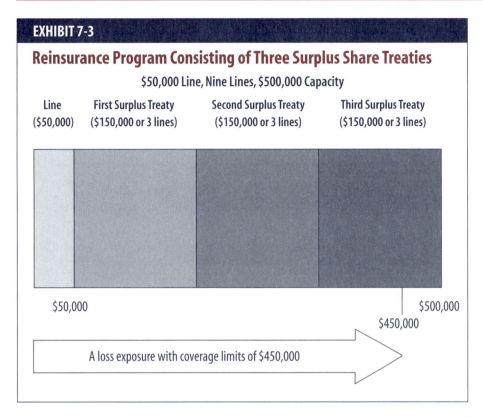

EXHIBIT 7-3

Reinsurance Program Consisting of Three Surplus Share Treaties

$50,000 Line, Nine Lines, $500,000 Capacity

EXHIBIT 7-4

Loss Allocation Among Three Surplus Share Treaties

$50,000 Line, Nine Lines, $500,000 Capacity

	Share of Loss Exposure			Loss		Share of Loss*
Primary Insurer	$50,000 ÷ $450,000	=	11.11%	× $10,000	=	$ 1,111
First Surplus	$150,000 ÷ $450,000	=	33.33%	× $10,000	=	3,333
Second Surplus	$150,000 ÷ $450,000	=	33.33%	× $10,000	=	3,333
Third Surplus	$100,000 ÷ $450,000	=	22.22%	× $10,000	=	2,222
						$10,000

* Rounded

A primary insurer usually purchases a first surplus treaty that has sufficient capacity to handle its normal coverage limit needs. Second and subsequent surplus treaties are purchased and priced (through a reduction in ceding commission percentages) to address the atypical coverage limit needs of a relatively small share of the primary insurer's policies. Primary insurers can, and often do, satisfy additional coverage limit needs by purchasing facultative reinsurance. However, primary insurers generally prefer to avoid the expense of facultative placements if a volume of loss exposures with large coverage limit needs is anticipated.

EXHIBIT 7-5

Premium Allocation Among Three Surplus Share Treaties

	Gross Premium		Share of Loss Exposure		Share of Gross Premium*	Ceding Commission*	Net Premium
Primary Insurer	$6,000	×	11.11%	=	$ 667	$2,133	$2,800
First Surplus	$6,000	×	33.33%	=	2,000	– 800	1,200
Second Surplus	$6,000	×	33.33%	=	2,000	– 800	1,200
Third Surplus	$6,000	×	22.22%	=	1,333	– 533	800
					$6,000	$ 0	$6,000

* Rounded

The primary insurer retains $667 of the $6,000 gross premium. The first and second surplus share reinsurers are owed the net amount of $1,200 each ($2,000 less the 40 percent ceding commission), and the third surplus share reinsurer is owed the net amount of $800 ($1,333 less the ceding commission). By remitting the premium to the reinsurers net of ceding commission, the primary insurer retains $2,800 ($667 + $2,133) of the $6,000 gross premium.

Functions of Surplus Share Treaties

Surplus share treaties serve three functions for primary insurers:

1. Increase large line capacity
2. Stabilize loss experience
3. Provide surplus relief

Some of these functions, while served by surplus share treaties, may be better served by other types of reinsurance.

Increase Large Line Capacity

Surplus share reinsurance is designed to provide primary insurers with flexibility in insuring large loss exposures provided the characteristics of those loss exposures meet predetermined parameters. Surplus share reinsurance is often said to provide the primary insurer with "automatic capacity" because the surplus share treaty incorporates the primary insurer's line guide and therefore expands and contracts underwriting capacity depending on the loss exposure's relevant attributes. Surplus share treaties provide the primary insurer with automatic access to additional large line capacity when the quality of the loss exposure justifies it. The alternative, and a relatively expensive one, is to purchase facultative reinsurance.

In most surplus share treaties, the primary insurer's underwriter uses judgment in setting the line on a loss exposure after consulting the recommendations contained in the line guide. Because the underwriter is able to use judgment in setting the line, the primary insurer could adversely select against the reinsurer in the cession of loss exposures. The second case in Exhibit 7-2 is an example in which the primary underwriter may be practicing adverse selection by ceding relatively undesirable loss exposures to the reinsurer.

To reduce the likelihood of adverse selection, while still providing the primary insurer with flexibility in setting the line for each loss exposure, the surplus share treaty often specifies a minimum line and maximum cession. Loss exposures for which the primary insurer is unwilling to commit to the minimum line cannot be ceded to the surplus share treaty. Reinsurers would be adversely selected against if they permitted primary insurers to reduce their line so far that they would only have a minimal participation in the financial consequences of their underwriting decisions.

The maximum cession under a surplus share treaty is stated as a dollar limit. However, the actual amount ceded under the treaty is based on a multiple of the primary insurer's line, subject to the limit imposed by the maximum cession. For example, a $1.2 million loss exposure for which the line guide suggests a $200,000 line and five-line capacity would meet the requirements of a surplus share treaty with a minimum line of $100,000 and a maximum cession of $2 million. The primary insurer would retain $200,000 of the loss exposure and $1 million would be ceded under the treaty. However, if the primary insurer's underwriter reduced the line on this loss exposure from $200,000 to $100,000, the amount ceded under the surplus share treaty would only be $500,000 (5 times the $100,000 line) and the primary insurer would need to consider retaining the additional liability (or coverage amount) or purchasing facultative reinsurance.

Finally, reinsurers often include a sliding scale commission provision in surplus share treaties to give the primary insurer a financial incentive to underwrite effectively and to cede quality loss exposures to the treaty.

Stabilize Loss Experience

Surplus share reinsurance stabilizes a primary insurer's loss experience by limiting the primary insurer's participation on each loss to its line. While this may be effective over a period of time, surplus share treaties usually do not provide primary insurers with sufficient protection from an accumulation of losses that could result from a catastrophic event. Primary insurers usually address their exposure to catastrophe losses by using catastrophe excess of loss reinsurance.

In addition to limiting losses to the primary insurer's line, surplus share reinsurance enables the primary insurer to develop size homogeneity within each category of loss exposure. Size homogeneity among loss exposures is desirable because it makes loss forecasting more accurate. For example, the potential for a primary insurer's loss ratio to fluctuate is greater when it insures loss exposures with varying coverage needs than when it insures loss exposures with the same coverage limit. The primary insurer's line guide uses loss exposure attributes (such as construction, occupancy, protection, and exposure) to categorize loss exposures based on potential loss severity and, therefore, to tailor the primary insurer's line to each category of loss exposure.

Provide Surplus Relief

Surplus share treaties and quota share treaties provide surplus relief in the same way. The primary insurer often cedes a large amount of premium, thereby decreasing its gross written premiums, and receives a ceding commission, thereby increasing its policyholders' surplus. Although pro rata reinsurance improves the primary insurer's capacity ratio, surplus share treaties are generally less effective than quota share treaties in providing surplus relief because less premium is ceded and therefore less ceding commission is received.

Surplus Share Treaties as Part of a Reinsurance Program

As previously mentioned, primary insurers use surplus share reinsurance for large, complex property loss exposures and when both large line capacity and surplus relief are needed.

New primary insurers, or primary insurers selling a new insurance product or entering a new territory, may choose to use quota share reinsurance until the volume of insurance policies sold increases such that loss experience stabilizes. With sufficient and credible loss experience, the primary insurer usually chooses to replace the quota share treaty with a surplus share treaty so that more premium is retained.

A surplus share treaty may be used as the only reinsurance treaty that applies to the primary insurer's insurance policies or it may be used in conjunction with a quota share treaty or excess of loss treaty. Surplus share treaties are often layered to provide the primary insurer with sufficient large line capacity.

Surplus share reinsurance, like quota share reinsurance, does not typically provide the primary insurer with the protection it would need if a catastrophe loss were to occur. Although the primary insurer's liability would be limited on each loss, surplus share reinsurance would not protect against an accumulation of losses. Catastrophe loss protection is best provided by a catastrophe excess of loss treaty.

A primary insurer will sometimes use per risk excess of loss reinsurance to increase its line and use a surplus share treaty to obtain greater large line capacity. For example, a primary insurer, would need a line of $100,000 to have the capacity under its nine-line surplus share treaty to insure loss exposures requiring $1 million in coverage limits. However, because of its restrictive line guide, this primary insurer is limited to a line of $50,000. This would limit the amount of coverage provided by the surplus share treaty to $500,000 ($50,000 + (9 × $50,000)). The primary insurer could purchase facultative per risk excess of loss reinsurance of

$50,000 xs $50,000. Under this arrangement, the primary insurer preserves its $50,000 line and is able to write $1 million in coverage limits.

When excess of loss reinsurance is used in this way, it is called underlying excess. Exhibit 7-6 illustrates how underlying excess of loss reinsurance supports the primary insurer's line. Surplus share treaties usually specify whether they will permit the primary insurer to reinsure its line in this way.

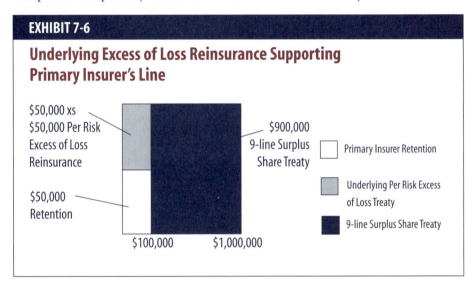

COMMON CLAUSES MODIFIED FOR USE IN SURPLUS SHARE TREATIES

This section discusses how some common clauses discussed in previous chapters are modified for use in surplus share treaties. These clauses are:

- Reinsuring clause
- Liability of the reinsurer clause
- Definitions clause
- Exclusions clause
- Reports and remittances clause

Reinsuring Clause

The reinsuring clause can be one all-encompassing clause, or it can be divided into separate clauses, such as the cover clause and the business reinsured clause shown in Exhibits 7-7 and 7-8, respectively. Whether presented as one clause or more than one clause, the wording is modified in the following three areas for a surplus share treaty:

1. Nature of cession
2. Statement of attachment
3. Description of the policies covered

> **EXHIBIT 7-7**
>
> ### Cover Clause
>
> The Company will cede, and the Reinsurer will assume, the Company's Surplus Liability on risks covered hereunder, subject to the limits set forth in the Retention and Limits Clause. The liability of the Reinsurer shall commence obligatorily and simultaneously with that of the Company.
>
> The Company shall make an entry of the amount reinsured in a book or on a form to be kept for the purpose; but, should the Company have intimation of a loss affecting any risk ceded or to be ceded before such entry has been made, the Company's Net Retention shall be fixed at the amount indicated for similar risks in its lists of limits or as shown by its book or practice, subject, however, to the limitations provided for herein. Any such case shall be advised to the Reinsurer immediately, full details being furnished in justification of the Net Retention fixed.
>
> Notwithstanding the obligation imposed upon the Company to cede its Surplus Liability, the Company shall have the right when it considers it in the interest of the Reinsurer to do so, to restrict or omit allotments of any particular risk in such a manner as to eliminate or restrict the liability of the Reinsurer.

> **EXHIBIT 7-8**
>
> ### Business Reinsured Clause
>
> This Agreement is to share with the Reinsurer the interests and liabilities of the Company under all Policies for Property Business in force, written or renewed by or on behalf of the Company during the term of this Agreement and ceded to this Agreement, subject to the terms and conditions herein contained.

The first modification is the nature of the cession. As with quota share treaties, surplus share treaties are usually obligatory for both the primary insurer and the reinsurer. The nature of cession is stated in the first paragraph of the sample cover clause shown in Exhibit 7-7. Included in the reinsurer's agreement to indemnify the primary insurer is a statement that indemnification is "subject to the limits set forth in the Retention and Limits Clause." That statement is included because the cession is based on the primary insurer's net retention. The retention and limits clause is discussed later in this chapter.

The second modification is the statement of attachment. For a new surplus share treaty, a risks attaching basis is easier for the primary insurer to administer from an underwriting perspective than a losses occurring basis. With a losses occurring basis of attachment, each in-force policy must be reviewed for the correct retention, and the percentage ceded must be recorded. This review must be carried out because the in-force portfolio may not fit the requirements of the new surplus share treaty in terms of minimum retention, maximum cession, or number of lines. Because of the administrative problems of having a new treaty apply to an in-force portfolio, many surplus share treaties apply on a risks attaching basis, in other words, only to policies that are issued or renewed on or after the treaty's effective date.

However, if the surplus share treaty is renewed with the same reinsurer, then switching to a losses occurring basis may be appropriate because the expiring treaty would have covered the in-force policies. The sample business reinsured clause that is shown in Exhibit 7-8 includes coverage for in-force policies and therefore applies on a losses occurring basis.

The third modification is the description of the policies covered. The reinsuring clause (or the business reinsured clause) incorporates the description that the primary insurer uses to identify the insurance policies to which the surplus share treaty applies. In surplus share treaties, the business covered is usually property insurance policies, so the description may be as simple as "fire and allied lines," "homeowners business," or, as shown in Exhibit 7-8, "all Policies for Property Business." Occasionally the description is more specific, such as "property business written in the Company's Farm Department," or "all property business written in Illinois, Ohio, and Indiana."

Liability of the Reinsurer Clause

The liability of the reinsurer clause establishes when the reinsurer assumes liability and on what basis. This wording may appear in a separate liability of the reinsurer clause or as part of the reinsuring clause. The final paragraph of Exhibit 7-7 contains wording that reflects the intent of the liability of the reinsurer clause.

For quota share treaties, when the primary insurer's underwriter accepts coverage, the reinsurer automatically assumes liability for its share of losses. For surplus share treaties, the primary insurer's underwriter usually consults the line guide, sets the line, and cedes the surplus liability when the insurance application is accepted. Even if a loss occurs before the line has been set, the primary insurer must apply its normal standards and practices in setting the line.

Definitions Clause

Definitions can be included throughout the reinsurance treaty, contained in a specific clause, or both. Exhibit 7-9 shows an example of a definitions clause. Three key definitions for a surplus share treaty, wherever located, are those for surplus liability, risk, and net retention.

EXHIBIT 7-9

Definitions Clause

The term "Property Business" as used in this Agreement shall mean all insurances and reinsurances written by the Company and classified as property.

The term "Policy" as used in this Agreement shall mean any binder, policy, or contract of insurance or reinsurance issued, accepted, or held covered provisionally or otherwise, by or on behalf of the Company.

The term "Net Retention" shall mean that portion of a risk retained by the Company for its net account and unreinsured in any manner except for Per Risk Excess of Loss reinsurance and Property Per Occurrence reinsurances.

The term "Surplus Liability" as used in this Agreement shall mean that portion of the Company's gross liability on any one risk which exceeds the Company's Net Retention.

"Risk" as used in this Agreement will be subject to definition solely by the Company.

"Loss occurrence" as used in this Agreement will mean the sum of all individual losses directly occasioned by any one disaster, accident, or loss or series of disasters, accidents, or losses arising out of one event, which occurs within the area of one state of the United States or province of Canada and states or provinces contiguous thereto and to one another. The duration and extent of any one loss occurrence will be limited to all individual losses sustained by the Company occurring during any period of 168 consecutive hours arising out of and directly occasioned by the same event except that the term "loss occurrence" will be defined further as follows:

A. As regards windstorm, hail, tornado, hurricane, and cyclone, including ensuing collapse and water damage, all individual losses sustained by the Company occurring during any period of 72 consecutive hours arising out of and directly occasioned by the same event. The event need not be limited to one state or province or states or provinces contiguous thereto.

B. As regards riot, riot attending a strike, civil commotion, vandalism, and malicious mischief, all individual losses sustained by the Company occurring during any period of 72 consecutive hours within the area of one municipality or county and the municipalities or counties contiguous thereto arising out of and directly occasioned by the same event. The maximum duration of 72 consecutive hours may be extended in respect of individual losses that occur beyond such 72 consecutive hours during the continued occupation of an insured's premises by strikers, provided such occupation commenced during the aforesaid period.

C. As regards earthquake (the epicenter of which need not necessarily be within the territorial confines referred to in the opening paragraph of this Article) and fire following directly occasioned by the earthquake, only those individual fire losses that commence during the period of 168 consecutive hours may be included in the Company's loss occurrence.

D. As regards freeze, only those individual losses directly occasioned by collapse, breakage of glass, and water damage (caused by bursting of frozen pipes and tanks) may be included in the Company's loss occurrence.

> Except for loss occurrences referred to in A. and B., the Company may choose the date and time when any such period of consecutive hours commences provided that it is not earlier than the date and time of the occurrence of the first recorded individual loss sustained by the Company arising out of that disaster, accident, or loss and provided that only one such period of 168 consecutive hours will apply with respect to one event.
>
> As respects those loss occurrences referred to in A. and B., if the disaster, accident, or loss occasioned by the event is of greater duration than 72 consecutive hours, then the Company may divide that disaster, accident, or loss into two or more loss occurrences provided no two periods overlap and no individual loss is included in more than one such period and provided that no period commences earlier than the date and time of the occurrence of the first recorded individual loss sustained by the Company arising out of that disaster, accident, or loss.
>
> No individual losses occasioned by an event that would be covered by 72 hours provisions may be included in any loss occurrence claimed under the 168 hours provisions.

Surplus liability is that liability amount ceded to the reinsurer. The surplus share treaty often expressly defines this term in the definitions clause. This term is discussed later in this chapter.

Risk is commonly defined in one of the following three ways:

1. All insured values under one roof
2. All insured values within four walls
3. All insured values at one location

A surplus share treaty usually contains a clause that refers to one of these definitions. For example, risk may be defined as follows:

> One risk shall be defined as respects the peril of fire as the total insured values within four walls, with the understanding, however, that the Company shall be the sole judge as to what constitutes one risk.

In this example, the primary insurer determines what is "one risk," and, because "four walls" is not defined, what constitutes "four walls." The reinsurer may agree to let the primary insurer use its inspection reports and other information to define "four walls" within the spirit of the treaty.

Net retention can specify what underlying reinsurance the primary insurer is allowed to have to support its retention. Net retention is discussed further in the definition of surplus liability later in this chapter.

Exclusions Clause

No standard list of exclusions exists for surplus share treaties and the variety of possible exclusions is extensive. Depending on what the primary insurer and the reinsurer negotiate, the surplus share treaty exclusions may be brief, for example, including only nuclear incident, pollution, war risks, terrorism, and insolvency fund exclusions. However, because surplus share treaties usually pertain to property insurance, the list of exclusions may be longer, for example, excluding specific causes of loss, types of insurance, or types of property. The exclusions may apply at all times, or they may not apply when the listed operations or causes of loss are only incidental to or a small part of the primary insurer's total operations. Exhibit 7-10 shows an example of an exclusions clause that may be found in a surplus share treaty.

EXHIBIT 7-10

Exclusions Clause

This Agreement does not cover:

A. Collision or upset, and towing

B. Theft, robbery, and pilferage, written as such

C. Conversion, embezzlement or secretion

D. Manufacturers' stock at factories or warehouses

E. Earthquake and flood when written as such

F. All excess of loss reinsurance assumed, except agency reinsurance being reinsurance of an individual risk in which a Company agent has authority to accept on behalf of the Company

G. Fleets' and dealers' legal liability risks

H. Financial Guarantee and Insolvency

I. Aircraft hulls

J. Satellites

K. Ocean Marine, except where covered by Inland Marine Floaters

L. Offshore drilling rigs

M. Original manufacture, storage, and transportation of petroleum products, except wholesale/retail of gasoline or fuel oil

N. Original manufacture, storage, and transportation of explosives. (An explosive substance is defined as any substance manufactured for the express purpose of exploding as differentiated from other commodities used industrially and which are fortuitously explosive, such as gasoline, celluloid, fuel gases, and dyestuffs.)

O. Difference-In-Conditions coverage, when written as such

P. Public utilities including dams, but not to exclude water utilities or electric utilities where the value of any individual generator does not exceed $1,000,000 total sum insured

Q. Mobile home parks, but not to exclude mobile homes written on an individual basis

R. Pools, Associations, Syndicates, and Insolvency Funds per the attached Pools, Associations, Syndicates, and Insolvency Funds Exclusion Clause No. 08-04.3

S. Property Business excluded by the attached Total Insured Value Exclusion Clause No. 08-04.4

T. Business excluded by the attached Nuclear Incident Exclusion Clauses:

> Nuclear Incident Exclusion Clause—Physical Damage—Reinsurance—U.S.A., No. 08-33
>
> Nuclear Incident Exclusion Clause—Physical Damage—Reinsurance—Canada, No. 08-34.2

U. Extra Contractual Obligations and Excess of Policy Limits amounts

The foregoing exclusions, other than H., R., S.,T., and U., will not apply when the operations or exposures outlined in those exclusions are only incidental to and a comparatively small part of the original insured's major activities or total operations.

Reports and Remittances Clause

The reports and remittances clause requirements for surplus share treaties are similar to those for quota share except that the primary insurer is required to record the net retention and cession amount for each loss exposure subject to the treaty and supply the information to reinsurer(s) via a bordereau. The first paragraph of the sample reports and remittances clause shown in Exhibit 7-11 specifies this record keeping requirement.

EXHIBIT 7-11

Reports and Remittances Clause

The Company shall maintain adequate records showing the particulars of the risk ceded and percents reinsured hereunder, and similar records of alterations, cancellations, rearrangements, and additions in which the Reinsurer is interested.

Within 45 days after the close of each month, the Company shall forward to the Reinsurer the following accounting and statistical data in connection with the month's transactions:

(1) Individual cession data plus summary by major line showing the written or return premium, commission or return commission, paid loss and paid loss adjustment expense, salvages and recoveries falling to the share of the Reinsurer, and balance due to or from the Reinsurer.

(2) Total amount of outstanding losses and unearned premium ceded hereunder.

The balance due to or from Reinsurer as set out in item (1) above shall be payable within 60 days of the close of the account month.

The Company shall also furnish the Reinsurer at the close of each quarter:

(1) Its unearned premium by major class,

(2) Paid loss and loss adjustment expenses by major class and year of occurrence,

(3) Outstanding losses by major class and year of occurrence, and

(4) Written premium by major class.

Continued on next page.

> The Company shall also furnish any other information to the Reinsurer as required for the filing of its Annual Statement. In the event of an industry designated catastrophe affecting this Agreement, the Company undertakes to appropriately designate losses paid and outstanding resulting therefrom on its normal accounts.

CLAUSES DESIGNED OR ADAPTED FOR SURPLUS SHARE TREATIES

The previous section covered common clauses that are modified for use in surplus share treaties. This section discusses clauses designed or adapted for use in surplus share treaties that enable them to operate as such. These clauses include:

- Surplus liability clause
- Net retention clause
- Retention and limits clause
- Method of cession clause

Surplus Liability Clause

Surplus liability clause
A surplus share treaty clause that defines the threshold at which the primary insurer will cede its liability to the reinsurer. The clause establishes a cession priority when several layers of surplus share treaties are used.

The **surplus liability clause** defines the threshold at which the primary insurer will cede its liability to the reinsurer. The clause establishes a cession priority, such as first, second, or third, when several layers of surplus share treaties are used. Not all surplus share treaties have a surplus liability clause. When the clause is not included, the retention and limits clause, described later in this section, can describe the cession limits.

Definition of First or Second Surplus

If surplus share treaties are organized into layers, the primary insurer usually uses the available capacity of the first surplus treaty before it cedes liability to the second surplus treaty, and so on. In the first surplus treaty, the surplus liability clause states that the surplus liability exceeds the primary insurer's net retention. Exhibit 7-12 shows an example of a surplus liability clause that makes the surplus share treaty in which it is included apply as first surplus treaty.

EXHIBIT 7-12

Surplus Liability Clause for a First Surplus Treaty

The term "Surplus Liability" as used in this Agreement shall mean that portion of the Company's gross liability on any one risk which exceeds the Company's Net Retention.

Source: Edwin B. Barber, CPCU, ARe Reinsurance Consultant

In a second surplus treaty, the surplus liability is the amount of liability that exceeds the primary insurer's net retention plus the cession to the first surplus treaty. A sample surplus liability clause for a second surplus treaty is shown in Exhibit 7-13.

> **EXHIBIT 7-13**
>
> **Surplus Liability Clause for a Second Surplus Treaty**
>
> "Second Surplus Liability" shall be defined as that portion of the gross line of the Company that remains on any risk after deducting the net retention of the Company plus the amount of liability ceded to its First Surplus Treaty.

Disclosure of Underlying Reinsurance Agreements

A primary insurer may reinsure its surplus share treaty's net retention via other reinsurance agreements such as a quota share treaty, another surplus share treaty, an excess of loss treaty, or a combination of treaties. Primary insurers reinsure their net retentions for two reasons:

1. To increase net retention to a level greater than their own financial resources may be able to support
2. To increase large line capacity available in the surplus share treaty

If the primary insurer does reinsure its net retention it must disclose those underlying reinsurance agreements in the surplus liability clause of the original treaty.

Net Retention Clause

The **net retention clause** defines the primary insurer's net retention. The definition of net retention can be contained in a separate net retention clause or can be included in the definitions clause, the reinsuring clause, or the retention and limits clause of the surplus share treaty. The net retention clause usually states whether or not the primary insurer is permitted to use underlying reinsurance to reinsure its net retention. Exhibit 7-14 shows both a clause that does not permit underlying reinsurance (except for catastrophe reinsurance) and a clause that does permit underlying reinsurance.

Net retention clause
A reinsurance treaty clause that defines the primary insurer's net retention.

> **EXHIBIT 7-14**
>
> **Net Retention Clauses**
>
> **Net Retention Defined Not to Permit Underlying Reinsurance**
>
> The term "net retention" as used herein shall mean the amount of liability on each risk that the Company elects to retain net for its own account and unreinsured in any way, except for catastrophe reinsurance.

Continued on next page.

> **Net Retention Defined to Permit Underlying Reinsurance**
>
> The term "net retention" as used herein shall mean the amount of liability on each risk that the Company elects to retain net for its own account. The Company's Per Risk Excess of Loss and Property Per Occurrence reinsurances shall be disregarded in establishing the Company's net retention.

Retention and Limits Clause

If a surplus share treaty does not include a surplus liability clause, the retention and limits clause can serve the same purpose. The retention and limits clause limits the amount of liability that the primary insurer can transfer to the reinsurer and establishes the primary insurer's minimum net retention. The sample retention and limits clause shown in Exhibit 7-15 specifies a $100,000 minimum net retention plus five lines, with a $1 million maximum cession for any one loss exposure.

Surplus share treaties usually express the maximum cession as a number of lines with a dollar amount as a cap. These treaties can also state the dollar limit on a probable maximum loss (PML) basis. Exhibit 7-16 provides an example that shows how the primary insurer's net retention and a maximum cession can be determined by PML.

EXHIBIT 7-15

Retention and Limits Clause

For the purpose of this treaty, cessions to this treaty shall be limited to five (5) times the net retention subject to a maximum of $1,000,000. Notwithstanding the provisions above, no risk shall be reinsured hereunder on which the net retention of the Company is less than $100,000.

EXHIBIT 7-16

Retention and Limits—Surplus Share Treaty—Probable Maximum Loss

For the purpose of this Agreement, the First Surplus shall be limited to:

(a) Two (2) times the net retention of the Company where its net retention is between $100,000 and $200,000.

(b) Four (4) times the net retention of the Company where its net retention is more than $200,000.

However, no cession shall be made hereunder for more than $5,000,000 any one risk nor more than $1,000,000 Probable Maximum Loss (PML) any one risk.

> No reinsurance shall be ceded hereunder on any subject of insurance on which the net retention of the Company at the time of cession is less than $100,000 any one risk.
>
> The net retention of the Company mentioned herein shall be understood to mean the amount of the net retention subject only to its Property Working Cover and/or catastrophe excess of loss reinsurance.

A surplus share treaty may include a per occurrence limit to restrict the amount of catastrophic losses indemnified by the treaty and protect the treaty's profitability from an accumulation of catastrophe related losses. If the treaty includes a per occurrence limit, it is added to the retention and limits clause, and a loss occurrence definition is included in the definitions clause. The loss occurrence definition in the definitions clause is similar to the loss occurrence language contained in the definitions clause discussed previously.

Method of Cession Clause

Surplus share treaties are used to provide large line capacity for complex property loss exposures. Consequently, one purpose of the **method of cession clause** is to address methods of ceding for policies covering multiple locations, multiple coverage parts, causes of loss insured within sublimits, and loss exposures insured on a blanket basis. A surplus share treaty addresses these typical complexities associated with insuring property loss exposures so that all the parties involved agree about what is ceded. Another purpose of the method of cession clause could be to reduce adverse selection by specifying how loss exposures are ceded to the treaty. The sample method of cession clause in Exhibit 7-17 illustrates one method for ceding when the loss exposures involved are large and complex.

Method of cession clause
A reinsurance treaty clause that addresses methods of ceding for policies covering multiple locations, multiple coverage parts, causes of loss insured within sublimits, and loss exposures insured on a blanket basis.

EXHIBIT 7-17

Method of Cession Clause

30 C
METHOD OF CESSION

It is agreed that when perils other than fire are written in conjunction with a fire line, these perils shall not be ceded except in conjunction with the fire line and then, as respects each peril, only for an amount not to exceed the amount ceded on the fire line.

In ceding reinsurance on any policy covering risks at two or more locations, the reinsurance allotted to the Reinsurer shall extend proportionately to all locations. In such a case, the Company shall comply with provisions of the minimum net retention requirement in respect to one location, but shall not be required to do so in respect to the other locations.

In ceding reinsurance on any policy comprising two or more items pertaining to one specific location, the reinsurance allotted to the Reinsurer shall extend proportionately to all such items, unless otherwise presented to the Reinsurer and accepted by it.

Continued on next page.

> When a risk is insured by the Company under more than one policy, the Company shall cede to the Reinsurer all or any part of the last policy or policies issued by the Company on the risk and shall pay to the Reinsurer the same rate of premium received by the Company under that particular policy or policies reinsured hereunder. In the event of loss, the Reinsurer shall participate pro rata in the liability of the Company on the risk in the proportion the total amount ceded hereunder bears to the total liability under all policies on the risk in effect at the time of the loss.

Source: Brokers & Reinsurance Markets Association (BRMA), http://www.brma.org/download/bcwrb030.doc (accessed February 5, 2004).

The method of cession clause states that the primary insurer can adjust the percentage ceded for coverage sublimits, but not to the reinsurer's detriment. For example, a primary insurer issues a commercial property policy for $1 million that has an earthquake sublimit of $100,000. The primary insurer's retention is $200,000 (20 percent). If the primary insurer cedes the same proportion of the liability for the earthquake coverage, it would retain $20,000 of the liability for that coverage. The primary insurer's underwriter can increase the retention on the earthquake coverage and cede less liability to the reinsurer. However, the underwriter cannot reduce the retention on the earthquake coverage to cede more liability to the reinsurer.

On multiple-location loss exposures, whether insured under one or multiple policies, the reinsurer assumes liability proportionately for all locations. If this procedure results in any of the locations having a net retention less than the treaty's required minimum net retention, both parties would ignore the treaty requirement to maintain the minimum net retention at those locations. However, the primary insurer must comply with the minimum net retention requirement at one location.

SURPLUS SHARE TREATY PRICING

As with quota share treaty pricing, surplus share treaty pricing depends on the amount of ceding commission the reinsurer pays to the primary insurer. The amount of ceding commission that the reinsurer is willing to pay depends on:

- The treaty's perceived profitability
- The treaty's limits
- The primary insurer's line
- Competition in the reinsurance marketplace

Unlike quota share reinsurance, the primary insurer's retention in a surplus share treaty varies with each cession depending on the primary insurer's line selected for each loss exposure and the coverage limit needs of each loss exposure. Consequently, determining the appropriate price for a surplus share treaty usually involves thoroughly analyzing the policies that will be subject to the treaty. This is accomplished by using a limits profile. Primary insurers also use limit profiles to evaluate the financial consequences of alternative lines. To specify the maximum amounts of insurance it will provide for particular categories of policies, a primary insurer uses a line guide. This section describes the use of limits profiles and line guides.

Limits Profile

A limits profile is a table in which the policies subject to the treaty have been categorized by coverage limit. The hypothetical homeowners data shown for Blue Granite Insurance Company in Exhibit 7-18 has policies categorized into $10,000 intervals for the dwelling coverage limits.

Based on these data, the primary insurer and reinsurer can determine the financial effect of a surplus share treaty with a retention set at various levels. Exhibit 7-19 shows the data from Exhibit 7-18 adjusted to reflect a retention of $120,000 and $130,000.

Under the $120,000 retention scenario, the primary insurer cedes $5,570,234 of premium (the total of column (4)) to the surplus share reinsurer. Using a $130,000 retention results in a smaller cession of premium ($4,430,415, shown at the bottom of column (6)).

If Blue Granite's policyholders' surplus is $5 million, then without reinsurance its capacity ratio would be 3.9 to 1 ($19.5 million ÷ $5 million = 3.9). This exceeds acceptable limits. Blue Granite could use a surplus share treaty with a $130,000 retention to reduce its capacity ratio to an acceptable level of 3 to 1 (($19.5 million − $4.4 million) ÷ $5 million = 3). Alternatively, it could reduce its capacity ratio to 2.8 to 1 by using a surplus share treaty with a $120,000 retention (($19.5 million − $5.5 million) ÷ $5 million = 2.8).

EXHIBIT 7-18

Homeowners Limits Profile for Blue Granite Insurance Company

Dwelling Coverage Limits	Policies		Premium	
	Count	Percent*	Amount	Percent*
$100,000–$110,000	323	0.75	$ 96,900	0.50
$110,001–$120,000	402	0.94	130,650	0.67
$120,001–$130,000	516	1.21	180,600	0.92
$130,001–$140,000	1,602	3.74	600,750	3.07
$140,001–$150,000	2,200	5.14	880,000	4.50
$150,001–$160,000	4,999	11.68	2,124,575	10.86
$160,001–$170,000	15,050	35.15	6,772,500	34.63
$170,001–$180,000	10,100	23.59	4,797,500	24.53
$180,001–$190,000	1,125	2.63	562,500	2.88
$190,001–$200,000	6,500	15.18	3,412,500	17.45
Totals	42,817	100.00%	$19,558,475	100.00%

* Rounded

EXHIBIT 7-19

Homeowners Limits Profile and Possible Retentions for Blue Granite Insurance Company

(1) Dwelling Coverage Limits	(2) Premium Amount	(3) $120,000 Retention Percentage Ceded	(4) Dollar Amount Ceded	(5) $130,000 Retention Percentage Ceded	(6) Dollar Amount Ceded
$100,000–$110,000	$ 96,900	0.00%	$ 0	0.00%	$ 0
$110,001–$120,000	130,650	0.00	0	0.00	0
$120,001–$130,000	180,600	4.00	7,224	0.00	0
$130,001–$140,000	600,750	11.11	66,743	3.70	22,228
$140,001–$150,000	880,000	17.24	151,712	10.34	90,992
$150,001–$160,000	2,124,575	22.58	479,729	16.13	342,694
$160,001–$170,000	6,772,500	27.27	1,846,861	21.21	1,436,447
$170,001–$180,000	4,797,500	31.43	1,507,854	25.71	1,233,437
$180,001–$190,000	562,500	35.14	197,663	29.73	167,231
$190,001–$200,000	3,412,500	38.46	1,312,448	33.33	1,137,386
Totals	$19,558,475		$5,570,234		$4,430,415

Notes:

1. The percentage ceded is based on the midpoint of the applicable Dwelling Coverage Limits range. It is therefore calculated as: (Midpoint − Retention) ÷ Midpoint.
2. Numbers are subject to rounding.

Line Guide

Primary insurers use line guides as underwriting tools to specify the maximum amounts of insurance that the primary insurer is prepared to provide for various categories of policies. Although line guides can be used for both property and liability insurance, most line guides are used for property insurance because total property loss exposures are easier to quantify than liability loss exposures. Property line guides usually include property loss exposure attributes, such as construction type, occupancy classification, and protection classification. For each class of loss exposure, the line guide indicates a suggested net retention. The insurer's reinsurance program typically is based on line guide information.

The sections that follow present a commercial property line guide and a homeowners line guide for the hypothetical Blue Granite Insurance Company.

Commercial Property Line Guide

An example of a simplified property line guide is shown in Exhibit 7-20. Some insurers use line guides that also include other elements such as the number of floors in the structure and how fire walls are used.

EXHIBIT 7-20

Commercial Property Line Guide

Commercial Property Line Guide
Basic Line ($000)

Construction Type	Protection Class			
	1–4	5–6	7–8	9–10
Frame	40	36	32	28
Masonry	45	41	36	31
Noncombustible	50	45	40	35
Fire-resistive	60	54	48	42

Occupancy Modifiers

Occupancy Class	Modifier
A	1.00
B	0.90
C	0.80
D	0.70
E	0.60
F	0.50

Instructions:

1. Select the *basic line,* based on construction type and protection class.
2. Identify the occupancy class and its applicable modifier. Multiply the basic line by the occupancy modifier to obtain the *modified line.*
3. Multiply the modified line by 2 for fully sprinklered risks of fire-resistive construction or multiply the modified line by 1.5 for fully sprinklered risks of noncombustible construction to obtain the *modified sprinkler line.*
4. Determine the *final line* by reducing the modified line or modified sprinklered line as appropriate for external exposures (such as a petrochemical plant 25 feet away) and for housekeeping and maintenance.

Line guides reflect the construction, occupancy, and protection classes of buildings. A building's construction has a direct bearing on the extent of damage a fire can cause as well as on the building's ability to resist damage from other causes of loss. Building construction classifications are typically based on the following three essential factors:

1. The material used for the load-bearing portions of the exterior walls
2. The material used in the building's roof and floors, especially the roof and floors' supports
3. The fire-resistive rating of materials used in the building's construction

The simplified line guide in Exhibit 7-20 uses four building construction classifications: frame, masonry, noncombustible, and fire-resistive. The frame construction classification includes structures that are most susceptible to damage by fire, while the fire-resistive classification includes structures that are least susceptible to damage by fire.

Occupancy refers to the insured's operations. The occupancy factor presented in the line guide reflects the hazards inherent in each type of operation. The Insurance Services Office (ISO) has developed an occupancy code that considers the loss exposure's basic occupancy, such as if the occupancy is an office, a habitational property, a sawmill, and so on. The scoring derived from the basic occupancy classification is then modified by combustibility and susceptibility factors. Combustibility is the material's ability to ignite and burn. ISO's approach ranks the combustibility of contents according to five classes, from noncombustible to rapid or flash burning. Susceptibility measures the extent to which fire and its effects will cause damage to materials typical of the occupancy. Even a relatively small fire can produce a large financial loss if the building's contents lose their value when contaminated by smoke. ISO indicates content susceptibility using five classifications that range from minimal damage to extreme loss.

The occupancy categories used in Exhibit 7-20 are illustrative. Category A is the least hazardous occupancy classification and category F is the most hazardous.

ISO uses a community's fire defense characteristics to quantify its fire protection services. ISO's public protection classification system grades communities from Class 1 (exemplary) to Class 10 (does not meet the minimum criteria). In classifying the public fire protection of communities, ISO considers fire alarm and communications systems, the local fire department, and the water supply. The line guide in Exhibit 7-20 groups public protection classes.

Commercial Line Guide Examples

The following three examples illustrate how a commercial line guide's consideration of construction, occupancy, and protection class affects an underwriter's decision about setting a loss exposure's final line or net retention. In all cases assume that the modified line equals the final line. Using Exhibit 7-20, assume that the occupancy modifier class A is the least hazardous loss exposure, such as an office.

Example 1—If the insurer insures an office in a building of fire resistive construction, located in a community with fire protection classified as protection class 4, the final line would be $60,000.

Example 2—If the insurer insures an office in a building of frame construction, located in a community with fire protection classified as protection class 7, the final line would be $32,000.

Example 3—If the insurer insures a restaurant (occupancy class F) of brick construction in a community with fire protection classified as protection class 6, the final line would be $20,500 ($41,000 × 0.50).

Homeowners Line Guide

In a homeowners line guide, public fire protection classification is usually the dominant factor. Homes are owner-occupied, so the occupancy criterion is insignificant. Construction characteristics are seldom considered because most homes are frame (or substantially frame) structures and are 100 percent subject to destruction by fire (100 percent PML). Exhibit 7-21 is an illustration of a simplified homeowners line guide. Protection class 1 is best and class 10 is worst.

EXHIBIT 7-21

Homeowners Line Guide

Protection Class	Maximum Line
1 to 4	$70,000
5 and 6	$60,000
7 and 8	$50,000
9 and 10	$40,000

Homeowners Line Guide Examples

An insurer receives an application for a one-story, two-bedroom, one-bath, frame construction home in protection class 3. The maximum line, using Exhibit 7-21, is $70,000. The insurer also insures a three-story, five-bedroom, four-bath, frame-construction colonial home with a protection class of 10. The maximum line using the same line guide is $40,000. Depending on the number of lines ceded to a surplus share treaty, the insurer may need additional reinsurance to provide the coverage amount needed.

SUMMARY

Surplus share treaties are a type of pro rata reinsurance commonly used in property reinsurance. As with quota share reinsurance, the primary insurer and reinsurer party to a surplus share treaty share in the underlying policy premium and losses for each loss exposure on a percentage basis. Unlike quota share treaties, the percentage of ceded liability varies with each loss exposure.

Surplus share treaties serve three functions for primary insurers:

1. Increase large line capacity
2. Stabilize loss experience
3. Provide surplus relief

Surplus share treaties contain many of the same types of clauses as other reinsurance treaties. Common clauses modified for use in a surplus share treaty include:

- Reinsuring clause
- Liability of the reinsurer clause
- Definitions clause
- Exclusions clause
- Reports and remittances clause

Clauses designed or adapted specifically for surplus share treaties include:

- *Surplus liability clause.* The surplus liability clause defines the threshold at which the primary insurer will cede its liability to the reinsurer and establishes a cession priority when several treaty layers are used.
- *Net retention clause.* The net retention clause defines the primary insurer's net retention and usually states whether or not the primary insurer is permitted to use underlying reinsurance to reinsure its net retention.
- *Retention and limits clause.* The retention and limits clause limits the amount of liability that the primary insurer can transfer to the reinsurer and establishes the primary insurer's minimum net retention.
- *Method of cession clause.* The method of cession clause addresses methods of ceding policies covering multiple locations, multiple coverage parts, causes of loss insured within sublimits, and loss exposures insured on a blanket basis.

As with quota share treaty pricing, surplus share treaty pricing depends on the amount of ceding commission the reinsurer pays to the primary insurer. The amount of ceding commission the reinsurer is willing to pay depends on:

- The treaty's perceived profitability
- The treaty's limits
- The primary insurer's line
- Competition in the reinsurance marketplace

Evaluating the usefulness of a surplus share treaty with a specific retention requires analyzing the insurance policies that are subject to the treaty using a limits profile. A primary insurer also needs to determine how much premium will be ceded at various retention amounts. The primary insurer uses line guides to communicate and control the amount of liability that individual primary insurer underwriters accept on individual loss exposures.

The next chapter examines the purpose, operation, and pricing of property per risk excess of loss treaties.

Chapter 8

Direct Your Learning

Property Per Risk Excess of Loss Treaties

After learning the content of this chapter, you should be able to:

- Explain the purpose and operation of property per risk excess of loss treaties.
- Explain the purpose and operation of clauses designed or adapted for property per risk excess of loss treaties.
- Explain the approaches to property per risk excess of loss treaty pricing.

OUTLINE

Overview of Property Per Risk Excess of Loss Treaties

Clauses Designed or Adapted for Property Per Risk Excess of Loss Treaties

Property Per Risk Excess of Loss Treaty Pricing

Summary

Develop Your Perspective

What are the main topics covered in the chapter?

This chapter describes the operation, contractual clauses, and the methods for pricing property per risk excess of loss treaties.

Identify the features of property per risk excess of loss reinsurance.

- What functions does a property per risk excess of loss treaty serve for a primary insurer?
- What are the two approaches used to price property per risk excess of loss treaties?

Why is it important to learn about these topics?

Property per risk excess of loss reinsurance provides a primary insurer with large line capacity and stabilizes loss experience. The ability to understand, analyze, and evaluate property per risk excess of loss treaties is important to enable you to determine whether they are helping your company or client-insurer achieve its objectives.

Review a property per risk excess of loss treaty.

- How are clauses designed or adapted for property per risk excess of loss treaties?

How can you use what you will learn?

Evaluate one of your company's or client-insurer's property per risk excess of loss treaties.

- Does this property per risk excess of loss treaty address your company's or client-insurer's needs?
- Does this property per risk excess of loss treaty provide your company or client-insurer with adequate protection from large property losses?

Chapter 8
Property Per Risk Excess of Loss Treaties

Property per risk excess of loss reinsurance can be used to satisfy the needs of primary insurers insuring large property loss exposures. Primary insurers can purchase property per risk excess of loss reinsurance on a facultative or treaty basis. The focus of this chapter is on property per risk excess of loss treaties. The chapter explains the following:

- How property per risk excess of loss treaties operate.
- How clauses have been designed or adapted for property per risk excess of loss treaties.
- How property per risk excess of loss treaties are priced.

OVERVIEW OF PROPERTY PER RISK EXCESS OF LOSS TREATIES

Property per risk excess of loss reinsurance covers property loss exposures and applies separately to *each loss* occurring to *each risk*. Primary insurers use per risk excess of loss reinsurance to protect against the adverse financial consequences of large losses.

As described in a previous chapter, excess of loss reinsurers indemnify primary insurers for losses that exceed the primary insurer's attachment point (or retention) up to a specified amount (the reinsurance limit). For property per risk excess of loss reinsurance, the attachment point and reinsurance limit apply to each loss exposure (risk) and to each loss. For example, a property per risk excess of loss treaty with a $50,000 attachment point and a $1 million reinsurance limit would respond to any loss sustained by any loss exposure that exceeded the $50,000 attachment point. Losses in excess of the $1 million reinsurance limit would be retained by the primary insurer unless liability for these losses is otherwise transferred to another reinsurer. Property per risk excess of loss reinsurance is often purchased in layers so that the primary insurer can obtain needed underwriting capacity.

Pro rata reinsurance usually applies on the same terms and conditions as specified in the underlying insurance policies; however, that is not always the case with excess of loss reinsurance. An excess of loss treaty may cover only one type of insurance and only selected causes of loss. For example, a property per risk excess of loss treaty may apply only to fire and lightning losses arising out of commercial property policies.

Additionally, excess of loss treaties may contain exclusions that do not appear in the underlying insurance policies and preclude coverage under the treaty. Pro rata reinsurance provides the primary insurer with broader coverage, but excess of loss reinsurance provides reinsurance coverage where it is needed most.

Property per risk excess of loss reinsurance serves many of the same functions as surplus share reinsurance but primary insurers may prefer property per risk excess of loss reinsurance. Some primary insurers consider the administrative work associated with surplus share treaties onerous because details about each surplus share cession must be reported to the reinsurer. Property per risk excess of loss treaties are easier to administer because a single attachment point applies to all loss exposures subject to the treaty and the same reinsurance rate applies to the entire policy portfolio. Also, some primary insurers do not want to cede the often significant amount of written premium as is required under surplus share treaties. Property per risk excess of loss reinsurance is priced based on the likelihood of loss in the reinsurer's layer and usually the reinsurance premium is a small percentage of the underlying written premiums.

Functions of Property Per Risk Excess of Loss Treaties

Property per risk excess of loss treaties serve the following functions:

- Increase large line capacity
- Stabilize loss experience

Increase Large Line Capacity

Property per risk excess of loss treaties increase large line capacity because the reinsurer usually assumes the entire exposure to loss above the primary insurer's retention. Therefore, the primary insurer is able to provide a larger policy limit than is possible or acceptable without reinsurance. For example, a primary insurer may have the financial capacity to assume policy limits of $100,000 on each homeowners policy it insures. However, the primary insurer needs to provide homeowners policies with policy limits of $500,000 to remain competitive. The primary insurer could purchase a $400,000 xs $100,000 property per risk excess of loss treaty so that the primary insurer's largest loss would be $100,000 on the $500,000 policy limits. The reinsurer would provide the remaining $400,000 of needed capacity. Exhibit 8-1 shows how property per risk excess of loss reinsurance provides large line capacity.

Stabilize Loss Experience

Primary insurers need stable profits if they are to grow and attract capital investment. Profits depend in part on underwriting results. Excessive losses—beyond those anticipated in the insurer's rates—lead to instability in underwriting results. Property per risk excess of loss treaties stabilize underwriting results because the primary insurer's loss is limited to the retention regardless of the size of the policy limits or the loss.

EXHIBIT 8-1

Example of Property Per Risk Excess of Loss Reinsurance

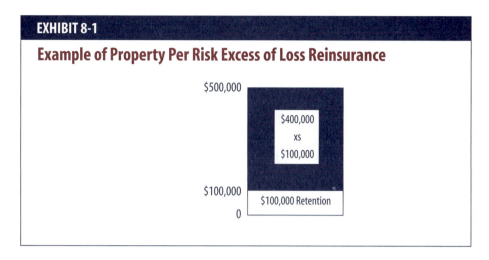

Property per risk excess of loss treaties can provide some protection from catastrophe losses but are not a substitute for a catastrophe reinsurance treaty. Property per risk excess of loss reinsurance would respond to catastrophe losses, but the primary insurer would have to absorb multiple retentions. Alternatively, an occurrence may cause minor damage on many loss exposures and the property per risk excess of loss treaty would not be triggered because the individual losses are well within the primary insurer's retention. For example, hailstorms can cause significant losses for insurers but the per risk loss is generally small. Finally, many property per risk excess of loss treaties contain a per occurrence limit that reduces the usefulness of those treaties in the case of a catastrophic occurrence. Catastrophe reinsurance treaties are designed and priced to respond to an accumulation of losses. Primary insurers usually coordinate their property per risk excess of loss and catastrophe reinsurance agreements.

Property Per Risk Excess of Loss Treaties as Part of a Reinsurance Program

Property per risk excess of loss reinsurance can be used on a facultative basis to reinsure individual loss exposures, as well as on a treaty basis involving the primary insurer's entire portfolio of property loss exposures.

Property per risk excess of loss reinsurance can be incorporated into a primary insurer's reinsurance program in several ways. For example, a primary insurer may use a multi-layered reinsurance program of property per risk excess of loss treaties to reinsure all of its property loss exposures. Alternatively, the primary insurer may purchase a pro rata treaty and a property per risk excess of loss treaty with either or both treaties responding to losses, depending on the circumstances of the loss and the structure of the treaties. Although an effective means of transferring the financial consequences of individual losses, property per risk excess of loss reinsurance is usually not intended to address a primary insurer's catastrophe protection needs. Therefore, the property per risk excess of loss reinsurance treaty's attachment point and reinsurance limits are usually selected in consideration of the primary insurer's catastrophe reinsurance program. Additionally, the primary insurer can purchase property per risk excess of loss reinsurance to provide needed large line capacity for specific loss exposures that have coverage needs beyond the primary insurer's reinsurance program.

CLAUSES DESIGNED OR ADAPTED FOR PROPERTY PER RISK EXCESS OF LOSS TREATIES

Some clauses are common to all types of excess of loss treaties. Because large property losses typically emerge and are settled relatively quickly, property per risk excess of loss treaties can usually be worded more simply than can casualty excess of loss treaties. The following section describes clauses that apply to excess of loss treaties in general and to property per risk excess of loss treaties in particular. Those clauses include the following:

- Retention and limits clause
- Loss notices and settlements clause
- Reinsurance premium clause
- Net retained lines clause
- Ultimate net loss clause
- Pools, associations, and syndicates exclusion clause
- Total insured value exclusion clause

Retention and Limits Clause

The retention and limits clause for a property per risk excess of loss treaty usually specifies that the retention and the reinsurance limit apply to any one risk and for each loss occurrence. Because of the importance of the definitions of risk and occurrence in establishing the reinsurer's liability, the retention and limits clause often defines them. Alternatively, some treaties define these terms in the definitions clause.

Property losses—even large ones—are typically easy to identify. The retention and limits clause usually contains straightforward language specifying how the retention and reinsurance limit operate. In the sample retention and limits clause that appears in Exhibit 8-2, the retention applies to "any one risk, each loss occurrence." The reference to loss occurrence means that a *new* retention and a *new* limit apply to each loss occurrence if a single insured risk experiences losses in two or more loss occurrences. The retention and limits clause can be modified to include the following:

- Co-participation provision
- Per occurrence limit
- Definition of one risk
- Annual aggregate deductible

EXHIBIT 8-2

Retention and Limits Clause

The Company shall retain and be liable for the first $100,000 of ultimate net loss as respects any one risk, each loss occurrence. The Reinsurer shall then be liable for the amount by which such ultimate net loss exceeds the Company's retention, but the liability of the Reinsurer shall not exceed $400,000 as respects any one risk, each loss occurrence.

The liability of the Reinsurer under this Contract in any one loss occurrence shall in no event exceed $1,200,000.

The Company shall be the sole judge of what constitutes one risk, with the following exceptions:

1. In no event shall a building and its contents be considered more than one risk;
2. As respects dwelling properties insured under Homeowners policies, the sum of Section I coverages shall be considered one risk;
3. In no event shall the insured values within four walls be considered more than one risk; and
4. In no event shall the insured values at any one location be considered more than one risk.

Co-participation provision. A co-participation provision requires the primary insurer to retain part of the loss above its retention. For example, a property per risk excess of loss reinsurer may require the primary insurer to retain in 5 percent of all losses above its retention. Exhibit 8-3 illustrates a Co-participation arrangement.

EXHIBIT 8-3

Excess of Loss Reinsurance With Co-Participation

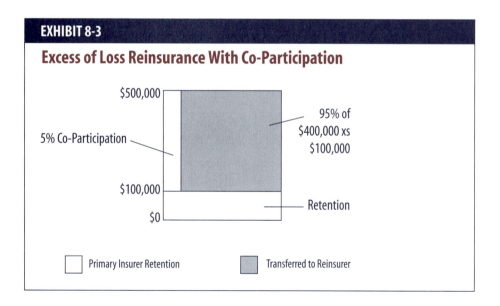

Per occurrence limit. Reinsurers often seek to limit the amount of loss that can be accumulated in a property per risk excess of loss treaty from a single loss occurrence. A primary insurer may try to transfer much of its catastrophe liability to reinsurers through its property per risk excess of loss treaties rather than through a catastrophe reinsurance agreement. Mindful of this possibility, reinsurers frequently insist on having a per occurrence limit in property per risk excess of loss treaties. The per occurrence limit is stated either as a dollar amount or as a multiple of the reinsurance limit of the property per risk excess of loss treaty. A per occurrence limit of $1.2 million is included in the sample retention and limits clause in Exhibit 8-2.

Definition of one risk. The term "one risk" should be defined in a property per risk excess of loss treaty because it is used to establish the primary insurer's retention and reinsurance treaty's limit. Usually, the primary insurer is the sole judge of what constitutes one risk, but the reinsurance treaty may include general guidelines. Nevertheless, the question of what is one risk can lead to disagreements between the primary insurer and the reinsurer. The sample retention and limits clause in Exhibit 8-2 includes parameters for the definition of one risk.

Annual aggregate deductible
A provision in which the primary insurer retains its normal retention on each loss plus an aggregate amount of the total losses during the year, up to the aggregate deductible amount.

Annual aggregate deductible. An **annual aggregate deductible** is a provision in which the primary insurer retains its normal retention on each loss plus an aggregate amount of the total losses during the year, up to the aggregate deductible amount. Annual aggregate deductibles are commonly found in property per risk excess of loss treaties. They allow the primary insurer to retain losses until the accumulation of losses during the treaty period becomes so large that the effect of any further losses on the primary insurer's underwriting results is undesirable. For example, assume that a primary insurer's past loss experience indicates that, during a typical year, losses between $100,000 and $500,000 contribute 3 percent to its loss ratio. The primary insurer's underwriting results are acceptable with that amount of aggregate loss each year. The primary insurer may establish a $400,000 xs $100,000 treaty with an annual aggregate deductible equal to 3 percent of earned premiums to limit the effect of losses over $100,000 to 3 percent of its loss ratio during a single year. Each loss over $100,000 is accumulated and retained by the primary insurer until the total amount exceeds the annual aggregate deductible. Then any additional losses are reimbursed by the reinsurer up to the treaty's limit.

Loss Notices and Settlements Clause

Loss notices and settlements clause
A reinsurance treaty clause that requires the primary insurer to notify the reinsurer of any loss amount that exceeds or is likely to exceed the primary insurer's retention.

The **loss notices and settlements clause** requires the primary insurer to notify the reinsurer of any loss amount that exceeds or is likely to exceed the primary insurer's retention.

Excess of loss treaties involve relatively few losses, but each loss that potentially exceeds the primary insurer's retention should be reported to the reinsurer. The reinsurer reviews most losses when they are first reported and again before the treaty anniversary because the reinsurer is responsible for all or most (when a co-participation or aggregate deductible provision applies) of the loss amounts above the retention. Once it is clear that a loss will exceed the retention, whatever the primary insurer does in settling the loss affects the reinsurer. The reinsurer must therefore remain vigilant and satisfied that the primary insurer is settling the loss properly. Therefore, the claim departments of the reinsurer and primary insurer must work together closely. Exhibit 8-4 shows an example of a loss notices and settlements clause.

EXHIBIT 8-4

Loss Notices and Settlements Clause

26 C
LOSS NOTICE

The Company shall advise the Reinsurer promptly of all losses which, in the opinion of the Company, may result in a claim hereunder and of all subsequent developments thereto which, in the opinion of the Company, may materially affect the position of the Reinsurer.

Inadvertent omission or oversight in dispatching such advices shall in no way affect the liability of the Reinsurer. However, the Company shall notify the Reinsurer of such omission or oversight promptly upon its discovery.

Source: Brokers & Reinsurance Markets Association (BRMA), http://www.brma.org/download/bcwrb026.doc (accessed February 11, 2004).

Reinsurance Premium Clause

Unlike pro rata reinsurers, excess of loss reinsurers do not share the primary insurer's premium. Therefore, excess of loss treaties contain a reinsurance premium clause that establishes exactly what the premium will be for the coverage provided. Exhibit 8-5 shows a sample reinsurance premium clause. Reinsurance premium clauses vary depending on the following conditions:

- Whether the treaty is provided for a specified term or is continuous until canceled
- Whether the subject premium base is net written premiums or net earned premiums
- Whether the treaty is written on a cut-off or run-off basis
- Whether the treaty has a flat rate, a provisional premium based on losses, or minimum and deposit premiums
- Whether any minimum and deposit premiums are equal to one another or are different amounts

The reinsurer expects to receive a minimum reinsurance premium for providing the primary insurer with large line capacity, regardless of whether the primary insurer incurs any losses covered by the per risk excess of loss treaty. The

EXHIBIT 8-5

Reinsurance Premium Clause

43 K

REINSURANCE PREMIUM

As premium for the reinsurance provided hereunder, the Company shall pay the Reinsurer _____ % of its net earned premium. Within _____ days after the end of each _____ , the Company shall report its net earned premium for the _____ . The premium due the Reinsurer, at the rate shown in the first paragraph, shall be paid by the Company with its report.

"Net earned premium" as used herein is defined as gross earned premium of the Company for the classes of business reinsured hereunder, less the earned portion of premiums ceded by the Company for reinsurance which inures to the benefit of this Contract. For purposes of calculating net earned premium,   (recite extraction calculation)   shall be considered subject premium.

Source: BRMA, http://www.brma.org/download/bcwrb043.doc (accessed February 11, 2004).

Deposit premium
The amount the primary insurer pays the reinsurer pending the determination of the actual reinsurance premium owed.

treaty often makes the minimum premium equal to the deposit premium. The **deposit premium** is the amount the primary insurer pays the reinsurer pending the determination of the actual reinsurance premium owed. The reinsurer must work with subject premium estimates provided by the primary insurer to determine the deposit premium. For example, a primary insurer may estimate that its treaty's underlying policies will generate $10 million in subject premium. Based on this estimate, as well as on the attachment point and reinsurance limit, the reinsurer develops a reinsurance rate. If the rate were 5.5 percent, the expected reinsurance premium would be $550,000 ($10,000,000 × 0.055). Assume that the reinsurer requires a minimum premium of 80 percent of the estimated reinsurance premium and that the minimum premium equals the deposit premium. In that case, the minimum premium and deposit premium would be $440,000 ($550,000 × 0.8).

Net Retained Lines Clause

Net retained lines clause
A reinsurance treaty clause that specifies that the reinsurance coverage applies only to the primary insurer's net retention.

The **net retained lines clause** specifies that the reinsurance coverage applies only to the primary insurer's net retention. For the reinsurer to establish a reinsurance rate for the coverage being provided, the assumed liability must be properly defined. In particular, the reinsurer will want to ensure that it is not liable for amounts that should have been paid by other reinsurers. The net retained lines clause provides this protection by defining the primary insurer's liability.

Exhibit 8-6 shows an example of a net retained lines clause.

> **EXHIBIT 8-6**
>
> ### Net Retained Lines Clause
>
> 32 B
> NET RETAINED LINES
>
> This Contract applies only to that portion of any policy which the Company retains net for its own account, and in calculating the amount of any loss hereunder and also in computing the amount or amounts in excess of which this Contract attaches, only loss or losses in respect of that portion of any policy which the Company retains net for its own account shall be included.
>
> The amount of the Reinsurer's liability hereunder in respect of any loss or losses shall not be increased by reason of the inability of the Company to collect from any other reinsurer(s), whether specific or general, any amounts which may have become due from such reinsurer(s), whether such inability arises from the insolvency of such other reinsurer(s) or otherwise.

Source: BRMA, http://www.brma.org/download/bcwrb032.doc (accessed February 11, 2004).

Ultimate Net Loss Clause

The **ultimate net loss clause** specifies the loss amount against which retention and reinsurance limit apply. The sample clause shown in Exhibit 8-7 defines ultimate net loss in terms of the following components:

- Loss
- Loss adjustment expenses
- Recoveries

Loss. The loss specified in Exhibit 8-7 is the primary insurer's actual loss after deducting recoveries from other reinsurance (called inuring reinsurance). In other words, if the primary insurer has purchased other reinsurance, the amounts recoverable under that other reinsurance must be deducted to determine the net loss subject to the excess of loss treaty.

Reinsurance programs are often designed so that underlying reinsurance is recognized by reinsurers offering high layers of reinsurance coverage. When this is desired, the definition of ultimate net loss is modified. For example, the ultimate net loss clause may specify "The amounts recoverable from the Company's quota share and first excess of loss treaties shall be ignored for the purposes of determining the ultimate net loss hereunder."

The ultimate net loss clause usually specifies that unrecoverable losses from other reinsurers do not affect this reinsurer's obligation to the primary insurer. For example, the sample ultimate net loss clause in Exhibit 8-7 refers to "recoveries," which refers to sums due, collectable or not, from other reinsurers.

Ultimate net loss clause
A reinsurance treaty clause that specifies the loss amount against which the retention and reinsurance limit apply.

> **EXHIBIT 8-7**
>
> **Ultimate Net Loss Clause**
>
> 54 A
>
> ULTIMATE NET LOSS
>
> The term "Ultimate Net Loss" means the actual loss, including loss adjustment expense, paid or to be paid by the Company on its net retained liability after making deductions for all recoveries, salvages, subrogations and all claims on inuring reinsurance, whether collectible or not; provided, however, that in the event of the insolvency of the Company, payment by the Reinsurer shall be made in accordance with the provisions of the Insolvency Article. Nothing herein shall be construed to mean that losses under this Contract are not recoverable until the Company's ultimate net loss has been ascertained.

Source: BRMA, http://www.brma.org/download/bcwrb054.doc (accessed February 11, 2004).

Loss adjustment expenses. As previously discussed, loss adjustment expenses can be significant. The ultimate net loss clause specifies whether (1) loss adjustment expenses are prorated between the primary insurer and the reinsurer(s) based on their respective shares of the loss or (2) whether the loss adjustment expenses are included in the loss amount.

With the first method, if the loss is $400,000 and the retention is $100,000, the reinsurer is responsible for $300,000, or 75 percent of the loss, and the primary insurer retains $100,000, or 25 percent of the loss. The loss adjustment expense is prorated on the same basis. Therefore, the reinsurer is responsible for 75 percent of the loss adjustment expense, and the primary insurer is responsible for 25 percent. Usually, the loss adjustment expense is not subject to the treaty limit when it is calculated on a pro rata basis. If the loss amount does not exceed the net retention, the reinsurer is not responsible for any of the loss adjustment expense.

With the second method, the resulting amount is subject to the net retention and the treaty limit. Therefore, the reinsurer may have to pay for a loss in which the actual loss amount does not exceed the net retention. When loss adjustment expenses are added to the loss, the primary insurer must carefully assess the loss adjustment expense potential in the types of insurance covered and purchase sufficient reinsurance limits.

Recoveries. Salvage, subrogation, and reversals and reductions of judgments all reduce the ultimate net loss. The primary insurer has a fiduciary responsibility to the reinsurer to pursue all avenues of possible recovery. The primary insurer must apply those recoveries to reduce the amount of the loss recoverable from excess of loss reinsurers. If the recovery is large enough to reimburse the reinsurer totally, the primary insurer can retain any remaining balance. If the primary insurer incurs expenses in the pursuit of recoveries, those expenses can be deducted from the recoveries before the primary insurer reimburses the reinsurer.

Pools, Associations, and Syndicates Exclusion Clause

The **pools, associations, and syndicates exclusion clause** excludes from coverage any liability emanating from the primary insurer's participation, directly or indirectly, through reinsurance in any of the following:

- Voluntary pools, associations, and syndicates that purchase their own reinsurance
- Involuntary pools such as FAIR plans, and coastal/windstorm pools

This clause is generally used in property per risk excess of loss and property catastrophe treaties. Reinsurers already participate either as members or as reinsurers in many of the pools, and therefore this exclusion is necessary to control their accumulation of pool liabilities. Losses from involuntary pools are excluded from property per risk excess of loss treaties because these losses are a primary insurer's cost of doing business in the states involved and should not be passed on to excess of loss reinsurers. Primary insurers subject to assessment by involuntary pools may request that this exclusion be amended to grant coverage under their catastrophe reinsurance agreements. For example, a primary insurer selling property insurance in one of the states with a windstorm pool is subject to an accumulation of losses from the insurance it sells and an assessment from the windstorm pool for losses that exceed the pool's financial resources. The additional clause to reinstate involuntary pool coverage for catastrophe reinsurance agreements is included in the sample pools, associations, and syndicates exclusion clause shown in Exhibit 8-8.

> **Pools, associations, and syndicates exclusion clause**
> A reinsurance treaty clause that excludes from coverage any liability emanating from the primary insurer's participation, directly or indirectly, through pools, associations, and syndicates.

EXHIBIT 8-8

Pools, Associations, and Syndicates Exclusion Clause

40 A
POOLS, ASSOCIATIONS, AND SYNDICATES EXCLUSION CLAUSE

Section A:

Excluding:

(a) All business derived directly or indirectly from any Pool, Association or Syndicate which maintains its own reinsurance facilities.

(b) Any Pool or Scheme (whether voluntary or mandatory) formed after March 1, 1968 for the purpose of insuring property whether on a country-wide basis or in respect of designated areas. This exclusion shall not apply to so-called Automobile Insurance Plans or other Pools formed to provide coverage for Automobile Physical Damage.

Section B:

It is agreed that business written by the Company for the same perils, which is known at the time to be insured by, or in excess of underlying amounts placed in the following Pools, Associations, or Syndicates, whether by way of insurance or reinsurance, is excluded hereunder:

Industrial Risk Insurers,

Continued on next page.

Associated Factory Mutuals,

Improved Risk Mutuals,

Any Pool, Association or Syndicate formed for the purpose of writing Oil, Gas or Petro-Chemical Plants and/or Oil or Gas Drilling Rigs,

United States Aircraft Insurance Group, Canadian Aircraft Insurance Group, Associated Aviation Underwriters, American Aviation Underwriters.

Section B does not apply:

(a) Where the Total Insured Value over all interests of the risk in question is less than $250,000,000.

(b) To interests traditionally underwritten as Inland Marine or stock and/or contents written on a blanket basis.

(c) To Contingent Business Interruption, except when the Company is aware that the key location is known at the time to be insured in any Pool, Association, or Syndicate named above, other than as provided for under Section B(a).

(d) To risks as follows:

> Offices, Hotels, Apartments, Hospitals, Educational Establishments, Public Utilities (other than railroad schedules) and builder's risks on the classes of risks specified in this subsection (d) only.

Where this clause attaches to Catastrophe Excesses, the following Section C is added:

Section C:

Nevertheless the Reinsurer specifically agrees that liability accruing to the Company from its participation in:

(1) The following so-called "Coastal Pools":

> Alabama Insurance Underwriting Association
>
> Florida Windstorm Underwriting Association
>
> Louisiana Insurance Underwriting Association
>
> Mississippi Windstorm Underwriting Association
>
> North Carolina Insurance Underwriting Association
>
> South Carolina Windstorm and Hail Underwriting Association
>
> Texas Catastrophe Property Insurance Association

AND

(2) All "Fair Plan" business for all perils otherwise protected hereunder shall not be excluded, except, however, that this reinsurance does not include any increase in such liability resulting from:

(i) The inability of any other participant in such "Coastal Pool" or "Fair Plan" to meet its liability.

(ii) Any claim against such "Coastal Pool" or "Fair Plan" or any participant therein, including the Company, whether by way of subrogation or otherwise, brought by or on behalf of any insolvency fund (as defined in the Insolvency Fund Exclusion Clause incorporated in this Contract).

Source: BRMA, http://www.brma.org/download/bcwrb040.doc (accessed February 20, 2004).

Total Insured Value Exclusion Clause

The **total insured value exclusion clause** excludes very large loss exposures from automatic coverage. Large loss exposures are defined as those needing amounts of insurance that exceed a specified amount, such as all loss exposures for which the total amount of insurance exceeds $250 million. Loss exposures needing significant amounts of insurance are sometimes insured in reinsurance transactions involving several primary insurers. For example, underwriters from several primary insurers may collaborate in the insuring of a large warehouse complex.

Property per risk excess of loss reinsurers have insisted on the use of a total insured value exclusion clause to control their accumulation of liability on a single loss exposure. If the clause were not included, the reinsurer could assume liability on the same loss exposure from several different primary insurers, with the total liability at an unacceptable level.

The exceptions to the sample total insured value exclusion clause in Exhibit 8-9 are loss exposures from offices, hotels, apartments, hospitals, educational establishments, public utilities, and builders risks. Generally, reinsurers consider these excepted categories of loss exposures to be desirable. Reinsurers also make an exception for a loss exposure insured in its entirety by the primary insurer. This latter exception makes sense because the reinsurer cannot have an unanticipated accumulation of liability if the primary insurer insures the entire loss exposure.

> **Total insured value exclusion clause**
> A reinsurance treaty clause that excludes very large loss exposures from automatic coverage.

EXHIBIT 8-9

Total Insured Value Exclusion Clause

53 B

TOTAL INSURED VALUE EXCLUSION CLAUSE

It is the mutual intention of the parties to exclude risks, other than Offices, Hotels, Apartments, Hospitals, Educational Establishments and Public Utilities (except Railroad Schedules), and Builders Risks on the above classes, where at the time of cession, the Total Insured Value over all interests exceeds $250,000,000. However, the Company shall be protected hereunder, subject to the other terms and conditions of this Contract, if subsequent to cession being made, the Company becomes acquainted with the true facts of the case and discovers that the mutual intention has been inadvertently breached; on condition that the Company shall at the first opportunity, and certainly by next anniversary of the original policy, exclude the risk in question.

It is agreed that this mutual intention does not apply to Contingent Business Interruption or to interests traditionally underwritten as Inland Marine or to Stock and/or Contents written on a blanket basis except where the Company is aware that the Total Insured Value of $250,000,000 is already exceeded for buildings, machinery, equipment and direct use and occupancy at the key location.

It is understood and agreed that this Clause shall not apply hereunder where the Company writes 100% of the risk.

Source: BRMA, http://www.brma.org/download/bcwrb053.doc (accessed February 11, 2004).

PROPERTY PER RISK EXCESS OF LOSS TREATY PRICING

Property per risk excess of loss treaty pricing can be approached in two general ways. Reinsurers often use both approaches and select the reinsurance rate that makes the most sense for the treaty being priced.

The following are the two approaches to pricing excess of loss reinsurance:

1. Exposure rating
2. Experience rating

Exposure rating considers the amount of liability inherent in the type of business covered by the treaty being priced. **Experience rating** considers the primary insurer's loss experience in the business covered by the treaty being priced. Both exposure rating and experience rating result in a reinsurance rate that is multiplied by the amount of subject premium to yield the reinsurance premium.

Before the reinsurer determines the exposure rating or experience rating the primary insurer and the reinsurer need to set retentions and reinsurance limits.

Exposure rating
An approach to reinsurance treaty pricing that considers the amount of liability inherent in the type of business covered by the treaty being priced.

Experience rating
An approach to reinsurance treaty pricing that considers the primary insurer's loss experience in the business covered by the treaty being priced.

Setting Retentions

Primary insurers usually set retentions after analyzing past losses. Loss analysis typically starts with categorizing losses by size and then identifying a level of losses that occur with sufficient frequency to make them predictable. Losses above this identified level are too unpredictable to safely retain. In setting retentions, primary insurers and reinsurers usually evaluate the last five or more years of loss experience, if available. To meaningfully compare different years of loss data, trend and loss development factors must be applied to adjust the dollar amount of losses to reflect prior-year to current economic conditions.

When setting a retention, the reinsurer and the primary insurer should also consider the primary insurer's financial strength, size, attitude toward accepting fluctuations in underwriting results, and the cost of reinsurance. Additionally, the property per risk excess of loss treaty should be considered in the context of the primary insurer's overall reinsurance program. For example, the treaty may be the only reinsurance purchased, or may be excess above a pro rata treaty. The context of the property per risk excess of loss treaty affects the extent to which it will be required to respond to losses.

Setting Reinsurance Limits

The reinsurance limit is strongly influenced by the treaty's role in the primary insurer's reinsurance program. For example, if the primary insurer's catastrophe reinsurance attaches at $10 million, the primary insurer may choose property per risk excess of loss reinsurance limits of $10 million.

The reinsurance limits can be set to reflect reinsurance costs. A primary insurer may not be willing to pay for reinsurance limits as high as it would like. Because property per risk excess of loss treaties are often layered, the primary insurer could choose different reinsurance limits for each layer to reduce costs. For example, if a primary insurer wanted total underwriting capacity of $10 million, the total reinsurance cost may be lower if the primary insurer purchased three treaty layers rather than one treaty. The primary insurer could purchase the following layers:

$$\$2,000,000 \text{ xs } \$1,000,000$$
$$\$3,000,000 \text{ xs } \$3,000,000$$
$$\$4,000,000 \text{ xs } \$6,000,000$$

The total cost for those three treaties may be less than the cost of one $9,000,000 xs $1,000,000 property per risk excess of loss treaty.

Exposure Rating

Reinsurers use exposure rating to identify the portion of the underlying premium that is available to fund losses in excess of the retention. Exposure rating assumes that more of the premium is needed to pay for small losses because they are more frequent than large losses. The following are the two exposure rating methods used to allocate underlying premiums to reinsurance layers:

- First loss scale
- Price per million

First Loss Scale

The first method of loss exposure rating for per risk excess of loss treaties is the first loss scale method. Several first loss scales are in general use. Some of these scales apply actuarial approaches and some apply non-actuarial approaches. Non-actuarial approaches may incorporate several hazard characteristics and individual loss exposure characteristics, such as construction, private and public fire protection, occupancy, amount of insurance, amount subject to a single loss, cause of loss, and type of coverage provided (such as building and personal property or business income). Many first loss scales incorporate these characteristics into tables to provide reinsurance underwriters with an appropriate price for the liability assumed.

Exhibit 8-10 is a simplified first loss scale based on hypothetical data that could be used to price a single loss exposure reinsured on a facultative basis. This exhibit is just one table from a multi-table first loss scale and it assumes that the primary insurer has a $100,000 retention. Column (1) lists amounts of insurance that the primary insurer may provide. Column (2) lists the expected average loss for each amount of insurance shown in column (1). Column (3) lists the percentage of each loss exposure retained for each amount of insurance (Retention ÷ Amount of insurance). Column (4) lists the expected retained loss, which is $22,084 for the $100,000 retention, as a percentage of expected average loss, (22,084 ÷ Expected average loss). Column (5) is the complement of column (4), calculated by subtracting column (4) from 100 percent. A reinsurer uses a first loss scale to determine the percentage of the premium the primary insurer must pay the reinsurer for the liability it transfers. The percentage of premium ceded is the same as the percentage of expected average loss ceded. For example, the primary insurer would pay the reinsurer 3.1 percent of the policy premium for a policy with an amount of insurance of $200,000.

EXHIBIT 8-10

Simplified First Loss Scale

Retention = $100,000

(1) Amount of Insurance	(2) Expected Average Loss	(3) Percentage Retained	(4) Percentage of Expected Average Loss Retained	(5) Percentage of Expected Average Loss Ceded
$100,000	$22,084	100.0%	100.0%	0.0%
112,500	22,150	88.9	99.7	0.3
125,000	22,217	80.0	99.4	0.6
137,500	22,284	72.7	99.1	0.9
150,000	22,364	66.7	98.7	1.3
162,500	22,443	61.5	98.4	1.6
175,000	22,558	57.1	97.9	2.1
187,500	22,673	53.3	97.4	2.6
200,000	22,791	50.0	96.9	3.1
212,500	22,908	47.1	96.4	3.6
225,000	23,041	44.4	95.8	4.2
237,500	23,173	42.1	95.3	4.7
250,000	23,321	40.0	94.7	5.3
262,500	23,468	38.1	94.1	5.9
275,000	23,594	36.4	93.6	6.4
287,500	23,720	34.8	93.1	6.9
300,000	23,875	33.3	92.5	7.5
312,500	24,030	32.0	91.9	8.1
325,000	24,162	30.8	91.4	8.6
337,500	24,295	29.6	90.9	9.1
350,000	24,430	28.6	90.4	9.6
362,500	24,565	27.6	89.9	10.1
375,000	24,717	26.7	89.3	10.7
387,500	24,869	25.8	88.8	11.2
400,000	25,000	25.0	88.3	11.7

Before a price is quoted, the reinsurer must determine whether the underlying insurance rate is adequate and the quality of the underwriting applied to the underlying loss exposure is satisfactory. If not, the reinsurer could apply the first loss scale and then adjust the reinsurance premium to offset the inadequate underlying insurance rate.

Exhibit 8-11 shows the application of a simplified first loss scale to a property per risk excess of loss treaty. The first loss scale method illustrated for a single loss exposure must be modified for a reinsurance treaty because the treaty applies to many loss exposures with various amounts of insurance. Rather than calculate a premium for each loss exposure, the data are summarized and average amounts are used for each amount of insurance. For example, the average amount of insurance for policies with amounts of insurance between $100,001 and $125,000 is $112,500. The average percentage retained (shown in column (5)) is the retention amount ($100,000) divided by the average amount of insurance.

In the example shown in Exhibit 8-11, the primary insurer wants a property per risk excess of loss treaty on commercial property policies insuring retail and wholesale occupancies and service businesses. The proposed treaty has a limit of $300,000 xs $100,000 each risk, each loss occurrence. The reinsurance underwriter obtains a listing of the primary insurer's subject premium applicable to each of the amounts of insurance ranges. If the primary insurer is unable to provide that information, underlying premiums can be estimated from a list of policy counts by amounts of insurance. Because such estimates are based on many assumptions, the exposure rate developed is less precise than if actual subject premium figures were available.

A reinsurer would also consider whether the primary insurer's policies insure multiple locations or if the policy limit is subject to a total loss from a single event. Additionally, a reinsurer would consider the loss exposure by cause of loss. For example, fire as a cause of loss may be considered to have greater loss potential than wind or other causes of loss because of the frequency and severity patterns of fire loss. These considerations form the basis of the retention factor shown in column (6). Column (7), the complement of column (6), shows the percentage of the average premium needed by the reinsurer to pay losses that exceed the retention. Column (8) shows the excess premium available to fund losses in excess of one retention (excess premium percentage × subject premium).

Modifications to the $401,092 total excess premium in Exhibit 8-11 may result from the following:

- Adequacy of underlying premiums
- Composition of policies subject to the treaty and their deductibles
- Quality of the primary insurer's underwriting
- Loading for the reinsurer's expenses, profit, and other considerations

EXHIBIT 8-11

Sisterdale Insurance Company

Calculation of Excess Premium Based on Policy Limit Profile

Amounts of Insurance Range Interval	(1) Policy Count	(2) Subject Premium	(3) Average Premium	(4) Average Amount of Insurance	(5) Average Percent Retained	(6) Retention Factor	(7) Excess Premium Percentage	(8) Excess Premium
$100,001–$125,000	980	$ 848,313	$ 865.63	$112,500	88.9%	99.7%	0.3%	$ 2,545
$125,001–$150,000	900	997,200	1,108.00	137,500	72.7	99.1	0.9	8,975
$150,001–$175,000	920	1,225,517	1,332.08	162,500	61.5	98.4	1.6	19,608
$175,001–$200,000	980	1,514,351	1,545.26	187,500	53.3	97.4	2.6	39,373
$200,001–$225,000	700	1,226,167	1,751.67	212,500	47.1	96.4	3.6	44,142
$225,001–$250,000	540	1,052,550	1,949.17	237,500	42.1	95.3	4.7	49,470
$250,001–$275,000	400	849,896	2,124.74	262,500	38.1	94.1	5.9	50,144
$275,001–$300,000	420	962,200	2,290.95	287,500	34.8	93.1	6.9	66,392
$300,001–$325,000	200	489,092	2,445.46	312,500	32.0	91.9	8.1	39,616
$325,001–$350,000	150	385,979	2,573.19	337,500	29.6	90.9	9.1	35,124
$350,001–$375,000	100	268,208	2,682.08	362,500	27.6	89.9	10.1	27,089
$375,001–$400,000	60	166,200	2,770.00	387,500	25.8	88.8	11.2	18,614
Totals	6,350	$9,985,673						$401,092

Adequacy of underlying premiums. A fundamental assumption of the first loss scale is that the underlying premiums charged by the primary insurer are sufficient to cover losses. Reinsurers should assess the adequacy of the primary insurer's rates when applying the first loss scale method.

Composition of the policies subject to the treaty and their deductibles. When applying the first loss scale method, the reinsurance underwriter must consider the composition of the policies subject to the treaty and their deductibles. For example, the reinsurance premium calculated from this method may be inadequate for highly protected loss exposures. Highly protected loss exposures are charged a relatively small underlying premium because of superior construction and extensive public and private loss protection systems. Because small losses on highly protected loss exposures are less likely than large losses, policyholders usually purchase underlying property policies with large deductibles. The underlying premiums for these policies are designed to cover unexpected but severe losses. Therefore, the first loss scale rates must be increased for the property per risk excess of loss coverage to make the rate commensurate with the liability assumed by the reinsurer. First loss scales have also been developed to reflect the loss characteristics of other types of loss exposures.

Quality of the primary insurer's underwriting. If the primary insurer's underwriter does not adequately investigate each loss exposure, loss frequency may increase, and the loss ratio may rise above expected levels. As with highly protected loss exposures, the reinsurer should increase the first loss scale rates to reflect poor quality underwriting and decrease the first loss scale rates to reflect high quality underwriting.

Loading for the reinsurer's expenses, profit, and other considerations. The reinsurer increases the first loss scale rate to provide for the following:

- A load to cover the reinsurer's operating expenses
- A load for profit and contingencies
- An additional surcharge if loss adjustment expenses are covered
- A catastrophe surcharge if the treaty covers multiple individual losses from one loss occurrence

These considerations are discussed more fully later in this chapter.

Price per Million

The second method of loss exposure rating for per risk excess of loss treaties is the price per million method. This method can be used when the underlying premium developed from the policies that exceed the attachment point is so small that the first loss scale method does not work well. Under the price per million method a reinsurer charges a set rate per million dollars of reinsurance limit purchased. The price per million rating method is used primarily for property facultative reinsurance when the attachment point of the treaty layer exceeds the largest loss that is likely to occur. This method can also be used to price property per risk excess of loss treaties when it is determined that the probability of a reinsurance loss is remote.

Experience Rating

In addition to exposure rating, reinsurers also use experience rating for property per risk excess of loss treaties. Experience rating provides an objective method of modifying the premium to reflect the quality of the primary insurer's underwriting, loss prevention, and claim handling capability. Experience rating uses the primary insurer's actual loss experience to develop the reinsurance rate. However, experience rating is appropriate only for those treaty layers that have enough losses to develop a credible rate. Experience rating involves the following four steps:

1. Collect required data
2. Trend losses
3. Develop the experience rate
4. Price the unused portion of the layer

Collect Required Data

The first step in experience rating is to collect the required data. For the reinsurance underwriter to accurately project future losses, the primary insurer must have enough losses in the treaty layer to provide credible data. If the primary insurer has little or no loss history in the treaty layer being priced, the reinsurer will need to rely on exposure rating.

Reinsurers need five to ten years of loss data from the primary insurer to use experience rating. Those loss data ideally will include all losses, not just those that exceeded the primary insurer's retention. Exhibit 8-12 shows a loss experience profile for Calloway Insurance Company.

The reinsurer must analyze the data to identify trends or loss experience irregularities. Based on the data in Exhibit 8-12, the reinsurer may conclude the following:

- Premium growth appears strong, perhaps too strong in a competitive insurance market. However, this growth may be due to an increase in policies sold at an inadequate price.
- Large losses are increasing, which may reflect lower underwriting standards, a change in the line guide, catastrophic losses, changes in territories, an increase in amounts of insurance, marketing changes, or a change in the distribution of loss exposures by protection class (insuring more unprotected or lightly protected loss exposures). The increase in large loss frequency is unlikely to simply be bad luck.
- Some claims have outstanding reserves. For example, the September 21, 2001, loss still has an outstanding reserve of $100,000. The reinsurer should investigate to determine (1) the probability of the loss settling within the reserve amount, (2) the quality of the claim adjusting, and (3) the possibility of legal actions that may result in extra-contractual obligations (ECO) or excess of policy limits (XPL) losses.

EXHIBIT 8-12

Loss Experience Profile for Calloway Insurance Company

Policy No.	Claim No.	Date of Loss	Paid	Outstanding Reserve	Total Incurred Losses
		1/1/99 – 12/31/99			
F10056	CF2035	2/13/99	$136,250	$ 0	$136,250
F10123	CF2173	4/21/99	172,400	0	172,400
H13285	PF1929	8/3/99	167,123	0	167,123
F10255	CF2102	11/30/99	385,250	0	385,250
		1/1/00 – 12/31/00			
F10325	CF2211	1/21/00	$183,500	$ 0	$183,500
F10681	CF2444	5/12/00	127,850	0	127,850
F12320	CF2589	8/22/00	386,750	0	386,750
H23450	PF2759	12/18/00	261,340	0	261,340
		1/1/01 – 12/31/01			
H23451	PF2825	3/2/01	$398,450	$ 0	$398,450
H24545	PF3021	8/21/01	141,250	0	141,250
F14451	CF3121	9/21/01	321,300	100,000	421,300
H25876	PF3124	10/12/01	276,250	0	276,250
F15135	CF3232	12/27/01	319,917	0	319,917
		1/1/02 – 12/31/02			
H25897	PF3135	5/23/02	$286,520	$ 0	$286,520
F14876	CF3357	7/21/02	312,750	0	312,750
H25914	PF3137	9/16/02	357,850	0	357,850
F16253	CF3257	11/13/02	414,250	0	414,250
H30034	PF3286	12/23/02	137,430	0	137,430
		1/1/03 – 12/31/03			
H33335	PF3456	2/16/03	$191,250	$ 0	$191,250
F16758	CF3373	3/11/03	345,112	5,000	350,112
F18182	CF3456	4/21/03	432,325	75,000	507,325
F19287	CF3578	6/7/03	278,750	0	278,750
H35768	PF3566	8/24/03	298,345	0	298,345
H37379	PF3634	9/27/03	231,890	3,500	235,390
F24345	CF3819	10/2/03	0	135,000	135,000

	Subject Earned Premium	Total Incurred Losses	Unadjusted Loss Cost
1999	$ 35,214,587	$ 861,023	2.45%
2000	36,459,781	959,440	2.63%
2001	38,588,396	1,557,167	4.04%
2002	40,721,340	1,508,800	3.71%
2003	43,938,000	1,996,172	4.54%
Total	$194,922,104	$6,882,602	3.53%

Trend Losses

The second step in experience rating is to trend the losses. Trending adjusts losses to what they would have been during the proposed treaty period and recognizes the effects of inflation on the costs to repair or replace damaged properties.

Trend factors should reflect the construction costs for the types of structures being reinsured. For losses on dwellings, a construction cost index may be used. For losses on commercial structures, the index should measure construction costs of commercial buildings. An example of such an index is shown in Exhibit 8-13.

EXHIBIT 8-13

Construction Costs Trends Index for Commercial Buildings

Year	Rate Index
1999	1.132
2000	1.076
2001	1.035
2002	1.017
2003	1.000

Exhibit 8-14 shows the losses calculated by applying the construction cost trends index in Exhibit 8-13 to the total incurred losses reported in Exhibit 8-12 and capping losses at the treaty reinsurance limit. The trended losses in Exhibit 8-14 reflect 2003 construction costs, so a further adjustment would be needed to reflect construction costs in a future proposed treaty term.

To calculate the ultimate treaty loss cost, the reinsurer divides losses by premiums. So, if the losses are trended, premiums must also be trended to adjust for changes in the primary insurer's rate level, and increases in loss exposure due to the effects of inflation on the value of property and the amount of coverage needed. A rate change index reflects the primary insurer's effective rate changes over the treaty's term.

The trended rate level reflects the rate that would currently be charged for the loss exposures insured during the experience period, just as the trended losses represent the amounts of the individual losses if they were currently incurred. To develop the rate change index, the reinsurer must receive effective rate change information from the primary insurer. Exhibit 8-15 shows a rate change index for Calloway Insurance Company.

EXHIBIT 8-14
Loss Experience Profile Trending for Calloway Insurance Company

Claim No.	Total Incurred Losses	Index	Indexed Losses	Trended Losses $300,000 xs $100,000
		1/1/99 to 12/31/99		
CF2035	$136,250	1.132	$154,235	$ 54,235
CF2173	172,400	1.132	195,157	95,157
PF1929	167,123	1.132	189,183	89,183
CF2102	385,250	1.132	436,103	300,000
	Total Excess Losses			$ 538,575
		1/1/00 to 12/31/00		
CF2211	$183,500	1.076	$197,446	$ 97,446
CF2444	127,850	1.076	137,567	37,567
CF2589	386,750	1.076	416,143	300,000
PF2759	261,340	1.076	281,202	181,202
	Total Excess Losses			$ 616,215
		1/1/01 to 12/31/01		
PF2825	$398,450	1.035	$412,396	$ 300,000
PF3021	141,250	1.035	146,194	46,194
CF3121	421,300	1.035	436,046	300,000
PF3124	276,250	1.035	285,919	185,919
CF3232	319,917	1.035	331,114	231,114
	Total Excess Losses			$1,063,277
		1/1/02 to 12/31/02		
PF3135	$286,520	1.017	$291,391	$ 91,391
CF3357	312,750	1.017	318,067	218,067
PF3137	357,850	1.017	363,933	263,933
CF3257	414,250	1.017	421,292	300,000
PF3286	137,430	1.017	139,766	39,776
	Total Excess Losses			$1,013,167
		1/1/03 to 12/31/03		
PF3456	$191,250	1.000	$191,250	$91,250
CF3373	350,112	1.000	350,112	250,112
CF3456	507,325	1.000	507,325	300,000
CF3578	278,750	1.000	278,750	178,750
PF3566	298,345	1.000	298,345	198,345
PF3634	235,390	1.000	235,390	135,390
CF3819	135,000	1.000	135,000	35,000
	Total Excess Losses			$1,188,847

EXHIBIT 8-15

Calloway Insurance Company Rate Change Index

Year	Rate Index
1999	0.951
2000	0.801
2001	0.762
2002	0.841
2003	1.000

Exhibit 8-16 displays the trended earned premium for Calloway Insurance Company. The subject earned premium from Exhibit 8-12 is multiplied by the rate change index in Exhibit 8-15 to determine the trended premium.

In some policies, the premium automatically increases with inflation because the value of an exposure unit increases with inflation. However, a trend factor is still necessary if losses are increasing faster than premiums.

Trended premiums indicate the premiums in current dollars to allow a better comparison between years. In Exhibit 8-16, Calloway's trended premium reflects more dramatic growth in 2002 and 2003 than the nontrended premiums suggest, which highlights the advantage of trending.

EXHIBIT 8-16

Calloway Insurance Company Trended Earned Premium

Year	Subject Earned Premium	Rate Index	Trended Premium
1999	$35,214,587	0.951	$33,489,072
2000	36,459,781	0.801	29,204,285
2001	38,588,396	0.762	29,404,358
2002	40,721,340	0.841	34,246,647
2003	43,938,000	1.000	43,938,000

Develop the Experience Rate

The third step in experience rating is to develop the experience rate. The number of years of experience used in the experience rate formula may be subject to negotiation. However, five to ten years is typical. If the policies subject to the treaty suffer catastrophic loss, the rating period may be extended to as many as fifteen years.

The experience rate is calculated as follows:

Experience rate = Trended losses ÷ Trended premium.

Exhibit 8-17 shows the experience rate calculation using the information developed in Exhibits 8-12 through 8-16.

The most recent three-year experience rate (3.035 percent) is higher than the five-year average (2.596 percent). The difference may indicate that the primary insurer is sacrificing its underwriting and pricing standards in its pursuit of premium growth. Based on that calculation, the reinsurer may anticipate an experience rate for the coming year of 2.5 percent to 3.5 percent, unless the primary insurer tightens underwriting and pricing requirements for the coming year. The reinsurer would not offer a lower reinsurance rate unless the treaty had generated profits in prior years or the reinsurer believed that a hard market would allow the primary insurer to increase insurance rates.

In this example, the reinsurance underwriter would probably select an experience rate based on the most recent three years of experience (3.035 percent).

EXHIBIT 8-17

Calloway Insurance Company Experience Rating Work Sheet

Year	(1) Trended Losses[1]	(2) Trended Premium[2]	(3) Experience Rate[3]
1999	$ 538,575	$ 33,489,072	1.608%
2000	616,215	29,204,285	2.110%
2001	1,063,227	29,404,358	3.616%
2002	1,013,167	34,246,647	2.958%
2003	1,188,847	43,938,000	2.706%
Total	$4,420,031	$170,282,362	2.596%
2001-2003 Total	$3,265,241	$107,589,005	3.035%

Notes:

[1] From Exhibit 8-14
[2] From Exhibit 8-16
[3] Column (1) ÷ Column (2)

Price the Unused Portion of the Layer

The fourth step in experience rating is to price the unused portion of the layer. Commonly, recent loss experience does not involve the entire treaty layer. For example, if the maximum loss recently experienced is $335,000 and the layer to be priced is $250,000 xs $250,000, the treaty limit between $335,000 and $500,000 would be referred to as the "unused limit." If the reinsurer used only experience rating and did not add a premium for the unused limit, that portion of the limit would be provided without charge to the primary insurer. Therefore, the reinsurer frequently adds a charge for the unused limit using exposure rating. If underlying policies with limits within the layer to be priced are being analyzed, that charge can be determined by a first loss scale method. If the primary insurer sells no policies with limits within the layer, the reinsurer may use the price per million method.

Establishing the Reinsurance Rate

The experience and exposure rating methods develop a rate that reflects only the costs associated with losses expected during the rating period, the **loss cost rate**. The loss cost rate must be increased to reflect the following factors:

- Internal expenses
- Retrocessional expenses
- Profit and contingencies
- Loss adjustment expenses
- Catastrophe charge

Loss cost rate
The rate that reflects only the costs associated with losses expected during the rating period.

Internal expenses. The reinsurer's internal expenses as a percentage of its written premiums typically range from about 1.7 percent to more than 6 percent. If a reinsurance intermediary is involved, the cost of brokerage must be added. Because reinsurers with lower internal expenses have a competitive advantage, the internal expenses used in establishing the reinsurance rate should reflect only those expenses incurred in reinsuring loss exposures similar to those being rated. For example, the expense of providing facultative reinsurance should not be included. If coverage is provided for a high layer of insurance with no losses expected, reinsurer loss adjustment expenses are not appropriate, nor are underwriting audit expenses. On the other hand, if the reinsurer expects multiple losses that involve the claim department and claim and underwriting audits, the reinsurer should load the reinsurance rate for such expenses.

Retrocessional expenses. Most reinsurers do not purchase property per risk excess of loss retrocessional coverage. However, when retrocessional coverage is purchased, the retrocessionaire's rate is applied to the premium charged for the treaty being rated. Those expenses must be added to the loss cost rate of the treaty being rated.

Profit and contingencies. A loading must be added for the reinsurer's profit and for any contingencies. Management should establish a loading of a predetermined percentage. The loading is generally in the 5 percent to 10 percent range and varies according to reinsurance market conditions.

Loss adjustment expenses. If loss adjustment expenses are included, an appropriate charge is added to reflect the reinsurer's expenses above the loss cost.

Catastrophe charge. Commonly, the catastrophe loss exposure in a property per risk excess of loss treaty is limited by incorporating a per loss occurrence limit. Usually, that limit is not greater than two or three times the per risk limit.

An accumulation of losses from one loss occurrence should be reinsured under a catastrophe treaty. However, if the property per risk excess of loss treaty is exposed to catastrophes, the reinsurance underwriter should evaluate the adequacy of the experience rate and add a charge suitable for the loss exposure.

The following illustrates the calculation of a final reinsurance rate:

Estimated Subject Premium	$10,000,000
Loss Cost Rate	0.035
Unused Limits Charge	0.007
Loadings (as a % of Reinsurance Premium):	
Internal Expense	0.037
Brokerage	0.050
Retrocessional Expense	0.073
Profit and Contingencies	0.050
Loss Adjustment Expenses	if applicable
Catastrophe Charge	if applicable

$$
\begin{aligned}
\text{Total loss cost} &= \text{Estimated subject premium} \times (\text{loss cost rate} + \text{unused limits charge}) \\
&= \$10{,}000{,}000 \times (0.035 + 0.007) \\
&= \$420{,}000.
\end{aligned}
$$

$$
\begin{aligned}
\text{Reinsurance premium} &= \text{Total loss cost} \div (1 - \text{the sum of the loadings}) \\
&= \$420{,}000 \div [1 - (0.037 + 0.050 + 0.073 + 0.050)] \\
&= \$420{,}000 \div 0.79 \\
&= \$531{,}646.
\end{aligned}
$$

In this illustration, the reinsurer would charge a reinsurance premium of $531,646 based on the estimated subject premium of $10 million and the premium is stated as a percentage of the subject premium, or 5.3 percent.

Selecting earned or written premiums as the subject premium base is negotiable. Generally, if the coverage is on a losses occurring basis, the reinsurance rate is based on earned premiums because the reinsurer assumes liability for losses occurring under any policies in force as of the treaty's effective date and time. If the coverage is on a risks attaching basis, the reinsurance rate is based on written premiums because the reinsurer assumes liability for losses occurring under policies issued or renewed on or after the treaty's effective date. The premium base could also be written premiums plus the unearned premium reserve at the beginning of the treaty period. The premium base ultimately selected is the one that the parties to the treaty agree best reflects the loss exposures covered.

Flat Rated Covers

Flat rate
A fixed rate that is not adjusted for losses occurring under the reinsurance treaty and that is applied to the primary insurer's prospective premiums.

Once the reinsurance rate is determined, that rate can be expressed as a flat rate. A **flat rate** (or prospective rate) is a fixed rate that is not adjusted for losses occurring under the reinsurance treaty and that is applied to the primary insurer's prospective premiums. Property per risk excess of loss treaties that have a fixed rate applying for the treaty term are often referred to as flat rated covers. The reinsurance rate is expressed as a percentage of subject premium. Because the subject premium is unknown, the primary insurer reports the actual subject premium at the end of the treaty period or at defined intervals. The amount of the reinsurance premium ultimately paid to the reinsurer(s) is determined once the primary insurer's final actual subject premium becomes known. The treaty usually requires a deposit premium and a minimum premium.

Loss Rated Covers

Loss rate
A rate that is determined from the actual losses sustained under a reinsurance treaty.

An alternative to a flat rate is a **loss rate**, in which the final rate is determined from the actual losses sustained under the treaty. A loss rated cover usually has three rates: a provisional rate, a minimum rate, and a maximum rate.

The provisional rate is generally set close to the reinsurance rate for the latest treaty term, or the loss cost rate after the loadings. That provisional rate is adjusted retrospectively based on the loss experience actually realized during the treaty term. The retrospective rate adjustment includes a provision for the reinsurer's profit, expenses, and contingencies, subject to the maximum and minimum rates.

The minimum and maximum rates are selected based upon the characteristics of the layer being rated, such as the size of the layer, the expected volatility of the loss experience, the indicated exposure rate, and administrative costs. For example, the minimum rate may be set at 50 percent of the provisional rate, and the maximum rate may be set at two to three times the provisional rate. The larger the layer, the wider the spread required between the minimum and maximum rates because a large loss during the treaty term will significantly affect the reinsurance rates charged.

The minimum rate includes an insurance charge that compensates the reinsurer for the possibility that losses may exceed the losses expected in the maximum rate *less* a credit for the possibility that actual losses may be less than the losses expected in the minimum rate.

Commonly, the minimum rate is a percentage of the exposure rate. For example, the minimum rate may be 40 percent of the exposure rate. Therefore, the primary insurer could potentially benefit from a 60 percent reduction in the exposure rate as a reward for high quality underwriting and the adequacy of underlying premiums. The maximum rate should also relate to the exposure rate. If the exposure rate is credible, the maximum rate should not be less than the exposure rate. When setting a maximum rate, the reinsurance underwriter must consider the adequacy of the exposure rate and the volatility of the loss experience. The maximum rate should help the reinsurer collect adequate premium in an adverse loss year. Therefore, the reinsurance underwriter may set the maximum rate at 125 to 150 percent of the exposure rate, or higher, particularly if the treaty provides a large reinsurance limit and the resulting loss experience is expected to be volatile.

SUMMARY

Property per risk excess of loss reinsurance covers property loss exposures and applies separately to *each loss* occurring to *each risk*. Primary insurers are indemnified for losses that exceed the property per risk excess of loss treaty's attachment point up to the treaty's reinsurance limit. Property per risk excess of loss reinsurance can be purchased on either a facultative or a treaty basis.

Primary insurers use property per risk of loss treaties to:

- Increase large line capacity
- Stabilize loss experience

Property per risk excess of loss reinsurance can be used alone or in conjunction with pro rata reinsurance, catastrophe excess of loss reinsurance, or property per risk excess of loss on a facultative basis.

Some clauses are common to all types of excess of loss treaties. This chapter describes the following clauses that apply to excess of loss treaties in general and to property per risk excess of loss treaties in particular:

- *Retention and limits clause*. The retention and limits clause for a property per risk excess of loss treaty usually specifies that the retention and reinsurance limit apply to any one risk and for each loss occurrence.
- *Loss notices and settlements clause*. The loss notices and settlements clause requires the primary insurer to notify the reinsurer of any loss amount that exceeds or is likely to exceed the primary insurer's retention.
- *Reinsurance premium clause*. The reinsurance premium clause establishes exactly what the premium will be for the coverage provided.
- *Net retained lines clause*. The net retained lines clause specifies that the reinsurance coverage applies only to the primary insurer's net retention.
- *Ultimate net loss clause*. The ultimate net loss clause specifies the loss amount against which the retention and reinsurance limit apply.
- *Pools, associations, and syndicates exclusion clause*. The pools, associations, and syndicates clause excludes from coverage any liability emanating from the primary insurer's participation, directly or indirectly, through pools, associations, and syndicates.
- *Total insured value exclusion clause*. The total insured value clause excludes very large loss exposures from automatic coverage.

Property per risk excess of loss treaties are priced using two approaches:

- Exposure rating
- Experience rating

Exposure rating considers the amount of liability inherent in the type of business covered by the treaty being priced. Experience rating considers the primary insurer's loss experience in the business covered by the treaty being priced. Reinsurers use both approaches and select the reinsurance rate that can be best justified. Regardless of the approach used to determine the projected costs associated with losses, the reinsurance rate must be adjusted to reflect the following factors:

- Operating expenses
- Retrocessional expenses
- Profits and contingencies
- Loss adjustment expenses
- Catastrophe charge

Reinsurers often use the reinsurance rate as a flat rate and apply it to the subject premium through the course of the treaty term (flat rated covers). Alternatively, the reinsurer uses a provisional rate, which is subsequently adjusted to reflect the actual loss experience under the treaty (loss rated covers).

The next chapter examines the purpose, operation, and pricing of casualty excess of loss treaties.

Chapter 9

Direct Your Learning

Casualty Excess of Loss Treaties

After learning the content of this chapter, you should be able to:

- Explain the purpose and operation of casualty excess of loss treaties.
- Explain the purpose and operation of common clauses modified for use in casualty excess of loss treaties.
- Explain the purpose and operation of clauses designed or adapted for casualty excess of loss treaties.
- Explain the approaches to casualty excess of loss treaty pricing.

OUTLINE

Overview of Casualty Excess of Loss Treaties

Common Clauses Modified for Use in Casualty Excess of Loss Treaties

Clauses Designed or Adapted for Casualty Excess of Loss Treaties

Casualty Excess of Loss Treaty Pricing

Summary

Develop Your Perspective

What are the main topics covered in the chapter?

This chapter describes the operation, contractual clauses, and the methods for pricing casualty excess of loss treaties.

Identify the purpose and operation of casualty excess of loss reinsurance.

- What functions does a casualty excess of loss treaty serve for a primary insurer?
- What are the two approaches used to price casualty excess of loss treaties?

Why is it important to learn about these topics?

Casualty excess of loss treaties are used to limit the primary insurer's exposure to losses arising out of a single occurrence. The ability to understand, analyze, and evaluate casualty excess of loss treaties is important to enable you to determine whether they are helping your company or client-insurer achieve its objectives.

Review a casualty excess of loss treaty.

- How are common clauses modified for use in property per risk excess of loss treaties?
- What clauses are designed specifically for casualty excess of loss treaties and how do they operate?

How can you use what you will learn?

Evaluate one of your company's or client-insurer's casualty excess of loss treaties.

- Does this casualty excess of loss treaty address the needs of your company or client-insurer?
- Does this casualty excess of loss treaty provide sufficient large line capacity, adequate loss stability from losses that accumulate from one occurrence, and the catastrophe protection needed by your company or client-insurer?

Chapter 9
Casualty Excess of Loss Treaties

Casualty excess of loss reinsurance covers losses arising out of the primary insurer's underlying casualty insurance policies. Casualty insurance is a type of insurance that provides coverage for bodily injury or property damage caused by the underlying insured's negligence. It includes liability insurance and other types of insurance that regulators historically did not allow to be categorized as either fire or marine insurance, such as automobile liability, general liability, employers liability, professional liability, errors and omissions insurance, aviation insurance, workers' compensation, plate glass insurance, and crime insurance. This chapter explains the following:

- How casualty excess of loss treaties operate
- How primary insurers use casualty excess of loss treaties to meet their reinsurance needs
- How casualty excess of loss treaties fit into a reinsurance program
- How common clauses are modified for use in casualty excess of loss treaties
- How clauses designed or adapted for casualty excess of loss treaties operate
- How casualty excess of loss treaties are priced

Casualty excess of loss reinsurance
A type of excess of loss reinsurance that covers losses arising out of the primary insurer's underlying casualty insurance policies.

OVERVIEW OF CASUALTY EXCESS OF LOSS TREATIES

Primary insurers purchase casualty excess of loss treaties to protect themselves from excessive liabilities arising from their underlying casualty insurance policies. Although the operation of casualty excess of loss reinsurance is practically identical to that of property per risk excess of loss reinsurance, the underlying characteristics of liability losses relative to property losses make these very different types of reinsurance. Liability losses involve bodily injury or property damage claims payable by the underlying insured to a third party. Liability losses often take time to manifest and settle, resulting in a significant delay in claim resolution. In contrast, property losses involve damage, destruction, taking, or loss of use of the insured's property. These first party losses are typically settled quickly because the insured usually knows the loss has occurred and the value of property losses is generally easy to ascertain. Because of these underlying differences between liability and property losses, the treaty clauses and pricing of casualty excess of loss reinsurance vary significantly from those of property per risk excess of loss reinsurance.

Functions of Casualty Excess of Loss Treaties

Casualty excess of loss treaties serve the following three functions for primary insurers:

1. Increase large line capacity
2. Stabilize loss experience
3. Provide catastrophe protection

Increase Large Line Capacity

Casualty excess of loss treaties enable primary insurers to issue policies with limits of liability that are larger than would otherwise be possible or acceptable. Large line capacity enables primary insurers with limited financial resources to compete more effectively in the marketplace by allowing them to provide coverage limits that underlying insureds need.

Stabilize Loss Experience

Casualty excess of loss treaties reduce the fluctuation in the primary insurer's loss experience by limiting the amount of loss sustained to the amount retained under the treaty. Stabilization of loss experience aids financial planning, supports growth, and can strengthen investors' confidence in the primary insurer.

Provide Catastrophe Protection

Clash covers, casualty excess of loss reinsurance treaties with high attachment points, protect primary insurers from the financial consequences of a single occurrence causing multiple losses under one policy or several policies. This catastrophe protection protects the primary insurer's earnings and policyholders' surplus.

Casualty Excess of Loss Treaties as Part of a Reinsurance Program

Casualty excess of loss reinsurance can be provided on a per policy basis or on a per occurrence basis. When provided on a per policy basis, the attachment point and reinsurance limit apply to losses arising from each policy. When provided on a per occurrence basis, the attachment point and reinsurance limit apply to losses arising from any one occurrence, regardless of the number of insureds, policies, or coverages involved. Because most casualty excess of loss treaties are on a per occurrence basis, this chapter focuses on that basis.

Excess of loss treaties are usually structured in layers. Multiple layers are used to increase the participation of reinsurers in the primary insurer's reinsurance program. The primary insurer may have a significant retention so the reinsurer of the first layer does not expect any losses during the treaty term. However, some excess of loss treaties are designed with a low attachment point so that the treaty is subject to losses during the treaty term. The reinsurance that applies to layers in which frequent losses are expected is called working cover. For example, the primary insurer may anticipate a significant number of losses will occur in its $50,000 xs $50,000 and $100,000 xs $100,000 layers. Working cover layers are priced to reflect the expected loss frequency. The layer between those reinsured by the working cover and the largest liability coverage limit offered by the primary insurer is called the policy-exposed layer.

Primary insurers may purchase clash cover to provide reinsurance coverage beyond the policy-exposed layer. Clash cover can provide coverage for the following:

- Single occurrences affecting multiple insureds or multiple types of insurance
- Extra-contractual obligations (ECO)
- Excess of policy limits (XPL) losses
- Excessive loss adjustment expenses

COMMON CLAUSES MODIFIED FOR USE IN CASUALTY EXCESS OF LOSS TREATIES

Some common clauses are modified for use in casualty excess of loss treaties. These clauses include:

- Reinsuring clause
- Definitions clause

Reinsuring Clause

As in property per risk excess of loss treaties, the reinsuring clause in a casualty excess of loss treaty specifies what types of insurance are covered under the treaty. Casualty excess of loss reinsurance is used to reinsure underlying casualty policies. Most casualty policies are liability policies that respond to bodily injury and property damage claims from third parties. Coverage for an underlying liability policy may be on either an occurrence or claims-made basis.

A liability policy issued on an occurrence basis responds to bodily injury and property damage that occur during the policy period. This occurrence trigger is the traditional approach used in liability policies to identify which primary insurance policy applies to a claim. A liability policy issued on a claims-made basis responds to bodily injury and property damage for those claims first made against the underlying insured during the policy period. This claims-made trigger is the approach used in types of liability insurance that have significant delays in claim reporting and settlement (long-tail liability), such as professional liability and directors and officers liability. The claims-made trigger makes identifying which primary insurance policy applies to a claim easier because the applicable policy is the one in force when the claim is first made. Liability policies issued on a claims-made basis have features that must be addressed in the casualty excess of loss treaty covering them. These features are usually addressed in the reinsuring clause. Three features of underlying claims-made policies that should be addressed in the reinsurance covering those claims-made policies include the following:

- Retroactive date
- Prior acts coverage
- Extended reporting period

Retroactive date
The date on or after which bodily injury or property damage must occur in order to be covered.

Retroactive date. The **retroactive date** is the date on or after which bodily injury or property damage must occur in order to be covered. A claims-made policy may contain no retroactive date, a retroactive date that is the same as the policy inception date, or a retroactive date that is before the policy inception date. Claims-made policies may appear to limit the primary insurer's exposure to long-tail liability. However, primary insurers are still exposed to long-tail liability for several reasons. If a claims-made policy has no retroactive date, it covers any claim first made against the underlying insured during the policy's term regardless of the occurrence date. If a claims-made policy has been in force for many years and has the original retroactive date, claims made during the current policy period for injury or damage that occurred during those prior policy periods would be covered.

Prior acts coverage
An extension of coverage for claims that would otherwise not be covered because they occurred prior to the retroactive date of the current claims-made policy and are not covered by the prior claims-made policy.

Prior acts coverage. **Prior acts coverage** is an extension of coverage for claims that would otherwise not be covered because they occurred prior to the retroactive date of the current claims-made policy and are not covered by the prior claims-made policy. For example, an insured that is moving its insurance coverage from one primary insurer to another may not be able to get the replacement insurer to keep the original retroactive date, therefore creating a coverage gap. Claims made during the new policy period that occurred prior to the new retroactive date would not be covered by either policy.

Extended reporting period
An additional period following the expiration of a claims-made policy during which the expired policy covers claims made against the insured, provided the injury occurred on or after the retroactive date (if any) and before policy expiration.

Extended reporting period. An **extended reporting period** is an additional period following the expiration of a claims-made policy during which the expired policy covers claims made against the insured, provided the injury occurred on or after the retroactive date (if any) and before policy expiration. The length of an extended reporting period can vary from months to years and in some cases is unlimited. If prior acts coverage or extended reporting periods are available under the underlying policies, the excess of loss treaty can cover those losses by stating that any claims made under such coverages will be covered under the treaty. The sample reinsuring clause in Exhibit 9-1 includes wording for prior acts coverage and extended reporting periods.

> **EXHIBIT 9-1**
>
> **Reinsuring Clause**
>
> A. By this Contract the Reinsurer agrees to reinsure the excess liability that may accrue to the Company under its policies, contracts, and binders of insurance or reinsurance (hereinafter called "policies") in force at the effective date hereof or issued or renewed on or after that date and classified by the Company as _____Casualty Insurance_____, subject to the terms, conditions, and limitations hereinafter set forth.
>
> B. As respects policies written on a claims-made basis, the Company may issue prior acts coverage (but for policy limits no greater than those the insured purchased from its immediately preceding carrier) and extended reporting coverage. Any claim under an extended reporting coverage provision or endorsement shall be deemed to have been reported on the day the original policy expired or was canceled. Premium, if any, for such extended reporting coverage period shall be considered fully earned by the Reinsurer on the last full day the original policy was in force.

Definitions Clause

An important definition to include in the definitions clause of a casualty excess of loss treaty is occurrence. The definition of occurrence used depends on the underlying coverage being reinsured. The following have occurrence definitions tailored to them:

- Products and completed operations coverage
- Occupational disease coverage
- Other losses coverage

Occurrence Definition for Products and Completed Operations Coverage

For products and completed operations coverage, the primary insurer may consider as one occurrence the accumulation of all injury or damage that occurs during a policy period to the same insured and that results from a single cause of loss. That definition of occurrence assumes that the single cause of loss resulted from an error in manufacturing the product or performing the operation that caused injury or damage. The injury or damage may occur at any time after the single act that created the bodily injury or property damage.

For example, an animal feed manufacturer allows the feed mixture to spoil and then packages and ships the poisonous feed to many cattle feedlots. Cattle become sick or die because of the improperly manufactured feed. When making a casualty excess of loss treaty claim, the feed manufacturer's insurer considers all the losses from the cattle feedlots to be one occurrence. The single act of packaging the spoiled feed resulted in many individual losses over a wide geographic area.

The sample definitions clause shown in Exhibit 9-2 contains an occurrence definition providing that all products and completed operations losses will be treated as one occurrence if they arise from the same "causative agency" during the same policy period. The date of loss is the beginning of the policy period.

EXHIBIT 9-2

Definitions Clause (Occurrence Definition for Products and Completed Operations Coverage)

A. "Occurrence" as used herein is defined as an accident or occurrence or a series of accidents or occurrences arising out of or caused by one event, except that:

1. As respects policies where the Company's limit of liability for Products and Completed Operations coverages is determined on the basis of the insured's aggregate losses during a policy period, all such losses proceeding from or traceable to the same causative agency shall, at the Company's option, be deemed to have been caused by one occurrence with a date of loss at the beginning of the policy period. Each renewal or annual anniversary date of the policy involved shall be deemed the beginning of a new policy period.

2. As respects Workers' Compensation and Employers Liability policies, each occupational or industrial disease case contracted by an employee of an insured shall be deemed to have been caused by a separate occurrence with a date of loss on:

   a. The date of disability for which compensation is payable if the case is compensable under the Workers' Compensation Law;

   b. The date disability due to the disease actually began if the case is not compensable under the Workers' Compensation Law;

   c. The date of cessation of employment if claim is made after employment has ceased.

3. As respects claims-made policies, an occurrence shall be deemed to have a date of loss on the date the loss is reported and/or claim is made under the original policy, except as provided in subparagraph 4 below. If the Company's losses arising out of a single occurrence are a result of more than one claim against a single insured, the Company may combine all such losses in a single occurrence, which shall be deemed to have a date of loss on the date the loss is first reported and/or claim is made under the policy or policies involved, except as provided in subparagraph 4 below.

4. As respects any extended reporting coverage provisions or endorsements under claims-made policies subject hereto, claims made against and/or reported to the Company during the extended reporting coverage period shall be deemed to have been reported on the last full day of the applicable policy period.

> B. "Loss adjustment expense" means all costs and expenses allocable to a specific claim that are incurred by the Company in the investigation, appraisal, adjustment, settlement, litigation, defense, or appeal of a specific claim, including court costs and costs of supersedeas and appeal bonds, and including 1) pre-judgment interest, unless included as part of the award or judgment; 2) post-judgment interest; and 3) declaratory judgment expense and any other legal expenses and costs incurred in connection with coverage questions and legal actions connected thereto.
>
> Loss adjustment expense does not include employee salaries, office expenses, and other overhead expenses.

Occurrence Definition for Occupational Disease Coverage

When workers' compensation policies are reinsured, the occurrence definition should address occupational disease. Occupational disease often involves more than one employee and potentially many employees. Therefore, the occurrence definition should specify whether the loss for each affected employee is considered a separate occurrence or whether the losses for all affected employees are considered one occurrence. The sample definitions clause in Exhibit 9-3 contains an occurrence definition that treats the loss for all employees as one occurrence. Other definitions clauses may specify that a separate retention and limit apply to the loss for each employee.

The date of loss for injuries sustained by an employee in the course of employment can be defined as the date of disability for which compensation is payable if covered by workers' compensation law, the date disability actually began if not covered by workers' compensation law, or the date of cessation of employment if the claim is made after employment has ended.

If losses for all affected employees are considered one occurrence, the occurrence definition limits that occurrence to all cases of occupational disease occurring under the same policy and during the same policy period. The date of loss for the occurrence is the first day of the policy period.

> ### EXHIBIT 9-3
>
> ### Definitions Clause (Occurrence Definition for Occupational Disease Coverage)
>
> "Occurrence" as used herein is defined as an accident or occurrence or a series of accidents or occurrences arising out of or caused by one event, except that as respects Workers' Compensation and Employers Liability policies, all occupational or industrial disease cases proceeding from or traceable to the same causative agency and assignable by the Company to the same policy and the same policy period shall be deemed to have been caused by one occurrence commencing at the beginning of the policy period. Each renewal or annual anniversary date of the policy involved shall be deemed the beginning of a new policy period.

Occurrence Definition for Other Losses Coverage

The occurrence definition for loss coverage other than for products and completed operations or occupational diseases may allow the primary insurer to accumulate all losses for injury or damage that occur during a continuous twelve-month period from the same event and to declare them as one occurrence. By using this definition, the primary insurer and reinsurer avoid arguments about the number of occurrences. For example, a sand and gravel pit operator uses dynamite over several months. Cracks appear in the foundations of nearby buildings. Determining which blast caused the damage is not necessary when the occurrence definition allows damages to be accumulated. Exhibit 9-4 shows an example of a definitions clause that may be used for this type of occurrence definition.

EXHIBIT 9-4

Definitions Clause (Occurrence Definition for Other Losses Coverage)

As respects third-party liability insurances other than those written and rated by the Reinsured as Products Liability and/or Completed Operations Liability, said term, at the option of the Reinsured, shall also mean all injuries or damage that occur during any one continuous period of twelve months and that result in claims against the same insured as defined in the original policies of the Reinsured, resulting from:

1. Infection, contagion, poisoning, or contamination proceeding from, or traceable to, the same causative agency; or

2. A series of operations, events, or occurrences arising out of operations at one specific site and that cannot be attributed to any single one of such operations, events, or occurrences, but rather to the cumulative effect of same.

CLAUSES DESIGNED OR ADAPTED FOR CASUALTY EXCESS OF LOSS TREATIES

The clauses in casualty excess of loss treaties tend to be more complex than those in property per risk excess of loss treaties because casualty excess of loss treaties deal with liability claims, which require settlement with third-party claimants. The clauses need to be specific enough to address standard coverage issues, and general enough to address the coverage distortions that can result when courts require coverage under policies when none was intended. The clauses that are designed or adapted for casualty excess of loss treaties include:

- Retention and limits clause
- Reinstatement clause
- Claims and loss adjustment expense clause

- Declaratory judgment expense clause
- Sunset and sunrise clauses
- Commutation clause

Retention and Limits Clause

Retention and limits clauses establish the amount of the primary insurer's retention and the reinsurer's limit of liability. The retention and limits clause for casualty excess of loss treaties should address the possibility of a single occurrence involving multiple insureds, multiple policies, or multiple coverages. Losses from multiple insureds could occur, for example, when the same insurer provides coverage for both the general contractor and the architect on a building that collapsed during construction. Losses from multiple policies could occur, for example, when the same insurer covers several automobiles involved in the same accident. Losses from multiple policies over a period of time could occur, for example, when an insured uses defective cement for several years to build a dam that eventually crumbled. If the cement manufacturer's general liability policy had renewed several times during the dam's construction, a claim would likely be made against each policy that had been in effect. Losses from multiple coverages occur, for example, when an insured automobile is involved in an at-fault accident causing bodily injury and property damage.

The sample retention and limits clause in Exhibit 9-5 addresses multiple insureds, multiple policies, and multiple coverages involved in a single occurrence. The sample clause's definitions of retention and reinsurance limit include all of the losses sustained by the primary insurer as the result of one occurrence. Stating the retention and reinsurance limit in this manner allows the primary insurer to more easily establish the maximum loss it can sustain in a single occurrence, rather than doing so under each policy or coverage part triggered by an occurrence.

EXHIBIT 9-5

Retention and Limits Clause

The Company shall retain and be liable for the first $ 500,000 of ultimate net loss (whether involving any one or any combination of the classes of business covered hereunder, regardless of the number of policies under which such loss is payable or the number of different interests insured) arising out of each occurrence. The Reinsurer shall then be liable for the amount by which such ultimate net loss exceeds the Company's retention, but the liability of the Reinsurer shall not exceed $ 1,000,000 as respects any one occurrence.

Reinstatement Clause

Although a casualty excess of loss treaty may limit the amount of coverage per occurrence, it may cover an unlimited number of occurrences during any one contract year. However, treaties with high attachment points, such as clash covers, usually specify a per occurrence limit and a maximum recovery in any one contract year. Such a treaty may have a **reinstatement clause** that reinstates the treaty's original per occurrence limit after a loss occurrence for a predetermined premium, subject to a maximum recovery for the contract year.

Reinstatement clauses are not as common in casualty excess of loss treaties as they are in property catastrophe treaties. Liability losses take longer to develop than property losses. Consequently, determining the percentage of the per occurrence limit that must be reinstated for a casualty excess of loss treaty is often difficult. Exhibit 9-6 shows an example of a reinstatement clause that may appear in a clash cover.

Reinstatement clause
A reinsurance treaty clause that reinstates the treaty's original per occurrence limit after a loss occurrence for a predetermined premium, subject to a maximum recovery for the contract year.

EXHIBIT 9-6

Reinstatement Clause

A. In the event all or any portion of the reinsurance hereunder is exhausted by loss, the amount so exhausted shall be reinstated immediately from the time the occurrence commences hereon. For each amount so reinstated the Company agrees to pay additional premium equal to the product of the following:

1. The percentage of the per occurrence limit reinstated (based on the ultimate net loss paid by the Reinsurer); multiplied by

2. The earned reinsurance premium for the contract year in which the occurrence commences (exclusive of reinstatement premium).

B. Whenever the Company requests payment by the Reinsurer of any ultimate net loss hereunder, the Company shall submit a statement to the Reinsurer of reinstatement premium due the Reinsurer. If the earned reinsurance premium for the contract year has not been finally determined as of the date of any such statement, the calculation of reinstatement premium due shall be based on the annual deposit premium and shall be readjusted when the earned reinsurance premium for the contract year has been finally determined. Any reinstatement premium shown to be due the Reinsurer as reflected by any such statement (less prior payments, if any) shall be payable by the Company concurrently with payment by the Reinsurer of the requested loss. Any return reinstatement premium shown to be due the Company shall be remitted by the Reinsurer as promptly as possible after receipt and verification of the Company's statement.

C. Notwithstanding anything stated herein, the liability of the Reinsurer hereunder for ultimate net loss shall not exceed $ __3,000,000__ as respects any one occurrence, nor shall it exceed $ __9,000,000__ as respects all occurrences with dates of loss during any one contract year.

The reinstatement clause deals with the following:

- Reinsurer's maximum liability
- Automatic reinstatement of the per occurrence limit
- Reinstatement premium

Reinsurer's Maximum Liability

A **contract year limit**, also called an aggregate limit, is the reinsurer's maximum liability for any one contract year for all losses arising out of all occurrences with dates of loss during that contract year. The contract year limit is usually a multiple of the per occurrence limit and can be as high as four or more times the per occurrence limit. So a treaty that allows three full reinstatements would have a contract year limit of four times the per occurrence limit (the original limit plus the three full reinstatements). The primary insurer and reinsurer negotiate the number of full reinstatements.

Contract year limit
The reinsurer's maximum liability for any one contract year for all losses arising out of all occurrences with dates of loss during that contract year.

Automatic Reinstatement of the Per Occurrence Limit

If the casualty excess of loss treaty has both per occurrence and contract year limits, each loss during the contract year reduces the available per occurrence limit and the contract year limit. For example, if the occurrence limit is $3 million and the contract year limit is $9 million, a $400,000 loss to the treaty reduces the $3 million occurrence limit to $2.6 million for any other losses from the same occurrence. The $9 million contract year limit is reduced to $8.6 million for any other occurrences with dates of loss during the contract year.

The reinstatement clause provides for the automatic reinstatement of the per occurrence limit as long as the contract year limit has not been exceeded during the contract year. Exhibit 9-7 shows how a series of losses during one contract year reduces the contract year limit until the occurrence limit cannot be reinstated.

EXHIBIT 9-7

Immediate Reinstatement

	Per Occurrence Limit	Contract Year Limit
	$3,000,000	$9,000,000
Occurrence 1 Loss $1,000,000	$2,000,000	$8,000,000
Immediate Reinstatement	$3,000,000	$8,000,000
Occurrence 2 Loss $3,000,000	$0	$5,000,000
Immediate Reinstatement	$3,000,000	$5,000,000
Occurrence 3 Loss $2,000,000	$1,000,000	$3,000,000
Immediate Reinstatement	$3,000,000	$3,000,000
Occurrence 4 Loss $3,000,000	$0	$0

Reinstatement Premium

In clash covers, the primary insurer may not be required to pay a reinstatement premium for one or more of the reinstatements provided. However, if there is a reinstatement premium, that premium is based on the percentage of the reinsurer's per occurrence limit that is reinstated. The reinstatement premium is calculated as follows:

$$\text{Reinstatement premium} = \text{Percentage of the per occurrence limit reinstated} \times \text{Earned reinsurance premium for the contract year.}$$

The reinstatement premium amount is pro rata regardless of the time remaining in the contract year; this is often referred to in the treaty contract as "pro rata as to amount and 100 percent as to time." For example, assume that the reinsurer's per occurrence limit is $3 million and that there is a loss of $1.8 million. This means that 60 percent of the per occurrence limit is reinstated. Therefore, a factor of 60 percent would apply in the reinstatement premium calculation to reflect the amount of per occurrence limit being reinstated.

The reinstatement premium is typically paid when the reinsurer settles the loss because the exact amount of the loss, and therefore the exact amount of the per occurrence limit to be reinstated, cannot be calculated until the loss is actually settled. If the final reinsurance premium for the contract year is not known at the time the reinstatement premium is paid, an estimated premium or the deposit premium can be used to calculate the reinstatement premium.

Claims and Loss Adjustment Expense Clause

Claims and loss adjustment expense clause
A reinsurance treaty clause that states the circumstances under which the primary insurer must report and the reinsurer must pay a liability claim, and how loss adjustment expense will be handled.

The **claims and loss adjustment expense clause** states the circumstances under which the primary insurer must report and the reinsurer must pay a liability claim, and how loss adjustment expense will be handled. Exhibit 9-8 shows an example of a claims and loss adjustment expense clause.

The claims and loss adjustment expense clause addresses the following areas:

- Reporting claims
- Binding the reinsurer to the primary insurer's settlement
- Sharing loss adjustment expense

Reporting claims. The first area that the claims and loss adjustment expense clause addresses is reporting claims. The primary insurer is required to report to the reinsurer any claims that exceed its retention. The sample claims and loss adjustment expense clause in Exhibit 9-8 also requires a claim to be reported when the claim reserve exceeds 50 percent of the retention or when specified serious injury occurs, regardless of the amount of the primary insurer's loss reserve.

Claims meeting the reporting requirements often develop to the point at which the excess of loss treaty is involved. Although the 50 percent of retention trigger in Exhibit 9-8 is a common percentage requirement, the percentage is often modified.

EXHIBIT 9-8

Claims and Loss Adjustment Expense Clause

A. Whenever a claim is reserved by the Company for an amount greater than 50% of its retention hereunder and/or whenever a claim appears likely to result in a claim under this Contract, the Company shall notify the Reinsurer. Further, the Company shall notify the Reinsurer whenever a claim involves a fatality, amputation, spinal cord injury, brain damage, blindness, extensive burns, or multiple fractures, regardless of liability, if the policy limits or statutory benefits applicable to the claim are greater than the Company's retention hereunder. (These are also known as significant injury criteria.) Inadvertent omission or oversight in dispatching such advices shall in no way affect the liability of the Reinsurer. However, the Company shall notify the Reinsurer of such omission or oversight promptly upon its discovery. The Reinsurer shall have the right to participate, at its own expense, in the defense or control of any claim or suit or proceeding involving this reinsurance.

B. All claim settlements made by the Company, provided they are within the terms of this Contract, shall be binding upon the Reinsurer, and the Reinsurer agrees to pay all amounts for which it may be liable upon receipt of reasonable evidence of the amount paid by the Company.

C. In the event of loss hereunder, loss adjustment expense incurred by the Company in connection therewith that does not reduce the Company's limit of liability under the policy involved shall be shared by the Company and the Reinsurer in the proportion that the ultimate net loss paid or payable by the Reinsurer bears to the total loss paid or payable by the Company, prior to any reinsurance recoveries, but after deduction of all salvage, subrogation, and other recoveries. However, if a verdict or judgment is reduced by any process other than by the trial court, resulting in an ultimate savings to the Reinsurer, or a judgment is reversed outright, the expenses incurred in securing such reduction or reversal shall be shared by the Company and the Reinsurer in the proportion that each benefits from such reduction or reversal, and the expenses incurred up to the time of the original verdict or judgment which do not reduce the Company's limit of liability under the policy involved shall be shared in proportion to each party's interest in such original verdict or judgment. The Reinsurer's liability for such loss adjustment expense shall be in addition to its liability for ultimate net loss.

The sample claims and loss adjustment expense clause in Exhibit 9-8 also provides that delayed notice does not release the reinsurer from its liability under the treaty if the reporting delay is accidental. Although reporting delays do not void reinsurance coverage, the reinsurer could be prejudiced by the primary insurer's failure to give notice in time for the reinsurer to participate in the claim's defense. As a result, a primary insurer may have to arbitrate coverage with the reinsurer. To avoid this, once the primary insurer discovers that it has failed to report a claim, it should inform the reinsurer immediately. The reinsurer could deny liability if the initial error is compounded by further delay.

After being notified of the claim, the reinsurer has the right to participate with the insurer in the claim defense at its own expense. The primary insurer's claim staff may welcome the expertise of the reinsurer's claim staff, particularly regarding complex claims.

Binding the reinsurer to the primary insurer's settlement. The second area that the claims and loss adjustment expense clause addresses is binding the reinsurer to the primary insurer's claim settlement. The reinsurer must respond promptly to the primary insurer's payment requests once the primary insurer has paid the claim and provided the reinsurer with proof of payment. This provision should eliminate disputes between the reinsurer and the primary insurer about the reinsurer's liability and payment schedule.

Sharing loss adjustment expense. The third area that the claims and loss adjustment expense clause addresses is the sharing of loss adjustment expense. Loss adjustment expenses can be included as part of the loss for the purpose of applying the retention and the reinsurance limit, or can be shared in the proportion that the primary insurer and reinsurer share the loss. The sample claims and loss adjustment expense clause in Exhibit 9-8 uses the latter approach.

Declaratory Judgment Expense Clause

> **Declaratory judgment action**
> A legal action in which the insurer (or insured) presents a coverage question to the court and asks the court to declare the rights of the parties under the applicable insurance policy.

In a **declaratory judgment action**, the insurer (or insured) presents a coverage question to the court and asks the court to declare the rights of the parties under the applicable insurance policy. The coverage question could involve issues such as whether there has been an occurrence, whether an exclusion applies, or whether the insurer is obligated to defend the insured in a specific situation. The declaratory judgment action's purpose is to resolve questions of coverage, not to enforce the contract.

A typical reinsurance question pertaining to a declaratory judgment action is whether the primary insurer's legal expenses for the action are covered under the reinsurance treaty. These expenses may be significant, and there is limited case law on whether they are covered if they are not specifically addressed by the treaty.

The following arguments support coverage for those expenses:

- Declaratory judgment expenses are like any other claim-related loss adjustment expense.
- The reinsurer benefits from successful declaratory judgment actions.
- The "follow the fortunes" doctrine requires coverage for declaratory judgment expenses.[1]

Arguments against coverage for declaratory judgment expenses include the following:

- Declaratory judgment expenses are not the result of claim handling but of an adversarial proceeding and therefore are not loss adjustment expenses.

- The treaty does not explicitly state that declaratory judgment expenses are covered.
- The "follow the fortunes" doctrine cannot create coverage where none exists.[2]

Reinsurers and primary insurers now frequently resolve this issue during treaty negotiations. This is particularly true when reinsurance covers liability insurance because declaratory judgment actions are more common in liability insurance than in property insurance. If declaratory judgment expenses are to be covered, the most common method is to include these expenses in the definition of loss adjustment expense so that both are treated in the same manner. Alternatively, the treaty can contain a separate **declaratory judgment expense clause** that states that the primary insurer's legal expenses in respect to a declaratory judgment action are covered by the treaty.

Declaratory judgment expense clause
A reinsurance treaty clause that states that the primary insurer's legal expenses in respect to a declaratory judgment action are covered by the treaty.

Sunset and Sunrise Clauses

The **sunset clause** limits the time after the treaty's expiration during which occurrences can be reported to the reinsurer. The time limit negotiated may be a period of months or years. Reinsurers use the sunset clause to help control long-tail liability claims. If no occurrences are reported to the reinsurer within the sunset period, the reinsurer can close out the treaty knowing that no additional losses will have to be covered. Sometimes, the sunset clause applies to each contract year of the reinsurance agreement. The sunset terms can be a separate clause or part of another clause, such as the retention and limits clause or the claims and loss adjustment expense clause. Exhibit 9-9 shows an example of a separate sunset clause.

Sunset clause
A reinsurance treaty clause that limits the time after the treaty's expiration during which occurrences can be reported to the reinsurer.

EXHIBIT 9-9

Sunset Clause

68 A

SUNSET

Notwithstanding Errors and Omissions provisions, if any, to the contrary, coverage hereunder shall apply only to losses reported by the Company to the Reinsurer within _____ years from the expiration of this Contract.

Source: Brokers & Reinsurance Markets Association (BRMA), http://www.brma.org/download/bcwrb068.doc (accessed February 17, 2004).

Reinsurance coverage is not available for losses unless they are reported before the sunset period expires. Primary insurers can purchase reinsurance, called sunrise coverage, to cover those losses. **Sunrise coverage** restores the coverage lost because of the operation of a sunset clause. Sunrise coverage can be provided using two methods. The first method is for the insurer to amend the sunset period in the existing treaty to extend

Sunrise clause
A reinsurance treaty clause that restores the coverage lost because of the operation of a sunset clause.

the duration of coverage in return for an additional premium. The second method is to add wording to a new treaty to cover losses not covered because of the sunset clause. Exhibit 9-10 is an example of a sunrise clause that could be added to a new treaty.

> **EXHIBIT 9-10**
>
> **Sunrise Clause**
>
> This Contract shall become effective on January 1, 2004, with respect to claims made on or after that date as respects occurrences with dates of loss during the period January 1, 2003, through December 31, 2003, that would have otherwise been covered under the Company's Casualty Excess of Loss Reinsurance Contract, effective January 1, 2003, were it not for the provisions of the Sunset Article as set forth in the above-mentioned contract, and shall continue in force thereafter until terminated.

Commutation Clause

Commutation clause
A reinsurance treaty clause that allows the primary insurer and reinsurer to close out liability for claims under the treaty after a stated time period from treaty expiration.

The **commutation clause** allows the primary insurer and reinsurer to close out liability for claims under the treaty after a stated time period from treaty expiration. This clause allows the reinsurer to determine its ultimate loss costs within a shorter period than if claims were allowed to develop over fifteen to twenty years or more. The commutation clause establishes the earliest point at which a commutation request can be contractually made. It also defines how an actuary or appraiser can determine ultimate costs and whether the actuary's or appraiser's recommendations are binding. Commutation clauses can be general and simple, or they can be specific and complex. Exhibit 9-11 shows an example of a commutation clause.

> **EXHIBIT 9-11**
>
> **Commutation Clause**
>
> 11 A
> COMMUTATION
>
> Either the Reinsurer or the Company may request commutation of that portion of any excess loss hereunder represented by any outstanding claim or claims after _____ years from the date of an occurrence. If both parties desire to commute a claim or claims, then within sixty (60) days after such agreement, the Company shall submit a statement of valuation of the outstanding claim or claims showing the elements considered reasonable to establish the ultimate net loss and the Reinsurer shall pay the amount requested.
>
> If agreement, as outlined in the paragraph above, cannot be reached, the effort can be abandoned or alternately the Company and the Reinsurer may mutually appoint an actuary or appraiser to investigate, determine and capitalize such claim or claims. If both parties then agree, the Reinsurer shall pay its proportion of the amount so determined to be the capitalized value of such claim or claims.

> If the parties, as outlined in the paragraphs above, fail to agree, they may abandon the effort or they may agree to settle any difference using a panel of three actuaries, one to be chosen by each party and the third by the two so chosen. If either party refuses or neglects to appoint an actuary within ____ days, the other party may appoint two actuaries. If the two actuaries fail to agree on the selection of a third actuary within ____ days of their appointment, each of them shall name two, of whom the other shall decline one and the decision shall be made by drawing lots. All the actuaries shall be regularly engaged in the valuation of Workers' Compensation claims and shall be Fellows of the Casualty Actuarial Society or of the American Academy of Actuaries. None of the actuaries shall be under the control of either party to this Contract.
>
> Each party shall submit its case to its actuary within ____ days of the appointment of the third actuary. The decision in writing of any two actuaries, when filed with the parties hereto, shall be final and binding on both parties. The expense of the actuaries and of the commutation shall be equally divided between the two parties. Said commutation shall take place in ___*(City, State)*___, unless some other place is mutually agreed upon by the Company and the Reinsurer.

Source: BRMA, http://www.brma.org/download/bcwrb011.doc (accessed February 17, 2004).

The commutation clause usually neither requires commutation nor specifies how to determine the claim's settlement value. Instead, it creates a general framework for the primary insurer and reinsurer to commute losses. The primary insurer and reinsurer should be comfortable with the reserve levels, the claim handling controls, and the probable settlement pattern in order to negotiate a settlement.

CASUALTY EXCESS OF LOSS TREATY PRICING

Casualty excess of loss treaties are priced using the same methods used for property per risk excess of loss treaties. These methods are exposure rating and experience rating. Reinsurers usually use both methods and select the reinsurance rate that appears appropriate for the insurance risk assumed.

Exposure Rating

The first method used to price casualty excess of loss treaties is exposure rating. Exposure rating uses insurance industry loss data for reinsurance pricing rather than the primary insurer's loss experience. In the example that follows, assume that Sisterdale Insurance Company (Sisterdale) is starting to sell a new insurance product, so it has no loss experience to establish a casualty excess of loss treaty price. Exhibit 9-12 shows a summary of the proposed casualty excess of loss treaty.

EXHIBIT 9-12

Sisterdale Insurance Company Proposed Casualty Excess of Loss Reinsurance Treaty

Underlying Insurance Covered: Private Passenger Automobile Liability

Basis: Combined Single Limit, Bodily Injury and Property Damage, Each Occurrence

Proposed Reinsurance Coverage (3 layers):
$50,000 xs $50,000
$400,000 xs $100,000
$500,000 xs $500,000

Maximum Limit Policy: $500,000

Estimated Subject Premium at Various Policy Limits:

Policy Limit	Estimated Subject Premium
$ 35,000	$ 2,000,000
50,000	3,000,000
100,000	3,000,000
200,000	200,000
300,000	1,000,000
400,000	100,000
500,000	700,000

Total Estimated Subject Premium: $10,000,000

Ceding Commission: 0%

Reinsurance Brokerage: 10%

Exhibit 9-13 shows the process that Sisterdale's reinsurer uses to calculate the indicated exposure rate for the $50,000 xs $50,000 layer in its casualty excess of loss treaty. Column (1) lists the policy limits that Sisterdale proposes to provide and Column (3) shows the estimated subject premium amounts that Sisterdale has projected that it will receive at each of the policy limits. Column (2) provides the increased limit factors that are developed by insurance advisory organizations to price coverage beyond basic policy limits. The increased limit factors reflect industry loss experience for providing liability insurance limits above basic policy limits.

Increased Limit Factors

Primary insurers price liability policies by determining the applicable basic rate (for basic coverage limits) and applying the appropriate increased limit factor for the coverage limits desired. Insurance advisory organizations collect premium and loss data to make the increased limit factors credible for primary liability policy pricing. Increased limit factors are also useful to reinsurers in calculating the portion of the underlying insurance premium associated with a reinsurance layer.

EXHIBIT 9-13

Sisterdale Insurance Company Calculation of Indicated Exposure Rate for the $50,000 xs of $50,000 Layer

(1) Policy Limit	(2) Increased Limit Factor	(3) Estimated Subject Premium	(4) Premium Fraction Ceded Excess of $50,000	(5) Premium Fraction Ceded Excess of $100,000	(6) Premium Ceded Excess of $50,000	(7) Premium Ceded Excess of $100,000	(8) Premium for Layer $50,000 xs $50,000
$35,000	1.00	$2,000,000	0	0	$ 0	$ 0	$ 0
$50,000	1.14	3,000,000	0	0	0	0	0
$100,000	1.30	3,000,000	16/130	0	369,231	0	369,231
$200,000	1.43	200,000	29/143	13/143	40,559	18,182	22,377
$300,000	1.49	1,000,000	35/149	19/149	234,899	127,517	107,382
$400,000	1.52	100,000	38/152	22/152	25,000	14,474	10,526
$500,000	1.55	700,000	41/155	25/155	185,161	112,903	72,258
TOTAL		$10,000,000			$854,850	$273,076	$581,774

(9)	Percentage of Estimated Subject Premium	5.82%
(10)	To Adjust to Net of Expenses	65%
(11)	Adjusted Percentage of Estimated Subject Premium (9) × (10)	3.78%
(12)	Allocated Loss Adjustment Expense Loading	10%
(13)	Reinsurer's Expected Loss Cost (11) ÷ 1−(12)	4.20%
(14)	Reinsurer's Loading Factor for Brokerage, Internal Expenses, and Profit and Contingencies	.25%
(15)	Indicated Exposure Rate (13) ÷ 1−(14)	5.60%

Column (2) in Exhibit 9-13 shows that $35,000 is the basic policy limit because the increased limit factor is 1.00. Policies with a $50,000 policy limit are priced using the basic policy limit rates and increased by a factor of 1.14. The 14 percent increase in the basic limit premium compensates the primary insurer for losses that exceed $35,000, based on industry-wide loss data. Similarly, a factor of 1.55 is used to increase basic policy limit rates for a policy with a $500,000 liability limit. Relative to a policy with a $35,000 liability limit, the $500,000 liability policy provides more than fourteen times the amount of coverage for only an additional 55 percent in premium. The reason for this relatively small charge for higher policy limits is that the probability of losses exceeding the basic policy limits is relatively remote.

Columns (4) and (5) are fractions that are used in columns (6) and (7) respectively to calculate how much of the projected premium shown in Column (3) is applicable to losses between $50,000 and $100,000 so that the first layer ($50,000 xs $50,000) of Sisterdale's casualty excess of loss treaty can be priced.

The fractions shown in columns (4) and (5) represent the difference between the increased limit factor for the applicable policy limit and the increased limit factor for the underlying coverage (1.14 for underlying coverage of $50,000 and 1.30 for underlying coverage of $100,000) divided by the increased limit factor for the policy limit. For simplicity, all amounts have been multiplied by 100. For example, consider a policy limit of $300,000 and an underlying coverage of $100,000. The increased limit factors for these amounts are 1.49 and 1.30 respectively. Therefore, the premium fraction ceded is 100 × [(1.49 – 1.30)/1.49] or 19/149. When that factor is applied to the written premium of $1,000,000, the result is $127,517, as shown in column (7).

Exhibit 9-13 uses the increased limit factors to determine the total premium dollars excess of $50,000 and excess of $100,000. Column (8) shows the amount of premium in a layer of $50,000 xs $50,000, which is the difference between the amount in column (6) and the amount in column (7).

The premiums in Exhibit 9-13 are written premiums that anticipate claim payments and expenses. Because the primary insurer does not receive a ceding commission, the primary insurer's expense portion of its premium is deducted to determine the premium ceded. Exact expense factors vary, but assume in this case that expenses are as follows:

Agents' Commissions	15%
Internal Expenses	10%
Boards, Bureaus, and Taxes	5%
Profit and Contingencies	5%
TOTAL	35%

Consequently, the percentage premium ceded to the reinsurer for the $50,000 excess of $50,000 layer is 65 percent (100 percent – 35 percent) of the amount shown in column (8) of Exhibit 9-13, or 3.78 percent of the total subject premium. The reinsurer expects the primary insurer's loss ratio to be 65 percent.

In addition to the increased limit factors, the reinsurance underwriter considers the following five factors that modify the reinsurance rate when exposure rating is used to price casualty excess of loss treaties:

1. Allocated loss adjustment expenses
2. Reinsurer's expenses
3. Extra-contractual obligations and excess of policy limits coverage
4. Clash cover
5. Policy limit mix

The first additional factor that reinsurance underwriters consider is allocated loss adjustment expenses. Reinsurance treaties typically indemnify the primary insurer for allocated loss adjustment expenses, either on a pro rata basis according to the proportion of the indemnity loss paid by the reinsurer, or as an addition to the total amount of indemnity paid. Increased limit factors do not include a loading for allocated loss adjustment expense, but rather include all of the allocated loss adjustment expense to the basic limit portion of the premium. Consequently, the reinsurer needs to include in the reinsurance premium an estimate of those allocated loss adjustment expenses if loss adjustment expenses are paid in addition to the indemnity loss payments. In Exhibit 9-13, an allocated loss adjustment expense loading of 1.10 is applied to the adjusted percentage of estimated subject premium to determine the reinsurer's expected loss cost.

The second additional factor that reinsurance underwriters consider is the reinsurer's expenses. As with primary insurance rates, the reinsurance rate must reflect expenses. For a reinsurer, those expenses include ceding commissions, brokerage, the reinsurer's internal expenses, a profit and contingency loading, and the reinsurer's net retrocessional cost, if any. In Exhibit 9-13, a reinsurer's expenses loading of 0.25 is applied to the reinsurer's expected loss cost to determine the indicated exposure rate.

The third additional factor that reinsurance underwriters consider is extra-contractual obligations and excess of policy limits coverage. If either of these coverages is to be provided by the reinsurance treaty, the reinsurer needs to include a charge for these additional potential sources of loss. Exhibit 9-13 does not include such a charge.

The fourth additional factor that reinsurance underwriters consider is clash cover. The treaty may provide reinsurance of an accumulation of net retentions resulting from a single occurrence that affects multiple insureds and multiple types of insurance. The reinsurance underwriter typically adjusts the exposure rate to reflect this loss potential, if applicable. No such adjustment is made in Exhibit 9-13.

The fifth additional factor that reinsurance underwriters consider is policy limit mix. If the casualty excess of loss treaty is provided on a flat rate, the reinsurer will want to periodically review the mix of policy limits being sold. If the actual policy limit distribution varies from the primary insurer's projections, it will affect the reinsurer's potential liability and the accuracy of the reinsurer's pricing. The reinsurer's loss ratio may not reflect that difference until a considerable length of time has elapsed.

One solution to this problem is to cede premiums to the reinsurer based on the actual policy limits sold rather than an estimate. The primary insurer reports each month's actual written premiums for each policy limit category and pays a premium based on a separate rate (called a cessions factor) for each policy limit category.

Another solution is to develop an average rate for the lower levels of reinsurance coverage that are expected to generate a predictable flow of losses. That

9.24 Reinsurance Principles and Practices

rate could be adjusted retrospectively at some future date on the basis of the reinsurer's actual losses. This solution involves the experience rating method of casualty excess of loss treaty pricing discussed next.

Experience Rating

The second method used to price casualty excess of loss treaties is experience rating. The goal of experience rating is to determine a loss cost rate for a future period that is based on actual past losses and the related subject premiums. This experience rate can then be compared to the exposure rate.

Assume Sisterdale has been developing a portfolio of private passenger automobile insurance for four years. During that time, numerous losses have been sustained, as shown in Exhibit 9-14.

EXHIBIT 9-14

Sisterdale Insurance Company Large Loss Listing $25,000 or More

(1) Year	(2) Claim No.	(3) Incurred Losses*	(4) $50,000 xs $50,000 Nominal Losses	(5) Trend Factor	(6) Trended Losses**	(7) $50,000 xs $50,000 Trended Losses
2000	970	$ 125,000	$ 50,000	$(1.06)^5$	$ 167,278	$ 50,000
	971	75,000	25,000	$(1.06)^5$	100,367	50,000
	972	45,000	0	$(1.06)^5$	60,220	10,220
	973	37,400	0	$(1.06)^5$	50,050	50
	974	120,000	50,000	$(1.06)^5$	160,587	50,000
	975	47,000	0	$(1.06)^5$	62,897	12,897
	976	152,000	50,000	$(1.06)^5$	203,410	50,000
	977	83,000	33,000	$(1.06)^5$	111,073	50,000
	978	170,000	50,000	$(1.06)^5$	227,498	50,000
	979	78,000	28,000	$(1.06)^5$	104,382	50,000
	980	74,500	24,500	$(1.06)^5$	99,698	49,698
		$1,006,900	$310,500		$1,347,460	$422,865
2001	981	$ 78,000	$ 28,000	$(1.06)^4$	$ 98,473	$ 48,473
	982	87,000	37,000	$(1.06)^4$	109,835	50,000
	983	58,000	8,000	$(1.06)^4$	73,224	23,224
	984	193,000	50,000	$(1.06)^4$	243,658	50,000
	985	79,000	29,000	$(1.06)^4$	99,736	49,736
	986	83,000	33,000	$(1.06)^4$	104,786	50,000
	987	120,000	50,000	$(1.06)^4$	151,497	50,000
	988	78,000	28,000	$(1.06)^4$	98,473	48,473
	989	65,000	15,000	$(1.06)^4$	82,061	32,061
	990	72,500	22,500	$(1.06)^4$	91,530	41,530
	991	83,500	334,500	$(1.06)^4$	105,417	50,000
		$ 997,000	$334,000		$1,258,690	$493,497

Casualty Excess of Loss Treaties 9.25

(1) Year	(2) Claim No.	(3) Incurred Losses*	(4) $50,000 xs $50,000 Nominal Losses	(5) Trend Factor	(6) Trended Losses**	(7) $50,000 xs $50,000 Trended Losses
2002	992	$ 67,000	$ 17,000	$(1.06)^3$	$ 79,798	$ 29,798
	993	98,000	48,000	$(1.06)^3$	116,720	50,000
	994	153,000	50,000	$(1.06)^3$	182,225	50,000
	995	88,000	38,000	$(1.06)^3$	104,809	50,000
	996	110,000	50,000	$(1.06)^3$	131,012	50,000
	997	82,000	32,000	$(1.06)^3$	97,663	47,663
	998	90,000	40,000	$(1.06)^3$	107,191	50,000
	999	41,000	0	$(1.06)^3$	48,832	0
	1000	112,000	50,000	$(1.06)^3$	133,394	50,000
		$ 841,000	$ 325,000		$1,001,644	$ 377,461
2003	1001	$ 81,000	$ 31,000	$(1.06)^2$	$ 91,012	$ 41,012
	1002	91,500	41,500	$(1.06)^2$	102,809	50,000
	1003	61,000	11,000	$(1.06)^2$	68,540	18,540
	1004	119,000	50,000	$(1.06)^2$	133,708	50,000
	1005	151,600	50,000	$(1.06)^2$	170,338	50,000
	1006	93,000	43,000	$(1.06)^2$	104,495	50,000
	1007	110,000	50,000	$(1.06)^2$	123,596	50,000
	1008	84,000	34,000	$(1.06)^2$	94,382	44,382
	1009	69,000	19,000	$(1.06)^2$	77,528	27,528
	1010	44,000	0	$(1.06)^2$	49,438	0
	1011	99,000	49,000	$(1.06)^2$	111,236	50,000
		$1,003,100	$ 378,500		$1,127,082	$ 431,462
Overall Total			$1,348,000			$1,725,285

* Includes the total amount of loss sustained by the primary insurer before taking into account the recoverable reinsurance. Losses include loss adjustment expenses.

** Rounded

In the trending of losses in Exhibit 9-14, an inflation rate of 6 percent is used. An experience rate for 2004 will be projected.

Trend factors apply to the entire loss amount, not just to the portion that lies within the $50,000 xs $50,000 layer. Some losses, such as claim numbers 972, 973, and 975, that did not exceed the attachment point as incurred, did exceed the attachment point after application of the trend factor. Other losses, such as claim numbers 971, 977, and 979, were within the $50,000 xs $50,000 layer on a nominal basis, but exceeded the layer after application of the trend factor. Overall, losses in 2003 increased as shown below.

	Before Trending	After Trending	Increase
2003 Incurred Losses	$1,003,100	$1,127,082	12.4%
2003 Nominal Losses	$378,500	$431,462	14.0%

Gross losses increased by 12.4 percent, but excess losses increased by 14 percent of the nominal values. Therefore, the reinsurer was more adversely affected by inflation than was the primary insurer.

Some delay usually occurs in reporting losses, particularly in liability and workers' compensation insurance. Also, the ultimate values of some losses are sometimes initially underestimated. The delay in loss reporting and underestimation of reported losses causes an increase of aggregate loss reserves over time, known as loss development. Exhibit 9-15 shows the typical development of a single loss as it may be recorded on the accounting records of the primary insurer and the reinsurer.

EXHIBIT 9-15
Value of a Single Loss

	12/31/00	12/31/01	12/31/02	12/31/03 (settled)	12/31/04
Value of loss occurring during 1999	0	39,000	58,000	65,000	65,000
Percentage increase from initial value		N/A	48.7%	66.7%	66.7%
Value to layer $50,000 xs $50,000	0	0	8,000	15,000	15,000
Percentage increase from initial value		N/A	N/A	87.5%	87.5%

If a primary insurer has sufficient loss data to determine a credible loss development pattern, the next step in experience rating is to chart the loss development to estimate the changes in loss reserves from year to year as they approach their ultimate values. Schedule P of a primary insurer's NAIC Annual Statement is a collection of such charts or "triangles" that are used as a measure of the insurer's loss reserve adequacy. Those estimates are then used to project the claims' future values.

The primary insurer's historical loss information is often insufficient to establish a credible projection. In such cases, industry loss development information may be used to establish the loss development patterns needed to achieve an acceptable level of data credibility. This approach reflects a combination of loss exposure and experience rating.

The cumulative effect of loss development and the method of estimating the ultimate value is shown in Exhibit 9-16.

EXHIBIT 9-16

Sisterdale Insurance Company Loss Development Using Age-to-Age Development Factors

Accident Year	Incurred Losses Age			
	1	2	3	4
2000	$298,463	$353,778	$363,671	**$422,865**
2001	$380,670	$473,231	**$493,497**	
2002	$322,064	**$377,461**		
2003	**$431,462**			

Bold figures are the trended $50,000 xs $50,000 totals from Exhibit 9-14.

Accident Year	Age-to-Age Development Factor Calculation Age			
	1–2	2–3	3–4	4
2000	1.185	1.028	1.163	
2001	1.243	1.043		
2002	1.172			
2003				
Average	1.200	1.036	1.163	Tail
Selected	1.200	1.036	1.163	1.082
Age-to-Ultimate Factor	1.564	1.303	1.258	1.082

Year	Loss Development				
	2003	2002	2001	2000	Total
Current Loss	$431,462	$377,461	$493,497	$422,865	$1,725,285
Age-to-Ultimate Factor	1.564	1.303	1.258	1.082	–
Ultimate Loss (Current loss × Age-to-ultimate factor)	$674,807	$491,832	$620,819	$457,540	$2,244,998
IBNR* (Ultimate current)	$243,345	$114,371	$127,322	$34,675	$519,713

* Incurred but not reported (Ultimate loss-current loss)

The age-to-age development factors are constructed by dividing each accident year's incurred losses at a point in time by that same accident year's incurred losses at the immediately preceding point in time. For example:

Age-to-age development
factor (2000: Years 1–2) = 2000 incurred losses at age 2 ÷ 2000 incurred losses at age 1
= 353,778 ÷ 298,463
= 1.185.

The resulting age-to-age development factors are averaged, and an appropriate factor is selected to adjust for any anomalies in the data. For the final time period, a tail factor is either selected from appropriate industry statistics or estimated.

> **Tail Factors**
>
> Analysts and others use loss development triangles to estimate the ultimate value of losses. In liability insurance typically only a limited number of years worth of development data are available. In those situations, the analyst selects a factor to estimate the amount of development expected beyond the range of the loss development triangle. This factor is called a tail factor. In Exhibit 9-16, the tail factor represents the expected development from age 4 to ultimate. Several methods can be used to estimate a tail factor. Some of those methods are beyond the scope of this text.

In this case, the tail factor was estimated using one-half of the previous increment (0.163 × 0.5 = 0.082).

The age-to-ultimate factors are calculated backwards from the final time period. For the final period, the age-to-ultimate factor is set at the selected age-to-age factor for that period. Then each age-to-ultimate factor is calculated by multiplying the proceeding period's age-to-ultimate factor by the selected age-to-age factor for the current period. For example:

Age-to-ultimate
factor Years 3–4 = Age-to-ultimate factor Year 4 × Selected age-to-age factor Years 3–4
= 1.082 × 1.163
= 1.258.

The aggregate losses for each year of development are recast to reflect the probable loss development to their ultimate aggregate value. This is done by multiplying the most recent valuation of actual losses incurred in each year of development by the applicable age-to-ultimate factor as in the following example:

2003 Ultimate loss = 2003 Current loss × Age-to-ultimate factor Years 1–2
= $431,462 × 1.564
= $674,807.

The difference between the current value of the losses and their ultimate value is the incurred but not reported (IBNR) reserve, as in the following example:

2003 IBNR = 2003 Ultimate loss − 2003 Current loss
= $674,807 − $431,462
= $243,345.

Estimated subject premium for this future period must reflect changes in manual rates and changes in exposure units. Sisterdale's records of rate changes can be used to adjust past premiums for current conditions. Broad economic data can be used to adjust for changes in exposure units to which the rates have been applied. The combined effect of those adjustments results in premium on-level factors with which the reinsurance underwriter can estimate an appropriate adjusted subject premium to be used for the period being priced.

Exhibit 9-17 displays the loss cost rate and experience rate calculations for Sisterdale.

EXHIBIT 9-17

Sisterdale Insurance Company Experience Rate Calculation

(1) Accident Year	(2) Adjusted Subject Premium	(3) Trended Excess Losses at 12/31/00 (Ex. 9-14)	(4) Age-to-Ultimate Development Factor (Ex. 9-16)	(5) Developed Ultimate Net Loss [(3) × (4)]	(6) Estimated Loss Cost Rate [(5) ÷ (2)]
2000	$10,000,000	$422,865	1.082	$ 457,540	4.58%
2001	11,500,000	$493,497	1.258	620,819	5.40%
2002	13,000,000	$377,461	1.303	491,832	3.78%
2003	13,500,000	$431,462	1.564	674,807	5.00%
Total	$48,000,000			$2,244,998	4.68% Avg.*†
Loss Adjustment Expense Loading (Ex. 9-13)					÷ 1−0.10
Reinsurance Loading Factor for Brokerage, Internal Expenses, and Profit and Contingencies (Ex. 9-13)					÷ 1−0.25
Experience Rate					6.93%

* Rather than using a simple average, many actuaries use a weighted average to reflect the premium size in each year.
† Calculated by 2,244,998 ÷ 48,000,000

Reinsurance Rate Evaluation and Selection

The reinsurance underwriter usually considers the result from each pricing method and selects a reinsurance rate that fits the insurance risk of the underlying policies and current reinsurance market conditions. In Sisterdale's case, the exposure rate is 5.60 percent, and the experience rate is 6.93 percent, as shown in Exhibits 9-13 and 9-17, respectively. Frequently, the two methods result in different rates. The reinsurer then attempts to reconcile the different rates to determine the best reinsurance price. No generally accepted method accomplishes this reconciliation. Reinsurance underwriters use their judgment to assign weights to each method based on the factors involved in a particular situation.

Factors to consider for exposure rates include the following:

- Accuracy and credibility of the projected distribution of subject premium by policy limits
- Accuracy of the increased limit factors in excess of the retention
- Possible loss adjustment expenses, extra-contractual obligations (ECO) losses, excess of policy limits (XPL) losses, and clash cover losses not contemplated by the increased limit factors

A change in the mix of policy limits would substantially affect the reinsurance rate. For example, at high-level attachment points, such as $1 million or above, the increased limit factors may not accurately reflect the possibility of loss due to the lack of credible loss data on which the factors are based. Additionally, ECO, XPL, and clash losses are not reflected in increased limit factors. Reinsurance underwriters must judge the probability and amount of those losses. Finally, loss adjustment expenses may affect the rate if they are added to the indemnity loss.

Factors to consider for experience rates include the following:

- Accuracy of the estimates of the claims cost inflation trend
- Accuracy of the estimates of excess loss development
- Accuracy of the current value of subject premium
- Adequacy of the statistical sampling
- Stability of the estimated excess loss costs

The underlying inflation trend assumptions must be appropriate. For example, the inflation trends on the cost of medical services may be very different from the inflation trends in building costs. One inflation trends index does not apply to all classes of business.

Excess loss development factors must be derived from a large enough number of losses to yield statistical credibility. Generally, the lower the attachment point of a layer and the smaller the amount of coverage in excess of the attachment point, the higher the level of data credibility.

The assumptions used to establish inflation affect the accuracy of premium on-level factors. The primary insurer should have accurate records of all rate-level changes during the experience period because many of those changes are filed with state insurance regulators.

The statistical sampling's adequacy depends, in part, on whether the entire layer or only a small portion of the layer has experienced losses. In the latter case, experience rates may not include a charge for the entire portion of the layer unless an adjustment is made.

The stability of the excess loss cost from year to year is also a factor. Sisterdale's exposure rate of 5.20 percent should remain fairly constant over time.

However, the experience rate fluctuates considerably by year. The reinsurance underwriter must decide whether an additional insurance risk charge should be added because of loss volatility. If the reinsurance underwriter is uncomfortable with loss volatility, a multiple-year, retrospectively rated treaty or a large insurance risk charge may be appropriate.

Upper Layers Pricing

For layers of coverage above the working cover, exposure rating is used more often than experience rating. As the attachment point or the size of the layer increases, the loss experience to the layer becomes less stable. Therefore, increased limit factors reflecting the loss potential based on insurance industry data are used. An exposure rate for Sisterdale may begin with the calculations in column (7) of Exhibit 9-13. The reinsurer could also compare Sisterdale's in-force policy portfolio (premiums and losses) with those of similar primary insurers in its portfolio of reinsurance agreements to determine whether the pricing appears to be reasonable. The instability of high layers may lead the reinsurer to include an additional insurance risk charge to justify the possibility of assuming unexpected losses. Lower loss frequency and greater uncertainty of profitable underwriting results for the reinsurer may justify the addition of a insurance risk charge.

Clash cover pricing, which attaches above all policy limits, is based on judgment and market competition because few, if any, losses are expected to be large enough to trigger coverage. Pricing the clash cover depends on the reinsurance underwriter's assessment of the possibility of ECO or XPL losses, the possibility of two or more insureds being involved in one occurrence, and the possibility of high loss adjustment expenses.

SUMMARY

Casualty excess of loss reinsurance covers losses arising out of the primary insurer's underlying casualty insurance policies. Primary insurers use casualty excess of loss treaties to:

- Increase large line capacity
- Stabilize loss experience
- Provide catastrophe protection

Casualty excess of loss reinsurance can be provided on a per policy basis or a per occurrence basis, but most casualty excess of loss treaties are on a per occurrence basis. Reinsurance coverage is often provided in layers, such as working cover, policy-exposed layers, and clash cover.

Some common clauses are modified for use in casualty excess of loss treaties. These common clauses include:

- Reinsuring clause
- Definitions clause

Other clauses are designed or adapted specifically for casualty excess of loss treaties. These clauses include:

- *Retention and limits clause.* The retention and limits clause for casualty excess of loss treaties should address the possibility of a single occurrence involving multiple insureds, multiple policies, or multiple coverages.
- *Reinstatement clause.* The reinstatement clause reinstates the treaty's original per occurrence limit after a loss occurrence for a predetermined premium, subject to a maximum recovery for the contract year.
- *Claims and loss adjustment expense clause.* The claims and loss adjustment expense clause states the circumstances under which the primary insurer must report and the reinsurer must pay a liability claim, and how loss adjustment expense will be handled.
- *Declaratory judgment expense clause.* The declaratory judgment expense clause states that the primary insurer's legal expenses in respect to a declaratory judgment action are covered by the treaty.
- *Sunset clause.* The sunset clause limits the time after the treaty's expiration during which occurrences can be reported to the reinsurer.
- *Sunrise clause.* The sunrise clause restores the coverage lost because of the operation of a sunset clause.
- *Commutation clause.* The commutation clause allows the primary insurer and reinsurer to close out liability for claims under the treaty after a stated time period from treaty expiration.

Two approaches to pricing casualty excess of loss treaties are exposure rating and experience rating. Exposure rating uses manual increased limit factors that primary insurers also use to determine the premium for the underlying policies. Increased limit factors are based on loss distributions constructed from insurance industry data. Exposure rating is useful when specific loss information is either unavailable or of insufficient quality or quantity to justify a high degree of confidence in that loss information. Experience rating is based on the primary insurer's past losses and related subject premiums. Actuarial techniques are used to adjust past losses to project probable future premiums and losses. The reinsurance underwriter usually combines the results of exposure rating and experience rating in determining the final rate.

The next chapter examines the purpose, operation, and pricing of catastrophe reinsurance.

CHAPTER NOTES

1. Leslie J. Davis, "Concerning the Coverage of Declaratory Judgment Expense," *Tort & Insurance Law Journal*, Spring 1995, p. 686.
2. Davis, p. 686.

Chapter 10

Direct Your Learning

Catastrophe Reinsurance

After learning the content of this chapter, you should be able to:

- Explain the purpose and operation of catastrophe treaties.
- Explain the purpose and operation of clauses designed or adapted for catastrophe treaties.
- Explain how catastrophe modeling operates.
- Explain how primary insurers and reinsurers use catastrophe modeling to determine their need for catastrophe reinsurance.
- Explain the approaches to catastrophe treaty pricing.
- Describe alternatives to traditional catastrophe reinsurance.

OUTLINE

Overview of Catastrophe Treaties

Clauses Designed or Adapted for Catastrophe Treaties

Catastrophe Modeling

Catastrophe Treaty Pricing

Alternatives to Traditional Catastrophe Reinsurance

Summary

Develop Your Perspective

What are the main topics covered in the chapter?

This chapter describes the operation, contractual clauses, and the methods for pricing catastrophe treaties. It also covers the operation and use of catastrophe models and alternative methods of managing catastrophe exposures.

Identify the purpose, operation, and methods for pricing of catastrophe reinsurance.

- What functions does a catastrophe treaty serve for a primary insurer?
- What are the main outputs of a catastrophe model?
- What elements affect catastrophe treaty pricing?
- What are the alternatives to traditional catastrophe reinsurance?

Why is it important to learn about these topics?

Catastrophe reinsurance treaties limit the financial consequences resulting from catastrophic events. The ability to understand, analyze, and evaluate catastrophe treaties is important to enable you to determine whether they are helping your company or client-insurer achieve its objectives.

Review a catastrophe treaty.

- What clauses are designed specifically for casualty excess of loss treaties and how do they operate?

How can you use what you will learn?

Evaluate one of your company's or client-insurer's catastrophe treaties.

- Does this catastrophe treaty address your company's or client-insurer's needs?
- Does this catastrophe treaty provide adequate protection to your company or client-insurer from the financial effect of catastrophe losses?

Chapter 10
Catastrophe Reinsurance

Catastrophe excess of loss reinsurance, usually called catastrophe reinsurance or catastrophe excess, provides primary insurers with protection from the financial consequences of an accumulation of losses arising from a catastrophic event. Catastrophic events occur infrequently, yet the severity of the loss they produce can threaten a primary insurer's solvency. Primary insurers use catastrophe treaties to safeguard their policyholders' surplus (net worth) should a catastrophic event occur. This chapter explains the following:

- How catastrophe treaties operate
- How clauses are designed or adapted for catastrophe treaties
- How catastrophe modeling can be used to estimate catastrophe losses
- How catastrophe treaties are priced
- How alternatives to traditional catastrophe reinsurance can provide the primary insurer with catastrophe protection

OVERVIEW OF CATASTROPHE TREATIES

Most primary insurers that sell property insurance purchase catastrophe reinsurance. The demand for catastrophe reinsurance results from natural and man-made disasters, such as tornadoes, hurricanes, terrorism, earthquakes, and winter storms to which property loss exposures are subjected. Exhibit 10-1 shows U.S. catastrophe losses by cause of loss between 1983 and 2002.

Coverage under a catastrophe treaty is triggered when accumulated losses arising out of a single event exceed the attachment point. Once losses exceed the attachment point, the reinsurer reimburses the primary insurer for losses until the reinsurance limit is reached. Unlike property per risk excess of loss, catastrophe reinsurance usually applies to all of the primary insurer's property business (such as all personal and commercial insurance covering property loss exposures) or a large subset of it (such as all property loss exposures in the states of Alabama, Mississippi, and Louisiana) rather than to losses sustained by individual loss exposures.

Catastrophe treaties often specify that they will not respond to a loss arising out of a single loss exposure, no matter how large the loss may be. In practice, most catastrophe treaties have a sufficiently high attachment point that many of the primary insurer's policies would have to be involved in a loss for the catastrophe treaty to respond. For example, if the largest property policy the primary insurer is willing to sell has a $1 million limit, the attachment point of the catastrophe treaty may be set at $10 million. As with other types of excess of loss reinsurance, catastrophe treaties typically contain a co-participation provision that requires the primary insurer to absorb a percentage of the loss that exceeds the attachment point.

EXHIBIT 10-1

Inflation-Adjusted U.S. Catastrophe Losses by Cause of Loss, 1983-2002[1]

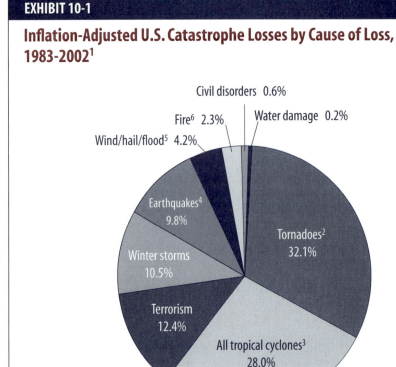

[1] Catastrophes are all events causing direct insured losses to property of $25 million or more in 2002 dollars. Adjusted for inflation by ISO.

[2] Excludes snow.

[3] Includes hurricanes and tropical storms.

[4] Includes other geologic events such as volcanic eruptions and other earth movement.

[5] Does not include flood damage covered by the federally administered National Flood Insurance Program.

[6] Includes wildland fires.

Source: Insurance Services Office, Inc. (ISO).

Used with permission from *The I.I.I. Insurance Fact Book 2004* (New York: Insurance Information Institute, 2004), p. 85.

For primary insurers that have geographically diversified loss exposures, and a limited exposure to catastrophe-related causes of loss, the price of catastrophe reinsurance is probably relatively low. However, for primary insurers that sell insurance almost exclusively in catastrophe-prone areas, catastrophe reinsurance is likely to be expensive and available only with a high attachment point relative to the size of the catastrophic exposure.

Function of Catastrophe Reinsurance

Primary insurers use catastrophe treaties to provide catastrophe protection, that is, to limit the financial consequences of catastrophic events. At a minimum, losses arising from a catastrophic event will destabilize underwriting results (increase the loss ratio and therefore increase the combined ratio), and could even lead to insurer insolvency.

Hurricane Andrew, a Category 5 hurricane on the Saffir-Simpson Hurricane Scale that made landfall on August 24, 1992, led to seven insurer insolvencies in Florida. Hurricane Iniki, also in 1992, led to the insolvency of Hawaii's largest insurer. In its 1996 study on managing catastrophe risk, the Insurance Services Office (ISO) stated that a megacastrophe that cost the property-casualty insurance industry $50 billion or more could result in insolvency for up to 36 percent of all insurers, depending on where the event occurs, and assuming current levels of reinsurance and its full collectibility.[1] Another ISO study stated that if Hurricane Andrew had hit Miami, losses could have exceeded $40 billion.[2] Despite making landfall south of Miami, Hurricane Andrew caused $15.5 billion in losses.[3] Significant catastrophes such as these have a widespread effect on the property-casualty industry by reducing policyholders' surplus and thereby limiting underwriting capacity.

With catastrophe reinsurance, a primary insurer can limit its losses to a predetermined retention per loss occurrence. This stabilizes loss experience results because losses in excess of the retention are passed on to reinsurers. The primary insurer's current and future reinsurance premium payments can spread the financial effects of catastrophe losses over several years.

Catastrophe treaties also help primary insurers avoid large fluctuations in earnings per share and wide swings in profits and losses that can cause adverse financial market reactions. By purchasing catastrophe treaties, primary insurers also achieve more statistically predictable loss experience. Although catastrophe treaties do not guarantee that primary insurers will have a constant loss ratio, they do flatten some of the loss ratio peaks for primary insurers. Exhibit 10-2 shows the combined ratios of reinsurers relative to the total property-casualty insurance industry.

EXHIBIT 10-2

Combined Ratios: Reinsurers and Total Industry, 1986-2002

The peaks of the combined ratio in 1992 and 2001 reflect years in which catastrophic losses were significant and in which the combined ratios for reinsurers were accordingly higher than those of the total insurance industry.

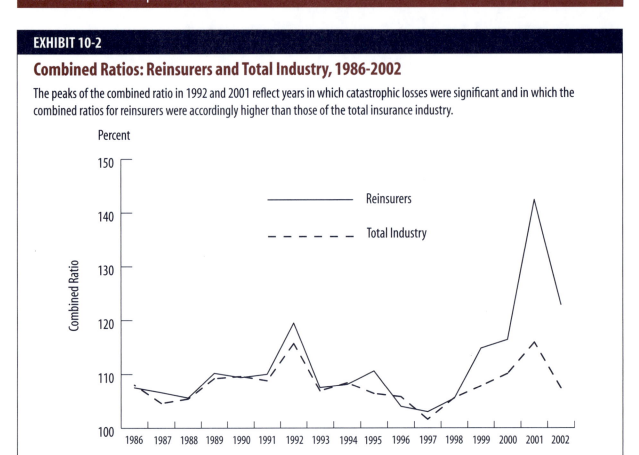

Catastrophe Reinsurance as Part of a Reinsurance Program

As with other forms of reinsurance, catastrophe reinsurance may be provided in layers. The primary insurer may also have a percentage co-participation in losses that exceed the attachment point, which encourages the primary insurer to exercise sound claim-handling practices even after the attachment point has been exceeded.

The primary insurer typically has other reinsurance that applies before the catastrophe treaty. This is known as inuring reinsurance because it inures to the benefit of (reduces the loss to) the catastrophe treaty. For example, the primary insurer might have purchased facultative, surplus share, quota share, or per risk excess of loss reinsurance to reduce the amount of loss to be covered by the catastrophe treaty. The catastrophe treaty only applies when the primary insurer's net retention (after the inuring reinsurance) exceeds the attachment point. Exhibit 10-3 illustrates how inuring reinsurance can benefit the catastrophe treaty.

EXHIBIT 10-3

Effect of Inuring Reinsurance

The primary insurer has a 60% quota share treaty and a $20 million xs $10 million catastrophe treaty. A policy covered by the treaties experiences a $30 million loss.

If the quota share treaty inures to the benefit of the catastrophe treaty, the loss exposures are as follows:

Loss	$30,000,000
Minus 60% quota share	(18,000,000)
Loss subject to catastrophe treaty	$12,000,000
Minus primary insurer's retention	(10,000,000)
Catastrophe coverage	$ 2,000,000

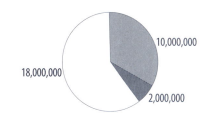

If the quota share treaty does not inure to the benefit of the catastrophe treaty, the loss exposures are as follows:

Loss	$30,000,000
Minus primary insurer's retention	(10,000,000)
Catastrophe coverage	$20,000,000
60% quota share of $10,000,000 retention	$ 6,000,000
40% primary insurer's net retention	$ 4,000,000

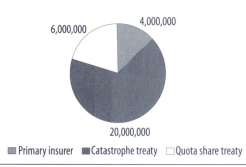

■ Primary insurer   ■ Catastrophe treaty   □ Quota share treaty

CLAUSES DESIGNED OR ADAPTED FOR CATASTROPHE TREATIES

Catastrophe treaties typically contain the common clauses that appear in other excess of loss treaties. Clauses designed or adapted for use in catastrophe treaties include the following:

- Term clause
- Retention and limits clause
- Ultimate net loss clause
- Loss occurrence clause
- Other reinsurance clause
- Reinstatement clause

Term Clause

The **term clause** defines the term of the reinsurance treaty. Catastrophe treaties usually have a one-year term, but they can be provided on a multiple-year term or on a continuous basis with annual termination provisions.

Term clause
A reinsurance treaty clause that defines the term of the reinsurance treaty.

Because many catastrophic events are seasonal, such as hurricanes and tornadoes, treaty terms that allow the primary insurer or reinsurer to terminate a catastrophe treaty before the end of an annual term are unusual. The term clause prevents one of the parties from canceling the agreement just before or after the catastrophe season.

Catastrophe treaties typically apply only to losses occurring during the treaty's term, so run-off coverage is not provided. However, they often include an extended expiration provision. The extended expiration provision provides that if the treaty expires while a loss occurrence is in progress, the reinsurer will indemnify the primary insurer as if the entire loss occurrence had occurred during the treaty's term. Therefore, the primary insurer has one retention under its expiring catastrophe treaty and does not have a second retention for the same loss occurrence under its renewal catastrophe treaty. The sample term clause shown in Exhibit 10-4 contains an extended expiration provision.

EXHIBIT 10-4

Term Clause

A. This Contract shall become effective on __January 1, 2004__, with respect to losses arising out of loss occurrences commencing on or after that date, and shall remain in force until __December 31, 2004__, both days inclusive.

B. If this Contract expires while a loss occurrence covered hereunder is in progress, the Reinsurer's liability hereunder shall, subject to the other terms and conditions of this Contract, be determined as if the entire loss occurrence had occurred prior to the expiration of this Contract, provided that no part of such loss occurrence is claimed against any renewal or replacement of this contract.

Retention and Limits Clause

The retention and limits clause in a catastrophe treaty should include the following:

- Net retention stated as the ultimate net loss per loss occurrence
- Co-participation provision
- Per loss occurrence limit

The ultimate net loss and loss occurrence clauses, discussed later in this section, define ultimate net loss and loss occurrence, both of which affect net retention. Those clauses provide that only the portion of each individual loss that is retained net by the primary insurer (not reinsured in any way) can be included in the amount of loss subject to the catastrophe treaty.

The primary insurer's retention under a catastrophe treaty must be greater than its retention for a single loss exposure. For example, if the primary insurer has a maximum net retention of $1 million per loss exposure, the retention on its catastrophe treaty must be more than $1 million. Generally, a catastrophe treaty that attaches just above the maximum loss exposure retention is expensive, so primary insurers usually have a catastrophe treaty retention equal to several per loss exposure retentions.

In addition to the retention, catastrophe treaties generally require the primary insurer to retain a co-participation percentage of the excess loss in order to encourage primary insurers to properly handle losses after the retention has been exceeded. The sample retention and limits clause in Exhibit 10-5 contains a co-participation provision.

EXHIBIT 10-5

Retention and Limits Clause

A. The Company shall retain and be liable for the first __$1,000,000__ of ultimate net loss arising out of each loss occurrence. The Reinsurer shall then be liable for __95%__ of the amount by which such ultimate net loss exceeds the Company's retention, but the liability of the Reinsurer shall not exceed __95%__ of __$4,000,000__ as respects any one loss occurrence.

B. In addition to its initial retention each loss occurrence, the Company shall retain __5%__ of the excess ultimate net loss to which this Contract applies.

The reinsurer's limit of liability is also stated in the retention and limits clause. The sample clause in Exhibit 10-5 states that the reinsurer's limit of liability "shall not exceed 95% of $4,000,000."

Ultimate Net Loss Clause

The ultimate net loss clause in a catastrophe treaty defines what constitutes a loss. Because of the importance of catastrophe reinsurance in protecting the primary insurer's assets, the definition of ultimate net loss should be clearly worded. This clause should reflect how the primary insurer and reinsurer intend for the primary insurer's various treaties to operate. For example, defining ultimate net loss on a gross loss basis means that the reinsurer does not benefit from the primary insurer's other reinsurance. To illustrate, a catastrophic event may trigger a recovery from facultative reinsurance agreements on specific loss exposures that are also subject to the catastrophe treaty. If the catastrophe treaty were on a gross loss basis, then the facultative reinsurance recoveries would not reduce the amount of the primary insurer's loss in determining if the catastrophe treaty's attachment point had been met. Consequently, catastrophe losses would possibly accumulate more quickly. The sample ultimate net loss clause shown in Exhibit 10-6 would not produce such a result. It specifies that ultimate net loss means actual loss retained by the primary insurer, so all other reinsurance inures to the benefit of the catastrophe treaty.

> **EXHIBIT 10-6**
>
> **Ultimate Net Loss Clause**
>
> 54 A
>
> ULTIMATE NET LOSS
>
> The term "Ultimate Net Loss" means the actual loss, including loss adjustment expense, paid or to be paid by the Company on its net retained liability after making deductions for all recoveries, salvages, subrogations and all claims on inuring reinsurance, whether collectible or not; provided, however, that in the event of the insolvency of the Company, payment by the Reinsurer shall be made in accordance with the provisions of the Insolvency Article. Nothing herein shall be construed to mean that losses under this Contract are not recoverable until the Company's ultimate net loss has been ascertained.

Source: Brokers & Reinsurance Markets Association (BRMA), http://www.brma.org/download/bcwrb054.doc (accessed February 18, 2004).

Generally, the ultimate net loss definition in a catastrophe treaty includes loss adjustment expenses incurred for catastrophe losses. Loss adjustment expenses do not include regular office expenses and salaries of the primary insurer's employees. However, expenses of regular employees who are temporarily diverted from their normal and customary duties and assigned to the field to adjust a catastrophe loss can be specifically included. Only those expenses actually incurred when settling claims are covered. Any salvage or recoveries that reduce the loss are deducted from ultimate net loss and applied when they are realized, without time limit. Consequently, reinsurers can benefit from salvage recoveries after loss payment.

To calculate ultimate net loss, reinsurers deduct losses on other applicable reinsurance from the actual loss sustained, whether those losses are recovered or not. Therefore, the loss to catastrophe reinsurers is not increased if the primary insurer cannot collect amounts due from other reinsurers under inuring reinsurance.

Loss Occurrence Clause

The loss occurrence clause defines what constitutes a catastrophic occurrence. The loss occurrence definition for a catastrophe treaty could be identical or very similar to the loss occurrence definition in a property per risk excess of loss treaty with a per occurrence limitation. The similarity exists because property per risk excess of loss reinsurers want to limit their losses from catastrophes. Exhibit 10-7 shows a sample loss occurrence clause that could be found in a catastrophe treaty.

In the sample clause shown in Exhibit 10-7, losses from causes of loss not specifically described are limited to those occurring within 168 consecutive hours.

EXHIBIT 10-7

Loss Occurrence Clause

27 E
LOSS OCCURRENCE

The term "Loss Occurrence" shall mean the sum of all individual losses directly occasioned by any one disaster, accident or loss or series of disasters, accidents or losses arising out of one event which occurs within the area of one state of the United States or province of Canada and states or provinces contiguous thereto and to one another. However, the duration and extent of any one "Loss Occurrence" shall be limited to all individual losses sustained by the Company occurring during any period of 168 consecutive hours arising out of and directly occasioned by the same event except that the term "Loss Occurrence" shall be further defined as follows:

(i) As regards windstorm, hail, tornado, hurricane, cyclone, including ensuing collapse and water damage, all individual losses sustained by the Company occurring during any period of 72 consecutive hours arising out of and directly occasioned by the same event. However, the event need not be limited to one state or province or states or provinces contiguous thereto.

(ii) As regards riot, riot attending a strike, civil commotion, vandalism and malicious mischief, all individual losses sustained by the Company occurring during any period of 72 consecutive hours within the area of one municipality or county and the municipalities or counties contiguous thereto arising out of and directly occasioned by the same event. The maximum duration of 72 consecutive hours may be extended in respect of individual losses which occur beyond such 72 consecutive hours during the continued occupation of an assured's premises by strikers, provided such occupation commenced during the aforesaid period.

(iii) As regards earthquake (the epicenter of which need not necessarily be within the territorial confines referred to in the opening paragraph of this Article) and fire following directly occasioned by the earthquake, only those individual fire losses which commence during the period of 168 consecutive hours may be included in the Company's "Loss Occurrence."

(iv) As regards "Freeze," only individual losses directly occasioned by collapse, breakage of glass and water damage (caused by bursting of frozen pipes and tanks) may be included in the Company's "Loss Occurrence."

For all "Loss Occurrences," other than (ii) above, the Company may choose the date and time when any such period of consecutive hours commences provided that it is not earlier than the date and time of the occurrence of the first recorded individual loss sustained by the Company arising out of that disaster, accident or loss and provided that only one such period of 168 consecutive hours shall apply with respect to one event, except for any "Loss Occurrence" referred to in subparagraph (i) above where only one such period of 72 consecutive hours shall apply with respect to one event, regardless of the duration of the event.

Continued on next page.

> As respects those "Loss Occurrences" referred to in (ii) above, if the disaster, accident or loss occasioned by the event is of greater duration than 72 consecutive hours, then the Company may divide that disaster, accident or loss into two or more "Loss Occurrences" provided no two periods overlap and no individual loss is included in more than one such period and provided that no period commences earlier than the date and time of the occurrence of the first recorded individual loss sustained by the Company arising out of that disaster, accident or loss.
>
> No individual losses occasioned by an event that would be covered by 72 hours clauses may be included in any "Loss Occurrence" claimed under the 168 hours provision.

Source: BRMA, http://www.brma.org/download/bcwrb027.doc (accessed February 18, 2004).

The final paragraph in Exhibit 10-7 addresses the possibility of a catastrophe involving more than one cause of loss with different hour limitations. For example, a hurricane could involve windstorm losses subject to the 72-hour limitation and flood losses subject to the 168-hour limitation. The primary insurer could consider all losses arising out of the hurricane as a single loss occurrence, subject to the hour limitations indicated.

Other Reinsurance Clause

Other reinsurance clause
A reinsurance treaty clause that specifies whether the retention applies only to the primary insurer's net retention or to both the primary insurer's net retention and the underlying reinsurance.

The **other reinsurance clause** specifies whether the retention applies only to the primary insurer's net retention or to both the primary insurer's net retention *and* the underlying reinsurance. If the stated retention does not apply to underlying reinsurance, the primary insurer is left with a gap in reinsurance coverage. For example, if the stated retention for a second layer $5 million xs $5 million catastrophe treaty that overlies a first layer $4 million xs $1 million catastrophe treaty does not include the first layer's retention, the primary insurer would have a $1 million net retention on the first layer and would then have an *additional* $4 million retention before the second layer would operate. Exhibit 10-8 illustrates this.

The problem illustrated in Exhibit 10-8 is overcome by simply acknowledging the underlying reinsurance layer. Exhibit 10-9 shows an example of an other reinsurance clause that acknowledges both a property per risk excess of loss and an underlying catastrophe treaty.

Reinstatement Clause

The reinstatement clause of a catastrophe treaty is drafted to reflect the possibility that multiple catastrophic occurrences can occur in a single year. Because of this possibility, the treaty, through the reinstatement clause, usually provides for an automatic reinstatement of the reinsurance limit. The reinstated reinsurance limit is usually provided for an additional premium. However, the reinstated reinsurance limit can only be used after the primary insurer has met its retention again. After the reinstated reinsurance limit has been exhausted, no coverage is provided under the treaty for future loss occurrences.

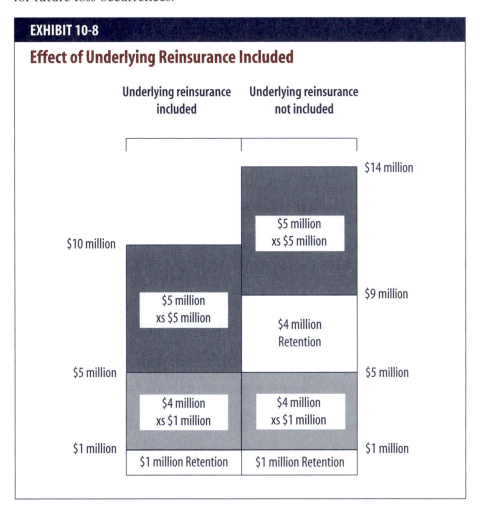

EXHIBIT 10-8
Effect of Underlying Reinsurance Included

EXHIBIT 10-9

Other Reinsurance Clause

The Company shall maintain in force property per risk excess of loss reinsurance, recoveries under which shall inure to the benefit of this Contract.

The Company shall be permitted to carry underlying catastrophe reinsurance, recoveries under which shall inure solely to the benefit of the Company and be entirely disregarded in applying all of the provisions of this Contract.

Typically, catastrophe treaties provide for immediate reinstatement of the limit to give the primary insurer the maximum possible limits without delay in case another loss occurrence involves the treaty. The sample reinstatement clause in Exhibit 10-10 provides for immediate reinstatement of the limit. This sample clause specifies a limit per loss occurrence and an overall maximum limit.

EXHIBIT 10-10

Reinstatement Clause

A. In the event all or any portion of the reinsurance hereunder is exhausted by loss, the amount so exhausted shall be reinstated immediately from the time the loss occurrence commences hereon. For each amount so reinstated the Company agrees to pay additional premium equal to the product of the following:

1. The percentage of the occurrence limit reinstated (based on the loss paid by the Reinsurer);

2. The earned reinsurance premium for the term of this Contract (exclusive of reinstatement premium).

B. Whenever the Company requests payment by the Reinsurer of any loss hereunder, the Company shall submit a statement to the Reinsurer of reinstatement premium due the Reinsurer. If the earned reinsurance premium for the term of this Contract has not been finally determined as of the date of any such statement, the calculation of reinstatement premium due shall be based on the annual deposit premium and shall be readjusted when the earned reinsurance premium for the term of this Contract has been finally determined. Any reinstatement premium shown to be due the Reinsurer as reflected by any such statement (less prior payments, if any) shall be payable by the Company concurrently with payment by the Reinsurer of the requested loss. Any return reinstatement premium shown to be due the Company shall be remitted by the Reinsurer as promptly as possible after receipt and verification of the Company's statement.

C. Notwithstanding anything stated herein, the liability of the Reinsurer hereunder shall not exceed __95%__ of __$4,000,000__ as respects loss or losses arising out of any one loss occurrence, nor shall it exceed __95%__ of __$8,000,000__ in all during the term of this Contract.

Typically, the reinsurer charges a pro rata amount of the original reinsurance premium as the reinstatement premium without adjusting for the length of the treaty's remaining term. Exhibit 10-11 provides an example of how the reinstatement premium is often calculated for catastrophe treaties. For simplicity, the example assumes that the catastrophe treaty has neither a co-participation provision nor inuring reinsurance.

EXHIBIT 10-11

Reinstatement Premium Calculation for a Catastrophe Treaty

Original limit = 100% of $4,000,000 xs $1,000,000

Gross amount of loss = $3,000,000

Original premium = $650,250

Reinstatement pro rata as to amount and 100% as to time

The reinstatement premium is calculated as follows:

Amount of loss applicable to the treaty	$3,000,000
Minus net retention	(1,000,000)
Amount recoverable	$2,000,000
Amount recoverable as a percentage of original limit*	0.50
Multiplied by the original premium	× 650,250
Reinstatement premium	$325,125

* $2,000,000 ÷ $4,000,000 = 50%

The example in Exhibit 10-11 shows a partial reinstatement because the amount recoverable from the reinsurer ($2 million) is less than the $4 million treaty limit for each loss occurrence. A gross loss of $5 million in the above example would have resulted in an amount recoverable of $4 million and payment of a reinstatement premium equal to the original premium.

Most property catastrophe occurrences are known immediately. The primary insurer and reinsurer know that some of the catastrophe treaty limit will be used, triggering a reinstatement. Although the extent of the loss is seldom known for some time, a reinstatement premium can be calculated after a reasonable estimate of the loss amount is made. The premium is typically due concurrently with loss payments made by the reinsurer and is periodically adjusted until the loss is completely settled.[4]

CATASTROPHE MODELING

Catastrophe models are computer programs that estimate losses from potential catastrophic events. In the U.S., the principal causes of loss modeled are hurricane, earthquake (shake loss plus the resulting fire loss), tornado, and hail. Catastrophe models may also be used for causes of loss such as winter freeze, brush fire, and terrorism. Primary insurers use catastrophe models to anticipate the financial effect of catastrophic events and to help them select reinsurance limits.

Catastrophe models
Computer programs that estimate losses from potential catastrophic events.

Users of catastrophe modeling information should understand what assumptions underlie the model and how results can be evaluated. Because results from different catastrophe models vary, a primary insurer often considers information derived from several catastrophe models.

Before computerized catastrophe models were introduced, primary insurers typically estimated a potential catastrophe's financial effect by tracking written premiums and associated aggregate liability by geographic area. Those estimates considered potential loss severity but not the specific probability that a catastrophe would occur. Computerized catastrophe models measure not only potential loss severity but also the probability that a catastrophic event will occur.

This section describes how catastrophe models work and how they are used. It also illustrates catastrophe modeling with an example. The section concludes by discussing catastrophe modeling issues.

How Catastrophe Modeling Operates

Most catastrophe models are proprietary and the owners of these models usually choose not to share the specifics of how their models operate. However, catastrophe models typically include the following three generic components:

1. Science component
2. Engineering component
3. Insurance component

Catastrophe models use insurer-supplied loss exposure data to produce a range of estimated losses that may result from the catastrophic event(s) being modeled. The inputs and outputs of catastrophe models and their use are described later in this section. Exhibit 10-12 shows the components of a catastrophe model along with its inputs and outputs.

Science Component

The first component of a catastrophe model is the science component. The **science component** simulates a catastrophic event. Meteorologists, seismologists, and geophysicists develop theories and identify variables to estimate a catastrophe's characteristics. For example, the science component may estimate the location of an earthquake's epicenter, whether the earthquake would occur between two of the earth's plates or within one plate, the earthquake's magnitude, and the soil conditions at the earthquake's location.

Catastrophe models may produce different results because they are based on different theories and variables. For example, over 100 years of data are available on hurricanes. However, the early data are not as detailed, sophisticated, or accurate as recent data. Also, the quantity of data on hurricanes may not be adequate to develop reliable estimates of future events. Therefore, scientists often must rely on incomplete data and consequently develop different theories about the potential frequency and severity of future hurricanes.

Science component
The element of a catastrophe model that simulates a catastrophic event.

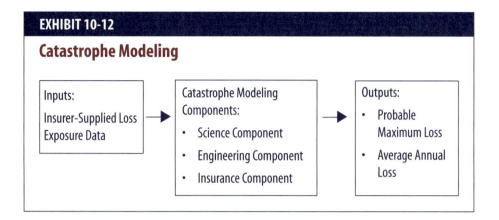

EXHIBIT 10-12

Catastrophe Modeling

Inputs: Insurer-Supplied Loss Exposure Data → Catastrophe Modeling Components: Science Component, Engineering Component, Insurance Component → Outputs: Probable Maximum Loss, Average Annual Loss

Engineering Component

The second component of a catastrophe model is the engineering component. The **engineering component** uses the information from the science component to estimate the extent of structural damage that would occur based on a simulated catastrophe. Those estimates incorporate information such as building construction, building height, building codes enforcement, and surrounding terrain that may affect the damaging forces or may contribute flying debris. The engineering component estimates how structural damage would affect a building and its contents and the amount of time that may be required to repair the damage.

Another reason why catastrophe models produce different results is because they use different engineering research to determine damageability. For example, research and professional opinions vary regarding the effects of hurricane winds and flying debris on different types of structures.

Engineering component
The element of a catastrophe model that uses the information from the science component to estimate the extent of structural damage that would occur based on a simulated catastrophic event.

Insurance Component

The third component of a catastrophe model is the insurance component. The **insurance component** evaluates the effect of a simulated catastrophe on the insurer's in-force policies and operating results. Depending on the magnitude of the simulated catastrophe, the primary insurer will sustain a range of losses. The insurance component usually reflects the coverage characteristics of the in-force policies, such as whether they are on an actual cash value basis or on a replacement cost basis.

Some catastrophe models include socioeconomic factors, such as the likelihood of fraud and theft following a catastrophe. Demand surge is another factor to consider in calculating the total insured loss. Demand surge occurs when repair costs increase dramatically following a catastrophe because of supply shortages. For example, the price of glass, roof shingles, and plywood could increase significantly in the affected area following a hurricane.

Insurance component
The element of a catastrophe model that evaluates the effect of the simulated catastrophe on the insurer's in-force policies and operating results.

How Catastrophe Modeling Is Used

Primary insurers use the results of catastrophe models to analyze the catastrophe exposure of their portfolio of in-force policies, develop marketing plans, and establish the underwriting acceptability of individual loss exposures. Reinsurers (and reinsurance intermediaries) use the results of catastrophe models to determine how an existing (or proposed) reinsurance program will respond under various catastrophe scenarios and to establish a rate for catastrophe reinsurance coverage. Reinsurers also use catastrophe modeling to manage the catastrophe exposure that they have assumed from their primary insurer clients and to aid in determining catastrophe retrocessional needs.

Two key outputs from catastrophe modeling are probable maximum loss and average annual loss.

Probable maximum loss (PML)
The amount of loss expected.

Probable maximum loss (PML) is the amount of loss expected. As an alternative to looking at the PML, the primary insurer could total all the amounts of insurance sold to develop the amount needed to cover a catastrophe. However, the disadvantage of this approach is that the amount sold does not equal the amount of loss expected. Exhibit 10-13 shows an example of a PML analysis.

EXHIBIT 10-13

PML Analysis

Confidence Level (Percent)	Return Period (Years)	Probable Maximum Loss ($ millions)
99.99	10,000	234
99.95	2,000	146
99.90	1,000	127
99.80	500	104
99.70	333	92
99.60	250	75
99.50	200	67
99.00	100	44
98.00	50	24
97.00	33	17
96.00	25	13
95.00	20	9
90.00	10	3

Exhibit 10-13 shows the confidence level percentage, return period in years, and PML in millions of dollars. The confidence level is assigned by the catastrophe model and indicates the confidence level in the other results shown. For example, a confidence level of 100 percent indicates absolute certainty, while a lower confidence level percentage indicates less certainty. Return period is the estimated number of years between catastrophic events that would cause the PML shown in the next column. According to the PML analysis shown in Exhibit 10-13, a $44 million catastrophe loss is expected every 100 years with a 99 percent probability and a $75 million catastrophe loss is expected every 250 years with a 99.6 percent probability. Based on this analysis, the primary insurer can make an informed decision as to the size of the reinsurance limit it should purchase.

The **average annual loss (AAL)** is the long-term average loss expected in any one year that represents the loss cost for the in-force polices for the cause of loss being modeled. When the analysis is performed on a ZIP Code level, the catastrophe model produces AAL values for each ZIP Code. ZIP Codes with high AAL values are particularly vulnerable to catastrophic loss. Because AAL values reflect all the components of the catastrophe model (science, engineering, and insurance), AAL values are more effective in identifying concentrations of catastrophe-prone in-force policies than a simple review of the geographic distribution of in-force policies.

Average annual loss (AAL)
The long-term average loss expected in any one year that represents the loss cost for the in-force polices for the cause of loss being modeled.

AAL analysis has several uses. Catastrophe models can generate policy-level AAL information so that reinsurance rates can be developed. The AAL can be allocated between the primary insurer's net retention and the reinsurance program to determine the AAL to the reinsurance program. If the cause of loss being modeled is the only cause of loss covered by the reinsurance program, a reinsurer could develop a rate by adding its own expense and profit factors to the AAL. Reinsurers and primary insurers can also use AAL information to compare the pricing of different reinsurance program proposals.

Example of Catastrophe Modeling

Andalusia Insurance Company (Andalusia) sells homeowners policies and policies for small commercial businesses, and has sold many policies in New York and New Jersey. Because the loss exposures for its existing in-force policy portfolio are located primarily on the coast, this insurer has a significant wind exposure.

Andalusia concluded its first catastrophe modeling analysis a year ago. That analysis yielded a 100-year PML of $20 million and a 250-year PML of $50 million, both with 100% confidence levels. Andalusia has $15 million of policyholders' surplus and catastrophe reinsurance with a per occurrence limit of $25 million. Its written premiums have grown 25 percent over the last year. Another catastrophe modeling analysis would show how that growth has affected Andalusia's loss exposure to hurricanes.

Andalusia begins the catastrophe modeling process by collecting information on its in-force policies to create its loss exposure data. Andalusia's information system maintains location information for each loss exposure insured. Andalusia's reinsurance intermediary requests detailed information shown in Exhibit 10-14 on each policy sold.

EXHIBIT 10-14

Information Required for Catastrophe Modeling

- Policy number
- Coverage form
- Type of insurance
- Location number (if multiple locations are covered under one policy)
- State code
- County code
- City
- ZIP Code (five-digit)
- Street number
- Street name
- Policy premium
- Policy limit
- Policy deductible
- Building limit
- Other structures limit
- Contents limit
- Loss of use limit
- Building height in stories
- Year built
- Occupancy type
- Construction class
- Wind peril exclusions

For a hurricane catastrophe model, the data must indicate whether wind is an excluded cause of loss. In some coastal areas, primary insurers exclude wind, and the insured often buys wind coverage from a state-sponsored coastal pool. However, in Andalusia's case, wind is an included source of loss.

If Andalusia cannot provide certain information, it can make assumptions about that information. However, the reliability of the results of the model depend on the quality of those assumptions.

The policy-level details can create a massive data file that often must be adjusted to match the catastrophe model's input criteria. For example, codes that indicate the coverage form used may need to be converted to the coverage codes used by the model. The primary insurer's information system may not capture required loss exposure data, such as the content limit for homeowners policies. Those data may need to be inserted into the data file based on Andalusia's assumptions. When the data file is ready, it is imported into the catastrophe model.

Catastrophe models that perform policy-level analysis must complete geocoding. **Geocoding** is a process of matching addresses with map positions. The catastrophe model tries to match policies to latitude and longitude. If the model cannot initially find a latitude-longitude match, it uses less and less detailed information until it finds one. For example, if street address level information is provided, the model first attempts to geocode at the street address. If the model cannot find the street address, it attempts to match at the five-digit ZIP Code level, then the city level, then the county level, until a latitude-longitude match is found.

Geocoding
A process of matching addresses with map positions.

The geocoded information is processed by the science, engineering, and insurance components of the catastrophic model to produce the following:

- Average annual loss (AAL) analysis
- Probable maximum loss (PML) analysis

The AAL analysis can be compared to the geographic distribution of in-force policies. Although geographic areas that have a large concentration of insured values usually have high AAL amounts as well, that is not always the case. AAL is a measure of vulnerability to the cause of loss being modeled, and a small number of strategically located policies may generate a relatively larger AAL than a larger number of policies in a lower risk area. Assume that Andalusia writes 25 percent of its New Jersey business in Bergen County (a northern New Jersey inland area) and 1 percent in Cape May County (a southern New Jersey coastal area). Based on geographic distribution, Andalusia may conclude that Bergen County is a serious hurricane exposure. However, a catastrophe model may show that Bergen County represents only 2 percent of the AAL and that Cape May County represents 40 percent. If the total premium collected in Cape May County were $100,000, but the AAL was $125,000, the premiums charged would be inadequate based on catastrophe modeling because the AAL from hurricanes exceeds the entire premium collected for the policies in the county.

Exhibit 10-15 shows Andalusia's PML analysis of estimated hurricane loss amounts at various return periods.

Andalusia's PML based on last year's information was $20 million at 100 years and $50 million at 250 years. Andalusia's new PML is $20 million at about 33 years and $50 million at about 160 years, so Andalusia's catastrophe exposure has worsened.

Based on that information, Andalusia could choose one or a combination of the following options:

- Purchase additional reinsurance.
- Sell fewer policies in vulnerable geographic areas.
- Offer different coverage or deductibles in vulnerable geographic areas.

Andalusia currently has catastrophe treaty limits of $25 million. It is probably not reasonable for Andalusia to purchase a catastrophe treaty for a 1,000-year event. This would require a large amount of reinsurance or significant additional capital. Similarly, Andalusia would not want to purchase reinsurance only for a 10-year event because this would leave Andalusia with a high loss exposure. Primary insurers generally attempt to address a range of losses for wind-related or earthquake events between the 100-year and 500-year return periods.

EXHIBIT 10-15

Andalusia's PML Analysis

Confidence Level (Percent)	Return Period (Years)	Estimated Loss ($)
99.90	1,000	96,798,825
99.80	500	88,630,502
99.70	333	76,741,547
99.60	250	64,455,436
99.50	200	54,325,774
99.00	100	43,719,520
98.00	50	29,466,350
97.00	33	20,644,539
96.00	25	15,796,420
95.00	20	11,460,244
90.00	10	7,434,366

Andalusia's senior management must determine its retention after considering the catastrophe model's projections. If Andalusia decides to purchase reinsurance for the 100-year event of $44 million, it should consider all events occurring above that point to ensure that none of them are likely events. For example, it may be that every event above the 100-year mark is a category 5 hurricane, the strongest category of hurricane on the Saffir-Simpson scale. Category 5 hurricanes are very rare in the Northeast, so Andalusia may be comfortable with not reinsuring events above the 100-year event. However, if some category 3 hurricanes are above the 100-year mark, Andalusia should consider reinsurance at that level. If Andalusia decides to manage a $44 million loss with additional catastrophe reinsurance, it will need to increase its reinsurance from $25 million to $44 million.

Andalusia could reduce its PML in several ways. Andalusia could develop plans to reduce the number of loss exposures in vulnerable geographic areas. The catastrophe model could be adjusted to determine the PML if specific loss exposures were removed from the portfolio. Andalusia may discover that nonrenewing selected loss exposures would reduce the PML to last year's level.

Andalusia may also decide to change coverages or deductibles. For example, it may choose to reduce the amount of additional living expense coverage offered because that coverage increases overall hurricane losses. Finally, Andalusia may decide to increase deductibles in coastal areas.

Catastrophe Modeling Issues

Catastrophe modeling is a significant departure from historical methods of primary insurer pricing and there are some issues about using catastrophe modeling in rate development. For example, in the past a primary insurer's actual historical losses may have been used to determine rates, but catastrophe models typically do not rely heavily on those historical losses. This could lead to a significant change in rates.

Another issue is that different models produce different outcomes because of the variation in the assumptions used to build each model. Also, new developments in the science, engineering, or insurance components can affect how a model works so that it produces different results even if the data have not changed.

Catastrophe models also place significant demands on primary insurers' information systems. The primary insurer's data must be compatible with the catastrophe model's input requirements. The information that the primary insurer must capture to make the best use of catastrophe models can increase primary insurer costs.

Finally, it can be difficult to evaluate catastrophe models because those who develop them are not willing to share their proprietary information. Despite all of these issues, it is likely that catastrophe model users will become more familiar with these models, will develop more accurate and reliable ways to gather data, and will discover new ways to use the information to benefit primary insurers, reinsurers, and the public.

CATASTROPHE TREATY PRICING

Over time, a reinsurer expects to receive premiums from a primary insurer that are adequate to cover the following:

- The reinsurer's share of the primary insurer's losses and loss adjustment expenses
- The reinsurer's own expenses
- The reinsurer's reasonable profit

Excess of loss treaties are frequently priced using experience rating and exposure rating techniques. However, experience rating is not generally used in pricing catastrophe treaties for the following reasons:

- Insufficient catastrophe losses occur to provide sufficient data to accurately estimate future losses and future premiums.
- Reinsured underlying policies can change so quickly that actual losses may not be useful in accurately estimating future losses.

However, a primary insurer's catastrophe loss experience data is still useful. It can be trended for any changes in the number of exposure units insured and the increased cost of construction. For example, assume that a particular region had a catastrophe loss in 1999 when 1,000 policies were in force. However, by 2003, the policy count for that particular region had changed. If the policy count had grown to 2,000 policies, the 1999 loss may be doubled. If the policy count had dropped to 500, because the primary insurer reduced the number of underlying policies sold following the loss, the estimated loss may be one-half the 1999 loss. The 1999 loss could also be adjusted for increased construction costs using a construction cost index. However, this type of trending is most appropriately used with exposure rating.

Catastrophe treaty pricing uses exposure rating based on trend analysis of a primary insurer's underlying policies. Catastrophe modeling is increasingly used to generate the expected loss information. Improvements in catastrophe modeling technology for measuring loss exposure have caused prices for catastrophe treaties to be based more on exposure and less on supply and demand.

Primary insurers charge insurance rates that include an amount for expected losses, including catastrophic losses. However, reinsurers charge rates for catastrophe treaties that are usually independent of, and seldom consider, the underlying insurance rates. Catastrophe treaty rates are based on other considerations, including the following:

- Attachment point
- Layers and limits
- Underlying insurance analysis
- Inuring reinsurance
- Payback of prior losses
- Reinsurance limit

Attachment Point

The attachment point is the amount of ultimate net loss that the primary insurer will retain in any one loss occurrence before reinsurance coverage is triggered. Catastrophe treaties usually have very high attachment points. The cost of a catastrophe treaty generally decreases as the attachment point increases.

Layers and Limits

A primary insurer may buy several layers of catastrophe reinsurance. The treaty layers should not overlap or leave gaps in coverage. Exhibit 10-16 illustrates possible layers for a medium-sized primary insurer.

Dividing a reinsurance program into layers allows the primary insurer to make optimal use of the reinsurance capacity available in the marketplace. Catastrophe reinsurance programs require a large amount of reinsurance capacity, more than any one reinsurer may be willing to provide. Consequently,

EXHIBIT 10-16
Illustration of Treaty Layer

Layer	Limit/Retention
1	$1.5 million xs $1 million
2	$2.5 million xs $2.5 million
3	$5 million xs $5 million
4	$5 million xs $10 million
5	$10 million xs $15 million

many reinsurers may take a percentage of each reinsurance layer. Also, reinsurers' underwriting guidelines often limit what they can provide per layer and per reinsurance program. Usually, their per program capacity is several times their per layer capacity. Therefore, if the primary insurer has only one layer for its total program, each reinsurer could be restricted to one participation in one layer rather than having a larger aggregate participation through several layers.

For example, assume that Descanso Re has a maximum capacity per treaty of $1 million and a reinsurance program capacity of $5 million. If a primary insurer has only one layer of $24 million xs $1 million, Descanso Re could authorize a participation of only $1 million. However, if the primary reinsurer's reinsurance program were split into five layers as shown in the table above, Descanso Re could authorize a participation of $5 million consisting of $1 million for each layer.

The low layers of a catastrophe reinsurance program experience more loss frequency than high layers because only the largest losses affect the high layers. Typically, the limits become larger in high layers to reflect this lower loss frequency and higher loss severity.

Some reinsurers prefer low layers that have high premiums and that experience more frequent losses. Others prefer high layers with low premiums and fewer losses. Some reinsurers prefer to skip layers, also called ventilate participation. For example, a reinsurer may participate in the first, third, fifth, and seventh layers. By layering the catastrophe reinsurance program, the primary insurer provides the maximum opportunity for reinsurers to participate in the program and facilitates placement.

Underlying Insurance Analysis

Reinsurers analyze the primary insurer's underlying insurance to determine whether they want to participate in a particular catastrophe reinsurance program, and to establish rates. Reinsurers consider the following in their analyses:

- Geographic distribution of loss exposures
- Estimated subject premium for the contract year to be rated

- Subject premium and loss history
- Property residual market facility participation
- Miscellaneous information

Geographic Distribution of Loss Exposures

The geographic distribution of loss exposures by region, state, county, or ZIP Code defines where the underlying loss exposures are physically located. The distribution can show premium, policy count, or total policy limits. Catastrophe modeling uses much of this information to perform catastrophe analysis.

The primary insurer's geographic distribution of loss exposures may change because of new marketing and underwriting strategies. Reinsurers must understand changes in the primary insurer's geographic distribution of loss exposures to accurately estimate the PML and to develop catastrophe rates.

Estimated Subject Premium for the Contract Year to Be Rated

Reinsurers also analyze the estimated subject premium for the contract year to be rated. Catastrophe treaty pricing is often expressed as a percentage of subject premium, either written or earned, for the treaty's term. Because the actual subject premium is not known until after the treaty's term, the primary insurer must estimate the subject premium for the reinsurer for pricing purposes. The dollar amount negotiated for the limit of reinsurance is stated as a percentage of this estimated subject premium. If at the end of the year the actual subject premium is greater than the estimate, the premium that the primary insurer must pay to the reinsurer increases. If actual subject premium is less than the estimate, the premium that the primary insurer must pay to the reinsurer decreases, usually subject to a minimum reinsurance premium. This assumes that any differences in the estimated subject premium and actual subject premium reflect loss exposure changes.

Subject Premium and Loss History

Subject premium and loss history are additional sources of information for the reinsurers' analyses. Usually, reinsurers analyze subject premium and catastrophe loss history for at least ten prior years to establish reinsurance rates. Reinsurers often request a history of catastrophe losses, usually stated as loss occurrence above a certain dollar amount, such as 50 percent of the proposed retention, to gain insight into past loss experience. Reinsurers analyze changes made to a primary insurer's underlying insurance from the time of those catastrophe losses to determine the potential for similar losses recurring.

Reinsurers need subject premium by state for the expiring contract year and estimated subject premium by state for the coming contract year to price the reinsurance coverage. States differ in their catastrophe loss exposures and their regulatory requirements for participation in involuntary catastrophe facilities, such as those discussed next. The judicial environment also differs by state.

Property Residual Market Facility Participation

Reinsurers also analyze the primary insurer's participation in property residual market facilities. Many states have formed property residual market facilities to provide property insurance that cannot be obtained in the voluntary market. Those facilities were created to address insurance availability problems. Generally, all primary insurers that sell insurance in the state must participate in the facility. Each primary insurer's participation in the facility is based on its share of the voluntary property market in the state.

When a catastrophe occurs, residual market facilities can incur large losses. Typically, residual market facilities pass on any deficits to primary insurers operating in the state according to the market share of the primary insurer. Because those assessments result from a specific loss occurrence, they are usually covered by catastrophe treaties by adding the assessments to a primary insurer's direct loss from the loss occurrence. Participation in property residual market facilities can be a significant component of a primary insurer's exposure to catastrophic events. To estimate potential assessments, reinsurers must know the primary insurer's participation in each such facility.

Coastal pools are examples of property residual market facilities that can cause catastrophe treaty losses. Several Gulf of Mexico and Atlantic coastal states have formed coastal pools to provide property insurance for loss exposures that are located in the coastal areas and that could not be insured in the voluntary market.

Many states also have Fair Access to Insurance Requirements (FAIR) plans. Most state FAIR plans were established in the 1960s after urban riots occurred in Los Angeles; Detroit; and Newark, New Jersey. Initially, those facilities provided insurance in urban areas where insurance in the voluntary market was unavailable. FAIR plans subsequently evolved and now have broad definitions that allow them to offer insurance in a variety of areas. Similar to coastal pools, FAIR plans could incur a significant loss from one loss occurrence, which would be passed on through assessments to primary insurers operating in the state.

Miscellaneous Information

Finally, reinsurers should obtain the following information when analyzing primary insurers' underlying policies:

- Rate change history for the subject policies
- Limits and deductibles for the subject policies, including summaries of subject policies in policy limit ranges
- Actual coverage history and proposed coverage changes

Analyzing this information enables the reinsurer to gain a better understanding of the primary insurer's underlying policies and the changes that may occur that will affect the current year's operating results.

Inuring Reinsurance

Inuring reinsurance reduces the amount of loss to the catastrophe treaty. Because of this, reinsurers should consider the amount of inuring reinsurance when pricing the catastrophe treaty. Also, premiums paid for pro rata inuring reinsurance reduce the amount of subject premium under the catastrophe treaty. Therefore, the reinsurance rate applies to a smaller amount of subject premium for a catastrophe treaty above pro rata inuring reinsurance than for one without pro rata inuring reinsurance. To price a catastrophe treaty, the reinsurer needs to review the current inuring reinsurance agreements in addition to past and projected agreements and rates. If a change to the inuring reinsurance is proposed, historical subject premiums and losses should be shown as if that projected structure were in place. This adjustment ensures a consistent evaluation of losses and premiums over time.

Payback of Prior Losses

Relationships between primary insurers and reinsurers are usually long term and are represented by either continuous reinsurance treaties or multiple renewals of term treaties. The goal of a reinsurance relationship is to spread the primary insurer's unexpected losses over time. The reinsurer expects that it will be paid back for indemnification payments made to the primary insurer. Many reinsurers use a "banking plan" in which they keep track of all the premiums they have received from a primary insurer and the losses that they have paid. Under such a plan, the primary insurer knows that a catastrophe loss payment by the reinsurer will be included in "the bank" and amortized over a specified number of years so that the reinsurer can be repaid. The number of years specified for the repayment of catastrophe losses significantly affects the reinsurance premium as the reinsurance relationship continues and catastrophe losses are incurred.

Two measures are often used in catastrophe treaty pricing to evaluate the reasonableness of the reinsurance premium relative to number of years it would take the reinsurer to recoup catastrophe loss payments. These two measures are:

1. Payback period
2. Rate on line

Payback period
The number of years that a treaty would need to continue at the present reinsurance premium for the reinsurer to recoup the payment of the reinsurance limit under the treaty.

The **payback period** specifies the number of years that a treaty would need to continue at the present reinsurance premium for the reinsurer to recoup the payment of the reinsurance limit under the treaty. The payback period is calculated as follows:

Payback period = Reinsurance limit ÷ Reinsurance premium paid.

For example, if the treaty's reinsurance limit is 95% of $10 million (or $9.5 million) and the premium paid is $1 million, the payback period would be 9.5 years. If a total loss to the treaty were to occur, it would take 9.5 years to pay back the layer with current pricing. In its evaluation, the reinsurer may be satisfied with a 9.5 year payback. However, the reinsurer may choose to increase the reinsurance premium and thereby shorten the payback period.

Rate on line (ROL), as with the payback period, is a measure of the appropriateness of the reinsurance premium relative to the reinsurance limit. Whereas the payback period is stated in years, the ROL is a percentage. ROL is calculated as follows:

Rate on line (ROL)
A measure of the appropriateness of the reinsurance premium relative to the reinsurance limit.

Rate on line = Reinsurance premium paid ÷ Reinsurance limit.

For example, if the treaty's reinsurance limit is 95% of $10 million (or $9.5 million) and the premium paid is $1 million, the rate on line would be 10.5 percent. Rate on line is the mathematical inverse of the payback period calculation.

Catastrophe treaty pricing reflects the amount of loss financing the reinsurer is willing to provide the primary insurer should a catastrophe loss occur. These measures, particularly rate on line, serve as a quick gauge of the treaty's pricing although the rate on line percentage is not the reinsurance rate. Reinsurers and reinsurer intermediaries often ask prospective primary insurer clients what their rate on line is to evaluate the price the primary insurer is currently paying for its catastrophe reinsurance coverage.

Reinsurer expectations for the appropriateness of the payback period and rate on line often depend on the layer of the catastrophe treaty being priced. A lower catastrophe treaty layer will often have a shorter payback period (or a higher rate on line) because lower layers are more likely to be exceeded by catastrophe losses and the reinsurer wants to be paid back before the next catastrophe loss occurs.

Although reinsurers have an expectation of being paid back for losses covered under catastrophe treaties, those expectations are usually only met in lower layers of the treaty in which the reinsurance premium can fund the treaty over a reasonable period of time. For example, a twenty year payback may be considered an appropriate reinsurance premium for one reinsurer, while a fifty year payback would not. The higher layers of a catastrophe treaty may be so high that no losses are expected. Consequently, the reinsurance premium charged is usually low and the payback period, if calculated, is many more years than is practical to consider. Therefore, for high layers of catastrophe reinsurance protection, the reinsurer is trying to ensure that the reinsurance premium will fund catastrophe losses.

Reinsurance Limit

An important consideration in catastrophe treaty pricing is setting the catastrophe reinsurance limit. The primary insurer, with the assistance of the reinsurer or reinsurance intermediary, uses catastrophe models to analyze their portfolio of in-force policies and determine a range of possible outcomes from catastrophic events. As shown earlier in this chapter, a catastrophe model can show the PML within certain time frames and can generate average annual loss figures. Using data such as this, the primary insurer can select a reinsurance limit that will protect it from the largest loss it expects to occur.

ALTERNATIVES TO TRADITIONAL CATASTROPHE REINSURANCE

Primary insurers sometimes seek alternative methods of managing their catastrophe exposures. A primary insurer may choose an alternative method to take advantage of the high credit quality of some of the capital markets or for greater capacity. Catastrophe reinsurance can be expensive after a single catastrophe or series of catastrophes reduces the global reinsurance capacity. A primary insurer may seek alternative methods if it wants to replace or supplement its current catastrophe reinsurance program.

Alternative methods rely on capital markets to securitize the insurance risk. That means that instead of purchasing reinsurance to cover its potential liabilities, the primary insurer uses security instruments to finance insurance risk. Among the methods most often used are:

- Lines of credit
- Catastrophe bonds
- Catastrophe options
- Catastrophe risk exchanges

Lines of Credit

Line of credit
An arrangement that allows borrowing up to a prescribed limit.

A **line of credit** is an arrangement that allows borrowing up to a prescribed limit. Lines of credit do not represent any risk transfer, they simply provide access to capital.

Catastrophe Bonds

Catastrophe bond
A bond issued by an insurer with a condition that if the issuer suffers a catastrophe loss greater than a specified amount, the obligation to pay interest and/or repay principal is deferred or forgiven.

A **catastrophe bond** is a bond issued by an insurer with a condition that if the issuer suffers a catastrophe loss greater than a specified amount, the obligation to pay interest and/or repay principal is deferred or forgiven. As long as catastrophe-related losses do not exceed the specified amount, investors earn a relatively high interest rate and receive a return of their principal. If catastrophe losses exceed the specified loss amount, the interest and/or principal forgone by bondholders is used to pay losses.

Catastrophe bonds are typically sold through a third party called a special purpose vehicle. The special purpose vehicle is paid a fee by the insurer for arranging and administering the deal, and pays interest and returns the principal on a specified date if the losses do not exceed the specified amount. Money paid into a special purpose vehicle is tax-deductible as a reinsurance expense.

Catastrophe Options

Catastrophe options are another means insurers use to transfer insurance risk to financial markets. A **catastrophe option** is an agreement that gives the purchaser the right to a cash payment if a specified index of catastrophe losses reaches a specified level. The catastrophe index, such as that provided by the Property Claims Service (PCS), keeps track of catastrophe losses by geographic region, by cause of loss, and by time of occurrence. The seller of the catastrophe option profits if the specified level on the catastrophe index is not reached.

Catastrophe options can be structured to imitate the operation of catastrophe reinsurance and some insurers are using catastrophe options to replace part of their reinsurance program. However, payments from catastrophe options and from catastrophe reinsurance are not triggered by the same events. For example, a catastrophe option would pay when hurricane-caused catastrophe losses in Florida exceed the specified amount even though the primary insurer holding the catastrophe option has sustained only minimal losses from the hurricane that are not sufficient to trigger the reinsurance. Alternatively, the primary insurer holding a catastrophe option may sustain significant losses from a hurricane that triggered the reinsurance but where the aggregate loss for the geographic region and time period covered by the index was insufficient to trigger an option payment.

Catastrophe options are attractive to capital market investors because insurance risk does not appear to be correlated with the risk associated with other securities. Therefore, they can be used to help to diversify an investment portfolio.

Catastrophe option
An agreement that gives the purchaser the right to a cash payment if a specified index of catastrophe losses reaches a specified level.

Catastrophe Risk Exchanges

A **catastrophe risk exchange** gives primary insurers a forum in which to trade insurance risk with other insurers. The insurance risk traded may differ by geographic area, type of property, or cause of loss insured against. An insurer with a geographic concentration of loss exposures can use a catastrophe risk exchange to reduce its losses from a single loss occurrence. An insurer can also diversify the kinds of property insured to make it less susceptible to heavy losses from a single cause of loss.

Catastrophe risk exchange
A forum in which primary insurers can trade insurance risk with other insurers.

SUMMARY

The function of catastrophe treaties is to limit the financial consequences of catastrophic events. As with other forms of reinsurance, catastrophe treaties may be structured in layers. Low layers have lower limits, higher loss frequency, and higher premiums than high layers.

Some clauses that are designed or adapted for catastrophe treaties include the following:

- *Term clause.* The term clause defines the term of the reinsurance treaty.
- *Retention and limits clause.* The retention and limits clause in a catastrophe treaty should include the net retention stated as the ultimate net loss per occurrence, a co-participation provision, and a per loss occurrence limit.
- *Ultimate net loss clause.* The ultimate net loss clause in a catastrophe treaty defines what constitutes a loss.
- *Loss occurrence clause.* The loss occurrence clause defines what constitutes a catastrophic occurrence.
- *Other reinsurance clause.* The other reinsurance clause specifies whether the retention applies only to the primary insurer's net retention or to both the primary insurer's net retention and the underlying reinsurance.
- *Reinstatement clause.* The reinstatement clause in a catastrophe treaty reflects the possibility that multiple catastrophic occurrences can occur in a single year.

Catastrophe models, computer programs that estimate losses from potential catastrophic events, can be used by primary insurers to anticipate the financial effect of catastrophic events. A catastrophe model typically includes the following three generic components:

1. Science component
2. Engineering component
3. Insurance component

Two key outputs from catastrophe modeling are probable maximum loss (PML) and average annual loss (AAL).

Catastrophe treaty pricing is affected by:

- Attachment point
- Layers and limits
- Underlying insurance analysis
- Inuring reinsurance
- Payback of prior losses
- Reinsurance limit

Primary insurers may seek alternative methods of managing their catastrophe exposures, such as:

- *Lines of credit.* A line of credit is an arrangement that allows borrowing up to a prescribed limit.
- *Catastrophe bonds.* A catastrophe bond is a bond issued by an insurer with a condition that if the insurer suffers a catastrophic loss greater than a specified amount, the obligation to pay interest and/or replay principal is deferred or forgiven.

- *Catastrophe options.* A catastrophe option is an agreement that gives the purchaser the right to a cash payment if a specified index of catastrophe losses reaches a specified limit.
- *Catastrophe risk exchanges.* A catastrophe risk exchange gives primary insurers a forum in which to trade insurance risk with other insurers.

The next chapter continues the discussion of catastrophe losses by examining aggregate excess of loss reinsurance.

CHAPTER NOTES

1. Insurance Services Office, Inc., *Managing Catastrophe Risk* (New York: Insurance Services Office, Inc., 1996), p. 3.
2. Insurance Services Office, Inc., *The Impact of Catastrophes on Property Insurance* (New York: Insurance Services Office, Inc., 1994). p. 10.
3. Craig Van Anne and Thomas Larsen, "Estimating Catastrophe Losses with Computer Models," *Contingencies*, March/April 1993, p. 45.
4. Complicated property losses can take years to settle. The business interruption portion of a loss may be litigated, extending the claim settlement process. Also, some properties are difficult to repair.

Chapter 11

Direct Your Learning

Aggregate Excess of Loss Treaties

After learning the content of this chapter, you should be able to:

- Explain the purpose and operation of aggregate excess of loss treaties.
- Explain the approaches to aggregate excess of loss treaty pricing.

OUTLINE

Overview of Aggregate Excess of Loss Treaties

Aggregate Excess of Loss Treaty Pricing

Summary

Develop Your Perspective

What are the main topics covered in the chapter?

This chapter describes the purpose and operation of aggregate excess of loss treaties, and discusses how these treaties are priced.

Describe the operation of aggregate excess of loss reinsurance.

- How does an aggregate excess of loss treaty fit into a primary insurer's reinsurance program?
- How is an aggregate excess of loss treaty priced?

Why is it important to learn about these topics?

Aggregate excess of loss treaties are a means through which primary insurers can protect their financial condition from the effects of catastrophe events and the accumulation of losses. The ability to understand, analyze, and evaluate aggregate excess of loss treaties is important to enable you to determine whether these treaties are helping your company or client-insurer achieve its objectives.

Review an aggregate excess of loss treaty.

- How does the retention and limits clause (if any) operate?

How can you use what you will learn?

Evaluate your company's or client-insurer's need for aggregate excess of loss reinsurance.

- Does your company's or client-insurer's reinsurance program include aggregate excess of loss reinsurance?
- Would aggregate excess of loss reinsurance, if available and reasonably priced, provide your company or client-insurer with additional protection from catastrophe losses and protection from accumulated losses?

Chapter 11
Aggregate Excess of Loss Treaties

Aggregate excess of loss treaties protect a primary insurer from losses that occur during a specified period that exceed either a certain dollar amount or a specified loss ratio. They are also known as stop loss treaties. Aggregate excess of loss reinsurance, while responding to catastrophe losses, provides broader stabilization of loss results than does catastrophe reinsurance, but may be more difficult to obtain. Aggregate excess of loss reinsurance is always purchased on a treaty basis because it is designed to apply to a large number of loss exposures. This chapter explains the following:

- How aggregate excess of loss treaties operate.
- How aggregate excess of loss treaties are priced.

OVERVIEW OF AGGREGATE EXCESS OF LOSS TREATIES

Aggregate excess of loss treaties cover an accumulation of losses that may arise from a catastrophe or from an unforeseen accumulation of several independent losses over a specified period, usually one year. The retention and limit of an aggregate excess of loss treaty can be stated either as a dollar amount or as a loss ratio.

Aggregate excess of loss treaties operate similarly to other types of excess of loss reinsurance. The following example illustrates how an aggregate excess of loss treaty with dollar amount retention and limit applies.

Barnley Insurance Company (Barnley) specializes in general liability insurance for policyholders that have significant product liability loss exposures. Barnley was concerned that a defective product could cause bodily injury to thousands of consumers and that even modest individual losses could accumulate to an amount that could not be handled without reinsurance.

Therefore, Barnley established a reinsurance program consisting of a casualty per occurrence excess of loss treaty and a 90% of $5 million xs $10 million aggregate excess of loss treaty. At the end of the year, Barnley's general liability in-force policies incurred $20 million in losses, $5 million of which was recovered from its casualty per occurrence excess of loss reinsurers, leaving Barnley with a net incurred loss of $15 million. The aggregate excess of loss treaty indemnified Barnley for $4.5 million of this $15 million net incurred loss. Exhibit 11-1 shows how Barnley's loss recovery was calculated.

EXHIBIT 11-1

Aggregate Excess of Loss Example for Barnley Insurance Company

Gross losses incurred	$20,000,000
Minus recovery from other (inuring) reinsurance	(5,000,000)
Net losses incurred	$15,000,000
Minus aggregate excess of loss retention	(10,000,000)
Loss covered by aggregate excess of loss	$ 5,000,000
Aggregate excess of loss recovery ($0.90 \times \$5,000,000$)	$ 4,500,000
Barnley's overall loss:	
Aggregate excess of loss retention	$10,000,000
Net loss after aggregate excess of loss recovery ($\$5,000,000 - \$4,500,000$)	500,000
Total overall loss	$10,500,000

Assuming Barnley had earned premiums of $20 million, the aggregate excess of loss treaty improved its loss ratio for its in-force policies from 75 percent ($15 million ÷ $20 million) to 52.5 percent ($10.5 million ÷ $20 million).

Aggregate excess of loss treaties that state the primary insurer's retention and the reinsurer's limit of liability in terms of a loss ratio are typically used to reinsure property loss exposures. The following example illustrates how an aggregate excess of loss treaty that uses loss ratio limits applies.

Minter Insurance Company (Minter) has a portfolio of in-force property policies and extensive catastrophe treaty protection. Even so, Minter's recent market-share growth has reduced its policyholders' surplus, and management does not want to jeopardize projected earnings. Based on past loss experience, Minter believes that it will have a 70 percent loss ratio, but could sustain in excess of a 75 percent loss ratio without significant repercussions from stockholders. Minter purchases an aggregate excess of loss treaty that covers 90 percent of losses in excess of a 75 percent loss ratio up to a 110 percent loss ratio (90% of 35% xs 75% loss ratio). Exhibit 11-2 shows how Minter's stop loss treaty would apply to a 100 percent net loss ratio.

EXHIBIT 11-2

Stop Loss Example for Minter Insurance Company

	Amounts	Aggregate Excess of Loss Treaty Recovery
Net earned premiums	$20,000,000	
Gross losses incurred	$25,000,000	
Minus recovery from other (inuring) reinsurance	(5,000,000)	
Net losses incurred and net loss ratio	$20,000,000	100%
Minus aggregate excess of loss treaty retention (75% of net earned premiums)	(15,000,000)	75%
Amount exceeding retention	$ 5,000,000	25%
Recovery from treaty (0.90 × $5,000,000)	$ 4,500,000	22.5%
Net loss after stop loss treaty ($20,000,000 − $4,500,000)	$15,500,000	77.5%

Before applying the aggregate excess of loss treaty, Minter had a loss ratio of 100 percent ($20 million ÷ $20 million). The treaty reduced Minter's loss ratio to 77.5 percent ($15.5 million ÷ $20 million).

Function of Aggregate Excess of Loss Treaties

The function of aggregate excess of loss treaties is to stabilize the primary insurer's loss results. Unlike other types of excess of loss reinsurance that have per risk or per occurrence limits, an aggregate excess of loss treaty has an attachment point and limit that encompass all net losses. Once losses exceed the primary insurer's retention, future losses are indemnified by the reinsurer up to the treaty limit. Therefore, aggregate excess of loss treaties are the most effective type of reinsurance in stabilizing primary insurers' loss ratios. However, the greater the loss stability provided by the aggregate excess of loss treaty, through low retentions and high limits, the more expensive the reinsurance coverage.

Aggregate Excess of Loss Treaties as Part of a Reinsurance Program

The primary insurer usually seeks recovery from aggregate excess of loss treaties after all other reinsurance recoveries. Aggregate excess of loss treaties protect primary insurers from overall adverse loss experience including the primary insurer's net retentions of otherwise unreinsured and partially reinsured in-force policies. Aggregate excess of loss treaties are most often used with property insurance, but they can also be used to control adverse loss experience arising from liability insurance. An aggregate excess of loss treaty can be designed to cover all in-force policies that a primary insurer sells, or a subset of in-force policies.

Aggregate excess of loss treaties are less commonly used than other types of excess of loss reinsurance. However, aggregate excess of loss treaties are often used to reinsure crop-hail insurance and to reinsure small insurers for various types of insurance. Crop-hail insurance indemnifies the farmer when hail damages or destroys crops. A primary insurer's crop-hail insurance in-force policies could be extremely profitable one year and have devastating losses the next. A primary insurer's reinsurance program for its crop-hail business may include a quota share treaty; first, second, and third layer surplus share treaties; and an aggregate excess of loss treaty. Such a program is justified because of the significant adverse loss potential.

An aggregate excess of loss treaty limits the effect of underwriting losses on policyholders' surplus. So, a small primary insurer may purchase an aggregate excess of loss treaty to protect its policyholders' surplus and therefore its balance sheet position.

Small insurers are not the only ones to use aggregate excess of loss treaties. Some large stock insurers purchase aggregate excess of loss treaties, generally with large retentions, so that unexpected losses do not have an adverse effect on the income statement. This helps to protect the insurer's projected earnings and therefore potentially its stock price.

Reinsurance marketplace dislocations (supply not meeting demand) can occur that create gaps in reinsurance programs. An inadequate catastrophe reinsurance program or unplaced layers of a catastrophe treaty result in additional retentions for primary insurers and are included in their net retention under the aggregate excess of loss treaty.

Retention and Limits Clause Adapted for Use in Aggregate Excess of Loss Treaties

Aggregate excess of loss treaties contain many of the same clauses that other excess of loss treaties contain, and the clauses for aggregate excess of loss do not vary a great deal from those discussed in previous chapters. Aggregate excess of loss treaty definitions of ultimate net loss and loss occurrence are often similar to the definitions in other excess of loss treaties. However, aggregate excess of loss treaties do not define an occurrence when the retention is stated as a loss ratio.

It is unusual for an aggregate excess of loss treaty to contain a reinstatement provision because the treaty's reinsurance limits are high enough to absorb the foreseeable worst-case loss year. Also, treaties that define limits in terms of the loss ratio do not include reinstatement provisions because only one final loss ratio exists for the year. If the reinsurer is unwilling to provide the reinsurance limits that the primary insurer wants, the primary insurer can try to purchase a second layer of aggregate excess of loss reinsurance to cover losses exceeding the first layer.

Aggregate excess of loss treaties typically contain a retentions and limits clause. This clause may contain both internal and outside retentions and limits, and can apply on a losses occurring or losses incurred basis.

Internal and Outside Retentions and Limits

For an aggregate excess of loss treaty with the retention and limit stated as dollar amounts, the primary insurer retains a flat dollar amount of aggregate loss during the treaty term. In some cases, an aggregate excess of loss treaty may have two retentions. The first retention is a lower or internal retention. The internal retention is usually a flat dollar amount applied to each loss (similar to a deductible), which the primary insurer would retain and apply on a per risk or per occurrence basis. Few of the primary insurer's losses will exceed the internal retention. The internal retention protects the treaty against smaller losses.

The second retention is an aggregate or outside retention. The outside retention may be higher than the primary insurer's annual net written premiums. For the treaty to respond, the sum of losses exceeding the internal retention must exceed the outside retention during the treaty term.

The aggregate excess of loss treaty may also have two reinsurance limits. The internal limit applies above the internal retention and is the maximum loss that can be applied to the outside retention. The outside limit is the most that the reinsurer will pay after the primary insurer meets the outside retention. Exhibit 11-3 illustrates a retention and limits clause that contains internal and outside retentions and limits.

In the sample clause shown in Exhibit 11-3, the primary insurer has an internal limit of $4 million in excess of an internal retention of $1 million for each loss occurrence, subject to an outside retention of $6 million. The primary insurer would have to experience more than one loss over $1 million to recover under the treaty. One $5 million loss would contribute $4 million toward the outside retention. Another $3 million loss would contribute an additional $2 million to the outside retention. Those two losses would meet the outside retention of $6 million. The next loss that exceeds $1 million would be recoverable under the aggregate excess of loss treaty. The maximum

> **EXHIBIT 11-3**
>
> ### Retention and Limits Clause With Internal and Outside Retentions
>
> No claim shall be made hereunder during any contract year until the Company's subject excess ultimate net loss arising out of loss occurrences commencing during the contract year exceeds $6,000,000 in the aggregate. The Reinsurer shall then be liable for 95 percent of the amount by which the Company's subject excess ultimate net loss for the contract year exceeds $6,000,000 in the aggregate, but the liability of the Reinsurer shall not exceed 95 percent of $10,000,000 in total during any one contract year.
>
> "Subject excess ultimate net loss" as used herein shall mean the amount by which the Company's ultimate net loss arising out of any one loss occurrence exceeds $1,000,000, but said amount shall not exceed $4,000,000 in excess of $1,000,000.
>
> In addition to its initial retention each loss occurrence and its aggregate retention each contract year, the Company shall retain 5 percent of the excess ultimate net loss to which this Contract applies.

single loss occurrence that can contribute to the treaty is $5 million because the internal limit is $4 million in excess of $1 million. Therefore, even if the primary insurer had an $11 million loss, only the $4 million in excess of the internal $1 million retention would count toward the outside retention and the outside limit. Exhibit 11-4 illustrates how the retention and limits clause applies to those losses.

In Exhibit 11-4, the first two losses combined satisfy the $6 million outside retention. The third loss for $11 million is split as follows:

- $1 million internal retention
- 95 percent of $4 million covered by the outside limit
- $6 million, plus 5 percent of $4 million, not reinsured or not covered by the treaty

Losses Occurring Basis

The retention and limits clause for an aggregate excess of loss treaty can apply to losses on a losses occurring or losses incurred basis. On a losses occurring basis, the reinsurance applies to losses that have an occurrence date within the treaty term. The retention and limits clause may indicate the following provisions:

- The reinsurance applies to the total of all losses that occur during the treaty term.
- The retention is the greater of a dollar amount or a loss ratio.

EXHIBIT 11-4

Aggregate Excess of Loss Internal and Outside Retentions and Limits

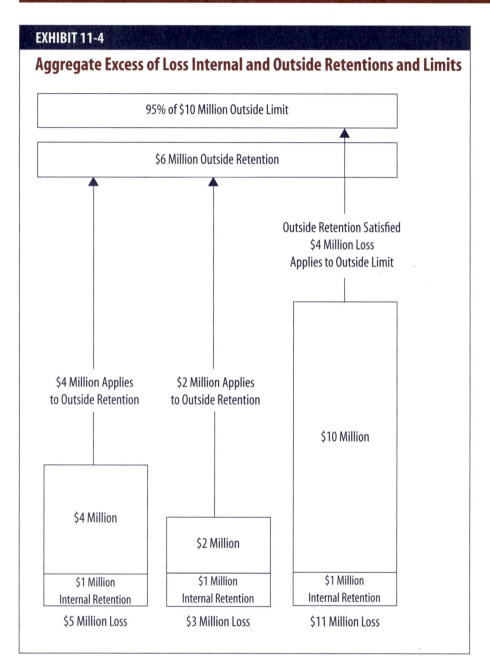

- The reinsurance limit is stated as a loss ratio or dollar amount (sometimes the lesser of the two).
- A co-participation provision is included.

Exhibit 11-5 is an example of a retention and limits clause attaching on a losses occurring basis. Ultimate net loss may be defined in the definitions clause, or elsewhere in the treaty.

> **EXHIBIT 11-5**
>
> ### Retention and Limits Clause—Losses Occurring Basis
>
> During the term of this Contract, the Company shall retain and be liable for an amount of ultimate net loss equal to the greater of $50,000,000 or 80 percent of its net earned premiums for the term of this Contract. The Reinsurer shall then be liable for 95 percent of the amount by which the Company's ultimate net loss exceeds its retention, but the liability of the Reinsurer shall not exceed 95 percent of $10,000,000 as respects the term of this Contract.
>
> In addition to its initial retention, the Company shall retain, net and unreinsured elsewhere, 5 percent of the excess ultimate net loss to which this Contract applies.

Losses Incurred Basis

The retention and limits clause on a losses incurred basis is the same as a losses occurring basis regarding retention, limit, and co-participation provision. The difference is in the coverage of reserve changes and the effect of settling prior years' claims during the treaty term. If a reserve for an outstanding loss is changed, the change affects incurred losses for the current year even though the actual loss occurred several years prior. Exhibit 11-6 is an example of a retention and limits clause on a losses incurred basis.

> **EXHIBIT 11-6**
>
> ### Retention and Limits Clause—Losses Incurred Basis
>
> No claim shall be made under this Contract for any accident year unless and until the Company shall have first incurred an amount of ultimate net loss on business covered during the accident year in excess of the greater of $10,000,000 or 80 percent of its net earned premium for the accident year. The Reinsurer shall then be liable for 95 percent of the amount by which the Company's ultimate net loss exceeds its retention, but the liability of the Reinsurer shall not exceed 95 percent of the lesser of $2,000,000 or 15 percent of the Company's net earned premium for the accident year under consideration.
>
> In addition to its initial retention, the Company shall retain, net and unreinsured elsewhere, 5 percent of the excess ultimate net loss to which this Contract applies.

The reserves usually include incurred but not reported (IBNR) reserves. The reinsurer entering into such a treaty should ascertain whether the IBNR reserves are adequate. If IBNR reserves are inadequate, the primary insurer may increase its IBNR reserves to reflect the reserve inadequacy and try to pass along that deficiency to the reinsurer.

The losses incurred basis is used much less frequently than the losses occurring basis because of unfavorable accounting treatment under Financial Accounting

Standards Board Statement No. 113 (FAS 113). Because incurred losses include prior years' reserves, FAS 113 treats a losses incurred basis treaty as a retroactive reinsurance agreement, which subjects it to a less favorable accounting treatment. Typically, retroactive reinsurance agreements are only used to help stabilize policyholders' surplus, or terminate the liabilities associated with specific types of insurance so that a merger or acquisition can proceed without these unwanted liabilities.

AGGREGATE EXCESS OF LOSS TREATY PRICING

The method of pricing aggregate excess of loss treaties is similar to other types of excess of loss reinsurance. Reinsurers develop a price by estimating the amount of losses that will fall between the primary insurer's retention and the reinsurance limit. However, as aggregate excess of loss treaties respond to large losses and significant loss accumulations, which are generally infrequent, the primary insurer's historical loss data typically has only limited usefulness in pricing. Therefore, reinsurers must use statistical techniques to determine expected losses enabling them to set retentions and limits.

Expected Losses

Actuaries use historical loss data and theoretical distributions to project expected losses. Although an in-depth discussion of theoretical distributions is beyond the scope of this text, an overview will provide insight into how actuaries price aggregate excess of loss treaties.

Actuaries, based on their experience and judgment, select a theoretical distribution that appears to model the known data. The actuary then extrapolates the "tail" of the theoretical distribution to estimate the probability of extremely large aggregate losses. Exhibit 11-7 illustrates an expected loss distribution for aggregate losses. For each aggregate loss amount on the horizontal axis in Exhibit 11-7, a probability between 0 percent and 100 percent exists that it will occur, as shown by the line in the exhibit. Generally, the attachment point is set at a level so that there is a low probability that aggregate losses will exceed it. Excess expected aggregate losses are represented by the shaded area (the tail), which indicates the amount the reinsurer needs to price.

After the reinsurer has an estimate of the distribution of aggregate losses, it can determine the retentions and limits.

Setting Retentions

As with other excess of loss treaties, establishing a useful and affordable attachment point for an aggregate excess of loss treaty depends on analyzing relevant loss and expense data. Past loss and expense data should be adjusted to reflect current dollars, rate changes, and changes in the underlying reinsurance program. Also, such data should be corrected to reflect the types of insurance included in the primary insurer's current in-force portfolio.

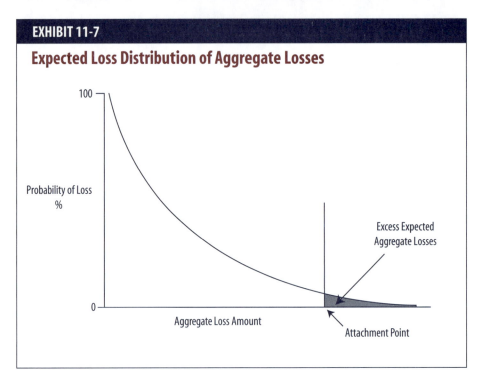

Once a loss and expense history is developed, the primary insurer and reinsurer can evaluate the level at which the attachment point may be set. The primary insurer usually prefers a low attachment point provided that the reinsurance premium is not too high. The reinsurer usually prefers an attachment point that does not guarantee the primary insurer a profit under the aggregate excess of loss treaty. Because a primary insurer's overall profitability includes its investment income in addition to operating profit, the reinsurer will likely want to consider the primary insurer's net investment income and overall operating results. Hypothetical loss and expense data that may be used to set the primary insurer's retention are shown in Exhibit 11-8.

With this information, the aggregate excess of loss treaty reinsurer can evaluate various possible attachment points that it can offer to the primary insurer. These attachment points will probably be sufficiently high that the primary insurer has a significant stake in efficiently handling the claims that do occur.

Setting Limits

One way to set aggregate excess of loss treaty limits is for the primary insurer to purchase the highest limits it can afford or is willing to purchase. Catastrophe models can provide information for determining the worst-case loss, and that information may be used to set a limit. The internal and outside limits may depend on the primary insurer's risk tolerance, its confidence in the probability that the reinsurance limits will not be exceeded, and its ability to absorb the net loss if the outside limit is exceeded. However, as with setting retentions, the ultimate factor in choosing limits is often the price.

EXHIBIT 11-8

Aggregate Excess of Loss Retention Information

Year	Earned Premium	Incurred Loss	Loss Ratio	Expense Ratio	Combined Ratio
1	$42,954,657	$26,301,136	61.23%	36.34%	97.57%
2	45,485,144	30,847,927	67.82	36.12	103.94
3	48,672,925	30,980,364	63.65	35.83	99.48
4	54,118,958	32,141,274	59.39	35.21	94.60
5	54,792,787	34,508,001	62.98	34.57	97.55
6	57,051,653	35,126,916	61.57	34.11	95.68
7	62,169,431	40,857,466	65.72	33.87	99.59
8	64,739,027	41,808,446	64.58	33.68	98.26
9	68,292,615	48,727,055	71.35	34.01	105.36
10	69,895,336	43,649,427	62.45	33.75	96.20
11 (est.)	71,992,197	44,275,080	61.50	33.57	95.07
Averages	$58,196,818	$37,201,909	63.92%	34.64%	98.48%

SUMMARY

Aggregate excess of loss treaties protect a primary insurer from losses that occur during a specified period that exceed either a certain dollar amount or the primary insurer's loss ratio. The operation of aggregate excess of loss treaties is similar to that of other types of excess of loss treaty. The function of aggregate excess of loss treaties is to stabilize the primary insurer's loss results.

A retention and limits clause may be adapted for use in an aggregate excess of loss treaty. It may include internal and outside retentions and limits, and it may specify that the treaty applies on a losses occurring or losses incurred basis.

Aggregate excess of loss treaty pricing involves estimating the losses that will fall between the primary insurer's retention and the reinsurance limit. Actuaries use theoretical distributions to estimate aggregate losses because primary insurer historical data is often insufficient to be of use.

The next chapter describes reinsurance audits and examines the types of audits a reinsurer may carry out on a primary insurer.

Chapter 12

Direct Your Learning

Reinsurance Audits

After learning the content of this chapter, you should be able to:

- Explain why reinsurance audits are conducted.
- Describe the steps in the reinsurance audit process.
- Describe the objectives, sources of information, and possible recommendations for each of the following types of reinsurance audits:
  - Underwriting audits
  - Transactional audits
  - Claim audits
- Describe the considerations involved when auditing a managing general agent.

OUTLINE

Overview of Reinsurance Audits

Authority to Conduct Audits

The Reinsurance Audit Process

Types of Reinsurance Audits

Managing General Agent Audits

Summary

Develop Your Perspective

What are the main topics covered in the chapter?

This chapter describes how reinsurance audits are used to evaluate an insurer's performance in important operational areas.

Compare the three types of reinsurance audits conducted by reinsurers.

- What is the common objective of these audits?
- What records are evaluated in the performance of an audit?

Why is it important to learn about these topics?

Reinsurance audits are a way for the reinsurer to get an understanding of the primary insurer's operations and for the primary insurer to understand the expectations of the reinsurer.

Consider the reinsurance audit process.

- What steps may be followed in a reinsurance audit?
- What sources of information may be evaluated in the performance of an audit?

How can you use what you will learn?

Examine an audit report on your company.

- What issues did the audit report address?
- What recommendations did the audit report make?

Chapter 12
Reinsurance Audits

An audit is a formal examination of an organization's or individual's records. One of the most common types of audit is an examination of a company's financial and accounting records by a certified public accountant (CPA). However, there are many other kinds of audits. This chapter describes reinsurance audits and the reinsurance audit process. The following types of reinsurance audit are discussed:

- Underwriting audit
- Transactional audit
- Claim audit

In addition, this chapter describes audits that a reinsurer may perform on a primary insurer's managing general agent.

OVERVIEW OF REINSURANCE AUDITS

A **reinsurance audit** is a specific type of audit that involves an examination of a primary insurer's or reinsurer's records and practices. It can result in suggestions for improving the insurer's controls, procedures, and operations. Reinsurance audits may be performed by an independent third party but are usually conducted by a party to the reinsurance transaction. Each party conducts an audit for a specific purpose. For example, before deciding whether to enter into a reinsurance agreement, a reinsurer may audit a primary insurer to evaluate its financial position, underwriting philosophy, operating systems, and internal controls. Alternatively, a primary insurer may audit a reinsurer before ceding business to it.

Reinsurance audit
An examination of a primary insurer's or reinsurer's records and practices.

A reinsurance intermediary is not usually subject to reinsurance audits because it is generally not a party to the reinsurance agreement. However, a reinsurance intermediary serving as a primary insurer's agent is functioning in a fiduciary capacity and could be subject to reinsurance audits.

The primary purpose of most reinsurance audits is to evaluate the business ceded under treaties the reinsurer has with the primary insurer. The information gathered for this purpose may be specific, such as data on individual claims against the primary insurer, or general, such as a description of the primary insurer's claim reserving practices. Reinsurance auditors usually evaluate the primary insurer's management, underwriting, and claim-handling philosophies, reinsurance accounting practices, and in-force policies.

Although most reinsurance audits are conducted by a reinsurer that is already doing business with a primary insurer, some are conducted by a reinsurer before it decides whether to do business with a primary insurer. An audit conducted by a reinsurer before committing to a new relationship is called a **pre-quote audit**. An audit made after a reinsurer has made a commitment to a primary insurer is called an **at-risk audit**.

One function of reinsurance is transferring underwriting expertise from a reinsurer to a primary insurer. A reinsurance audit can help fulfill that function. For example, during an underwriting audit, a reinsurer could provide advice on a type of insurance that the primary insurer plans to sell.

The reinsurance auditor should be familiar with the specific provisions of the treaty being reviewed. Understanding the treaty enables the auditor to evaluate whether the primary insurer's records and operations comply with treaty provisions.

Pre-quote audit
A reinsurance audit that a reinsurer conducts on a primary insurer's operations before committing to a new relationship.

At-risk audit
A reinsurance audit that a reinsurer conducts on a primary insurer's operations after the reinsurer has made a commitment to the primary insurer.

AUTHORITY TO CONDUCT AUDITS

A reinsurer's authority to audit a primary insurer is derived from the reinsurance agreement. Most reinsurance agreements contain an access to records clause, which gives the reinsurer the authority to inspect the primary insurer's records that relate to the business conducted between the parties. An example of an access to records clause is shown in Exhibit 12-1.

EXHIBIT 12-1

Access to Records Clause

The Reinsurer or its duly authorized representative shall have the right to examine, at all offices of the Company at all reasonable times, all books and records of the Company relating to any business which is the subject of this Agreement. This right shall survive the termination of the Agreement and shall continue so long as either party has any rights or obligations under this Agreement. Upon request, the Company shall supply the Reinsurer, at the Reinsurer's expense, with copies of any such books or records.

THE REINSURANCE AUDIT PROCESS

Not all audits are conducted the same way. However, a reinsurance audit generally includes the following six steps:

1. Establish objectives.
2. Determine approach.
3. Gather information.
4. Review the primary insurer's records.
5. Evaluate the primary insurer's practices.
6. Write a summary report and hold an exit conference.

Steps 1, 2, and 3 are generally performed off-site before the reinsurer's auditors travel to the primary insurer's office. Steps 4, 5, and 6 are usually performed on-site while the auditors are at the primary insurer's offices. The composition of the audit team reflects the audit's scope. For example, the auditors for a claim audit could include reinsurer claim personnel as well as the reinsurer account representative who is responsible for the primary insurer account. Exhibit 12-2 summarizes the six-step sample reinsurance audit process.

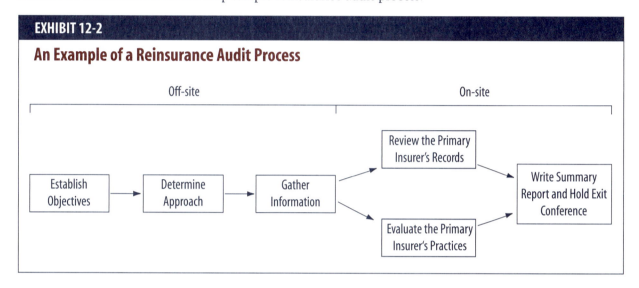

EXHIBIT 12-2

An Example of a Reinsurance Audit Process

Establish Objectives

The first step in the sample audit process is to establish objectives. Many audit objectives target specific concerns, such as primary insurer underwriting and claim handling procedures. Other audit objectives are general and relate to broad issues, such as loss and premium trends and the quality of a primary insurer's management.

An audit's objectives determine its scope, that is, whether it will include underwriting, transactional, and claim audit elements. For example, one objective may be to verify whether the correct policies for the treaty are submitted (underwriting audit). A second objective may be to review the adequacy of the primary insurer's loss and loss adjustment expense reserves (claim audit).

Determine Approach

The second step in the sample audit process is to determine approach. The auditors may choose either a structured or a flexible audit approach. A structured audit approach involves formal procedures to sample and evaluate the primary insurer's data. A flexible approach allows more latitude in the procedures used to sample and evaluate data. A primary insurer's attitude may influence the reinsurer's decision about which approach to use. Some primary insurers view a structured audit as confrontational. However, they may be more amenable to an informal review that takes a flexible approach.

Gather Information

The third step in the sample audit process is to gather information. Audit objectives influence the type of information the auditors must gather. For example, if one of the underwriting audit objectives is to ascertain whether the correct policies are submitted to the reinsurer, a random sample of the primary insurer's policies should be gathered as well as data on whether each policy was submitted to the reinsurance treaty.

The auditors should determine sources for the required information and, if feasible, design forms to facilitate its collection. Before starting an audit, the auditors should communicate their information needs to the primary insurer directly or through the reinsurance intermediary (if one is involved). This advance communication helps to ensure that the necessary information is available to the auditors once they arrive at the primary insurer's office.

Review the Primary Insurer's Records

The fourth step in the sample audit process is to review the primary insurer's records. Again, an audit's objectives determine which of the primary insurer's records the auditors should review. An underwriting audit could involve a review of the primary insurer's underwriting and treaty files. A transactional audit could involve a review of the primary insurer's bordereaux and summary account statements, as well as a sample of policy and claim files. A claim audit could involve a review of the primary insurer's open reserves, loss development reports, and loss payments.

Evaluate the Primary Insurer's Practices

The fifth step in the sample audit process is to evaluate the primary insurer's practices. In doing so, the auditors should consider three types of primary insurer operating controls:

1. Input controls
2. Processing controls
3. Output controls

Input controls
Procedures that help to ensure that accurate data are input to information systems.

Processing controls
Procedures that help to ensure that data are processed correctly after they are entered into an information system.

Input controls help to ensure that accurate data are input to information systems. For example, a primary insurer's internal auditors often sample documents from policy and claim files and compare them with actual data entered into the system.

Processing controls help to ensure that data are processed correctly after they are entered into an information system. These controls apply to the primary insurer's information system and involve workflows. For example, processing controls can prevent policy and claim information from being recorded under the wrong contracts and can prevent errors in calculating commissions or reserves. Processing controls can also involve physical workflows. For example, auditors may verify that the primary insurer's mailroom promptly sends claim notices to claim examiners.

Output controls reconcile output reports with input data. For example, a premium bordereau (output report) can be verified by comparing it with the input sheets that were used to enter premium data.

Output controls
Procedures that reconcile output reports with input data.

The scope of the operating control evaluation depends on the planned scope of the review of the primary insurer's records. For example, when the auditors plan to review underwriting and claim files, they should evaluate those operating controls related to the primary insurer's underwriting and claim operations. However, regardless of the review's scope, all three types of controls should be evaluated.

To evaluate operating controls, the auditor can use the following sources of information:

- Audit reports developed by the primary insurer's internal and external auditors
- Questionnaires designed by reinsurance auditors and completed by the primary insurer
- First-hand observation of primary insurer's procedures

Primary insurers are subject to audits performed by state insurance regulators, external accounting auditors, and internal auditors. Each of these audits reviews the insurer's operating controls to determine if material mistakes or intentional misrepresentations are occurring in financial reporting. Problems identified in these audits may be relevant to reinsurance reporting as well.

Reinsurance auditors often rely on questionnaires to gather basic information on the primary insurer's controls. For example, the claim component of a questionnaire may ask what authority is granted to individual claim representatives to settle claims and how use of that authority is monitored. Other questions may address how losses that exceed 50 percent of the primary insurer's retention and losses involving particular types of injuries (such as brain injury, burns, disfigurement, paralysis, and death) are handled. Completed questionnaires assist in audit planning and enable reinsurance auditors to familiarize themselves with the primary insurer's functional areas. The auditor may need to tailor the content of the questionnaire to the primary insurer under review. For example, a questionnaire developed for a captive insurer or a small insurer selling a single type of insurance could differ significantly from that for a large multi-line property-casualty insurer.

Another source of information reinsurance auditors typically use to evaluate operating controls is to observe first-hand the procedures primary insurer employees follow in recording and reporting reinsurance transactions. For example, an auditor may ask a primary insurer underwriter to show how he or she would code a policy that would not be subject to the treaty or one that would be automatically included were it not facultatively reinsured. While participating in this walk-through of regular activities, the auditor may witness procedures that are inconsistent with the reinsurance treaty's terms.

Write a Summary Report and Hold an Exit Conference

The sixth step in the sample audit process is to write a summary report and hold an exit conference. To facilitate the timely resolution of audit findings, the auditors write summaries and distribute them to the primary insurer's personnel. These summaries document the expectations of the reinsurer and whether or not the expectations are being met. These summaries usually specify why unmet expectations are a problem for the reinsurer and what actions, if any, the reinsurer will take if the problems are not corrected. The summaries can also serve as an agenda for the exit conference, which should be scheduled at the conclusion of the audit. The exit conference provides an opportunity for the primary insurer and the reinsurer to review and discuss the findings. During this conference, the reinsurer should convey to the primary insurer both favorable and unfavorable audit findings and suggest ways the primary insurer can improve its controls, procedures, and operations. Having looked at the general reinsurance audit process, this chapter will now examine specific types of reinsurance audits.

TYPES OF REINSURANCE AUDITS

There are several different types of reinsurance audits. This section examines the objectives of, guidelines for, and possible recommendations resulting from the following types of reinsurance audits carried out by a reinsurer or a primary insurer:

- Underwriting audit
- Transactional audit
- Claim audit

Underwriting audit
A reinsurance audit that examines the primary insurer's coverage, pricing, and risk selection decisions.

Transactional audit
A reinsurance audit that examines the premium, loss, and commission data reported by a primary insurer to a reinsurer.

Claim audit
A reinsurance audit that examines a primary insurer's claim reporting, claim payment, and reserving practices.

An **underwriting audit** examines a primary insurer's coverage, pricing, and risk selection decisions. A **transactional audit** examines the premium, loss, and commission data reported by a primary insurer to a reinsurer. A **claim audit** examines the primary insurer's claim reporting, claim payment, and reserving practices. Exhibit 12-3 presents the types of reinsurance audits discussed in this section, the objectives of each, and the records reviewed or employees consulted by each.

Underwriting Audits

Underwriting audits involve reviewing the primary insurer's coverage, pricing, and risk selection decisions. The objectives of underwriting audits include the following:

- Verify that the primary insurer cedes the correct policies to the reinsurance treaty.
- Gain familiarity with a primary insurer's management, underwriters, and in-force policies.
- Recommend strategies to improve the underwriting operations of the primary insurer.

EXHIBIT 12-3

Types of Reinsurance Audits

Type of Audit	Objectives	Records Reviewed/ Employees Consulted
Underwriting	• Assess coverage, pricing and selection decisions.	• Underwriting and treaty files
	• Gain familiarity with primary insurer's underwriting philosophy.	• Underwriters • Underwriting managers • Senior management
Transactional	• Verify accuracy of premium, loss, and commission data submitted to reinsurer.	• Summary account • Bordereaux
	• Evaluate primary insurer's reinsurance reporting controls.	• Reinsurance reporting records and transaction audit manuals
Claim	• Determine whether claims are covered by a treaty under review.	• Open claim reports
	• Monitor trends in losses.	• Loss development reports
	• Assess primary insurer's claim staff and claim-handling procedures.	• Claim procedure manuals • Claim department personnel
	• Discover information for a disputed claim.	• Claim report

An underwriting audit's success depends on the type and quality of information available for review. Employees can be a valuable source of information. The auditors should interview the primary insurer's key employees, including senior managers, underwriting managers, and underwriters. Senior managers can provide information about underwriting policy, operating controls, organizational structure, and future direction. Underwriting managers and underwriters know how procedures are implemented, including how items are processed. During the interviews, the auditors should also try to determine the workload and authority of the underwriters as well as the extent and suitability of any delegation of underwriting authority to producers.

Another source of underwriting audit information is the primary insurer's underwriting files. These files help the auditors determine whether the treaty is operating as originally intended. The underwriting files selected for review should include active ones, representing the loss exposures subject to the treaty, and files for loss exposures the primary insurer nonrenewed, canceled, and declined. The sample of underwriting files should also help the auditors to determine whether the primary insurer's risk selection and rating plan are applied consistently, are documented appropriately, and address all loss exposures adequately. Any deviations from underwriting guidelines and rating plans by the primary insurer should be recorded and discussed with the primary insurer's management.

As part of the review of underwriting files, the auditors should analyze a primary insurer's historical pricing levels. This analysis helps the auditors determine the primary insurer's commitment to long-term price adequacy. This is particularly important to a reinsurer that provides pro rata reinsurance because all premiums and losses are shared in the same proportion between the primary insurer and the reinsurer. If the primary insurer's premiums do not adequately cover incurred losses, both the primary insurer and the reinsurer share in an equally unprofitable portfolio.

The auditors should also evaluate the primary insurer's ability to select loss exposures that yield profitable underwriting results. Reviewing selected underwriting files, including active files and those for nonrenewed, canceled, and declined risks, reveals the primary insurer's selection process. The files should document the insured characteristics of each loss exposure. The auditors should ascertain that the primary insurer has procedures to handle high hazard or unusual loss exposures. Questions the auditors could ask the primary insurer include the following:

- Do you exclude high hazard or unusual loss exposures?
- Do you require inspections or other engineering services for high hazard or unusual loss exposures that you insure?
- Do you adjust pricing for high hazard or unusual loss exposures that you insure?
- How do you determine whether a high hazard or unusual loss exposure is submitted to the reinsurance treaty?

The auditors should verify that the primary insurer is accepting loss exposures in accordance with its underwriting guide. The underwriting guide helps the primary insurer determine the type of additional information that may be needed to accept a loss exposure. For example, it indicates when inspections or additional financial information are necessary. The auditors should verify that each selected underwriting file complies with the primary insurer's underwriting guide.

The last source of underwriting audit information is treaty information. This includes contract wording, placement information, accounting records, correspondence, and loss experience reports. To help analyze these sources to identify any underwriting problems, auditors can interview the primary insurer's claim and accounting personnel. One problem that could be found is that the loss exposures submitted to the treaty do not meet certain underwriting standards and are not of a sufficient quantity, given the treaty's terms. This is a problem because the reinsurer expects a minimum level of quality for loss exposures, and expects the primary insurer to submit a minimum number of loss exposures (for a pro rata treaty) or a minimum amount of written premiums from subject policies (for an excess of loss treaty).

If the function of the reinsurance treaty is to increase the primary insurer's premium capacity, the auditors should verify that the additional capacity is used to insure loss exposures that are acceptable to the reinsurer. A review of selected policies subject to the treaty should verify that there is a process to achieve this outcome. Reviewing selected underwriting files can also verify that the treaty does not include loss exposures that are specifically excluded. If the primary insurer believes such loss exposures are covered under the treaty, then the reinsurer may need to discuss these loss exposures with the primary insurer, as well as the purpose and intent of the exclusions.

At the conclusion of an underwriting audit, the auditors should understand the strengths and weaknesses of the primary insurer's underwriting. At this point, the auditors write a summary report and hold an exit conference. The auditors may recommend that the primary insurer change its selection process so that loss exposures of appropriate quality are submitted to the treaty. The auditors may also recommend that the primary insurer modify its overall pricing. Any recommendations should be discussed with the primary insurer's management.

Transactional Audits

Transactional audits examine the premium, loss, and commission data a primary insurer reports to a reinsurer. Ideally, auditors should use a structured approach for a transactional audit. The objectives of a transactional audit include the following:

- Verify the accuracy of premium, loss, and commission data the primary insurer reports to the reinsurer.
- Determine whether the primary insurer is complying with the reinsurance treaty terms.
- Evaluate the primary insurer's reinsurance reporting controls.

Transactional audits provide the reinsurer with an understanding of how the primary insurer processes transactions that are subject to the reinsurance treaty. As with other types of audits, the success of a transactional audit depends on the type and quality of information available for review. Information sources include premium and loss accounts prepared by the primary insurer, and interviews with key employees. Before starting a transactional audit, the auditors should request a summary account statement from the primary insurer that includes data on written premiums, ceding commissions, and paid losses. The summary account gives the auditors information on the total size of the primary insurer's premiums and losses as well as on the operation of the reinsurance treaty. Exhibit 12-4 shows an example of a summary account.

Some auditors submit test data (hypothetical premiums and losses) to the primary insurer for processing in their information system. Based on the reinsurance treaty terms, the auditors know the outputs (ceded premiums, commissions, and ceded losses) the primary insurer's system should produce.

For example, the transactional auditors' test premium data may include annual and six-month policies, policies canceled at policy inception, policies canceled during the policy term, policies paid in full at inception, and policies subject to adjustment beyond the policy term. Similarly, the test loss data may include losses in various stages of settlement.

EXHIBIT 12-4

Example of a Reinsurance Summary Account

Summary Account
80 Percent Quota Share
25 Percent Ceding Commission

	Primary Insurer	Reinsurer
Gross Written Premiums	$8,000,000	
Ceded Premium		$6,400,000
Ceding Commission		(1,600,000)
Paid Losses	$4,500,000	
Ceded Paid Losses		(3,600,000)
Paid Loss Adjustment Expenses	100,000	
Ceded Loss Adjustment Expenses		(80,000)
Net Due Reinsurer		**$1,120,000**

Auditors should conduct interviews with the primary insurer's management and staff, including representatives from key departments such as underwriting, claims, accounting, and information systems. Management interviews provide the auditors with an overview of the reinsurance reporting system and its major functions. Staff interviews provide details on how premium, loss, and commission data are processed.

In addition to the information gathered through interviews, auditors gather premium, loss, and commission data. For pro rata reinsurance agreements, auditors should request the premium and loss bordereaux that support premium, loss, and commission data on the summary accounts. The auditors should then compare data on the bordereaux with the totals shown on the summary accounts. If the auditors cannot reconcile those accounts with the supporting premium bordereaux, they should consult with the primary insurer to determine the cause of the discrepancy. If an error is discovered, the auditors should calculate the additional amount due to either the reinsurer or the primary insurer. If a reinsurance intermediary is involved in the reinsurance placement, he or she should be advised of any adjustments to the premium and loss bordereaux.

The auditors should request documentation for the premium totals shown on the summary accounts. This documentation may consist of treaty files or written and earned premium amounts shown in the primary insurer's NAIC Annual Statement. Auditors could review a sample of premium adjustments to determine whether the premium adjustments are calculated correctly.

The auditors should also verify loss and loss adjustment expense totals on the summary accounts. Information on paid losses, reserves, and loss adjustment expenses (both paid and reserved) can be derived from the primary insurer's NAIC Annual Statement. The auditors could sample claim files and verify the summary account data for each loss. For example, the auditors could verify the policy and claim file numbers, insured's name, claimant's name, paid loss amounts, paid loss adjustment expenses, salvage, subrogation, and current outstanding loss and loss adjustment expense reserves. Finally, the auditors should review a sample of policies ceded to the treaty. During this review, the auditors should ask questions about premium, losses, and commissions for each policy. Those questions may include the following:

- For what years has reinsurance coverage been provided?
- Can the reinsurer's share of each policy's premium be traced to the premium bordereaux?
- Is premium sent to the reinsurer in a timely manner?
- Is each policy's premium applied to the correct underwriting period?
- Are all paid losses and paid loss adjustment expenses adequately supported by the contents of the claim file?
- Can all paid losses and paid loss adjustment expenses be traced to the loss bordereaux?
- Is the reinsurance commission properly calculated for each bordereau?
- Do the commission totals on the bordereaux match the totals on the summary accounts?

This policy and claim file review enables the auditors to evaluate the accuracy of the premium, loss, and commission data reported to the reinsurer and helps them to identify areas for improvement.

Evaluating reinsurance reporting controls is also part of a transactional audit. To facilitate this evaluation, auditors prepare questionnaires that address the four key functions of the primary insurer: underwriting, accounting, claims, and information systems. The underwriting, accounting, and information systems questionnaires indicate how the primary insurer's business is marketed and underwritten, how a premium is recorded and collected, and how a premium is reported and remitted to reinsurers. The claim questionnaire indicates how coverage is verified and how losses are shown on the primary insurer's accounting records and reported to reinsurers.

After all applicable information is gathered and analyzed for the transactional audit, auditors write a summary report and hold an exit conference.

One of the key reasons for conducting a transactional audit is to improve the primary insurer's recording and reporting procedures for premium and losses. Therefore, the auditors may recommend that the primary insurer change its procedures to better comply with reinsurance treaty terms. Specific suggestions for the primary insurer may include ways to improve the procedure for reconciling premium and loss bordereaux with summary accounts and ways to speed the reporting of losses to the reinsurer.

Claim Audits

Claim audits could involve reviewing a specific claim, specific types of claims, or the primary insurer's claim procedures, including its controls and the qualifications of its claim staff. Because of the increasing volume of asbestos, environmental, and toxic tort claims, claim audits for long-tail liability business have increased in importance. The objectives of a claim audit can include the following:

- Review a single claim or series of claims to verify that they are covered by the underlying policy and are adequately reserved.
- Monitor trends in incurred losses.
- Review and evaluate the primary insurer's general reserving practices.
- Assess the primary insurer's claim-handling systems and controls.
- Evaluate the credentials and skills of the primary insurer's claim staff.

As with the other reinsurance audits, the success of a claim audit depends on the type and quality of information available for review. Information sources include interviews with key employees, open claim reserve reports, loss development reports, and copies of internal claim procedure manuals. The auditors should conduct interviews with management and selected claim department personnel. These interviews should reveal information about each person's workload, claim-settling authority, and involvement in setting loss and loss adjustment expense reserves. The interviews should also indicate the primary insurer's general claim-handling and claim-settling philosophy. Questions the auditors could ask include the following:

- Have there been changes to claim reporting practices?
- Have there been changes to reserving practices?
- What is the claims representative's average case load?
- Have changes been made recently in claim representatives' claim authority?

Another source of claim audit information is the primary insurer's open claims and loss development reports. These reports should indicate whether claims are reported late to the primary insurer. If a primary insurer's reserves develop unexpectedly over time because of late reported claims or increases in case reserves, the auditors should carefully examine the primary insurer's current level of incurred but not reported (IBNR) reserves. Inadequate primary insurer IBNR reserves usually indicate that the reinsurer has inadequate loss and loss adjustment reserves, particularly when excess of loss reinsurance is involved.

Finally, a primary insurer's internal claim procedure manuals can provide important claim audit information. These manuals describe the process the primary insurer uses to set reserves. They specify when and how reserves should be set and how changes in reserves should be made. Procedures should be included in the manual that require notification of a claim manager when significant reserve changes occur. Procedures should also be in place to notify the reinsurer of claims that potentially could exceed the primary insurer's retention. The manuals should also describe the process for reporting claims that are covered by the reinsurance treaty and may indicate the primary insurer's general claim-handling philosophy.

Claim auditors often examine individual claim files to assess the primary insurer's claim procedures. The selected files usually involve those claims that may trigger coverage from the reinsurance treaty and those that will likely involve a significant claim for the reinsurer. The auditors should look for evidence that the primary insurer encourages early, comprehensive investigation of liability and damage. For example, when investigating a new claim, the primary insurer should determine whether the claim is covered by the policy, and estimate the claim's value as soon as possible. In some instances, the auditors may suggest a strategy to manage the claim to an early settlement or recommend that the reserve be increased; however, the primary insurer is generally not required to follow the auditors' advice. Based on the auditors' findings, the reinsurer can establish an additional case reserve on its accounting records to reflect what it believes will be the ultimate value of the claim.

At the conclusion of a claim audit, the auditors write a summary report and hold an exit conference with the primary insurer's claim personnel. The auditors may suggest that the primary insurer should increase reserves on specific losses, or that it should settle claims more aggressively. The auditors may also request that specific claims not yet reported to the reinsurer by the primary insurer be reported as soon as possible, or may require additional documentation for claims not yet paid by the reinsurer.

MANAGING GENERAL AGENT AUDITS

A reinsurer could perform any of the types of audits discussed in this chapter on a primary insurer's managing general agent, if appropriate, and should present the findings to both the managing general agent and the primary insurer it represents. A **managing general agent (MGA)** is an authorized agent of the primary insurer that manages all or part of the primary insurer's insurance activities, usually in a specific geographic area. The extent of this authority varies and depends on the written contract between the MGA and the primary insurer. For example, an MGA could have complete underwriting and claim authority on behalf of a primary insurer.

Managing general agent (MGA)
An authorized agent of the primary insurer that manages all or part of the primary insurer's insurance activities, usually in a specific geographic area.

The auditors are responsible for making a qualitative evaluation of the relationship between the MGA and the primary insurer. If the primary insurer takes a hands-off approach with the MGA, the auditors may have to take additional steps to verify that the MGA is meeting its obligations under the contract. If the primary insurer's relationship with the MGA includes regular audits of the MGA to verify compliance with the contract, the auditors should review those audit reports. Exhibit 12-5 shows one possible relationship between an MGA and a primary insurer.

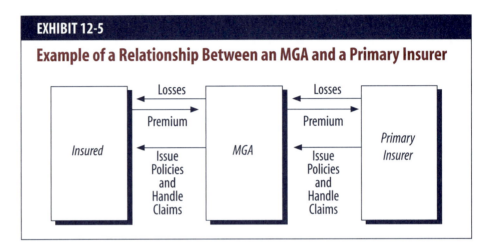

EXHIBIT 12-5

Example of a Relationship Between an MGA and a Primary Insurer

When auditing an MGA, the auditors should establish objectives and gather information that goes beyond the normal audit inquiry. For example, the auditors should take special care to understand the nature, scope, and quality of the agency relationship between the MGA and the primary insurer. In addition, the auditors should decide whether the MGA has the financial strength and technical expertise to protect the interests of both the primary insurer and the reinsurer.

The auditors should also review the written contract that governs the relationship between the primary insurer and the MGA. The contract specifies the authority that the primary insurer delegated to the MGA, including underwriting authority for specific types of insurance, claim investigation and settlement authority, and reinsurance placement authority. In addition, the contract usually specifies the MGA's premium and loss reporting obligations to the primary insurer as well as the compensation to be provided to the MGA.

The auditors should review the underwriting authority of the MGA and note any restrictions on premiums, limits, types of insurance, or geographic exposure. The auditors should then analyze the insurance ceded to the reinsurer to make sure it complies with the MGA's underwriting authority. Inconsistencies should be brought to the MGA's and the primary insurer's attention. The auditors should also review the internal operating controls of the MGA and ascertain whether it is complying with record keeping and reporting requirements.

Finally, the auditors should assess the competency and financial strength of the MGA. Although the primary insurer is ultimately responsible for the MGA's actions, any weakness in the MGA's operations could result in unprofitable underwriting results for both the primary insurer and the reinsurer, particularly when the MGA practices poor claim administration and underwriting. Auditors should carefully evaluate an MGA that does not have a sufficient financial stake in the policies it issues but has an incentive to sell insurance to earn commissions, whether that business is profitable or not.

SUMMARY

Both the primary insurer and the reinsurer can benefit from the reinsurance audit process. Well-conducted, sound reinsurance audits can improve communication between the primary insurer and reinsurer, and foster enduring professional relationships that focus on mutually identifying and resolving problems. A primary insurer sometimes audits a reinsurer to verify solvency; however, this chapter examined reinsurance audits from the point of view of a reinsurer auditing a primary insurer. A reinsurer's authority to audit a primary insurer is derived from the access to records clause in the reinsurance agreement.

The reinsurance audit process may include the following six steps:

1. Establish objectives.
2. Determine an approach.
3. Gather information.
4. Review primary insurer records.
5. Evaluate the primary insurer's operating controls.
6. Write a summary report and hold an exit conference.

This chapter examines the following types of reinsurance audit:

- *Underwriting audit.* An underwriting audit examines the primary insurer's coverage, pricing, and loss exposure selection decisions.
- *Transactional audit.* A transactional audit examines the premium, loss, and commission data reported by a primary insurer to a reinsurer.
- *Claim audit.* A claim audit examines a primary insurer's claim reporting, claim payment, and reserving practices.

At the beginning of a reinsurance audit, the auditor usually interviews the primary insurer's senior staff and then interviews the staff of the department involved in the audit (underwriters, claim supervisors, and accounting supervisors). Audits are generally concluded with a summary report and an exit conference. The contents of the report should be discussed with the primary insurer and be made available for future audits.

Some reinsurance audits focus on a managing general agent (MGA). When auditing an MGA, the reinsurance auditor should focus on the nature and scope of the MGA's authority, the relationship between the MGA and the primary insurer, and the MGA's stability.

The next chapter examines the impact of reinsurance regulation on both primary insurers and reinsurers.

Chapter 13

Direct Your Learning

Reinsurance Regulation

After learning the content of this chapter, you should be able to:

- Describe the role of state insurance regulators in regulating the following aspects of insurers:
  - Licensing
  - Rates and forms
  - Financial and market conduct examinations
- Explain how the National Association of Insurance Commissioners (NAIC) uses each of the following regulatory tools:
  - NAIC Annual Statement
  - NAIC model laws
  - NAIC accreditation program
  - NAIC association examinations
  - Insurance Regulatory Information System (IRIS)
  - NAIC risk-based capital system
- Describe the concerns of and activities taken by insurance regulators about each of the following:
  - Credit for a reinsurance transaction
  - Creditworthiness of reinsurers
  - Creditworthiness of reinsurance intermediaries

OUTLINE

State Insurance Regulation

National Association of Insurance Commissioners (NAIC)

Regulatory Concerns About the Use of Reinsurance

Summary

Develop Your Perspective

What are the main topics covered in the chapter?

This chapter describes state insurance regulation as it applies to reinsurers, the regulatory tools used by the National Association of Insurance Commissioners (NAIC), and the ongoing regulatory concerns about using reinsurance.

Identify the regulatory framework for insurance.

- What aspects of insurers' business are regulated by state regulators?
- What regulatory tools are used by the NAIC?

Why is it important to learn about these topics?

The primary goal of insurance regulation is to protect insurer solvency. Understanding the regulatory framework will enable you to understand how regulations safeguard the insurer's ability to pay claims.

Consider how insurance regulations affect reinsurance.

- What are the key regulatory concerns that insurance regulators have about the use of reinsurance?
- How do state insurance regulators address creditworthiness concerns?

How can you use what you will learn?

- To what extent does your company or client-insurer rely on reinsurance?
- How is the solvency of your company or client-insurer affected by the financial caliber of its reinsurers?

Chapter 13
Reinsurance Regulation

Reinsurers are subject to many of the same regulations as are primary insurers. This chapter focuses on those aspects of insurance regulation that are particularly applicable to reinsurers. It also focuses on how the financial strength of reinsurers is directly regulated to ensure their solvency and to protect the solvency of primary insurers. Finally, it discusses the key regulatory concerns about the use of reinsurance and how these concerns have been addressed.

STATE INSURANCE REGULATION

In the United States, primary insurers and reinsurers are predominately regulated at the state level. State insurance departments create and enforce state insurance regulations. A fundamental purpose of these regulations is to protect insurer solvency so that contractual commitments to insureds and claimants can be met. The authority granted to the state insurance departments is broad so that the complexity and variety of insurance issues can be addressed.

It can be difficult for states to regulate reinsurers that are incorporated in a different state or a different country. However, insolvency remains a key concern. If a reinsurer fails to honor a primary insurer's claims, the reinsurer could financially impair or cause the eventual insolvency of that primary insurer. State insurance regulators work with one another through the National Association of Insurance Commissioners (NAIC), discussed later in this chapter, to identify reinsurers that are struggling financially. Ultimately, the responsibility for regulating reinsurer solvency rests with the reinsurer's state of domicile. However, if any state finds a reinsurer's solvency to be in jeopardy, that state can suspend or revoke the reinsurer's license to operate in the state or can classify the reinsurer as unauthorized.

State insurance regulators regulate the following aspects of insurers:

- Licensing
- Rates and forms
- Financial and market conduct examinations

Licensing

Most insurers are licensed or authorized to sell insurance in one or more states. An **authorized insurer**, or **admitted insurer**, is an insurer to which a state insurance department has granted a license to sell insurance in that state. The license stipulates which types of insurance the insurer is permitted to sell. An insurer that is incorporated in the same state in which it is selling insurance is known as a **domestic insurer**. An insurer that is incorporated in a state different from the one in which it is selling insurance is known as a **foreign insurer**. An insurer that is incorporated outside the United States is called an **alien insurer**.

A fundamental requirement for obtaining an insurance license is having adequate financial strength in the form of policyholders' surplus and, in the case of a stock insurer, in the form of capital. Each state determines the minimum amount of capital and policyholders' surplus that an insurer must have to be licensed in the state. The minimum amount of capital and policyholders' surplus required varies by state and by the type of insurance that the insurer wants to sell. If an insurer fails to meet the financial requirements, or fails to operate consistently with state insurance laws, state regulators can revoke or suspend the insurer's license.

A reinsurer that is authorized to do business in the primary insurer's state of domicile is called an **authorized reinsurer**. Authorized reinsurers include licensed reinsurers and reinsurers otherwise accredited to do business in the state (or licensed in a state with similar laws). An **accredited reinsurer** is an insurer that is otherwise unauthorized to do business in the same state as the primary insurer but that is granted approval to assume reinsurance by meeting the state insurance department's requirements. These requirements usually involve:

- Filing a formal acknowledgment of the jurisdiction of the state
- Submitting to financial examinations by the state
- Providing evidence that the reinsurer is licensed as an insurer or reinsurer in at least one other state, or, in the case of an alien reinsurer, is lawfully entered through another state
- Meeting specific policyholders' surplus requirements
- Filing annual financial statements

An **unauthorized reinsurer** is a reinsurer that is not licensed or otherwise authorized to do business in the primary insurer's state of domicile. Unauthorized reinsurers are usually alien reinsurers doing business in the U.S.

A reinsurer's authorization status is critical to the primary insurer because it determines the conditions required for a transaction to qualify for accounting treatment as a reinsurance transaction in the primary insurer's financial statements.

Authorized insurer or admitted insurer
An insurer to which a state insurance department has granted a license to sell insurance in that state.

Domestic insurer
An insurer that is incorporated in the same state in which it is selling insurance.

Foreign insurer
An insurer that is incorporated in a state different from the one in which it is selling insurance.

Alien insurer
An insurer that is incorporated outside the United States.

Authorized reinsurer
A reinsurer that is authorized to do business in the primary insurer's state of domicile.

Accredited reinsurer
A reinsurer that is otherwise unauthorized to do business in the same jurisdiction as the primary insurer but that is granted approval to assume reinsurance by meeting the state insurance department's requirements.

Unauthorized reinsurer
A reinsurer that is not licensed or otherwise authorized to do business in the primary insurer's state of domicile.

A reinsurance agreement with an *authorized reinsurer* benefits the primary insurer's financial results because it transfers financial obligations (liabilities for unearned premium reserves and loss reserves) from the primary insurer to the reinsurer, thereby increasing the primary insurer's policyholders' surplus. Additionally, the primary insurer can treat amounts owed by the reinsurer, usually loss payments, as an asset.

A reinsurance agreement with an *unauthorized reinsurer* does not necessarily provide the primary insurer with the accounting benefit that a transaction with an authorized reinsurer provides. Specifically, the primary insurer is not allowed to transfer its financial obligations to the reinsurer unless those financial obligations are collateralized by the unauthorized reinsurer.

Rates and Forms

State insurance regulators have authority over many of the rates charged by authorized primary insurers. Likewise, state insurance regulators must approve the coverage forms used by authorized primary insurers. The coverage forms define the financial obligations that the primary insurers have assumed from insureds. The rates provide the financial basis that primary insurers use to pay covered losses.

Reinsurance rates are not subject to the filing and approval regulations applicable to most primary insurance rates. However, this does not mean that reinsurance rates are not affected by state insurance regulation. Rate regulation of primary insurers indirectly affects any subsequent reinsurance transaction. Inadequate primary insurance rates will usually result in inadequate reinsurance premiums. When reinsurers are unable to obtain an adequate premium for the underlying loss exposure, they must restrict coverage, reduce ceding commissions, or decline the coverage. Consequently, rate regulation of primary insurers can affect the availability of reinsurance in the marketplace.

State insurance regulators do not require the same prior approval or informational filings for reinsurance treaties and facultative certificates as they often do for primary coverage forms. Instead, regulators influence the content of reinsurance agreements by requiring that they contain specific clauses. Most states require the following clauses in reinsurance agreements with primary insurers:

- *Insolvency clause.* This states that the reinsurer is not relieved of its responsibility under the reinsurance agreement should the primary insurer become insolvent.
- *Service of suit clause.* This requires an alien reinsurer to have an agent within the U.S. who can accept the formal delivery of writs, summonses, or other legal notices on the reinsurer's behalf.
- *Intermediary clause.* This requires the reinsurer to accept financial responsibility for funds transferred to it by a primary insurer through an intermediary.

Financial and Market Conduct Examinations

The insurance statutes in various states require or permit the state's insurance department to periodically examine the financial affairs and market conduct of all insurers, including reinsurers authorized to do business in the state. The state insurance department is usually required to examine all domestic insurers at least once every three to five years and can initiate an examination whenever it is deemed expedient. Authorized foreign and alien insurers are also examined periodically in conformance with NAIC association examinations. NAIC association examinations are described later in this chapter.

Financial examination
An analysis of an insurer's operations and financial condition to determine if the insurer meets the financial requirements to sell insurance in a particular state.

A **financial examination** is an analysis of an insurer's operations and financial condition to determine if the insurer meets the financial requirements to sell insurance in a particular state. A team of state insurance department examiners confirms that financial reporting procedures and requirements are being followed. This confirmation includes verifying that assets shown on financial statements actually exist and are properly valued, as well as determining that all liabilities have been identified and are properly valued. Examiners audit and verify underwriting results and investment income (including capital gains and losses on the sale of investment assets). They also examine premiums earned, losses and loss adjustment expenses paid and incurred, changes in unpaid loss and loss adjustment expense reserves, and all reinsurance in force by type of insurance. If the examination uncovers problems, the insurance department usually has broad powers to attempt to correct whatever problems are identified.

Market conduct examination
An analysis of an insurer's practices in four operational areas: sales and advertising, underwriting, ratemaking, and claim handling.

A **market conduct examination** is an analysis of an insurer's practices in four operational areas: sales and advertising, underwriting, ratemaking, and claim handling. Market conduct examinations usually focus on how insurers treat insurance applicants, insureds, and claimants. Although subject to market conduct examinations, reinsurers are usually not subjected to as extensive an examination as primary insurers because of their lack of or limited direct involvement with applicants, insureds, or claimants.

National Association of Insurance Commissioners (NAIC)
An organization of insurance regulators that coordinates insurance regulation activities among the various insurance departments and provides a forum to discuss, develop, and coordinate regulatory policy among the jurisdictions.

NATIONAL ASSOCIATION OF INSURANCE COMMISSIONERS (NAIC)

The **National Association of Insurance Commissioners (NAIC)** is an organization of insurance regulators that coordinates insurance regulation activities among the various insurance departments and provides a forum to discuss and develop regulatory policy. The insurance commissioners of each of the fifty states, the District of Columbia, American Samoa, Guam, Puerto Rico, and the U.S. Virgin Islands are members. The NAIC uses a variety of regulatory tools.

> **NAIC Regulatory Tools**
> - NAIC Annual Statement
> - NAIC model laws
> - NAIC accreditation program
> - NAIC association examinations
> - Insurance Regulatory Information System (IRIS)
> - NAIC risk-based capital system

NAIC Annual Statement

The **NAIC Annual Statement** is a specified format for financial reporting. An NAIC committee reviews and revises the NAIC Annual Statement format or "blank" annually so that it continues to meet the reporting needs of state insurance departments. Insurers file an NAIC Annual Statement on or before March 1 with the insurance department for each state in which the insurer is authorized to transact business. The common reporting format simplifies the task of solvency surveillance by state insurance departments and reduces the reporting burden for insurers operating in multiple jurisdictions.

NAIC Annual Statement
A specified format for financial reporting.

Insurer financial reporting requirements have developed separately from those of noninsurers. Accounting rules and procedures used to prepare the NAIC Annual Statement are called **statutory accounting principles (SAP)**. These procedures are conservative and generally value insurer assets and liabilities as if the insurer were to be immediately liquidated. This approach requires that assets are understated and liabilities are overstated, resulting in an intentional understatement of the net worth (policyholders' surplus) of the insurer as compared to the accounting approach used by noninsurers.

Statutory accounting principles (SAP)
Accounting rules and procedures used to prepare the NAIC Annual Statement.

State insurance regulators use the NAIC Annual Statement to determine the extent to which a primary insurer relies on reinsurance. Reinsurance transactions usually modify a primary insurer's financial position. The detailed information contained in the NAIC Annual Statement schedules enable state insurance regulators to determine if reinsurance transactions have masked underlying financial instability.

NAIC Model Laws

When a new problem or issue arises in the insurance industry, the NAIC may respond by developing an **NAIC model law** written in a style similar to that of a state statute that reflects the NAIC's position. Each state legislature then considers the model law for possible enactment. A model law may not be passed in its exact form by every state legislature, but it provides a common basis for drafting state laws. Consequently, certain aspects of insurance regulation are relatively uniform among states. The NAIC has proposed over 200 model laws. Many of them influence reinsurance reporting requirements, but only a few are considered directly applicable to reinsurance transactions. Two of these, the Credit for Reinsurance Model Act and the Reinsurance Intermediary Model Act, are discussed later in this chapter.

NAIC model law
A document written in a style similar to that of a state statute that reflects the NAIC's position on problems or issues in the insurance industry.

NAIC Accreditation Program

NAIC accreditation program
A formal program to provide consistency of solvency regulation among the states and improve the standards of solvency regulation and financial examinations conducted in all states.

The **NAIC accreditation program** is a formal program to provide consistency of solvency regulation among the states and improve the standards of solvency regulation and financial examinations conducted in all states. The program sets requirements that a state's insurance department must meet to gain accreditation, including the state's ability and authority to examine and regulate an insurer's corporate and financial affairs. Under this program, states that have been accredited by the NAIC cannot accept the results of insurer examinations performed by states that have not been accredited. The Credit for Reinsurance Model Act and the Reinsurance Intermediary Model Act are two of the model laws required in the minimum standard for state insurance department accreditation. States within the program are subject to annual review and reaccreditation every five years.

NAIC Association Examinations

NAIC association examination
A financial examination of an insurer by a team of state insurance regulators representing zones in which the insurer operates.

An **NAIC association examination**, also called a zone examination, is a financial examination of an insurer by a team of state insurance regulators representing zones in which the insurer operates. The NAIC recommends an association examination for insurers licensed in more than one zone or in more than three jurisdictions in a single zone. The fifty-four separate regulatory jurisdictions are divided by the NAIC into four zones for purposes of conducting association examinations.

Whether a particular insurer is examined by one jurisdiction or more than one jurisdiction depends on the insurer's geographic scope of operations and the amount of insurance sold in each jurisdiction. If an insurer has annual direct written premiums of $1 million or more in a zone, or if at least 20 percent of its insurance sold (regardless of the dollar amount) is in a zone, that zone is invited to participate in the examination.

The insurance department of the insurer's state of domicile notifies the NAIC secretary when it proposes to examine an insurer. The NAIC secretary checks the premium volume shown in the insurer's most recent NAIC Annual Statement and notifies each zone's chairman of its eligibility for participation. The zone chairman designates one of the states within the zone to appoint an examiner to be the zone representative on the examination team. If all states within the zone waive participation, the entire zone waives participation and is not represented. An examiner-in-charge from the domiciliary state heads the examination team and is assisted by his or her staff and examiners representing each participating zone. The examiner-in-charge is responsible for outlining the examination program in accordance with the provisions of the *NAIC Financial Condition Examiners' Handbook*. Zone representatives can request investigation into areas of special interest to their state or members of their zone.

The examination report is prepared before the close of the examination and is presented to the insurer's officers for review and discussion. It contains summary financial statements from the insurer's most recent NAIC Annual Statement along with an analysis of specific changes resulting from the examination. The report also discusses any adverse findings and any material changes in the financial statements.

Insurance Regulatory Information System (IRIS)

The **Insurance Regulatory Information System (IRIS)** is a set of financial ratios developed by the NAIC to evaluate an insurer's financial strength. The primary purpose of using the IRIS ratios is to identify insurers that are in the early stages of financial difficulty. The IRIS results are sent to the insurance regulators in the insurer's state of domicile and are entered onto the NAIC's computer system, where the results can be accessed by all state insurance regulators. IRIS test results can also help identify any specific areas that need immediate attention. Test results can determine priorities for special on-site examinations.

> **Insurance Regulatory Information System (IRIS)**
> A set of financial ratios developed by the NAIC to evaluate an insurer's financial strength.

Several of the IRIS ratios are affected by reinsurance or are used to evaluate an insurer's dependence on reinsurance. The capacity ratio is used to measure an insurer's ability to sell more insurance and therefore to grow its market share.

The capacity ratio compares an insurer's net written premiums (which represent its exposure to potential claims) to its policyholders' surplus (which represents its financial capacity for absorbing losses). If losses and expenses exceed net written premiums, an insurer must use its surplus to meet its obligations. Therefore, an insurer's net written premiums should not become too large relative to its policyholders' surplus.

State insurance regulators review a number of financial ratios to evaluate an insurer. However, the capacity ratio is considered key because it indicates that an insurer might have become financially overextended by selling too much insurance. A capacity ratio that is greater than 3 to 1 is typically considered to be outside acceptable limits. One use of reinsurance is to provide insurers with surplus relief, which enables them to keep their capacity ratio within acceptable limits.

Another IRIS ratio affected by reinsurance is the surplus aid to surplus ratio. This ratio evaluates the insurer's dependence on ceding commissions from reinsurance. If the ceding commission on unearned ceded premiums exceeds 25 percent of the insurer's policyholders' surplus, the ratio is considered unsatisfactory.

The IRIS change in surplus ratio considers the percentage change in the insurer's policyholders' surplus during the year. A 10 percent or greater decrease in policyholders' surplus or an increase of 50 percent or greater is considered unusual and may trigger scrutiny. Large increases in policyholders' surplus may result from several factors, one of which is reinsurance transactions that provide surplus relief.

NAIC Risk-Based Capital System

NAIC risk-based capital system
A system developed by the NAIC to determine the minimum amount of capital an insurer needs to support its operations, given its risk characteristics.

The **NAIC risk-based capital system** is a system developed by the NAIC to determine the minimum amount of capital an insurer needs to support its operations, given its risk characteristics. In the context of the risk-based capital system, risk characteristics are categorized as follows:

- Asset risk—the risk that an asset's value will be lower than expected
- Underwriting risk—the loss volatility of the types of insurance sold
- Credit risk—the risk that the insurer will be unable to collect monies owed to it

The NAIC has developed a complex set of formulas for calculating risk-based capital, which have been adopted by many states. These formulas attempt to make the minimum capital required for an insurer a function of the insurer's risk characteristics. Before adopting the NAIC formulas, state insurance codes made little or no allowance for the risk differentials among insurers when specifying minimal capital requirements.

REGULATORY CONCERNS ABOUT THE USE OF REINSURANCE

Reinsurance is an essential tool of insurer management, yet the specifics of its use have been an ongoing regulatory issue. State insurance regulators have three key regulatory concerns.

> **Key Regulatory Concerns About the Use of Reinsurance**
> - The standards by which an insurer should be allowed to take credit for a reinsurance transaction
> - The creditworthiness of reinsurers
> - The creditworthiness of reinsurance intermediaries

Credit for a Reinsurance Transaction

State insurance regulators have allowed primary insurers to take credit for a reinsurance transaction on their financial statements based on the reinsurer's authorization status and other conditions, rather than on the actual value of the economic benefit that the reinsurance transaction provides. However, some reinsurance agreements, categorized as finite risk reinsurance agreements, depart from traditional reinsurance transactions in that only a limited amount of insurance risk is transferred from the primary insurer to the reinsurer. Consequently, state insurance regulators have adopted requirements that must be met for a reinsurance agreement to be treated as a reinsurance transaction.

Finite risk reinsurance agreements are the focus of these requirements because they have been used to greatly enhance the appearance of a primary insurer's financial condition without actually doing so. These agreements often contain complex and sophisticated provisions that have caused state insurance regulators and accounting organizations to revisit the criteria under which credit for reinsurance is granted. The following sections describe:

- NAIC Credit for Reinsurance Model Act
- The effect of reinsurance on a primary insurer's balance sheet
- Accounting pronouncements affecting reinsurance

NAIC Credit for Reinsurance Model Act

The Credit for Reinsurance Model Act allows a primary insurer to take credit for reinsurance as an asset on its NAIC Annual Statement if the reinsurer is licensed or accredited in the state in which the primary insurer is domiciled. The primary insurer can also take credit for reinsurance if the reinsurer is licensed or accredited in another state that has standards similar to the state in which the primary insurer is domiciled. The model act also allows primary insurers to take credit for unauthorized reinsurance if the reinsurer's obligations are secured with collateral, such as trust accounts, letters of credit, and trust funds.[1]

The Effect of Reinsurance on the Balance Sheet

State insurance regulators focus solvency examinations on the adequacy of an insurer's capital as shown on its balance sheet. As previously discussed, state insurance regulators use the capacity ratio to determine if an insurer has sold more insurance relative to its financial resources than is considered financially prudent. This section describes how reinsurance affects the balance sheet, how statutory accounting principles (SAP) force insurers to limit market share expansion, and how reinsurance transactions facilitate market share growth.

Under SAP, income and expenses are mismatched. SAP requires insurers to establish an **unearned premium reserve**, which is a balance sheet liability representing premiums that have been paid but have not yet been earned. This unearned premium reserve is maintained to repay insureds should they decide to cancel their policies. Premiums are recognized as income only as they are earned. In contrast, SAP requires that policy-related expenses be charged immediately. Because the insurer is required to charge these expenses against income it has not yet earned, it must take money from its policyholders' surplus to pay these initial expenses. The more insurance that is sold, the greater the reduction in policyholders' surplus. This is referred to as the surplus drain caused by growth in written premiums.

Unearned premium reserve
A balance sheet liability representing premiums that have been paid but have not yet been earned.

A primary insurer may purchase pro rata reinsurance to alleviate surplus drain. Pro rata reinsurance reduces net written premiums (the numerator of the capacity ratio) because ceding the reinsurance premium transfers a portion of the obligation to maintain unearned premium reserve to the reinsurer.

Policyholders' surplus (the denominator of the capacity ratio) increases by the amount of ceding commission received from the reinsurer. The net effect is a reduction in the capacity ratio.

To illustrate, assume that Spring Insurance Company (Spring) opened for business on December 31, 2003. On that date, it had $500,000 in cash and $1.5 million in investments. On January 1, 2004, it sold and collected $5 million of written premiums, on one-year policies. In selling these policies, Spring incurred $1.5 million in expenses for producer commissions, premium taxes, and internal costs, such as underwriting and policy issuance.

Exhibit 13-1 shows the balance sheet for Spring on January 1, 2004, as it would have appeared if Spring had not purchased reinsurance and if it had ceded half of its premiums to a reinsurer and received a 30 percent ceding commission on the reinsurance premium.

EXHIBIT 13-1

Balance Sheet for Spring Insurance Company, January 1, 2004

	Without Reinsurance	With Reinsurance
Assets		
Cash	$4,000,000[1]	$2,250,000[2]
Investments	1,500,000	1,500,000
Total Assets	$5,500,000	$3,750,000
Liabilities		
Unearned Premium Reserve	$5,000,000	$2,500,000[3]
Total Liabilities	5,000,000	2,500,000
Policyholders' Surplus	500,000	1,250,000
Total Liabilities and Policyholders' Surplus	$5,500,000	$3,750,000
Capacity Ratio	10 to 1	2 to 1

[1] $500,000 (existing cash) + $5,000,000 (written premiums) − $1,500,000 (policy acquisition expenses).

[2] $500,000 (existing cash) + $2,500,000 (50 percent of $5,000,000 written premiums) + $750,000 (the ceding commission; 30 percent of $2,500,000) − $1,500,000 (policy acquisition expenses).

[3] Spring's unearned premium reserve was reduced from $5,000,000 to $2,500,000 because the reinsurer assumed responsibility for maintaining this liability when it assumed the $2,500,000 in written premiums.

Spring's capacity ratio has been reduced to 2 to 1 from 10 to 1 because of the purchase of pro rata reinsurance. First, net written premiums decreased from $5 million to $2.5 million because of the reinsurance cession. Second, policyholders' surplus increased from $500,000 to $1.25 million because of the reimbursement of $750,000 of prepaid expenses, equal to the 30 percent ceding commission paid by the reinsurer on the $2.5 million of written premiums ceded.

Exhibit 13-1 illustrates the surplus relief function of reinsurance—reducing surplus drain that results from having to maintain an unearned premium reserve.

In the past, some reinsurance transactions were structured so that poorly capitalized primary insurers received surplus relief without any transfer of insurance risk. These transactions were usually structured using one of two methods. The first method was to have a reinsurance transaction in which all the primary insurer's losses were reimbursed by the reinsurer and eventually paid back by the primary insurer. The second method was to have a reinsurance transaction that commenced on the last day of the calendar year and terminated on the first day of the following year to improve the balance sheet for NAIC Annual Statement purposes only. These methods for circumventing solvency regulation have largely disappeared because changes in accounting rules have eliminated the benefit that insurers sought through these methods.

These changes in accounting rules were primarily directed at finite risk reinsurance transactions. Because the potential for these transactions is to obscure the insurer's true financial condition, several accounting requirements were developed. These accounting requirements are discussed next.

Accounting Pronouncements Affecting Reinsurance

In the late 1970s and early 1980s, state insurance regulators and accounting organizations began questioning whether certain transactions should continue to qualify for accounting treatment as reinsurance transactions. In 1992, the Financial Accounting Standards Board (FASB) issued its Statement No. 113, "Accounting and Reporting for Reinsurance of Short-Duration and Long-Duration Contracts" (FAS 113). Long-duration contracts are those that are expected to remain in force for an extended period, such as endowment contracts. All other contracts, including the majority of property and liability contracts, are classed as short-duration contracts. According to FAS 113, a short-duration transaction qualifies for reinsurance accounting treatment if the following two requirements are met:

1. The reinsurer assumes significant insurance risk under the reinsured portions of the underlying insurance contracts.
2. It is reasonably possible that the reinsurer may realize a significant loss from the transaction.

FAS 113 defines "insurance risk" as including both underwriting risk and timing risk. Underwriting risk is described as the uncertainty about the ultimate amount of any premiums, commissions, claims, and claim settlement expenses. Timing risk is described as the uncertainty about the timing of premiums, commissions, claims, and claim settlement expenses. "Reasonably possible" and "significant loss" are not specifically defined. Therefore, FAS 113 provides limited guidance about whether a particular transaction can be accounted for as reinsurance.

These accounting requirements, which apply to insurer financial statements that are based on Generally Accepted Accounting Principles (GAAP), greatly affect the insurer's ability to use finite risk reinsurance to improve its financial condition. Although FAS 113 does not apply to the NAIC Annual Statement, the NAIC has adopted similar requirements in its Statement of Statutory Accounting Principles (SSAP) No. 61, "Life, Deposit-Type and Accident and Health Reinsurance," and SSAP No. 62, "Property and Casualty Reinsurance." Also, regulators in some states prohibit certain types of finite risk reinsurance transactions.

Creditworthiness of Reinsurers

Primary insurers that have reinsurance agreements with authorized or otherwise accredited reinsurers are permitted to show amounts owed to them by reinsurers as assets on their balance sheets. These reinsurance recoverables, such as the amounts owed to primary insurers for unreimbursed losses, are often significant. Because state insurance regulators are concerned about whether primary insurers will be able to collect these amounts from reinsurers, and the effect that the failure to collect them would have on the solvency of primary insurers, the NAIC requires insurers to provide extensive information about their reinsurance transactions in Schedule F of the NAIC Annual Statement. These Schedule F requirements are discussed in more detail in the next chapter.

Reinsurance agreements with unauthorized reinsurers do not qualify for reinsurance accounting treatment by the primary insurer unless the reinsurer provides collateral in the form of letters of credit, trust agreements, or funds deposited by and withheld from reinsurers.

A letter of credit is a form of payment guarantee issued by a bank. To be acceptable collateral, a letter of credit must be clean, be irrevocable, contain an evergreen clause, and be issued by an approved bank. A clean letter of credit is one that is not conditioned on the delivery of any other documents or materials that would inhibit obtaining the funds. An irrevocable letter of credit cannot be modified or revoked without the beneficiary's consent, once the beneficiary is established. An evergreen clause automatically renews the letter of credit for a specific time unless the issuer of the letter of credit signifies its intent not to renew the letter at expiration. An approved bank is a U.S. financial institution that meets the following conditions:

- Is organized or licensed under state or federal laws
- Is regulated, supervised, and examined by U.S. federal or state bank regulatory authorities
- Is determined by the NAIC Securities Valuation Office to have adequate financial condition and standing

Trust agreements, surety bonds, cash, and other liquid assets also could constitute acceptable collateral for many insurance and reinsurance transactions.

Some unauthorized alien reinsurers choose to collateralize their obligations to U.S. insurers through multi-beneficiary trust funds. Reinsurers must fund these trusts with 100 percent of their gross liabilities, plus an additional buffer amount of $20 million. (Lloyd's of London is required to maintain an additional buffer amount of $100 million.) Trusts must be funded in the form of cash, marketable securities meeting specific standards, or letters of credit.

International reinsurers have proposed reducing the 100 percent funding requirement for multi-beneficiary trusts. They contend that these trust funds serve only as collateral; losses arising out of U.S. claims are actually paid from the international reinsurers' loss reserves, not from the trust funds. International reinsurers also argue that maintaining a fully funded trust for U.S. claims in addition to their own loss reserves increases their cost of capital to operate in the U.S., which is one of only a few countries that impose this requirement.

To offset the drain on policyholders' surplus resulting from doing business with unauthorized reinsurers, primary insurers may withhold amounts due to the reinsurers. These amounts consist mostly of the reinsurance premium that the primary insurer owes the reinsurer but also may include salvage and subrogation recoveries, as well as other miscellaneous amounts. The amounts withheld as deposits are usually negotiated in the reinsurance agreement and expressed as a percentage of the reinsurance premium. If the amounts withheld are inadequate to cover the reinsurer's obligations, then subsequent losses are billed to the reinsurer.

In severe cases, a commutation agreement may be the best way to limit problems with collecting reinsurance recoverables. A **commutation agreement** specifies how to value, settle, and discharge all obligations between parties to a reinsurance agreement. In return for cash, the primary insurer withdraws the liability for outstanding losses and loss adjustment expenses related to the commuted reinsurance agreement. However, a commutation agreement does not necessarily enable a primary insurer to collect from a delinquent reinsurer.

Commutation agreement
An agreement that specifies how to value, settle, and discharge all obligations between parties to a reinsurance agreement.

Creditworthiness of Reinsurance Intermediaries

State insurance regulators addressed creditworthiness of reinsurance intermediaries after the Pritchard & Baird case. Regulatory action in the aftermath of this case required that reinsurers assume the credit risk associated with using a reinsurance intermediary. The sections that follow contain a description of the Pritchard & Baird case and how it was resolved, the state of New York's regulatory response, and the NAIC model law that resulted from the case.

Pritchard & Baird Case

The reinsurance intermediary firm of Pritchard & Baird was one of the largest reinsurance intermediaries in the U.S., doing business with over 900 insurers and reinsurers.

Contrary to industry practice, Pritchard & Baird deposited all monies, including those of its primary insurer and reinsurer clients, into a single bank account. Without the knowledge of its clients, the firm's principal owners withdrew increasing amounts of money from the firm's account, characterizing them as "loans." Because of inadequate accounting records, the total amount of those withdrawals could not be determined. By 1975, the firm was having difficulty paying its clients. One primary insurer filed suit, and Pritchard & Baird was forced into bankruptcy.

The reinsurers argued that Pritchard & Baird acted as the agent for the primary insurers, so payments by reinsurers to Pritchard & Baird constituted payment to the primary insurers and payments by the primary insurers to Pritchard & Baird did not constitute payments to the reinsurers. Consequently, any losses from the bankruptcy should fall on the primary insurers.

The primary insurers took the opposite position and argued that Pritchard & Baird acted as agent for the reinsurers, so that payments to Pritchard & Baird constituted payment to the reinsurers and payment by the reinsurers to Pritchard & Baird did not constitute payment to the primary insurers. Consequently, any losses from the bankruptcy should fall on the reinsurers.

To determine the nature of Pritchard & Baird's agency relationship, the court reviewed Pritchard & Baird's operating method, which included the following:

- Pritchard & Baird would approach a primary insurer and request authorization to negotiate reinsurance agreements on its behalf.
- After obtaining such authorization, Pritchard & Baird would approach reinsurers to find the reinsurance agreement most favorable to the primary insurer.
- Pritchard & Baird sometimes recommended reinsurance agreements with direct writing reinsurers if those reinsurers offered the agreement most favorable to the primary insurer, even though the direct reinsurers would not pay commissions to Pritchard & Baird.
- When an agreement was reached, Pritchard & Baird would draft the necessary documents, present them to the primary insurer for approval, and, after obtaining such approval, send them to the reinsurer for execution.
- Primary insurers wrote premium checks payable to Pritchard & Baird. The checks were deposited in Pritchard & Baird's bank account, and, after deducting its commission, Pritchard & Baird sent its own check to the reinsurer for payment of the reinsurance premium.
- Reinsurers sent claim checks that were payable to primary insurers to Pritchard & Baird who, in turn, forwarded them to the primary insurers.

After reviewing the operating method of Pritchard & Baird, the court held that the primary insurers, and not the reinsurers, exercised primary supervision of Pritchard & Baird. This conclusion was reached because Pritchard & Baird received prior authorization and approval from the primary insurers for many of its activities. Pritchard & Baird was presumed to have acted as an agent for the primary insurers, therefore the court decided that the losses resulting from Pritchard & Baird's failure to send premiums to the reinsurers should fall on the primary insurers. However, this decision does not mean that every reinsurance intermediary is considered to be an agent of the primary insurer. In other cases the courts have concluded that reinsurance intermediaries represent reinsurers. Determining which party an intermediary represents depends on the degree of control exercised by the primary insurer compared to the control exercised by the reinsurer.

New York Regulation 98

Largely as a result of the Pritchard & Baird case, the New York legislature in 1976 required the licensing of reinsurance intermediaries and authorized the New York Insurance Department to examine and regulate reinsurance intermediaries. In 1982, the New York Insurance Department adopted Regulation 98, which applies to primary insurers licensed in New York (wherever domiciled). To take credit for ceded reinsurance on their financial statements, these primary insurers must have an intermediary clause in their reinsurance agreements when reinsurance intermediaries are involved in reinsurance transactions. Many other states followed New York's lead and required an intermediary clause.

As the intermediary clause specifies that payments made by the primary insurer to a reinsurance intermediary are deemed to have been received by the reinsurer, the reinsurer assumes the credit risk if the reinsurance intermediary defaults. The clause makes the reinsurance intermediary the reinsurer's agent for the purpose of receiving and transmitting funds, which is opposite of the decision reached in the Pritchard & Baird case. This relationship addresses the concern that placing the reinsurance intermediary's credit risk on the primary insurer could lead to solvency problems for the primary insurer and consequently harm insureds. The intermediary clause does not address the question of whom the reinsurance intermediary represents for other purposes, such as receiving and transmitting information. This question must still be answered by reviewing the parties' apparent intent.

New York Regulation 98 also states the following explicit obligations of reinsurance intermediaries:

- The reinsurance intermediary must have written authority from the primary insurer before it negotiates or accepts any reinsurance agreement for the primary insurer. The written authorization must indicate at least the following: (1) the name of the primary insurer (and affiliates, if any), (2) the types of insurance to be reinsured, (3) the kinds of reinsurance or retrocessions to be negotiated on that specific transaction, (4) the amounts of insurance, and (5) the effective date and the expiration date of the authority.
- When the reinsurance intermediary negotiates a reinsurance agreement, it must give prompt written notice to the primary insurer. Such notice must be accompanied by written evidence that the assuming reinsurer or reinsurers have agreed to assume the liability for certain loss exposures.

- If the reinsurance intermediary places reinsurance with a reinsurer that is not licensed in, or accredited by, the state of New York, the reinsurance intermediary must make a reasonable inquiry about the financial strength of such reinsurer. At the primary insurer's request, the reinsurance intermediary must furnish any information obtained in its inquiry along with a recent financial statement of the reinsurer. The primary insurer can release the reinsurance intermediary from this duty in writing if it chooses.
- The reinsurance intermediary must notify the primary insurer of any conflicts of interest that the intermediary has at the beginning of the relationship or that may arise in the future. Such conflicts could arise from ownership or control of the reinsurance intermediary by a reinsurer, ownership of a reinsurer by the reinsurance intermediary, retrocessional placements by the reinsurance intermediary on a reinsurer's behalf, underwriting agency agreements, or similar relationships or transactions.
- The reinsurance intermediary must maintain records adequate to permit an audit of its activities to ensure that it has complied with all statutes and regulations. Regulation 98 specifies the minimum information required. The information must be maintained for at least ten years.
- The reinsurance intermediary must deposit funds received from primary insurers and reinsurers in at least one bank account separate from the accounts in which the reinsurance intermediary's funds are deposited. Funds can be withdrawn from these accounts only (1) to transmit funds to primary insurers or reinsurers in the normal course of business, (2) to pay commissions due to the reinsurance intermediary and, if authorized in writing, to pay for interest on the deposited funds, (3) to pay commissions due to others, and (4) to pay federal excise taxes.

Regulation 98 represents the first significant attempt to regulate reinsurance intermediaries either in the U.S. or abroad.

NAIC Reinsurance Intermediary Model Act

In December 1989, the NAIC introduced the Reinsurance Intermediary Model Act. Several technical amendments to the act were added in June 1990. The purpose of the act is to specify requirements for reinsurance intermediaries, including licensing, and to give state insurance departments examination authority over reinsurance intermediaries. The majority of states have adopted the Reinsurance Intermediary Model Act or similar legislation.

The Reinsurance Intermediary Model Act has several provisions similar to New York's Regulation 98. It differs in that it requires the licensing of reinsurance intermediaries and it distinguishes between reinsurance intermediary brokers and reinsurance intermediary managers. A reinsurance intermediary broker places reinsurance cessions on a primary insurer's behalf, but does not have the power to bind the primary insurer. A reinsurance intermediary manager does have the power to bind the primary insurer. New York has retained Regulation 98, rather than adopt the Reinsurance Intermediary Model Act.

Provisions of the Reinsurance Intermediary Model Act that apply to reinsurance intermediary brokers are as follows:

- The reinsurance intermediary broker must obtain a license in each state in which it does business. An exception to this requirement is that if the reinsurance intermediary broker does not have an office in a state in which it does business, it must either be licensed in the state as a nonresident reinsurance intermediary or be licensed in a state having substantially similar laws.
- The reinsurance intermediary broker must have a written authorization with each primary insurer it works with. At a minimum, the written authorization must specify that (1) the primary insurer can terminate its authority at any time, (2) the reinsurance intermediary broker must account for all transactions and remit all funds due the primary insurer within thirty days of receipt, (3) the reinsurance intermediary broker must hold all funds in a fiduciary capacity in a qualified U.S. financial institution, (4) the reinsurance intermediary broker must comply with any written standards of the primary insurer about cession and retrocession of liability for all loss exposures, and (5) the reinsurance intermediary broker must disclose any relationship with any reinsurer with which it does business.
- The reinsurance intermediary broker must keep books and records that provide proof of the placement for at least ten years after each agreement expires.
- The primary insurer must have access to, and the right to copy and audit, all accounts and records maintained by the reinsurance intermediary broker.

The Reinsurance Intermediary Model Act also includes several sections on licensing, agreement provisions, and prohibited acts for reinsurance intermediary managers.

SUMMARY

Primary insurers and reinsurers are predominantly regulated at the state level. A fundamental purpose of these regulations is to ensure insurer solvency so that contractual commitments to insureds and claimants can be met. State insurance regulators regulate the following aspects of primary insurers and reinsurers:

- Licensing
- Rates and forms
- Financial and market conduct examinations

The National Association of Insurance Commissioners (NAIC) is an organization of insurance regulators that coordinates insurance regulation activities among the various insurance departments. NAIC regulatory tools include the following:

- *NAIC Annual Statement.* The NAIC Annual Statement is a specified format for financial reporting.
- *NAIC model laws.* NAIC model laws are documents written in a style similar to that of state statutes that reflect the NAIC's position on problems or issues in the insurance industry.
- *NAIC accreditation program.* The NAIC accreditation program is a formal program to provide consistency of solvency regulations among the states and improve the standards of solvency regulation and financial examinations conducted in all states.
- *NAIC association examinations.* The NAIC association examinations are financial examinations of insurers by teams of state insurance regulators representing the zones in which the insurers operate.
- *Insurance Regulatory Information System (IRIS).* The Insurance Regulatory Information System is a set of financial ratios developed by the NAIC to evaluate an insurer's financial strength.
- *NAIC risk-based capital system.* The NAIC risk-based capital system is a system developed by the NAIC to determine the minimum amount of capital an insurer needs to support its operations, given its risk characteristics.

State insurance regulators' key concerns regarding reinsurance are the standards by which an insurer should be allowed to take credit for a reinsurance transaction, and the creditworthiness of reinsurers and reinsurance intermediaries. Reinsurance agreements have been subject to regulatory scrutiny because these agreements can be used to obscure financial problems. The Pritchard & Baird case led to tighter regulation of reinsurance intermediaries, such as New York Regulation 98 and the NAIC Reinsurance Intermediary Model Act.

This chapter discussed some elements of the NAIC Annual Statement in a regulatory context. The following chapter focuses in more detail on the reinsurance aspects of the NAIC Annual Statement.

CHAPTER NOTES

1. NAIC Model Regulation Service, *Model Law on Credit for Reinsurance and Credit for Reinsurance Model Regulation*, July 1994, pp. 785–786.
2. *In the matter of Pritchard & Baird, Inc.*, 8 B. R. 265 (D.N.J. 1980).

Chapter 14

Direct Your Learning

Reinsurance Aspects of the NAIC Annual Statement

After learning the content of this chapter, you should be able to:

- Describe the major assets and liabilities found on the balance sheet of an insurer's NAIC Annual Statement, particularly those that pertain to reinsurance transactions.

- Describe the information contained in the following parts of an insurer's NAIC Annual Statement.
  - Underwriting and Investment Exhibit
  - Schedule F
  - Schedule P

OUTLINE

Balance Sheet With Supporting Exhibits and Schedules

Underwriting and Investment Exhibit

Schedule F

Schedule P

Summary

Develop Your Perspective

What are the main topics covered in the chapter?

This chapter provides an overview of the NAIC Annual Statement, including a discussion of the balance sheet, income statement, and two schedules often used by reinsurers: Schedule F and Schedule P.

Consider the content of the NAIC Annual Statement.

- Which elements of an insurer's balance sheet and income statement are typically affected by reinsurance?
- What information is contained in Schedule F and Schedule P?

Why is it important to learn about these topics?

Understanding the financial data in the NAIC Annual Statement will help you to assess an insurer's financial strength and a primary insurer's reliance on reinsurance.

Review an NAIC Annual Statement.

- To what extent is the company depending on reinsurance for financial leverage?

How can you use what you will learn?

Examine your company's NAIC Annual Statement.

- What would your company's balance sheet look like without reinsurance?
- To what extent is your company relying on loss reimbursements from reinsurers with a history of being slow in paying their debts?

Chapter 14
Reinsurance Aspects of the NAIC Annual Statement

As discussed in the previous chapter, the NAIC Annual Statement (referred to in this chapter as Annual Statement) is the uniform financial report filed annually by all insurers, both primary insurers and reinsurers, with the insurance department of each state in which the insurer is authorized to do business. The Annual Statement is prepared according to statutory accounting principles (SAP) and is designed to provide state insurance regulators with the information needed to regulate the insurer's solvency. It is also the means through which state insurance departments are able to require near uniform financial reporting from all insurers.

The Annual Statement is a complex and lengthy financial document, consisting of a balance sheet (assets, liabilities, and policyholders' surplus), a statement of income, and a cash flow statement that are backed by supporting exhibits and schedules. The Annual Statement Blank consists of over one hundred pages but a completed Annual Statement for a large insurer usually contains many more pages because of schedules listing investment securities and investment transactions. The Annual Statement is the primary source of insurer financial information.

A thorough discussion of the Annual Statement is beyond the scope of this text. Therefore, this chapter focuses on those elements of an insurer's balance sheet and income statement that are affected by reinsurance transactions. Additionally, two major Annual Statement schedules are described: Schedule F and Schedule P. Schedule F contains information pertinent to the insurer's reinsurance activities. Schedule P contains loss and loss adjustment expense (LAE) information by type of insurance.

BALANCE SHEET WITH SUPPORTING EXHIBITS AND SCHEDULES

The balance sheet is found on pages 2 and 3 of the Annual Statement Blank. It includes assets and liabilities similar to those found on the balance sheet of any business. For example, cash and real estate are included as assets. It also includes many assets and liabilities that are unique to insurance operations, such as reinsurance recoverable, reinsurance payable, and the unearned premium reserve.

A reinsurer may analyze a primary insurer's Annual Statement balance sheet to measure the primary insurer's financial strength and to determine the primary insurer's reinsurance needs.

Assets

SAP categorizes assets as admitted or nonadmitted. **Admitted assets** are those assets that are approved by a state insurance department for inclusion on an insurer's Annual Statement balance sheet. Typically, admitted assets must meet minimum liquidity requirements and have a predictable market value. **Nonadmitted assets** are assets that are not permitted by a state insurance department to be shown on an insurer's Annual Statement balance sheet. This is typically because they are not readily marketable. Examples of nonadmitted assets are agents' balances over ninety days past due and investment securities that are in default. Nonadmitted assets are shown on the Annual Statement but not on the balance sheet. Therefore, insurer investments in these assets reduce policyholders' surplus.

Admitted asset
An asset that is approved by a state insurance department for inclusion on an insurer's Annual Statement balance sheet.

Nonadmitted asset
An asset that is not permitted by a state insurance department to be shown on an insurer's Annual Statement balance sheet.

> **Page Numbers and Line References**
>
> Page numbers and line references are used throughout this chapter to help identify exactly where the information being described can be found on the Annual Statement Blank. However, the Annual Statement Blank is revised annually by the NAIC Blanks Committee. These changes can cause page numbers and line references to change.

Page 2 of the Annual Statement Blank is the assets side of the balance sheet, which summarizes the insurer's admitted assets. Supporting schedules provide more detail about particular categories of assets. For most property-casualty insurers, investment securities are the largest admitted asset. Consequently, the first nine items are reserved for investment (or invested) assets, such as bonds and stocks. Exhibit 14-1 shows the assets page from the Annual Statement Blank.

The assets side of the balance sheet provides only summary information about the insurer's invested assets, but it does give some indication of the insurer's investment risk. An insurer that maintains a low-risk investment portfolio (for example, bonds rather than stocks) may be able to assume relatively higher risk in its underwriting operations and vice versa. An insurer with a high-risk investment portfolio may need additional reinsurance protection to guard against simultaneous losses in its investment and underwriting operations.

EXHIBIT 14-1

Assets

ANNUAL STATEMENT FOR THE YEAR 2004 OF THE

ASSETS

	1 Assets	Current Year 2 Nonadmitted Assets	3 Net Admitted Assets (Cols. 1 - 2)	Prior Year 4 Net Admitted Assets
1. Bonds (Schedule D)				
2. Stocks (Schedule D):				
2.1 Preferred stocks				
2.2 Common stocks				
3. Mortgage loans on real estate (Schedule B):				
3.1 First liens				
3.2 Other than first liens				
4. Real estate (Schedule A):				
4.1 Properties occupied by the company (less $......... encumbrances)				
4.2 Properties held for the production of income (less $......... encumbrances)				
4.3 Properties held for sale (less $......... encumbrances)				
5. Cash ($......, Schedule E-Part 1), cash equivalents ($......., Schedule E-Part 2) and short-term investments ($......., Schedule DA)				
6. Contract loans (including $......... premium notes)				
7. Other invested assets (Schedule BA)				
8. Receivable for securities				
9. Aggregate write-ins for invested assets				
10. Subtotals, cash and invested assets (Lines 1 to 9)				
11. Investment income due and accrued				
12. Premiums and considerations:				
12.1 Uncollected premiums and agents' balances in the course of collection				
12.2 Deferred premiums, agents' balances and installments booked but deferred and not yet due (including $......... earned but unbilled premiums)				
12.3 Accrued retrospective premiums				
13. Reinsurance:				
13.1 Amounts recoverable from reinsurers				
13.2 Funds held by or deposited with reinsured companies				
13.3 Other amounts receivable under reinsurance contracts				
14. Amounts receivable relating to uninsured plans				
15.1 Current federal and foreign income tax recoverable and interest thereon				
15.2 Net deferred tax asset				
16. Guaranty funds receivable or on deposit				
17. Electronic data processing equipment and software				
18. Furniture and equipment, including health care delivery assets ($..........)				
19. Net adjustment in assets and liabilities due to foreign exchange rates				
20. Receivables from parent, subsidiaries and affiliates				
21. Health care ($..........) and other amounts receivable				
22. Other assets nonadmitted				
23. Aggregate write-ins for other than invested assets				
24. Total assets excluding Separate Accounts, Segregated Accounts and Protected Cell Accounts (Lines 10 to 23)				
25. From Separate Accounts, Segregated Accounts and Protected Cell Accounts				
26. Total (Lines 24 and 25)				
DETAILS OF WRITE-INS				
0901.				
0902.				
0903.				
0998. Summary of remaining write-ins for Line 9 from overflow page				
0999. Totals (Lines 0901 through 0903 plus 0998) (Line 9 above)				
2301.				
2302.				
2303.				
2398. Summary of remaining write-ins for Line 23 from overflow page				
2399. Totals (Lines 2301 through 2303 plus 2398) (Line 23 above)				

Source: NAIC Annual Statement Blank–P/C, 2004 edition. Permission for reprinting given by the NAIC. Further reprint or redistribution strictly prohibited.

The investment portfolio is subject to a variety of risks, including:

- Potential variation in the market price of investments
- Possible default by the issuers of investment securities
- Lack of liquidity

Liquidity is the ease with which an asset can be converted to cash with little or no loss of value. Insurers sometimes must liquidate investments to pay claims, especially for catastrophe losses.

Bonds

Bonds are typically the largest single invested asset category for a property-casualty insurer. Many insurers, especially small insurers, invest a high proportion of their assets in bonds because bonds are considered the safest long-term investment available. Although a bond's market price can vary widely over time as interest rates change, insurers include bonds at their amortized value on their Annual Statement balance sheet. The **amortized value** is a value that reflects the payment of principal and interest over time. This makes the Annual Statement value of a bond immune from current market prices, which rise and fall with interest rate changes. Consequently, an insurer's policyholders' surplus is not severely affected by a decline in the market price of its bonds unless the bonds must be sold.

The assets side of the balance sheet does not indicate the quality of an insurer's bond portfolio, the bonds' market value, or their maturity dates. However, detailed information on each bond the insurer holds is shown in Schedule D—Part 1. The information includes the interest rate, maturity date, book value (usually amortized value), par value, fair value (market value), and accrued interest. Part 1A of Schedule D shows the quality ratings and maturities of all bonds in summary form. Other parts of Schedule D show bonds acquired or disposed of during the year.

Bonds with long maturities generally are of higher risk. The market prices of bonds vary inversely with market interest rates, rising when interest rates fall and falling when interest rates rise. This effect is more severe for long-maturity bonds than for short-maturity bonds because a long-maturity bond's interest rate is locked in for a longer time period. If market interest rates rise shortly after a long-maturity bond is issued, the holder is locked into the lower interest rate for a longer time period than the holder of a short-maturity bond and therefore the market value of the former declines.

Common Stocks

Common stocks typically are the second largest invested asset category for property-casualty insurers. However, many insurers, especially small ones, do not hold large amounts of common stocks. Common stocks are usually shown on the Annual Statement balance sheet at their market value on the last business day of the year. Fluctuations in stock prices can cause substantial variations in the insurer's policyholders' surplus. Details for common stocks are shown in Schedule D—Part 2—Section 2 of the Annual Statement.

Liquidity
The ease with which an asset can be converted to cash with little or no loss of value.

Amortized value
A value that reflects the payment of principal and interest over time.

Many insurers invest substantial amounts in the stocks of their subsidiaries and affiliated companies. Usually, no established market exists for these securities, so substantial holdings of the stocks of subsidiaries and affiliates have a significant liquidity risk. The risk is increased if the insurer also has significant reinsurance arrangements with the subsidiaries and affiliates. The value of investments in subsidiaries is usually the value of the subsidiary's policyholders' surplus. Schedule D—Summary by Country, shown at the beginning of Schedule D in the Annual Statement, shows the total investment in bonds, preferred stock, and common stock of the insurer's parent, subsidiaries, and affiliates. Additional details for stocks of parent, subsidiaries, and affiliates are shown in Schedule D—Part 6.

Short-Term Investments

The third largest category of invested assets for property-casualty insurers typically is cash, cash equivalents, and short-term investments. This category is a catchall because it includes certain bonds, bills, notes, commercial paper, certificates of deposit, and shares in money market funds. All short-term investments have a maturity period of one year or less. They are usually matched with liabilities that the insurer must pay within a year, such as loss reserves for short-tail types of insurance.

Reinsurance-Related Assets

In many cases, only three asset items on an insurer's Annual Statement balance sheet deal directly with reinsurance. These are "Amounts recoverable from reinsurers" on line 13.1, "Funds held by or deposited with reinsured companies" on line 13.2, and "Other amounts receivable under reinsurance contracts" on line 13.3.

Line 13.1 on the assets side of the balance sheet is used by primary insurers to show the total amounts recoverable from all reinsurers. Recoverables by individual reinsurers are listed in the primary insurer's Schedule F—Part 3 of the Annual Statement.

For regulatory purposes, an unauthorized reinsurer may deposit assets equal to the unearned premiums and losses payable (including loss reserves) under its reinsurance agreements with primary insurers. Line 13.2 on the assets side of the balance sheet is used by a reinsurer and represents those funds deposited with a primary insurer. These amounts are an asset of the reinsurer.

Line 13.3 on the assets side of the balance sheet is used for amounts recoverable under reinsurance contracts that do not fit into line 13.1.

Other Annual Statement assets that may involve reinsurance transactions include the following:

- Line 12.1, "Uncollected premiums and agents' balances in the course of collection" includes a reinsurer's uncollected premiums from primary insurers.

- Line 20, "Receivables from parent, subsidiaries and affiliates." This asset includes some reinsurance elements if a reinsurance relationship exists among the parent, the subsidiary, and affiliates, especially if a parent purchased reinsurance centrally for the benefit of all subsidiaries and affiliates.

The amounts of reinsurance in lines 12.1 and 20 should be small for most insurers and reinsurers.

Liabilities, Surplus, and Other Funds

Page 3 of the Annual Statement is the liabilities side of the balance sheet, which lists the insurer's liabilities, policyholders' surplus, and other funds. Exhibit 14-2 shows page 3 from the Annual Statement Blank. Lines 1 through 26 show liabilities. Lines 27 through 35 show surplus and other funds. The figure on line 36, which shows the total of liabilities, surplus, and other funds, should equal the total asset figure shown on line 26 of page 2. Losses and loss adjustment expenses (LAE) usually constitute the largest liability of a property-casualty insurer (lines 1 and 3). The unearned premium reserve (line 9) is usually the second largest liability but it may be the largest liability of an insurer that sells only property insurance.

Loss and Loss Adjustment Expense Reserves

Line 1 of the liabilities side of the balance sheet is labeled "Losses." It represents the insurer's liability to make payments for losses that have already occurred but have not yet been settled. This liability is usually called the loss reserve. Line 2 shows the amount a reinsurer is obligated to pay under reinsurance it has assumed for losses that have already been paid by the primary insurers. Line 3 shows an insurer's obligation to pay LAE related losses that have already occurred. Lines 1, 2, and 3, together, constitute the insurer's loss and LAE reserves.

The total reserve for losses (line 1) is supported by detailed loss information (by type of insurance) shown on the Underwriting and Investment Exhibit, Part 2A. Additional details of loss reserves are shown in Schedule P of the Annual Statement. The total reserve for unpaid LAE also appears on Part 2A, line 34, Column 9 of the Underwriting and Investment Exhibit. Additional details about LAE, by type of insurance, can be found in Schedule P—Part 1 of the Annual Statement. Both the Underwriting and Investment Exhibit and Schedule P are discussed in more detail later in this chapter.

Reinsurance Liabilities

The amount indicated on line 2 of the liabilities side of the balance sheet, "Reinsurance payable on paid loss and loss adjustment expenses," is taken from Schedule F—Part 1, Column 6 of the Annual Statement. It represents the amount that the reinsurer filing the statement must pay under assumed reinsurance for losses already paid by primary insurers. This liability is the counterpart of the "Amounts recoverable from reinsurers" that a primary insurer would show on line 13.1 of the assets side of its balance sheet.

EXHIBIT 14-2

Liabilities, Surplus, and Other Funds

ANNUAL STATEMENT FOR THE YEAR 2004 OF THE

LIABILITIES, SURPLUS AND OTHER FUNDS	1 Current Year	2 Prior Year
1. Losses (Part 2A, Line 34, Column 8)		
2. Reinsurance payable on paid loss and loss adjustment expenses (Schedule F, Part 1, Column 6)		
3. Loss adjustment expenses (Part 2A, Line 34, Column 9)		
4. Commissions payable, contingent commissions and other similar charges		
5. Other expenses (excluding taxes, licenses and fees)		
6. Taxes, licenses and fees (excluding federal and foreign income taxes)		
7.1 Current federal and foreign income taxes (including $.......... on realized capital gains (losses))		
7.2 Net deferred tax liability		
8. Borrowed money $........and interest thereon $		
9. Unearned premiums (Part 1A, Line 37, Column 5) (after deducting unearned premiums for ceded reinsurance of $.............and including warranty reserves of $...............)		
10. Advance premium		
11. Dividends declared and unpaid:		
11.1 Stockholders		
11.2 Policyholders		
12. Ceded reinsurance premiums payable (net of ceding commissions)		
13. Funds held by company under reinsurance treaties (Schedule F, Part 3, Column 19)		
14. Amounts withheld or retained by company for account of others		
15. Remittances and items not allocated		
16. Provision for reinsurance (Schedule F, Part 7)		
17. Net adjustments in assets and liabilities due to foreign exchange rates		
18. Drafts outstanding		
19. Payable to parent, subsidiaries and affiliates		
20. Payable for securities		
21. Liability for amounts held under uninsured accident and health plans		
22. Capital notes $....................and interest thereon $		
23. Aggregate write-ins for liabilities		
24. Total liabilities excluding protected cell liabilities (Lines 1 through 23)		
25. Protected cell liabilities		
26. Total liabilities (Lines 24 and 25)		
27. Aggregate write-ins for special surplus funds		
28. Common capital stock		
29. Preferred capital stock		
30. Aggregate write-ins for other than special surplus funds		
31. Surplus notes		
32. Gross paid in and contributed surplus		
33. Unassigned funds (surplus)		
34. Less treasury stock, at cost:		
34.1 .... shares common (value included in Line 28 $.......................)		
34.2 .... shares preferred (value included in Line 29 $.......................)		
35. Surplus as regards policyholders (Lines 27 to 33, less 34) (Page 4, Line 38)		
36. TOTALS (Page 2, Line 26, Col. 3)		
DETAILS OF WRITE-INS		
2301.		
2302.		
2303.		
2398. Summary of remaining write-ins for Line 23 from overflow page		
2399. Totals (Lines 2301 through 2303 plus 2398) (Line 23 above)		
2701.		
2702.		
2703.		
2798. Summary of remaining write-ins for Line 27 from overflow page		
2799. Totals (Lines 2701 through 2703 plus 2798) (Line 27 above)		
3001.		
3002.		
3003.		
3098. Summary of remaining write-ins for Line 30 from overflow page		
3099. Totals (Lines 3001 through 3003 plus 3098) (Line 30 above)		

Source: NAIC Annual Statement Blank—P/C, 2004 edition. Permission for reprinting given by the NAIC. Further reprint or redistribution strictly prohibited.

"Ceded reinsurance premiums payable" on line 12 indicates premiums owed by the primary insurer filing the statement to its reinsurer. It is the counterpart of line 12.1 on the assets side of the balance sheet. Another liability amount dealing with reinsurance is found on line 13, "Funds held by company under reinsurance treaties." This is the counterpart of line 13.2 on the assets side of the balance sheet, and represents funds from reinsurers that the primary insurer filing the statement holds under reinsurance treaties. These funds are usually held so that the primary insurer filing the statement can take credit on its Annual Statement for reinsurance purchased from unauthorized reinsurers just as it can when dealing with authorized reinsurers. Only the total funds are reported on line 13, but details can be found in Schedule F—Part 3.

Line 16, "Provision for reinsurance," is taken from Schedule F—Part 7. The section of this chapter on Schedule F covers this provision in detail.

Exhibit 14-3 summarizes the reinsurance-related assets and liabilities found on the Annual Statement Blank, including their line number references. Where one line entry is the counterpart of another line entry, those entries are placed side by side in the exhibit. For example, line 13.1 under Primary Insurer Assets is the counterpart of line 2 under Reinsurer Liabilities.

Liability for Unearned Premiums

The liability for unearned premiums is shown on line 9 of the liabilities side of the balance sheet. This total is supported by Part 1A of the Underwriting and Expense Exhibit, which shows unearned premium by type of insurance. Calculating the unearned premium reserve is a straightforward procedure. However, the unearned premiums are based on the premiums charged by the insurer. If those premiums are inadequate to pay losses and expenses, then the unearned premium reserve will be inadequate to pay future losses and expenses.

The other liabilities shown on the Annual Statement balance sheet of a property-casualty insurer do not differ significantly from those shown on the balance sheet of any other business.

Capital and Surplus

Lines 27 through 35 of the liabilities side of the balance sheet deal with the insurer's capital and policyholders' surplus. The entries are similar to those shown in that section of the balance sheet for noninsurance businesses. The major difference is the inclusion of "Surplus as regards policyholders" (line 35), which is not used in most noninsurance businesses.

UNDERWRITING AND INVESTMENT EXHIBIT

The Underwriting and Investment Exhibit begins on page 4 of the Annual Statement and contains several schedules. The first part of the Underwriting and Investment Exhibit is the Statement of Income.

EXHIBIT 14-3

Reinsurance-Related Assets and Liabilities

Primary Insurer	Reinsurer
Assets	**Liabilities**
Amounts recoverable from reinsurers (line 13.1)	Reinsurance payable on paid loss and loss adjustment expenses (line 2)
Receivables from parent, subsidiaries, and affiliates (line 20)*	
Other amounts receivable under reinsurance contracts (line 13.3)	
Liabilities	**Assets**
Funds held by company under reinsurance treaties (line 13)	Funds held by or deposited with reinsured companies (line 13.2)
Ceded reinsurance premiums payable (line 12)	Uncollected premiums and agents' balances in the course of collection (line 12.1)
Provision for reinsurance (line 16)	

* Used by a primary insurer if it has reinsurance arrangements with its parent, subsidiaries, or affiliates.

Statement of Income

The Statement of Income in the Underwriting and Investment Exhibit is similar in structure to those used by noninsurance businesses, although much of the terminology used is specific to the insurance business. It includes earned premiums, expenses incurred, and the resulting net underwriting gain or loss. A reinsurer is interested in a primary insurer's income statement because it is one indicator of the primary insurer's financial strength.

The Statement of Income shows profit or loss for only the current year and the prior year. However, the Five-Year Historical Data Exhibit (which appears later in the Annual Statement) shows the income for the current year and previous four years. Exhibit 14-4 shows the Statement of Income page from the Underwriting and Investment Exhibit in the NAIC Annual Statement Blank.

Part 1—Premiums Earned

Part 1 of the Underwriting and Investment Exhibit shows premiums earned by type of insurance. It also shows the components of premiums earned.

EXHIBIT 14-4

Underwriting and Investment Exhibit; Statement of Income

ANNUAL STATEMENT FOR THE YEAR 2004 OF THE

UNDERWRITING AND INVESTMENT EXHIBIT STATEMENT OF INCOME	1 Current Year	2 Prior Year
UNDERWRITING INCOME		
1. Premiums earned (Part 1, Line 34, Column 4)....................		
DEDUCTIONS		
2. Losses incurred (Part 2, Line 34, Column 7).....................		
3. Loss expenses incurred (Part 3, Line 25, Column 1)............		
4. Other underwriting expenses incurred (Part 3, Line 25, Column 2).............		
5. Aggregate write-ins for underwriting deductions..................		
6. Total underwriting deductions (Lines 2 through 5)............		
7. Net income of protected cells................................		
8. Net underwriting gain (loss) (Line 1 minus Line 6 plus Line 7)............		
INVESTMENT INCOME		
9. Net investment income earned (Exhibit of Net Investment Income, Line 17)............		
10. Net realized capital gains (losses) (Exhibit of Capital Gains (Losses))............		
11. Net investment gain (loss) (Lines 9 + 10)............		
OTHER INCOME		
12. Net gain (loss) from agents' or premium balances charged off (amount recovered $................................ amount charged off $................................)		
13. Finance and service charges not included in premiums............		
14. Aggregate write-ins for miscellaneous income............		
15. Total other income (Lines 12 through 14)............		
16. Net income before dividends to policyholders and before federal and foreign income taxes (Lines 8+11+15)............		
17. Dividends to policyholders............		
18. Net income, after dividends to policyholders but before federal and foreign income taxes (Line 16 minus Line 17)............		
19. Federal and foreign income taxes incurred............		
20. Net income (Line 18 minus Line 19) (to Line 22)............		
CAPITAL AND SURPLUS ACCOUNT		
21. Surplus as regards policyholders, December 31 prior year (Page 4, Line 38, Column 2)............		
GAINS AND (LOSSES) IN SURPLUS		
22. Net income (from Line 20)............		
23. Change in net unrealized capital gains or (losses)............		
24. Change in net unrealized foreign exchange capital gain (loss)............		
25. Change in net deferred income tax............		
26. Change in nonadmitted assets (Exhibit of Nonadmitted Assets, Line 26, Col. 3)............		
27. Change in provision for reinsurance (Page 3, Line 16, Column 2 minus Column 1)............		
28. Change in surplus notes............		
29. Surplus (contributed to) withdrawn from protected cells............		
30. Cumulative effect of changes in accounting principles............		
31. Capital changes:		
31.1 Paid in............		
31.2 Transferred from surplus (Stock Dividend)............		
31.3 Transferred to surplus............		
32. Surplus adjustments:		
32.1 Paid in............		
32.2 Transferred to capital (Stock Dividend)............		
32.3 Transferred from capital............		
33. Net remittances from or (to) Home Office............		
34. Dividends to stockholders............		
35. Change in treasury stock (Page 3, Lines 34.1 and 34.2, Column 2 minus Column 1)............		
36. Aggregate write-ins for gains and losses in surplus............		
37. Change in surplus as regards policyholders for the year (Lines 22 through 36)............		
38. Surplus as regards policyholders, December 31 current year (Line 21 plus Line 37) (Page 3, Line 35)............		
DETAILS OF WRITE-INS		
0501.		
0502.		
0503.		
0598. Summary of remaining write-ins for Line 5 from overflow page............		
0599. Totals (Lines 0501 through 0503 plus 0598) (Line 5 above)............		
1401.		
1402.		
1403.		
1498. Summary of remaining write-ins for Line 14 from overflow page............		
1499. Totals (Lines 1401 through 1403 plus 1498) (Line 14 above)............		
3601.		
3602.		
3603.		
3698. Summary of remaining write-ins for Line 36 from overflow page............		
3699. Totals (Lines 3601 through 3603 plus 3698) (Line 36 above)............		

Source: NAIC Annual Statement Blank–P/C, 2004 edition. Permission for reprinting given by the NAIC. Further reprint or redistribution strictly prohibited.

The premiums earned figure is calculated by adding net premiums written in the current year and unearned premiums as of December 31 of the prior year and then subtracting unearned premiums of the current year. The earned premium entry on the Statement of Income (line 1) is the total in Part 1, line 34, Column 4. Exhibit 14-5 shows Part 1 of the Underwriting and Investment Exhibit in the Annual Statement Blank.

Part 1B—Premiums Written

Part 1B of the Underwriting and Investment Exhibit shows premiums written by type of insurance. It also shows the components of net premiums written. The net premiums written figure is calculated by adding direct business and reinsurance assumed (from affiliates and non-affiliates) and subtracting reinsurance ceded (to affiliates and non-affiliates). Reinsurers can use Part 1B to evaluate a primary insurer's mix of business. This view of a primary insurers policy portfolio is often viewed in conjunction with Schedule T—Exhibit of Premiums Written, which shows written premium allocated by state (or territory). Reinsurers can use Schedule T to determine the geographic distribution of the primary insurer's policy portfolio. Taken together, the Underwriting and Investment Exhibit and Schedule T provide a comprehensive overview of a primary insurer's operations.

Parts 1 and 1B of the Underwriting and Investment Exhibit list all the types of insurance an insurer could sell, including entries for excess of loss reinsurance. Pro rata reinsurance, whether assumed or ceded, is shown by the type of insurance to which it pertains. For example, an insurer's quota share reinsurance transactions (ceded and assumed) for fire business would be shown in their components on line 1. Nonproportional assumed reinsurance transactions are categorized as property (line 30), liability (line 31), and financial (line 32). Part 1B of the Underwriting and Investment Exhibit becomes even more useful when analyzed in conjunction with Part 2, which shows loss experience by type of insurance. Exhibit 14-6 shows Part 1B of the Underwriting and Investment Exhibit in the Annual Statement Blank. Exhibit 14-7 shows Schedule T—Exhibit of Premiums Written from the Annual Statement Blank.

Part 2—Losses Paid and Incurred

Part 2 of the Underwriting and Investment Exhibit shows losses by type of insurance. Losses paid and incurred are categorized as either direct business, reinsurance assumed, or reinsurance recovered. These categories do not distinguish between reinsurance transactions with affiliates and those with other reinsurers. Part 2 uses premium earned data from Part 1 to calculate the loss ratio for each type of insurance (Column 8). Exhibit 14-8 shows Part 2 of the Underwriting and Investment Exhibit in the Annual Statement Blank.

EXHIBIT 14-5

Underwriting and Investment Exhibit; Part 1—Premiums Earned

ANNUAL STATEMENT FOR THE YEAR 2004 OF THE

UNDERWRITING AND INVESTMENT EXHIBIT
PART 1—PREMIUMS EARNED

Line of Business	1 Net Premiums Written per Column 6, Part 1B	2 Unearned Premiums Dec. 31 Prior Year- per Col. 3, Last Year's Part 1	3 Unearned Premiums Dec. 31 Current Year- per Col. 5 Part 1A	4 Premiums Earned During Year (Cols. 1 + 2 - 3)
1. Fire				
2. Allied lines				
3. Farmowners multiple peril				
4. Homeowners multiple peril				
5. Commercial multiple peril				
6. Mortgage guaranty				
8. Ocean marine				
9. Inland marine				
10. Financial guaranty				
11.1 Medical malpractice—occurrence				
11.2 Medical malpractice—claims-made				
12. Earthquake				
13. Group accident and health				
14. Credit accident and health (group and individual)				
15. Other accident and health				
16. Workers' compensation				
17.1 Other liability—occurrence				
17.2 Other liability—claims-made				
18.1 Products liability—occurrence				
18.2 Products liability—claims-made				
19.1,19.2 Private passenger auto liability				
19.3,19.4 Commercial auto liability				
21. Auto physical damage				
22. Aircraft (all perils)				
23. Fidelity				
24. Surety				
26. Burglary and theft				
27. Boiler and machinery				
28. Credit				
29. International				
30. Reinsurance-Nonproportional Assumed Property				
31. Reinsurance-Nonproportional Assumed Liability				
32. Reinsurance-Nonproportional Assumed Financial Lines				
33. Aggregate write-ins for other lines of business				
34. TOTALS				
DETAILS OF WRITE-INS				
3301.				
3302.				
3303.				
3398. Sum. of remaining write-ins for Line 33 from overflow page				
3399. Totals (Lines 3301 through 3303 plus 3398) (Line 33 above)				

Source: NAIC Annual Statement Blank–P/C, 2004 edition. Permission for reprinting given by the NAIC. Further reprint or redistribution strictly prohibited.

Reinsurance Aspects of the NAIC Annual Statement   **14.15**

EXHIBIT 14-6

Underwriting and Investment Exhibit; Part 1B—Premiums Written

ANNUAL STATEMENT FOR THE YEAR 2004 OF THE

UNDERWRITING AND INVESTMENT EXHIBIT
PART 1B—PREMIUMS WRITTEN
Gross Premiums (Less Return Premiums), Including Policy and Membership Fees
Written and Renewed During Year

	1	Reinsurance Assumed		Reinsurance Ceded		6
		2	3	4	5	Net Premiums
	Direct	From	From Non-	To	To Non-	Written
Line of Business	Business (a)	Affiliates	Affiliates	Affiliates	Affiliates	Cols. 1+2+3-4-5
1. Fire..............................						
2. Allied lines.................						
3. Farmowners multiple peril...........						
4. Homeowners multiple peril............						
5. Commercial multiple peril..........						
6. Mortgage guaranty.............						
8. Ocean marine.................						
9. Inland marine..............						
10. Financial guaranty...........						
11.1 Medical malpractice—occurrence........						
11.2 Medical malpractice—claims-made......						
12. Earthquake..................						
13. Group accident and health............						
14. Credit accident and health (group and individual)...........						
15. Other accident and health.........						
16. Workers' compensation...........						
17.1 Other liability—occurrence.........						
17.2 Other liability—claims-made.........						
18.1 Products liability—occurrence...........						
18.2 Products liability—claims-made.........						
19.1,19.2 Private passenger auto liability...........						
19.3,19.4 Commercial auto liability...........						
21. Auto physical damage..........						
22. Aircraft (all perils)..........						
23. Fidelity......................						
24. Surety.......................						
26. Burglary and theft............						
27. Boiler and machinery........						
28. Credit.......................						
29. International...............						
30. Reinsurance-Nonproportional Assumed Property.............	xxx					
31. Reinsurance-Nonproportional Assumed Liability...........	xxx					
32. Reinsurance-Nonproportional Assumed Financial Lines.......	xxx					
33. Aggregate write-ins for other lines of business.............						
34. TOTALS						
DETAILS OF WRITE-INS						
3301.						
3302.						
3303.						
3398. Sum. of remaining write-ins for Line 33 from overflow page........						
3399. Totals (Lines 3301 through 3303 plus 3398) (Line 33 above)						

(a) Does the company's direct premiums written include premiums recorded on an installment basis? Yes ( ) No ( )
If yes: 1. The amount of such installment premiums $............................
        2. Amount at which such installment premiums would have been reported had they been recorded on an annualized basis $............

P/C

Source: NAIC Annual Statement Blank–P/C, 2004 edition. Permission for reprinting given by the NAIC. Further reprint or redistribution strictly prohibited.

EXHIBIT 14-7

Schedule T—Exhibit of Premiums Written

ANNUAL STATEMENT FOR THE YEAR 2004 OF THE

SCHEDULE T—EXHIBIT OF PREMIUMS WRITTEN
Allocated by States and Territories

States, Etc.	1 Is Insurer Licensed? (Yes or No)	Gross Premiums, Including Policy and Membership Fees Less Return Premiums and Premiums on Policies Not Taken		4 Dividends Paid or Credited to Policyholders on Direct Business	5 Direct Losses Paid (Deducting Salvage)	6 Direct Losses Incurred	7 Direct Losses Unpaid	8 Finance and Service Charges Not Included in Premiums	9 Direct Premium Written for Federal Purchasing Groups (Included in Col. 2)
		2 Direct Premiums Written	3 Direct Premiums Earned						
1. Alabama...........AL									
2. Alaska...........AK									
3. Arizona...........AZ									
4. Arkansas...........AR									
5. California...........CA									
6. Colorado...........CO									
7. Connecticut...........CT									
8. Delaware...........DE									
9. Dist. Columbia...........DC									
10. Florida...........FL									
11. Georgia...........GA									
12. Hawaii...........HI									
13. Idaho...........ID									
14. Illinois...........IL									
15. Indiana...........IN									
16. Iowa...........IA									
17. Kansas...........KS									
18. Kentucky...........KY									
19. Louisiana...........LA									
20. Maine...........ME									
21. Maryland...........MD									
22. Massachusetts...........MA									
23. Michigan...........MI									
24. Minnesota...........MN									
25. Mississippi...........MS									
26. Missouri...........MO									
27. Montana...........MT									
28. Nebraska...........NE									
29. Nevada...........NV									
30. New Hampshire...........NH									
31. New Jersey...........NJ									
32. New Mexico...........NM									
33. New York...........NY									
34. No. Carolina...........NC									
35. No. Dakota...........ND									
36. Ohio...........OH									
37. Oklahoma...........OK									
38. Oregon...........OR									
39. Pennsylvania...........PA									
40. Rhode Island...........RI									
41. So. Carolina...........SC									
42. So. Dakota...........SD									
43. Tennessee...........TN									
44. Texas...........TX									
45. Utah...........UT									
46. Vermont...........VT									
47. Virginia...........VA									
48. Washington...........WA									
49. West Virginia...........WV									
50. Wisconsin...........WI									
51. Wyoming...........WY									
52. American Samoa...........AS									
53. Guam...........GU									
54. Puerto Rico...........PR									
55. U.S. Virgin Islands...........VI									
56. Canada...........CN									
57. Aggregate other alien...........OT	XXX								
58. Totals	(a)								
DETAILS OF WRITE-INS									
5701.	XXX								
5702.	XXX								
5703.	XXX								
5798. Sum. of remaining write-ins for Line 57 from overflow page	XXX								
5799. Totals (Lines 5701 through 5703+5798) (Line 57 above)	XXX								

Explanation of basis of allocation of premiums by states, etc.

(a) Insert the number of yes responses except for Canada and Other Alien.

Source: NAIC Annual Statement Blank–P/C, 2004 edition. Permission for reprinting given by the NAIC. Further reprint or redistribution strictly prohibited.

EXHIBIT 14-8

Underwriting and Investment Exhibit; Part 2—Losses Paid and Incurred

ANNUAL STATEMENT FOR THE YEAR 2004 OF THE

UNDERWRITING AND INVESTMENT EXHIBIT
PART 2—LOSSES PAID AND INCURRED

	1	2	3	4	5	6	7	8
		Losses Paid Less Salvage						
Line of Business	Direct Business	Reinsurance Assumed	Reinsurance Recovered	Net Payments (Cols. 1 + 2 - 3)	Net Losses Unpaid Current Year (Part 2A, Col. 8)	Net Losses Unpaid Prior Year	Losses Incurred Current Year (Cols. 4 + 5 - 6)	Percentage of Losses Incurred (Col. 7, Part 2) to Premiums Earned (Col. 4, Part 1)
1. Fire								
2. Allied lines								
3. Farmowners multiple peril								
4. Homeowners multiple peril								
5. Commercial multiple peril								
6. Mortgage guaranty								
8. Ocean marine								
9. Inland marine								
10. Financial guaranty								
11.1 Medical malpractice—occurrence								
11.2 Medical malpractice—claims-made								
12. Earthquake								
13. Group accident and health								
14. Credit accident and health (group and individual)								
15. Other accident and health								
16. Workers' compensation								
17.1 Other liability—occurrence								
17.2 Other liability—claims-made								
18.1 Products liability—occurrence								
18.2 Products liability—claims-made								
19.1, 19.2 Private passenger auto liability								
19.3, 19.4 Commercial auto liability								
21. Auto physical damage								
22. Aircraft (all perils)								
23. Fidelity								
24. Surety								
26. Burglary and theft								
27. Boiler and machinery								
28. Credit								
29. International								
30. Reinsurance- Nonproportional Assumed Property	XXX							
31. Reinsurance- Nonproportional Assumed Liability	XXX							
32. Reinsurance- Nonproportional Assumed Financial Lines	XXX							
33. Aggregate write-ins for other lines of business								
34. TOTALS								
DETAILS OF WRITE-INS								
3301.								
3302.								
3303.								
3398. Sum. of remaining write-ins for Line 33 from overflow page								
3399. Totals (Lines 3301 through 3303 + 3398) (Line 33 above)								

Source: NAIC Annual Statement Blank–P/C, 2004 edition. Permission for reprinting given by the NAIC. Further reprint or redistribution strictly prohibited.

Part 2A—Unpaid Losses and Loss Adjustment Expenses

Part 2A of the Underwriting and Investment Exhibit shows total estimated loss and loss adjustment expense by type of insurance. The supporting details for these totals appear in Schedule P. Exhibit 14-9 shows Part 2A of the Underwriting and Investment Exhibit in the Annual Statement Blank.

Part 2A shows unpaid net losses excluding those incurred but not reported (IBNR) in Column 4 as well as including IBNR in Column 8. The loss data from Parts 2 and 2A, when combined with the premium data from Part 1B, can roughly indicate an insurer's profitability from reinsurance operations. Unfortunately, the data on incurred losses for reinsurance transactions with affiliates cannot be separated from those with non-affiliates.

Column 8 of Part 2A shows net unpaid losses by type of insurance and in total. The total figure on line 34 of column 8 is carried over to line 1 of the liabilities section of the balance sheet on page 3 of the Annual Statement (Exhibit 14-2). Column 9 of Part 2A shows the reserve for unpaid LAE by type of insurance and in total. The total from line 34 is carried over to line 3 of the liabilities section of the balance sheet.

Although an analysis of the Underwriting and Investment Exhibit can provide substantial insights into an insurer's reinsurance operations, the principal source of reinsurance information in the Annual Statement is Schedule F.

SCHEDULE F

Schedule F
The NAIC Annual Statement Schedule that shows specific information about ceded and assumed reinsurance, as well as portfolio transfers.

Schedule F of the Annual Statement shows specific information about ceded and assumed reinsurance, as well as portfolio transfers. It also includes a restated balance sheet, which shows the insurer's assets and liabilities on a gross basis before the effects of reinsurance transactions are netted out. One significant purpose of Schedule F is to calculate the provision for reinsurance on line 16 of the liabilities side of the primary insurer's balance sheet (see Exhibit 14-2). When an insurer posts a liability to the balance sheet without a corresponding increase in assets, its policyholders' surplus is reduced. Therefore, an insurer will want to minimize this provision for reinsurance. The components of the provision for reinsurance are explained later in this section.

Schedule F consists of eight parts:

- Part 1—Assumed Reinsurance
- Part 2—Portfolio Reinsurance
- Part 3—Ceded Reinsurance
- Part 4—Aging of Ceded Reinsurance
- Part 5—Provision for Unauthorized Reinsurance
- Part 6—Provision for Overdue Authorized Reinsurance
- Part 7—Provision for Overdue Reinsurance
- Part 8—Restatement of Balance Sheet to Identify Net Credit for Ceded Reinsurance

EXHIBIT 14-9

Underwriting and Investment Exhibit; Part 2A—Unpaid Losses and Loss Adjustment Expenses

ANNUAL STATEMENT FOR THE YEAR 2004 OF THE

UNDERWRITING AND INVESTMENT EXHIBIT
PART 2A—UNPAID LOSSES AND LOSS ADJUSTMENT EXPENSES

1		Reported Losses			Incurred But Not Reported			
		2	3	4	5	6	7	8	9
Line of Business	Direct	Reinsurance Assumed	Deduct Reinsurance Recoverable from Authorized and Unauthorized Companies	Net Losses Excl. Incurred But Not Reported (Cols. 1+2-3)	Direct	Reinsurance Assumed	Reinsurance Ceded	Net Losses Unpaid (Cols. 4 + 5 + 6 − 7)	Unpaid Loss Adjustment Expenses
1. Fire									
2. Allied lines									
3. Farmowners multiple peril									
4. Homeowners multiple peril									
5. Commercial multiple peril									
6. Mortgage guaranty									
8. Ocean marine									
9. Inland marine									
10. Financial guaranty									
11.1 Medical malpractice—occurrence									
11.2 Medical malpractice—claims-made									
12. Earthquake									
13. Group accident and health								(a)	
14. Credit accident and health (group and individual)								(a)	
15. Other accident and health									
16. Workers' compensation									
17.1 Other liability—occurrence									
17.2 Other liability—claims-made									
18.1 Products liability—occurrence									
18.2 Products liability—claims-made									
19.1, 19.2 Private passenger auto liability									
19.3, 19.4 Commercial auto liability									
21. Auto physical damage									
22. Aircraft (all perils)									
23. Fidelity									
24. Surety									
26. Burglary and theft									
27. Boiler and machinery									
28. Credit									
29. International					XXX				
30. Reinsurance- Nonproportional Assumed Property	XXX				XXX				
31. Reinsurance- Nonproportional Assumed Liability	XXX				XXX				
32. Reinsurance- Nonproportional Assumed Financial Lines	XXX								
33. Aggregate write-ins for other lines of business									
34. TOTALS									

DETAILS OF WRITE-INS

3301.
3302.
3303.
3398. Sum of remaining write-ins for Line 33 from overflow page
3399. Totals (Lines 3301 through 3303 + 3398) (Line 33 above)

(a) Including $..........for present value of life indemnity claims.

Source: NAIC Annual Statement Blank–P/C, 2004 edition. Permission for reprinting given by the NAIC. Further reprint or redistribution strictly prohibited.

Parts 3 through 6 provide data for the provision for overdue reinsurance appearing in Part 7. Each of the eight parts is discussed in this section.

Schedule F—Part 1

Schedule F—Part 1 shows the reinsurance assumed by the reinsurer. It includes paid and reserved loss and LAE amounts as well as funds deposited with, and letters of credit posted on behalf of, the primary insurer. Schedule F—Part 1 is shown in Exhibit 14-10. As an example, two primary insurers are listed, ABC Insurance and XYZ Insurance. The total reinsurance on paid losses and LAE ($15,009,973) in column 6 is an amount payable that appears on line 2 on the liabilities side of the reinsurer's balance sheet.

Another significant item in Schedule F—Part 1 is in column 12, "Funds Held by or Deposited With Reinsured Companies." This is the amount the reinsurer deposits with the primary insurer and it appears on line 13.2 of the assets side of the reinsurer's balance sheet. For the reinsurer filing the sample statement in Exhibit 14-10, the amount deposited with ABC Insurance and XYZ Insurance, is $21,328,400.

Schedule F—Part 2

Schedule F—Part 2 shows all of the insurer's ceded and assumed portfolio reinsurance transactions during the current year. Portfolio reinsurance transactions involve blocks of business already written by insurers. A portfolio reinsurance transaction can involve either known losses (loss portfolio transfers) or known and unknown losses. Loss portfolio transfers are usually extraordinary events, and this schedule highlights those transactions for additional scrutiny. Schedule F—Part 2 shows the name of the portfolio reinsurer, the date of the reinsurance contract (agreement), the amount of the original (underlying) premium, and the amount of the reinsurance premium. Schedule F—Part 2 is shown in Exhibit 14-11.

Schedule F—Part 3

Schedule F—Part 3 provides details about reinsurance ceded by the insurer and is shown in Exhibit 14-12. Both authorized and unauthorized reinsurers should be listed here. Amounts are shown for reinsurance recoverable on paid losses and paid LAE, known case loss and LAE reserves, IBNR loss and LAE reserves, unearned premiums, and contingent commissions. Column 19 shows the amounts that reinsurers deposited with the primary insurer. Those amounts must be posted on line 13 of the liability side of the primary insurer's balance sheet.

EXHIBIT 14-10

NAIC Annual Statement; Schedule F—Part 1

ANNUAL STATEMENT FOR THE YEAR 2004 OF THE

SCHEDULE F—PART 1
Assumed Reinsurance as of December 31, Current Year (000 Omitted)

1	2	3	4	5	6	7	8	9	10	11	12	13	14
					\multicolumn{2}{c}{Reinsurance On}							
Federal ID Number	NAIC Company Code	Name of Reinsured	Domiciliary Jurisdiction	Assumed Premium	Paid Losses and Loss Adjustment Expenses	Known Case Losses and LAE	Cols. 6 + 7	Contingent Commissions Payable	Assumed Premiums Receivable	Unearned Premium	Funds Held By or Deposited With Reinsured Companies	Letters of Credit Posted	Amount of Assets Pledged or Compensating Balances to Secure Letters of Credit
		ABC Insurance			10,009,973	14,000,000	24,009,973				14,658,400	0	0
		XYZ Insurance			5,000,000	6,000,000	11,000,000				6,670,000	0	0
9999999 Totals					15,009,973	20,000,000	35,009,973				21,328,400		

P/C

Source: NAIC Annual Statement Blank–P/C, 2004 edition. Permission for reprinting given by the NAIC. Further reprint or redistribution strictly prohibited.

14.22 Reinsurance Principles and Practices

EXHIBIT 14-11
NAIC Annual Statement; Schedule F—Part 2

ANNUAL STATEMENT FOR THE YEAR 2004 OF THE

SCHEDULE F—PART 2
Premium Portfolio Reinsurance Effected or (Canceled) during Current Year

1	2	3	4	5	6
Federal ID Number	NAIC Company Code	Name of Company	Date of Contract	Original Premium	Reinsurance Premium

0199999 Total Reinsurance Ceded by Portfolio

0299999 Total Reinsurance Assumed by Portfolio

Source: NAIC Annual Statement Blank–P/C, 2004 edition. Permission for reprinting given by the NAIC. Further reprint or redistribution strictly prohibited.

EXHIBIT 14-12
NAIC Annual Statement; Schedule F—Part 3

ANNUAL STATEMENT FOR THE YEAR 2004 OF THE

SCHEDULE F—PART 3
Ceded Reinsurance as of December 31, Current Year (000 Omitted)

1	2	3	4	5	6	7	8	9	10	11	12	13	14	15	16	17	18	19
									Reinsurance Recoverable On						Reinsurance Payable			
Federal ID Number	NAIC Company Code	Name of Reinsurer	Domiciliary Jurisdiction	Reinsurance Contracts Ceding 75% or More of Direct Premiums Written	Reinsurance Premiums Ceded	Paid Losses	Paid LAE	Known Case Loss Reserves	Known Case LAE Reserves	IBNR Loss Reserves	IBNR LAE Reserves	Unearned Premiums	Contingent Commissions	Cols. 7 through 14 Totals	Ceded Balances Payable	Other Amounts Due to Reinsurers	Net Amount Recoverable From Reinsurers Cols. 15 − [16 + 17]	Funds Held by Company Under Reinsurance Treaties
		Prompt Re			2,430,000	6,000,000	700,000	4,000,000	0	8,200,000	0			18,900,000	2,100,000	0	16,800,000	0
		Overdue Re				5,100,000	365,000	3,800,000	0	6,100,000	0			15,365,000	0	0	15,365,000	0
		Slowpay Re				9,300,000	141,000	2,100,000	0	21,200,000	0			32,741,000	0	0	32,741,000	12,767,376
9999999 Totals					2,430,000	20,400,000	1,206,000	9,900,000	0	35,500,000	0			67,006,000	2,100,000	0	32,741,000	12,767,376

NOTE: Report the five largest provisional commission rates included in the cedant's reinsurance treaties. The commission rate to be reported is by contract with ceded premium in excess of $50,000:

1	2	3
Name of Company	Commission Rate	Ceded Premium
1)		
2)		
3)		
4)		
5)		

36

P/C

Source: NAIC Annual Statement Blank–P/C, 2004 edition. Permission for reprinting given by the NAIC. Further reprint or redistribution strictly prohibited.

The example given in Exhibit 14-12 shows three authorized reinsurers, Prompt Re, Overdue Re, and Slowpay Re whose names describe how promptly they reimburse the primary insurer for paid losses and LAE. The figures shown in Exhibit 14-12 are carried through subsequent exhibits to illustrate how a provision for reinsurance is calculated. Columns 7 and 8 of Exhibit 14-12 show that the paid losses and paid LAE recoverable total $21,606,000 ($20,400,000 + $1,206,000). The amounts in columns 9, 10, and 11, which total $45,400,000 ($9,900,000 + 0 + $35,500,000), are those that are yet to be recovered from the reinsurers on outstanding loss reserves. Columns 16 and 17 show the ceded balances payable to reinsurers, which are subtracted from the total recoverables to determine the net amount recoverable from reinsurers in Column 18. Column 19 shows the amount held by the primary insurer under its reinsurance treaties. Exhibit 14-12 shows $12,767,376 held under the treaty with Slowpay Re.

Schedule F—Part 4

Schedule F—Part 4, shown in Exhibit 14-13, illustrates the aging of ceded reinsurance recoverable on paid losses and paid LAE. The amount recoverable is divided between the amount that is current (Column 5) and the amount overdue by a certain number of days (Columns 6 through 10). For example, for Overdue Re, $1,000,000 is overdue for more than 120 days. The percentage overdue is calculated in column 12 by dividing the total overdue (Column 10) by the total due (Column 11). The longer reinsurance recoverables remain uncollected, the more likely it is that the insurer will not be able to collect them.

Schedule F—Part 5

Schedule F—Part 5 calculates the provision for unauthorized reinsurance, which is part of the overall provision for reinsurance that a primary insurer must show on line 16 of the liabilities side of the balance sheet. Schedule F—Part 5 is shown in Exhibit 14-14.

As discussed previously, the effect of the provision for reinsurance is to reduce policyholders' surplus. Therefore, the requirement to make provision for unauthorized reinsurance may act as a disincentive to do business with an unauthorized reinsurer.

If the reinsurer provides the primary insurer with collateral in respect of the reinsurance recoverables, then the amount of the provision for unauthorized reinsurance may be reduced. The amounts of collateral are listed on Schedule F—Part 5, and include funds that a reinsurer deposits with the primary insurer (Column 6) and letters of credit furnished by a reinsurer to the primary insurer (Column 7). However, even if all the recoverables are fully secured, a provision for unauthorized reinsurance would still have to be made if any amounts are either more than ninety days past due or are in dispute. In practice, a primary insurer may redeem some or all of the collateral so that no losses are overdue by more than ninety days.

EXHIBIT 14-13
NAIC Annual Statement; Schedule F—Part 4

ANNUAL STATEMENT FOR THE YEAR 2004 OF THE

SCHEDULE F—PART 4
Aging of Ceded Reinsurance as of December 31, Current Year (000 Omitted)

1	2	3	4	5	6	7	8	9	10	11	12	13
					Reinsurance Recoverable on Paid Losses and Paid Loss Adjustment Expenses							
							Overdue					
Federal ID Number	NAIC Company Code	Name of Reinsurer	Domiciliary Jurisdiction	Current	1 to 29 Days	30 - 90 Days	91 - 120 Days	Over 120 Days	Total Overdue Cols. 6 + 7 + 8 + 9	Total Due Cols. 5 + 10	Percentage Overdue Col. 10/Col. 11	Percentage More Than 120 Days Overdue Col. 9/Col. 11
		Prompt Re		4,300,000	1,400,000	1,000,000	0	0	2,400,000	6,700,000	36%	0
		Overdue Re		1,800,000	900,000	965,000	800,000	1,000,000	3,665,000	5,465,000	67%	18%
		Slowpay Re		2,000,000	2,400,000	2,641,000	900,000	1,500,000	7,441,000	9,441,000	79%	16%
9999999 Totals				8,100,000	4,700,000	4,606,000	1,700,000	2,500,000	13,506,000	21,606,000		

Source: NAIC Annual Statement Blank–P/C, 2004 edition. Permission for reprinting given by the NAIC. Further reprint or redistribution strictly prohibited.

EXHIBIT 14-14
NAIC Annual Statement; Schedule F—Part 5

ANNUAL STATEMENT FOR THE YEAR 2004 OF THE

SCHEDULE F—PART 5
Provision for Unauthorized Reinsurance as of December 31, Current Year (000 Omitted)

1	2	3	4	5	6	7	8	9	10	11	12	13	14	15	16	17
Federal ID Number	NAIC Company Code	Name of Reinsurer	Domiciliary Jurisdiction	Reinsurance Recoverable all Items Schedule F Part 3, Col. 15	Funds Held By Company Under Reinsurance Treaties	Letters of Credit	Ceded Balances Payable	Miscellaneous Balances	Other Allowed Offset Items	Sum of Cols. 6 through 10 but not in excess of Col. 5	Subtotal Col. 5 minus Col. 11	Recoverable Paid Losses & LAE Expenses Over 90 Days past Due not in Dispute	20% of Amount in Col. 13	Smaller of Col. 11 or Col. 14	Smaller of Col. 11 or 20% of Amount in Dispute Included in Col. 5	Total Provision for Unauthorized Reinsurance Smaller of Col. 5 or Cols. 12+15+16
9999999 Totals																

1. Amounts in dispute totaling $_____ are included in Column 5.
2. Amounts in dispute totaling $_____ are excluded from Column 13.
3. Column 5 excludes $_____ recoverables on ceded IBNR on contracts in force prior to July 1, 1984 and not subsequently renewed.

Source: NAIC Annual Statement Blank–P/C, 2004 edition. Permission for reprinting given by the NAIC. Further reprint or redistribution strictly prohibited.

Schedule F—Part 6

Schedule F—Part 6, shown in Exhibit 14-15, establishes the amounts overdue from each authorized reinsurer. It also determines whether a reinsurer can be categorized as "slow-paying" by reference to a particular percentage. This percentage is calculated by dividing the reinsurance recoverable on paid losses and paid LAE more than ninety days overdue (Column 4) by the sum of reinsurance recoverable on paid losses and paid LAE (Column 5) and the amounts received in the prior ninety days (Column 6). If this percentage is 20 percent or above, the reinsurer is categorized as a slow-paying reinsurer. Schedule F—Part 7 deals with slow-paying reinsurers. If the percentage is less than 20 percent, then a penalty of 20 percent of the amount overdue by more than ninety days is added to the provision for reinsurance on the balance sheet.

In the example in Exhibit 14-15, the percentage figure for Overdue Re is 19 percent, while for Slowpay Re it is 23 percent. Therefore, Slowpay Re is categorized as a slow-paying reinsurer. Schedule F—Part 6 calculates the 20 percent penalty amount for Overdue Re in Column 11 ($360,000). The penalty amount for dealing with Slowpay Re is calculated in Schedule F—Part 7.

Schedule F—Part 7

Schedule F—Part 7 calculates the provision for overdue reinsurance, and is shown in Exhibit 14-16 with the sample reinsurance recoverable of $32,741,000 (Column 4) from Slowpay Re. The amount withheld and letter of credit amount total $21,112,441 ($12,767,376 + $8,345,065) for a net reinsurance recoverable of $11,628,559 (Column 11), 20 percent of this amount ($2,325,712) is calculated at the bottom of Schedule F—Part 7. This penalty is added to the penalties from Schedule F—Part 5 and Schedule F—Part 6 to determine the total provision for reinsurance ($2,685,712). The total provision is the amount that appears on line 16 of the liabilities side of the primary insurer's balance sheet. Exhibit 14-17 summarizes how the total provision for reinsurance is determined.

Schedule F—Part 8

Schedule F—Part 8 is a restatement of the balance sheet to identify reinsurance, and is shown in Exhibit 14-18. Assets and liabilities are restated to show the insurer's balance sheet gross of ceded reinsurance. The figures in this part are intended to indicate the primary insurer's dependence on reinsurance.

EXHIBIT 14-15
NAIC Annual Statement; Schedule F—Part 6

ANNUAL STATEMENT FOR THE YEAR 2004 OF THE

SCHEDULE F—PART 6
Provision for Overdue Authorized Reinsurance as of December 31, Current Year

1 Federal ID Number	2 NAIC Company Code	3 Name of Reinsurer	4 Reinsurance Recoverable on Paid Losses and LAE More Than 90 Days Overdue (a)	5 Total Reinsurance Recoverable on Paid Losses and Paid LAE (b)	6 Amounts Received Prior 90 Days	7 Col. 4 divided by (Cols. 5 + 6)	8 Amounts in Col. 4 for Companies Reporting less than 20% in Col. 7	9 Amounts in Dispute Excluded from Col. 4 for Companies Reporting less than 20% in Col. 7	10 20% of Amount in Col. 9	11 Amount Reported in Col. 8 × 20% + Col. 10
		Prompt Re.	0	6,700,000	900,000	0%	0	0	0	0
		Overdue Re.	1,800,000	5,465,000	3,900,000	19%	1,800,000	0	0	360,000
		Slowpay Re.	2,400,000	9,441,000	1,000,000	23%	0	0	0	0
9999999 Totals			4,200,000	21,606,000	5,800,000		1,800,000	0	0	360,000

(a) From Schedule F-Part 4 Columns 8 + 9, total authorized, less $_____ in dispute.
(b) From Schedule F-Part 3 Columns 7 + 8, total authorized, less $_____ in dispute.

P/C

Source: NAIC Annual Statement Blank–P/C, 2004 edition. Permission for reprinting given by the NAIC. Further reprint or redistribution strictly prohibited.

EXHIBIT 14-16
NAIC Annual Statement; Schedule F—Part 7

ANNUAL STATEMENT FOR THE YEAR 2004 OF THE

SCHEDULE F—PART 7
Provision for Overdue Reinsurance as of December 31, Current Year

1	2	3	4	5	6	7	8	9	10	11	12
Federal ID Number	NAIC Company Code	Name of Reinsurer	Reinsurance Recoverable All Items	Funds Held By Company Under Reinsurance Treaties	Letters of Credit	Ceded Balances Payable	Other Miscellaneous Balances	Other Allowed Offset Items	Sum of Cols. 5 through 9 but not in Excess of Col. 4	Col. 4 minus Col. 10	Greater of Col. 11 or Schedule F - Part 4 Cols. 8 + 9
		Slowpay Re	32,741,000	12,767,376	8,345,065				21,112,441	11,628,559	11,628,559
9999999	Totals		32,741,000	12,767,376	8,345,065	0	0	0	21,112,441	11,628,559	

1. Total 11,628,559
2. Line 1 x .20 2,325,712
3. Schedule F-Part 6 Col. 11 360,000
4. Provision for Overdue Authorized Reinsurance (Lines 2 + 3) 2,685,712
5. Provision for Unauthorized Reinsurance (Schedule F-Part 5, Col. 17 x 1000) 0
6. Provision for Reinsurance (sum Lines 4 + 5) (Enter this amount on Page 3, Line 16) 2,685,712

P/C

Source: NAIC Annual Statement Blank–P/C, 2004 edition. Permission for reprinting given by the NAIC. Further reprint or redistribution strictly prohibited.

EXHIBIT 14-17

Schedule F Provision for Reinsurance

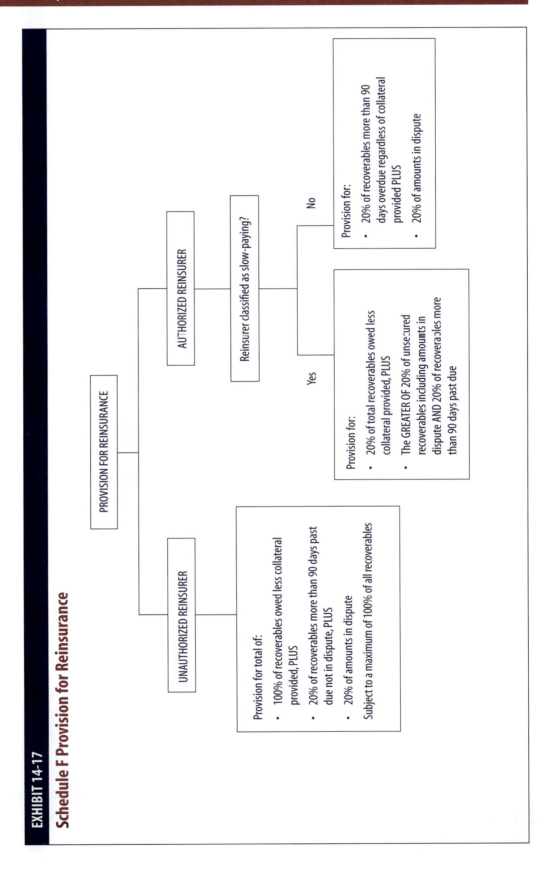

Reinsurance Aspects of the NAIC Annual Statement   14.31

EXHIBIT 14-18

NAIC Annual Statement; Schedule F—Part 8

ANNUAL STATEMENT FOR THE YEAR 2004 OF THE

SCHEDULE F-PART 8
Restatement of Balance Sheet to Identify Net Credit for Reinsurance

	1 As Reported (Net of Ceded)	2 Restatement Adjustments	3 Restated (Gross of Ceded)
ASSETS (Page 2, Col. 3)			
1. Cash and invested assets (Line 10).................................			
2. Premiums and considerations (Line 12)...........................			
3. Reinsurance recoverable on loss and loss adjustment expense payments (Line 13.1)............			
4. Funds held by or deposited with reinsured companies (Line 13.2)...........			
5. Other assets..			
6. Net amount recoverable from reinsurers........................			
7. Totals (Line 26)..			
LIABILITIES (Page 3)			
8. Losses and loss adjustment expenses (Lines 1 through 3)...........			
9. Taxes, expenses, and other obligations (Lines 4 through 8).........			
10. Unearned premiums (Line 9).......................................			
11. Advance premiums (Line 10).......................................			
12. Dividends declared and unpaid (Line 11.1 and 11.2).................			
13. Ceded reinsurance premiums payable (net of ceding commissions) (Line 12).....			
14. Funds held by company under reinsurance treaties (Line 13)............			
15. Amounts withheld or retained by company for account of others (Line 14).........			
16. Provision for reinsurance (Line 16).................................			
17. Other liabilities (Lines 15 and 17 through 23)......................			
18. Total liabilities excluding protected cell business (Line 26 minus Line 25).........			
19. Surplus as regards policyholders (Line 35).........................		XXX	
20. Totals (Line 36)			

NOTE: Is the restatement of this exhibit the result of grossing up balances ceded to affiliates under 100 percent reinsurance or pooling arrangements?   Yes [ ]   No [ ]

If yes, give full explanation: _____

_____

41   P/C

Source: NAIC Annual Statement Blank–P/C, 2004 edition. Permission for reprinting given by the NAIC. Further reprint or redistribution strictly prohibited.

SCHEDULE P

Evaluating an insurer's loss reserves is important in determining the insurer's financial condition. The total estimated liabilities for losses and loss adjustment expenses appear in lines 1, 2, and 3 on the liabilities side of the balance sheet and in Part 2A of the Underwriting and Investment Exhibit. The supporting data for this information is contained in Schedule P. The importance of loss reserves is emphasized by the size and complexity of **Schedule P**, which shows detailed historical information on paid and reserved losses and LAE. Schedule P consists of seven parts plus interrogatories, but this chapter focuses on Parts 1 through 4.

Each of these four parts is composed of subparts for each type of insurance. Part 1 also has a summary of parts 1 through 4, which includes all classes of insurance combined.

Schedule P
The NAIC Annual Statement Schedule that shows detailed historical information on paid and reserved losses and LAE.

Schedule P—Part 1

Schedule P—Part 1 provides detailed information on historical losses and loss expenses. It provides an analysis of premiums earned and of loss and loss expenses. Exhibit 14-19 shows the Schedule P—Part 1—Summary. It includes premiums earned, loss and loss expense payments, losses unpaid, defense and cost containment, unpaid, adjusting other unpaid and total losses and loss expenses incurred.

The relevant data are shown by year for the most recent ten years. An additional line shows aggregate data for all years prior to the past ten. The parts of the Schedule that should not contain numerical data are marked "XXX."

Schedule P—Part 2

Schedule P—Part 2 provides a history and development of incurred net losses and defense and cost containment expenses. As with Schedule P—Part 1, Schedule P—Part 2 contains subparts for each type of insurance. In each subpart, Column 11 shows the amount of loss development during the past year, and Column 12 shows the loss development over the past two years. A positive number in either column indicates an increase in incurred losses, while a negative number indicates a decrease. Exhibit 14-20 shows the Schedule P—Part 2—Summary.

Schedule P—Part 3

Schedule P—Part 3 provides a history of cumulative net paid losses, and defense and cost containment expenses. It also includes the number of claims closed with loss payment and without loss payment. Again, there are subparts for each type of insurance. Exhibit 14-21 shows the Schedule P—Part 3—Summary.

EXHIBIT 14-19

Schedule P—Part 1—Summary

ANNUAL STATEMENT FOR THE YEAR 2004 OF THE

SCHEDULE P—ANALYSIS OF LOSSES AND LOSS EXPENSES

SCHEDULE P—PART 1—SUMMARY

($000 Omitted)

	Premiums Earned			Loss and Loss Expense Payments								12
	1	2	3	Loss Payments		Defense and Cost Containment Payments		Adjusting and Other Payments		10	11	
Years in Which Premiums Were Earned and Losses Were Incurred	Direct and Assumed	Ceded	Net (Cols. 1–2)	4 Direct and Assumed	5 Ceded	6 Direct and Assumed	7 Ceded	8 Direct and Assumed	9 Ceded	Salvage and Subrogation Received	Total Net Paid (Cols. 4 - 5 + 6 - 7 + 8 - 9)	Number of Claims Reported-Direct and Assumed
1. Prior	XXX	XXX	XXX									XXX
2. 1995												XXX
3. 1996												XXX
4. 1997												XXX
5. 1998												XXX
6. 1999												XXX
7. 2000												XXX
8. 2001												XXX
9. 2002												XXX
10. 2003												XXX
11. 2004												XXX
12. Totals	XXX	XXX	XXX									XXX

	Losses Unpaid				Defense and Cost Containment Unpaid				Adjusting and Other Unpaid		23	24	25
	Case Basis		Bulk + IBNR		Case Basis		Bulk + IBNR						
	13	14	15	16	17	18	19	20	21	22			
	Direct and Assumed	Ceded	Direct and Assumed	Ceded	Direct and Assumed	Ceded	Direct and Assumed	Ceded	Direct and Assumed	Ceded	Salvage and Subrogation Anticipated	Total Net Losses and Expenses Unpaid	Number of Claims Outstanding Direct and Assumed
1.													XXX
2.													XXX
3.													XXX
4.													XXX
5.													XXX
6.													XXX
7.													XXX
8.													XXX
9.													XXX
10.													XXX
11.													XXX
12.													XXX

	Total Losses and Loss Expenses Incurred			Loss and Loss Expense Percentage (Incurred/Premiums Earned)			Nontabular Discount		34	Net Balance Sheet Reserves After Discount	
	26	27	28	29	30	31	32	33	Inter-Company Pooling Participation Percentage	35	36
	Direct and Assumed	Ceded	Net	Direct and Assumed	Ceded	Net	Loss	Loss Expense		Losses Unpaid	Loss Expenses Unpaid
1.	XXX	XXX	XXX	XXX	XXX	XXX			XXX		
2.											
3.											
4.											
5.											
6.											
7.											
8.											
9.											
10.											
11.											
12.	XXX	XXX	XXX	XXX	XXX	XXX			XXX		

Note: Parts 2 and 4 are gross of all discounting, including tabular discounting. Part 1 is gross of only nontabular discounting, which is reported in Columns 32 and 33 of Part 1. The tabular discount, if any, is reported in the Notes to Financial Statements which will reconcile Part 1 with Parts 2 and 4.

Source: NAIC Annual Statement Blank–P/C, 2004 edition. Permission for reprinting given by the NAIC. Further reprint or redistribution strictly prohibited.

EXHIBIT 14-20

Schedule P—Part 2—Summary

ANNUAL STATEMENT FOR THE YEAR 2004 OF THE

SCHEDULE P—PART 2—SUMMARY

	INCURRED NET LOSSES AND DEFENSE AND COST CONTAINMENT EXPENSES REPORTED AT YEAR END ($000 OMITTED)										DEVELOPMENT	
Years in Which Losses Were Incurred	1 1995	2 1996	3 1997	4 1998	5 1999	6 2000	7 2001	8 2002	9 2003	10 2004	11 One Year	12 Two Year
1. Prior............	....	....	....	....	....	....	....	....	....	....	....	....
2. 1995............	....	....	....	....	....	....	....	....	....	....	....	....
3. 1996............	XXX	....	....	....	....	....	....	....	....	....	....	....
4. 1997............	XXX	XXX	....	....	....	....	....	....	....	....	....	....
5. 1998............	XXX	XXX	XXX	....	....	....	....	....	....	....	....	....
6. 1999............	XXX	XXX	XXX	XXX	....	....	....	....	....	....	....	....
7. 2000............	XXX	XXX	XXX	XXX	XXX	....	....	....	....	....	....	....
8. 2001............	XXX	XXX	XXX	XXX	XXX	XXX	....	....	....	....	....	....
9. 2002............	XXX	XXX	XXX	XXX	XXX	XXX	XXX	....	....	....	....	....
10. 2003............	XXX	XXX	XXX	XXX	XXX	XXX	XXX	XXX	....	....	....	XXX
11. 2004............	XXX	XXX	XXX	XXX	XXX	XXX	XXX	XXX	XXX	....	XXX	XXX
										12. Totals		

Source: NAIC Annual Statement Blank–P/C, 2004 edition. Permission for reprinting given by the NAIC. Further reprint or redistribution strictly prohibited.

EXHIBIT 14-21

Schedule P—Part 3—Summary

ANNUAL STATEMENT FOR THE YEAR 2004 OF THE

SCHEDULE P—PART 3—SUMMARY

	CUMULATIVE PAID NET LOSSES AND DEFENSE AND COST CONTAINMENT EXPENSES REPORTED AT YEAR END ($000 OMITTED)										11	12
Years in Which Losses Were Incurred	1 1995	2 1996	3 1997	4 1998	5 1999	6 2000	7 2001	8 2002	9 2003	10 2004	Number of Claims Closed With Loss Payment	Number of Claims Closed Without Loss Payment
1. Prior............	000	....	....	....	....	....	....	....	....	....	XXX	XXX
2. 1995............	....	....	....	....	....	....	....	....	....	....	XXX	XXX
3. 1996............	XXX	....	....	....	....	....	....	....	....	....	XXX	XXX
4. 1997............	XXX	XXX	....	....	....	....	....	....	....	....	XXX	XXX
5. 1998............	XXX	XXX	XXX	....	....	....	....	....	....	....	XXX	XXX
6. 1999............	XXX	XXX	XXX	XXX	....	....	....	....	....	....	XXX	XXX
7. 2000............	XXX	XXX	XXX	XXX	XXX	....	....	....	....	....	XXX	XXX
8. 2001............	XXX	XXX	XXX	XXX	XXX	XXX	....	....	....	....	XXX	XXX
9. 2002............	XXX	XXX	XXX	XXX	XXX	XXX	XXX	....	....	....	XXX	XXX
10. 2003............	XXX	XXX	XXX	XXX	XXX	XXX	XXX	XXX	....	....	XXX	XXX
11. 2004............	XXX	XXX	XXX	XXX	XXX	XXX	XXX	XXX	XXX	....	XXX	XXX

Source: NAIC Annual Statement Blank–P/C, 2004 edition. Permission for reprinting given by the NAIC. Further reprint or redistribution strictly prohibited.

EXHIBIT 14-22

Schedule P—Part 4—Summary

ANNUAL STATEMENT FOR THE YEAR 2004 OF THE

SCHEDULE P—PART 4—SUMMARY

Years in Which Losses Were Incurred	BULK AND IBNR RESERVES ON NET LOSSES AND DEFENSE AND COST CONTAINMENT EXPENSES REPORTED AT YEAR END ($000 OMITTED)									
	1	2	3	4	5	6	7	8	9	10
	1995	1996	1997	1998	1999	2000	2001	2002	2003	2004
1. Prior.........	....	....	....	....	....	....	....	....	....	....
2. 1995.........	....	....	....	....	....	....	....	....	....	....
3. 1996.........	XXX	....	....	....	....	....	....	....	....	....
4. 1997.........	XXX	XXX	....	....	....	....	....	....	....	....
5. 1998.........	XXX	XXX	XXX	....	....	....	....	....	....	....
6. 1999.........	XXX	XXX	XXX	XXX	....	....	....	....	....	....
7. 2000.........	XXX	XXX	XXX	XXX	XXX	....	....	....	....	....
8. 2001.........	XXX	XXX	XXX	XXX	XXX	XXX	....	....	....	....
9. 2002.........	XXX	XXX	XXX	XXX	XXX	XXX	XXX	....	....	....
10. 2003.........	XXX	XXX	XXX	XXX	XXX	XXX	XXX	XXX	....	....
11. 2004.........	XXX	XXX	XXX	XXX	XXX	XXX	XXX	XXX	XXX	....

Source: NAIC Annual Statement Blank–P/C, 2004 edition. Permission for reprinting given by the NAIC. Further reprint or redistribution strictly prohibited.

Schedule P—Part 4

Schedule P—Part 4 contains a history of bulk and incurred but not reported (IBNR) reserves by type of insurance. The data shown in Part 4 form a loss development triangle. Over time the bulk and IBNR reserves are replaced by case reserves reported and claim payments made. Exhibit 14-22 shows the Schedule P—Part 4—Summary.

SUMMARY

All insurers, both primary insurers and reinsurers, are required to file an NAIC Annual Statement (Annual Statement) with the insurance department of each state in which the insurer is authorized to do business. The Annual Statement is prepared according to statutory accounting principles (SAP) and is designed to provide state insurance regulators with the information needed to regulate the insurer's solvency.

The Annual Statement is a complex and lengthy financial document, consisting of a balance sheet, a statement of income, and a cash flow statement, backed by supporting exhibits and schedules. This chapter concentrated on aspects of the Annual Statement related to reinsurance transactions by discussing the balance sheet, income statement, and supporting Schedules F and P.

The largest categories of assets on the Annual Statement balance sheet of an insurer typically are bonds, common stocks, and short-term investments. The most common reinsurance-related asset for a reinsurer is funds deposited by the reinsurer with primary insurers, and for a primary insurer is amounts recoverable from reinsurers.

The largest liability on an insurer's Annual Statement balance sheet typically is loss and loss adjustment expense reserves. For a reinsurer, the other key liability is the amount payable by the reinsurer on paid losses already paid by the primary insurer. For a primary insurer, the other key liabilities are the deposit amounts held by the primary insurer under reinsurance treaties, the provision for reinsurance, and the unearned premium amount.

The Annual Statement Underwriting and Investment Exhibit includes the Statement of Income, which shows the premium income, net of ceded reinsurance, by types of insurance. The Underwriting and Investment Exhibit also shows premiums earned, premiums written, losses paid and incurred, and unpaid losses and LAE, all by type of insurance.

Schedule F shows specific information on ceded and assumed reinsurance, as well as portfolio transfers. It establishes the primary insurer's provision for reinsurance based on reinsurance ceded to both authorized and unauthorized reinsurers. Schedule F also includes a restated balance sheet, which shows assets and liabilities gross of ceded reinsurance and indicates the primary insurer's dependence on reinsurance.

Schedule P shows detailed information by type of insurance on losses and LAE, both paid and reserved. It also contains historical losses in a loss triangle format and is therefore useful in calculating the insurer's IBNR amount.

The next chapter describes the methods that primary insurers and reinsurers use to estimate reserves for losses and loss adjustment expenses.

Chapter 15

Direct Your Learning

Reserves

After learning the content of this chapter, you should be able to:

- Describe the relationship over time between incurred losses, paid losses, and reserves.
- Describe the effect of inadequate reserves on an insurer's financial position.
- Describe the methods for establishing case and bulk reserves.
- Describe salvage and subrogation and their effect on reserves.
- Explain the difficulties excess of loss reinsurers encounter when applying reserving methods.

OUTLINE

Loss and Loss Adjustment Expense Reserves

Methods for Establishing Reserves

Salvage and Subrogation

Reserving Methods for Excess of Loss Reinsurers

Summary

Develop Your Perspective

What are the main topics covered in the chapter?

This chapter describes the reserves maintained by primary insurers and reinsurers and loss reserving methods.

Identify the different types of reserves.

- What are the different methods of establishing reserves?
- How are reserves affected by salvage and subrogation?

Why is it important to learn about these topics?

Understanding loss reserving methods will help you to develop a better understanding of the significance that reserves have in the determination of primary insurer (and reinsurer) profitability and solvency.

Consider the factors that affect an excess of loss reinsurer's reserves.

- What strategies may an excess of loss reinsurer use to address monetary inflation, social inflation, and claims that have long loss development periods?

How can you use what you will learn?

Review the financial statements of your company.

- Have reserves been increased to address under-reserving or decreased to address over-reserving?

Chapter 15
Reserves

Primary insurers and reinsurers must establish reserves, which are estimates of the amounts they will have to pay in the future for losses that have already occurred. Reserves, which consist of reserves for both losses and loss adjustment expenses (LAE), affect the insurers' financial reports, including their NAIC Annual Statements.

Insurers must estimate reserves as precisely as possible in order to accurately report their financial position. However, estimating reserves is difficult because, in most cases, the amount that the insurer will eventually pay for a claim is uncertain. For example, the insurer may not know all of the facts about the underlying claim when estimating reserves.

This chapter describes the methods that primary insurers and reinsurers use to estimate reserves. Generally, reserves are easier to estimate for property insurance than for liability insurance because property losses are easier to value and usually settle more quickly than liability losses. Consequently, most of this chapter is devoted to the complex task of estimating reserves for liability insurance. However, many of the methods described also apply to reserves for property insurance. In addition, this chapter describes some of the difficulties that reinsurers encounter when estimating reserves for excess of loss reinsurance.

LOSS AND LOSS ADJUSTMENT EXPENSE RESERVES

Reserves consist of loss reserves and loss adjustment expense reserves. For a primary insurer, losses are the amounts that it is obligated to pay to claimants under primary insurance policies. A reinsurer's losses are the amounts that it is obligated to pay to primary insurers under reinsurance agreements. Losses can be separated into paid losses and loss reserves.

Loss adjustment expenses are amounts required to defend and settle a primary insurer's claims. These expenses include court costs related to a specific claim and expenses associated with the claim function that cannot be allocated to a particular claim. As with losses, loss adjustment expenses include paid and reserved amounts. **Loss adjustment expense reserves** are estimates of the future cost of defending and settling claims for losses that have already occurred. A reinsurer's obligation to share a primary insurer's loss adjustment expenses is determined by its reinsurance agreement with the primary insurer.

Loss adjustment expense reserves
Estimates of the future cost of defending and settling claims for losses that have already occurred.

Paid losses
The amounts already paid to claimants.

Loss reserves
Estimates of the amounts to be paid in the future for losses that occurred in the past.

Incurred losses
The sum of paid losses and loss and loss adjustment expense reserves.

Allocated loss adjustment expenses (ALAE)
Loss adjustment expenses associated with specific claims.

Unallocated loss adjustment expenses (ULAE)
Loss adjustment expenses that cannot be readily associated with a specific claim.

Paid losses are the amounts already paid to claimants. **Loss reserves** are estimates of the amounts to be paid in the future for losses that occurred in the past. **Incurred losses** are the sum of paid losses and loss and loss adjustment expense reserves as shown in the following formula.

Incurred losses = Paid losses + Loss reserves + Loss adjustment expense reserves.

Paid losses, reserves, and incurred losses are usually accumulated on an accident-year basis, which means they are related to all accidents that occur in a twelve-month period. As loss payments are made during the accident year, paid losses increase and reserves decrease by an equal amount. Therefore, incurred losses are unchanged. However, incurred losses do change when a reserve is amended because of additional information on a claim or because a new claim is reported. An accident year's accounts can be kept open for many years until all losses that occurred in that year are paid.

Before 1998, loss adjustment expenses were categorized in the Annual Statement as either allocated or unallocated. **Allocated loss adjustment expenses (ALAE)** were those loss adjustment expenses associated with specific claims. For example, the fees paid to a lawyer in the defense of a particular claim. **Unallocated loss adjustment expenses (ULAE)** were the loss adjustment expenses that could not be readily associated with a specific claim. For example, the general expenses associated with operating the insurer's claim function, such as claim representative salaries and expenses.

Beginning in 1998, the NAIC changed the loss adjustment expense categories for their Annual Statement purposes to (1) defense and cost containment and (2) adjusting and other. The NAIC made these changes partly because the insurance industry was not being consistent in how it reported expenses. For example, insurers that incurred expenses related to using independent adjusting firms usually recorded those expenses as ALAE because they could readily be associated with a particular claim. Insurers that incurred expenses related to using their own in-house claim staff usually recorded those expenses as ULAE because allocating their staff's time among claims was difficult.

Despite the change in the NAIC Annual Statement terminology, many insurance professionals continue to use the former terms and to relate defense and cost containment expenses to ALAE and the adjusting and other category expenses to ULAE. Because the actuarial techniques used to estimate unpaid LAE consider whether the expense can be directly associated with a particular claim, most actuarial literature continues to refer to loss adjustment expenses as ALAE and ULAE. This chapter also uses the ALAE and ULAE terminology.

The Life Cycle of Incurred Losses

Primary insurers and reinsurers periodically update their estimates of incurred losses for past accident years. These updates reflect the latest information on individual losses for each past year, including recent loss payments, and late reported losses. The final paid amount for all losses in an accident year is called the **ultimate loss**.

Exhibit 15-1 shows the life cycle of incurred losses relating to a single accident year. In this example, incurred losses increase from zero months to seventy-two months after the start of the accident year, at which point incurred losses equal ultimate losses. However, losses are not fully paid until 108 months after the start of the accident year.

Ultimate loss
The final paid amount for all losses in an accident year.

EXHIBIT 15-1

Life Cycle of Incurred Losses for a Single Accident Year

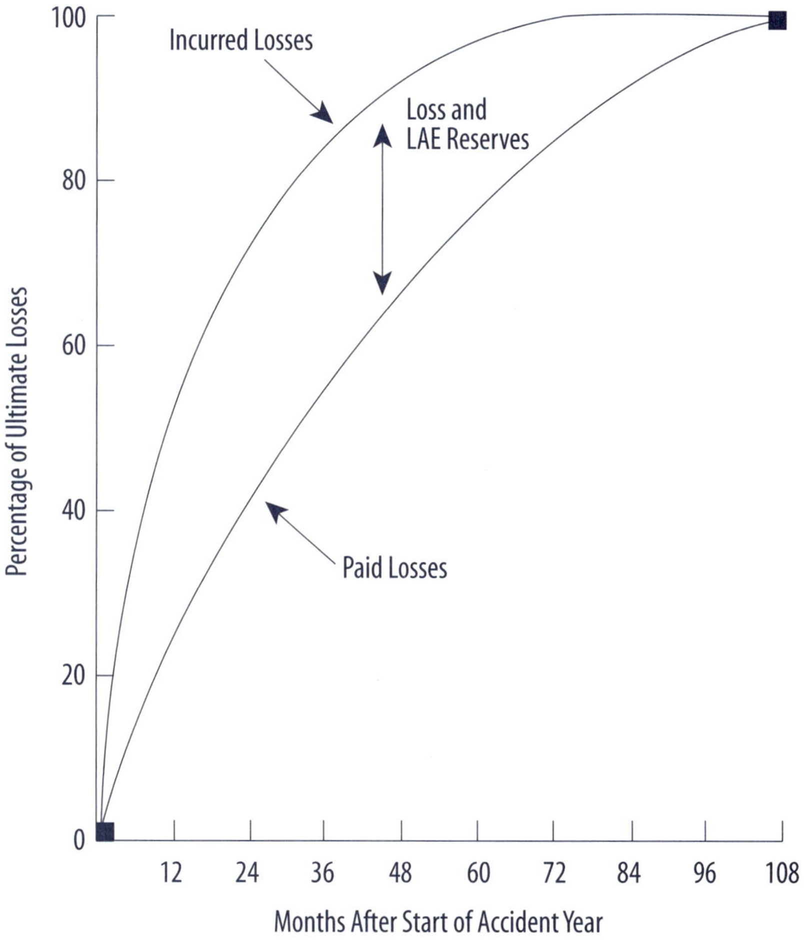

Primary insurers and reinsurers try to estimate accurate loss reserves as soon as possible after the end of an accident year. If loss reserves are accurate, then incurred losses equal ultimate losses at that point in time. In practice, an accident year's incurred losses often are less than ultimate losses for some time after the end of the accident year. Information received after the end of an accident year usually causes loss reserves to increase, therefore also causing incurred losses to increase for the accident year. For example, many years

Loss development
The increase or decrease of incurred losses over time.

after a loss occurs, an insurer may have to make a large payment as a result of a court judgment. This payment may not have been anticipated when reserves were established and it causes incurred losses to increase for the accident year. The increase or decrease of incurred losses over time is called **loss development**. In Exhibit 15-1, incurred losses develop over the period from zero to seventy-two months.

Implications of Inadequate Reserves

Reserves affect the incurred losses figures that are charged as expenses on an insurer's income statement and recorded as liabilities on its balance sheet. If reserves are initially understated and later increased, net income and policyholders' surplus will decrease when the understatement is recognized. For example, given a ratio of reserves to policyholders' surplus of 2 to 1, an error of 10 percent in estimating reserves would cause an error of 20 percent in the stated policyholders' surplus. The two tables in Exhibit 15-2 illustrate this relationship.

EXHIBIT 15-2

Effect of Understated Reserves on Policyholders' Surplus

Table 1—Primary Insurer Balance Sheet

Assets		Liabilities	
Cash	$25,000,000	Unearned Premiums	$10,000,000
		Reserves	10,000,000
		Policyholders' Surplus	5,000,000
Total Assets	$25,000,000	Total Liabilities and Surplus	$25,000,000

Table 2—Primary Insurer Balance Sheet With 10 Percent Adjustment to Reserves

Assets		Liabilities	
Cash	$25,000,000	Unearned Premiums	$10,000,000
		Reserves	11,000,000
		Policyholders' Surplus	4,000,000
Total Assets	$25,000,000	Total Liabilities and Surplus	$25,000,000

The reserves of $10 million in Table 1 of Exhibit 15-2 are underestimated by 10 percent. When the underestimation is recognized in Table 2, the reserves are increased by 10 percent to $11 million, and policyholders' surplus decreases by 20 percent, from $5 million to $4 million.

Because the primary insurer's pricing relies on historical loss data, inadequate reserves can result in reduced premium revenues. Therefore, in the long term, if a primary insurer does not have adequate reserves it may not have the funds necessary to pay claims. A pattern of inadequate reserving may ultimately lead to the primary insurer's insolvency.

Significance of Primary Insurer Reserves for the Reinsurer

Loss reserves present the largest uncertainty on a primary insurer's and reinsurer's balance sheet. Reinsurers establish their loss reserves on reserve data recorded by the primary insurer. Therefore, reinsurers have a direct interest in the reserve adequacy of the primary insurers they reinsure.

Reinsurers providing pro rata reinsurance are responsible for a proportional share of the loss reserves established by the primary insurer. Because the liability of pro rata reinsurance exists from the first dollar of loss, a pro rata reinsurer usually follows the reserving practices of its primary insurers. Consequently, if a primary insurer understates reserves, that understatement affects both the primary insurer and its pro rata reinsurer to the same degree.

Reinsurers providing excess of loss reinsurance are responsible only for those losses that exceed the attachment point. Because the liability of excess of loss reinsurers does not exist until the attachment point is exceeded, the reinsurer may be unaware of substantial losses until these losses directly affect them. Consequently, if a primary insurer understates reserves, that underestimation may have a significant effect on the excess of loss reinsurer's reserves.

Both pro rata and excess of loss reinsurers are exposed to the inherent time lag in loss reporting from primary insurers. Even primary insurers experience a time lag between the occurrence of a loss and the creation of a claim file in the primary insurer's information system.

As explained earlier, property insurance losses are usually reported and reserved sooner than casualty insurance losses. In general, property insurance losses are readily discovered and reported. However, casualty insurance losses often involve delays in discovery that result in delays in claim reporting. Mass tort claims, such as those for asbestosis-related injuries, usually involve extreme delays in reporting. For example, mesothelioma, the cancer typically associated with exposure to asbestos, may not manifest until decades following the claimant's initial exposure.

Although long loss reporting delays significantly affect the adequacy of primary insurer reserves, the financial consequences of these delays also have a substantial effect on the excess of loss reinsurer. Reinsurance premiums are based partly on a primary insurer's reserves. If these reserves are understated, the reinsurance premiums charged to primary insurers may be inadequate for the loss exposures that are reinsured.

Reinsurers are interested in the long-term survival prospects of primary insurers. If a primary insurer has inadequate reserves, it may indicate that the primary insurer is in financial difficulty, possibly facing insolvency. A reinsurer that deals with an insolvent primary insurer could experience problems, including lengthy and expensive litigation regarding the disposition of outstanding claims.

METHODS FOR ESTABLISHING RESERVES

There are two general methods for establishing reserves for losses and loss adjustment expenses.

> **Methods for Establishing Reserves**
> 1. Case reserves
> 2. Bulk reserves

Case reserves
Reserves established for the settlement of individual claims.

Bulk reserves
Reserves established for the settlement of an entire group of claims.

Case reserves are reserves established for the settlement of individual claims, and **bulk reserves** are reserves established for the settlement of an entire group of claims. For some categories of claim, reserves can be set using either the case or bulk reserve method. For example, for reported losses for which the amount of payment is uncertain, loss reserves could be set for each individual loss (case) or for the whole group of losses (bulk). Exhibit 15-3 shows a breakdown of the different elements of reserves and the types of claim or expense they are used for. The following sections describe methods for setting case and bulk reserves for both losses and loss adjustment expenses.

Case Reserves

Primary insurers establish a claim file for each reported loss. This file includes an estimate of the ultimate loss that will be paid to the claimant. The claim representative's estimate of the ultimate loss, less any payments already made, makes up the case loss reserve for the file. Allocated loss adjustment expense reserves can also be established for each individual claim.

Case reserves can be established for the following three categories of loss reserves:

1. Reported losses—payment certain
2. Reported losses—payment uncertain
3. Allocated loss adjustment expenses

Reported Losses—Payment Certain

The reserve for reported losses for which the amount of payment is certain is the easiest of the loss reserves to calculate. Because the claimant and the insurer have already agreed on the amount of the payment, calculating this type of reserve is simply a matter of adding the agreed settlement amounts for all claims. Calculating reserves in the other categories is more complex.

EXHIBIT 15-3

Breakdown of Reserves

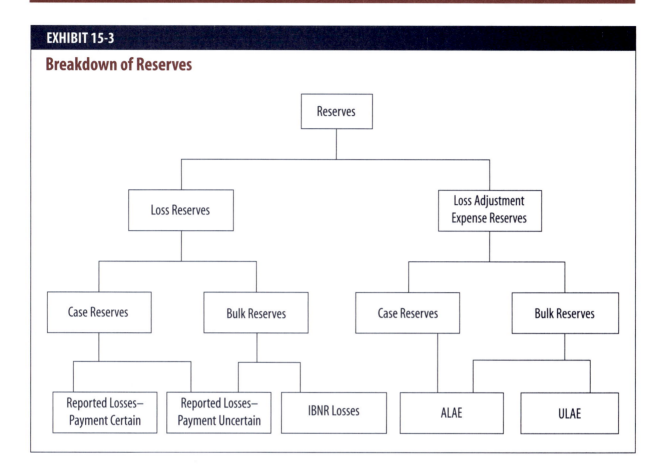

Reported Losses—Payment Uncertain

More expertise is necessary to determine the amount to reserve for reported losses for which the amount of payment is uncertain. The insurer must estimate the ultimate loss using known information about the claim, historical loss data for similar claims, and the judgment of the individual making the estimate. If the claimant later reports additional facts that affect the value of the claim, the insurer will have to adjust the reserve accordingly.

There are three methods that are commonly used to determine the case loss reserves for reported losses when the amount of payment is uncertain.

Three Methods of Determining Case Loss Reserves
1. The judgment method
2. The average or factor method
3. The tabular method

Judgment method
A method to establish a case loss reserve based largely on experience with similar claims.

The first method of determining case loss reserves is the judgment method. With the **judgment method**, a claim representative estimates the value of each claim based largely on experience with similar claims. This method does not involve any statistical analysis. One potential weakness of the judgment method is that its accuracy depends on the quality and extent of the claim representative's experience. Two people may estimate vastly different figures for the same loss. Even reserves established by the same person for similar losses could vary from time to time.

Average method
A method to establish a case loss reserve by using an average amount for specific categories of claims.

The second method for determining case loss reserves is based on statistical data and is generally called the average method or the factor method. The **average method** establishes a case loss reserve by using an average amount for specific categories of claims. The case reserve for specific categories of claims is set at an average amount. The average amount is based on an analysis of past claims and is trended for inflationary changes, changes in amounts insured, or other factors that may cause future payments to differ from past payments. The average method is most suitable for types of insurance in which claims are relatively frequent, reported and paid promptly, and not subject to extreme variations. Automobile physical damage is an example of a type of insurance with these characteristics. For example, every auto collision claim may be reserved at a value of $1,500, and that value is not changed until the claim is paid. The insurer may feel that setting more accurate reserves on this type of claim is not worth the expense associated with the extra effort.

Under the average method, the reserves for some individual claims are inadequate, and the reserves for other claims are excessive. However, if the average is accurate, the aggregate loss reserve accurately reflects the ultimate loss amounts for all outstanding claims. If used alone, the average method may produce inadequate reserves for those types of liability insurance that have a wide variation in claim amounts and long delays in settlements (such as medical malpractice insurance and product liability insurance). In these cases, the average method and the judgment method are sometimes used together. Using this combined reserving approach, an average value is assigned to each claim as soon as it is reported. For example, every auto bodily injury claim may initially be reserved for an average value of $10,000. In sixty days, or as soon as additional information becomes available on the claim, the reserve is adjusted, based on judgment.

Tabular method
A method to establish a case loss reserve that establishes an average amount of all claims that have similar characteristics in terms of the claimant's age, health, and marital status.

The third method of determining case loss reserves is the **tabular method**, which establishes an average amount of all claims that have similar characteristics in terms of the claimant's age, health, and marital status. It is useful for calculating case loss reserves for lost income benefits under workers' compensation insurance or structured settlement amounts under liability insurance.

The tabular method uses rates and factors from one or more actuarial tables to calculate the present value of future loss payments. This present value amount becomes the case loss reserve for those payments. The following tables are examples of those that can be used:

- Morbidity tables, showing the likelihood of sickness or injury
- Mortality tables, showing the likelihood of death
- Annuity tables, showing the likelihood of survival
- Remarriage tables, showing the likelihood of remarriage by a widow or widower[1]

Calculating Case Reserves by Using the Tabular Method

Suppose a lost income benefit of $300 per week for life is payable to a fifty-year-old permanently disabled male worker. A case loss reserve for this benefit can be calculated by using mortality tables and present value factors. Mortality tables can be used to derive one-year probabilities of survival at each age. Because this person is disabled, the factors in the mortality table may need to be adjusted to reflect the mortality for a disabled person. Special mortality tables for this purpose have been developed. Using present value factors and the results of the mortality table values, actuaries can calculate the present value factor for an annual annuity of $1 payable to this person for life. Assume this present value factor is 16.412. The case reserve is calculated by multiplying the present value factor by the annual benefit amount. In this example, the case reserve would be $256,027 ($300 per week × 52 weeks × 16.412).

Each case loss reserve calculated by the tabular method can be considered an average reserve for all claims with the same characteristics (for example, claimants with the same age, health, and marital status). Consequently, the tabular method is likely to yield an appropriate total reserve for a large number of individual claims. However, the case reserve for any given claim can vary substantially from the amount ultimately paid for that claim. The primary weakness of the tabular method is that its applicability is limited to when a fixed amount of benefits is paid over a period of time, such as a person's life. However, for those situations, it is the preferred method.

Allocated Loss Adjustment Expenses

Case reserves for allocated loss adjustment expenses (ALAE) can be established by using the judgment method or by adding a fixed percentage to each case loss reserve. The judgment method of establishing case ALAE reserves suffers from the same weaknesses as the judgment method of establishing case loss reserves. For some types of insurance, simply adding a percentage to each loss reserve can produce accurate aggregate reserves for ALAE.

Correcting Case Reserves

At any point in time, the total case reserves for reported losses are likely to be inadequate because they tend to develop, or increase, over time. One method for correcting inadequate total case reserves is to increase the case reserve for each claim. The simplest way to do this is to add the same percentage to each. These increases are often called "additional case reserves."

A more time-consuming method of correcting understated case reserves is to review each open claim file, increasing only those reserves that are inadequate. This approach assumes that either (1) the reviewers can more accurately determine loss reserve amounts than those who established the original claim reserve, or (2) more information has become available on the claim.

For their own financial reporting purposes, reinsurers may supplement the primary insurer's case reserves. A reinsurer's claims personnel may review the primary insurer's claim files and add amounts that they feel are necessary to account for loss development. The reinsurer's total case reserves then consist of the primary insurer's case reserves and the reinsurer's additional case reserves.

Bulk Reserves

Bulk reserves can be established for the following categories of claim reserves:

- Reported losses—payment uncertain
- IBNR reserves
- Loss adjustment expenses, both allocated and unallocated

Reported Losses—Payment Uncertain

Reserves for reported losses when the amount of payment is uncertain can be calculated on a bulk basis by subtracting the amount already paid for losses from a certain percentage of total earned premium. For example, an actuary may estimate general liability losses at 70 percent of an earned premium of $13 million, or $9.1 million. However, if $3 million has already been paid on these losses, then this amount is subtracted from the reserve, reducing the reserve from $9.1 million to $6.1 million.

IBNR Reserves

Incurred but not reported (IBNR) losses are losses that have occurred but have not yet been reported. Because these losses have occurred, loss payments should be estimated and reserved for. The IBNR loss category also includes a reserve for reported losses that are expected to develop; that is, the final payment for these losses is expected to exceed the amount that they are currently reserved for. (This component of IBNR is sometimes called IBNER, incurred but not enough reserved.) For liability insurance, IBNR loss reserves are difficult to estimate because tremendous uncertainty exists as to the number and size of losses yet to be reported, as well as to the development of reported losses.

A primary insurer always has a liability for IBNR losses. Because estimating the number and average size of individual claims that may be reported late is difficult, IBNR reserves are, by their nature, a bulk reserve.

IBNR reserves are residual reserves because, at any point in time, they equal the difference between incurred losses and ultimate losses. The following formula shows this relationship:

IBNR reserves = Ultimate losses − Incurred losses.

There are three basic methods of estimating IBNR reserves, although there are many acceptable alternative approaches.

> **Three Basic Methods of Estimating IBNR Reserves**
> 1. The loss ratio method
> 2. The percentage method
> 3. The loss triangle method

The first method of estimating IBNR reserves is the loss ratio method. The **loss ratio method** assumes that the ultimate loss ratio will equal the loss ratio that was considered when calculating premium rates. Therefore, if the premium rates assumed a loss ratio of 80 percent, the ultimate losses are assumed to equal 80 percent of earned premiums. Deducting paid and reserved amounts for reported losses from the ultimate loss amounts yields the IBNR reserve.

The loss ratio method may be useful in the early stages of developing IBNR reserves for long-tail liability insurance. However, the loss ratio method should be used only for the first year or two after losses are incurred. More sophisticated and responsive methods should be used as soon as the actual reported losses provide an adequate basis for projecting IBNR reserves.

One weakness of the loss ratio method is that the actual loss ratio seldom equals the anticipated loss ratio. In fact, the difference between them can be substantial. If the actual loss ratio is less than the anticipated loss ratio, the loss ratio method results in redundant reserves. If the actual loss ratio is greater than the anticipated loss ratio, the method results in inadequate reserves. Furthermore, if the premium rates charged were inadequate (as evidenced by an underwriting loss), the reinsurer needs to recognize the inadequate subject premium rates used by the primary insurer when calculating the anticipated loss ratio.

Despite these weaknesses, the loss ratio method is often used in the early stages of development for long-tail liability insurance because, during this time, the loss triangle method is not completely reliable. After twenty-four months, the loss triangle method is likely to be more reliable than the loss ratio method.

Loss ratio method
A method of estimating the IBNR reserve that assumes that the ultimate loss ratio will equal the loss ratio that was considered when calculating premium rates.

Percentage method
A method of estimating the IBNR reserve that uses historical relationships between IBNR reserves and reported losses to develop percentages that are used in IBNR forecasts.

The second method of estimating IBNR reserves is the percentage method. The **percentage method** uses historical relationships between IBNR reserves and reported losses to develop percentages that are used in IBNR forecasts. For example, if the IBNR losses were 30 percent of total incurred losses over a period of years, IBNR losses for a particular year may be estimated at 30 percent of incurred losses for that year. In its application, the percentage method develops a separate percentage for each accident year. If the trend (upward or downward) in the percentage of IBNR losses is measurable, the percentage used for projecting IBNR losses should reflect that trend.

The number of months necessary for losses to develop to their ultimate level varies depending on the type of insurance. The percentage method is an acceptable method for estimating property loss reserves because they can be estimated with reasonable accuracy soon after they are reported. This method is likely to be less accurate for liability loss reserves, which typically take longer to develop.

Exhibit 15-4 shows an IBNR calculation using the percentage method. In this example, IBNR losses are assumed to equal 20 percent of reported losses for the most recent accident year—twelve months of development (twelve months after the start of the policy year), 10 percent for the prior accident year—twenty-four months of development, and 5 percent for the next prior accident year—thirty-six months of development. Losses are assumed to be fully developed at forty-eight months after the start of the accident year. The IBNR reserve for each accident year is calculated by multiplying the reported losses for that accident year by the IBNR factor. The total IBNR reserve for the four accident years in Exhibit 15-4 is $1,723,258.

EXHIBIT 15-4

Calculation of IBNR Reserve for X4 From Hypothetical Data Using the Percentage Method

Historical Accident Year	Reported Losses ($)	Evaluation Point (Months of Development)	IBNR Factor	IBNR Reserve ($)
X1	4,725,679	48	0.00	0
X2	4,887,963	36	0.05	244,398
X3	4,878,845	24	0.10	487,885
X4	4,954,876	12	0.20	990,975
Total	$19,447,363			$1,723,258

The third method for estimating IBNR reserves is the loss triangle method, which is also known as the loss development method, the chain link method, the chain ladder method, and the link ratio method. The **loss triangle method** uses historical loss data to calculate loss development factors with which to estimate IBNR reserves This method is commonly used to determine IBNR reserves for liability insurance, particularly liability insurance that requires many years to fully develop. The loss triangle method is subject to wide variability in the first year or two of loss development, and is more complex than the other reserving methods already presented. As with all loss reserving methods, this method will not produce reliable results unless the historical data and the actuarial assumptions are accurate.

Loss triangle method
A method to estimate IBNR reserves that uses historical loss data to calculate loss development factors.

A loss triangle is a display of historical loss data in the shape of a triangle. The data usually consists of the total reported losses for each historical year, although other data, such as losses paid, number of claims paid, or average claim size can be used. The nature of the estimates derived from a loss triangle depends on the data used in the triangle. The data in a reported losses triangle is used to project the development of total loss amounts for each historical year. IBNR loss reserves can then be derived based on this projected loss development. Because loss triangles analyze historical loss development patterns to forecast future loss development, a major assumption of the loss triangle method is that the historical pattern of development will continue.

The loss data used in a loss triangle may or may not include ALAE. If the loss data includes ALAE, then the forecasted loss amounts will also include ALAE. (In some cases, separate loss triangles are used to estimate ALAE.)

This section describes a loss triangle based on incurred losses not including ALAE.

The four major steps for calculating IBNR reserves from a loss triangle, each of which is described in this section, are as follows:

1. Organize historical data in a loss triangle format.
2. Calculate twelve-month loss development factors from the loss triangle.
3. Calculate ultimate loss development factors from the twelve-month development factors.
4. Use ultimate loss development factors to calculate the IBNR reserve.

The first step in the loss triangle method is to organize historical data in a loss triangle format. A simplified loss triangle using the severity of reported losses is shown in Exhibit 15-5. It assumes that ultimate losses can be accurately estimated at seventy-two months after the start of an accident year.

EXHIBIT 15-5

Loss Triangle Based on Incurred Losses ($000)

Accident Year	Months of Development (after beginning of accident year)					
	12	24	36	48	60	72 Ultimate
X1	10,000	10,200	10,300	10,350	10,375	10,375
X2	12,000	12,300	12,500	12,600	12,650	12,650
X3	14,000	14,500	14,750	14,850	14,900	
X4	16,000	16,600	16,900	17,050		
X5	18,000	18,800	19,200			
X6	20,000	21,000				
X7	22,000					

Each row of data in Exhibit 15-5 shows historical estimates of the incurred loss amounts for the accident year shown at the left end of the row. For example, the first row shows data for accident year X1. On December 31, X1 (twelve months after the start of the X1 accident year), the primary insurer estimated its incurred losses for accident year X1 to be $10,000,000. On December 31, X2 (twenty-four months after the start of the X1 accident year), the estimate for X1 accident-year losses had increased to $10,200,000. By December 31, X6 (seventy-two months after the start of the X1 accident year), the estimate for X1 losses had reached $10,375,000. At that point, the primary insurer assumed that the incurred losses reserves for accident year X1 had reached their ultimate value.

The lowest diagonal of the table, running from $22,000,000 on the left to $12,650,000 on the right, shows the estimate for each year's losses as of December 31, X7, the latest year for which data are available. On December 31, X8, another diagonal of severity data should be added below the figures in the table.

The second step in the loss triangle method is to calculate twelve-month loss development factors from the loss triangle. Exhibit 15-6 uses the data in Exhibit 15-5 to calculate loss development factors based on changes in incurred losses over successive twelve-month periods. These factors are called twelve-month loss development factors (also known as age-to-age loss development factors and link ratios). For example, the first factor for X1 (1.020) shows the change in the company's estimates of X1 accident-year losses from December 31, X1, to December 31, X2. It was calculated by dividing the twenty-four month figure for X1 by the twelve-month figure for X1 ($10,200,000 ÷ $10,000,000 = 1.020). Each of the other figures in the triangle in Exhibit 15-6 was calculated in the same manner. The X7 year has no twelve-month loss development factor because two successive estimates are required to calculate a loss development factor, and only one estimate is available.

EXHIBIT 15-6

Calculating Twelve-Month Loss Development Factors

Accident Year	Twelve-Month Loss Development Factors				
	12 to 24	24 to 36	36 to 48	48 to 60	60 to Ultimate
X1	1.020	1.010	1.005	1.002	1.000
X2	1.025	1.016	1.008	1.004	1.000
X3	1.036	1.017	1.007	1.003	
X4	1.038	1.018	1.009		
X5	1.044	1.021			
X6	1.050				
Average	1.036	1.016	1.007	1.003	1.000
5-Year Average	1.039	1.016	1.007	1.003	1.000
3-Year Average	1.044	1.019	1.008	1.003	1.000
Selected	1.044	1.019	1.008	1.003	1.000

The lower section of Exhibit 15-6 shows the derivation of twelve-month loss development factors that are used to estimate ultimate loss amounts for each historical accident year. The row labeled "Average" shows the average of all of the twelve-month loss development factors above it. The next row shows the average of the twelve-month factors for the five most recent years above it.[2] The third row shows the average of the twelve-month loss development factors for the three most recent years.

The last row in the exhibit (labeled "Selected") shows the twelve-month factors that an analyst may choose. Selecting twelve-month factors is a matter of judgment. In Exhibit 15-6, the averages show an increasing trend. That is, the three-year average is greater than the five-year average, and, in the first column, the five-year average is greater than the overall average. Therefore, an analyst would probably select the largest of the three averages, without modification.

> ### Selecting Twelve-Month Loss Development Factors
>
> The selection process involves a comparison of the average factors for various periods, such as those used in Exhibit 15-6. The time periods used reflect the types of claims being estimated. The following approach may be helpful in selecting a factor:
>
> - If the three averages show an increasing trend, select the largest factor.
> - If the three averages show a decreasing trend, select the smallest factor.
> - If the three averages do not show a trend, select the factor intermediate in value.
>
> A selected factor can be adjusted if, in the actuary's opinion, it is inconsistent with the loss data or other adjacent factors. For example, most actuaries would expect each twelve-month loss development factor to be smaller than the factor immediately preceding it because as losses age, loss development tends to slow down. For example, for X1, the twenty-four-to-thirty-six-month factor (1.010) is lower than the twelve-to-twenty-four-month factor (1.020).

Ultimate loss development factor
A factor that is applied to the most recent estimate of incurred losses for a specific accident year to estimate the ultimate incurred loss for that year.

The third step in the loss triangle development method is to calculate ultimate loss development factors from the twelve-month loss development factors. An **ultimate loss development factor** is a factor that is applied to the most recent estimate of incurred losses for a specific accident year to estimate the ultimate incurred loss for that year.

Exhibit 15-7 shows the calculation of ultimate loss development factors. Each selected factor from Exhibit 15-6 is multiplied by the other selected factors to its right to calculate an ultimate loss development factor.

EXHIBIT 15-7

Calculating Ultimate Loss Development Factors

Time Period	Ultimate Loss Development Factor
60 Months to Ultimate	$1.000 = 1.000$
48 Months to Ultimate	$1.003 \times 1.000 = 1.003$
36 Months to Ultimate	$1.008 \times 1.003 \times 1.000 = 1.011$
24 Months to Ultimate	$1.019 \times 1.008 \times 1.003 \times 1.000 = 1.030$
12 Months to Ultimate	$1.044 \times 1.019 \times 1.008 \times 1.003 \times 1.000 = 1.076$

The fourth step in the loss triangle method is to use ultimate loss development factors to calculate the IBNR reserve. Multiplying the ultimate loss development factor from Exhibit 15-7 by the latest evaluation of losses for each year (Exhibit 15-5) gives an estimate of ultimate losses for each accident year, as shown in column 5 of Exhibit 15-8. The IBNR reserve (column 6) is calculated by subtracting incurred and reported losses (column 2) from estimated ultimate losses (column 5).

The data in Exhibit 15-5 are consistent, making it easy for the analyst to arrive at reasonable loss development factors. Most loss triangles are less consistent and include anomalous data items.

Such anomalies may result from chance variations in loss frequency or severity, from changes in rules of law, or from delays in adjusting claims. They may also result from conscious decisions made by claim personnel to increase or decrease the level of case reserves. The level of case reserves may also change when responsibility for handling a claim passes from one person to another.

EXHIBIT 15-8
Calculating IBNR Reserves Using Loss Development Factors

(1) Historical Accident Year	(2) Incurred and Reported Losses ($000)	(3) Months of Development	(4) Ultimate Loss Development Factor	(5) Estimated Ultimate Losses ($000)	(6) IBNR Reserve ($000)
X1	10,375	72	1.000	10,375	0
X2	12,650	72	1.000	12,650	0
X3	14,900	60	1.000	14,900	0
X4	17,050	48	1.003	17,101	51
X5	19,200	36	1.011	19,411	211
X6	21,000	24	1.030	21,630	630
X7	22,000	12	1.076	23,672	1,672
Total	$117,175			$119,739	$2,564

Systematic increases in loss reserves over time indicate a consistent practice of carrying inadequate case reserves. These systematic increases create larger than normal loss development factors.

After a period of systematic increases in loss reserves, knowing whether the reserves are still inadequate, or whether they are now correct, is difficult. However, the typical assumption is that the reserves are still inadequate. The loss triangle itself does not indicate the adequacy of loss reserves. That determination requires a careful analysis of individual claim files or, in many cases, additional data on individual claims.

Loss Adjustment Expenses

Bulk reserves can be used for both allocated and unallocated loss adjustment expenses. Bulk reserves for ALAE can be estimated by applying a percentage factor to either earned premiums or incurred losses. The percentage factor is determined by analyzing the insurer's experience. For example, if experience shows that ALAE average 25 percent of incurred losses, then 25 percent is applied to current incurred losses to estimate the reserve for ALAE.

One disadvantage of this method of estimating ALAE is that the calculation assumes that no changes have occurred that affect the factor. If changes have occurred, the factor must be adjusted. Another disadvantage results from the manner in which losses are usually settled. Small losses, especially those settled without payment, are usually settled more quickly than large losses. Consequently, total loss reserves at any given time are likely to include a disproportionate number of large losses. Because large losses usually involve proportionately more ALAE than small losses, the percentage method may underestimate the ALAE reserve. Calculating ALAE using the loss triangle method may overcome this problem.

By definition, ULAE cannot be attributed to specific claims. Consequently, the reserve for such expenses must be estimated on a bulk basis. The reserve for ULAE is usually estimated as a percentage of the sum of incurred losses and ALAE. The insurer determines the percentage based on experience.

Because ULAE consist of budgeted items, the total amount to be paid in a given year is easy to estimate at the beginning of the year. However, some of the ULAE paid in a given year will be related to losses incurred in earlier years particularly for long-tail liability insurance. Allocating current expenses to prior accident years is common, but such allocations may distort current accident year expense.

Combined Methods of Reserving

This section discusses ways in which the various methods of reserving can be combined in order to use the strengths of two or more methods. There are a variety of combined methods that can be used. This section covers the following methods:

- The two-part combination method
- The Bornhuetter-Ferguson method
- The three-part combination method

Two-Part Combination Method

To realize the advantages of both the loss ratio method and the loss triangle method, some actuaries have suggested that a weighted average of the two methods be used with the weights varying with the number of months after the start of the policy year. Exhibit 15-9 shows a set of weights that may be used for estimating liability loss reserves.

At the end of the accident year (twelve months of development), the reserve would be based entirely on the loss ratio method because the reported loss data are not mature enough to estimate ultimate losses using the loss triangle method. Starting at twenty-four months of development, the loss reserve can be partially based on the loss triangle method. At sixty months of development and thereafter, the reserve is based solely on the loss triangle method.

The weights shown in Exhibit 15-9 are based on judgment. Different weights could be selected for different types of insurance.

EXHIBIT 15-9
Weights for Combining the Loss Ratio Method and the Loss Triangle Method

Months of Development (after start of accident year)	Weights	
	Loss Ratio Method	Loss Triangle Method
12	100%	0%
24	50%	50%
36	25%	75%
48	10%	90%
60 or more	0%	100%

Bornhuetter-Ferguson Method

A variation of the two-part combination method that does not rely on judgmental weights is called the Bornhuetter-Ferguson method.[3] The **Bornhuetter-Ferguson method** estimates the IBNR reserve using expected losses and an IBNR factor. It is frequently used when the losses reported to the insurer are not sufficiently mature to use the loss triangle method. Immature loss data occurs because of the delay between the time a loss occurs and when it is reported to the insurer. This delay is more pronounced for liability insurance than for property insurance. Likewise, reinsurers experience an even longer delay in loss reporting because they establish reserves only after the primary insurer does. Losses arising out of casualty excess of loss treaties generally suffer the most delay. The reinsurer's reported losses can be zero for the first two or three years before retentions are exceeded and primary insurers report known claims to their reinsurers.

Bornhuetter-Ferguson method
A method of estimating the IBNR reserve using expected losses and an IBNR factor.

One weakness of the Bornhuetter-Ferguson method is the level of inherent subjectivity that is involved in selecting IBNR factors, which can be estimated using a variety of techniques applied to industry data or historical insurer data. Even small changes in assumptions can cause wide variations in IBNR reserves and thereby net income, sometimes changing a profit to a loss or vice versa.

Exhibit 15-10 illustrates how the Bornhuetter-Ferguson method is used to calculate IBNR loss reserves for a casualty excess of loss treaty.

The ultimate earned premiums (column 2) are multiplied by an initial expected loss ratio (column 3) to yield initial expected losses (column 4). Then an expected percentage of unreported losses (column 5)—an estimate of losses that have occurred but have not yet been reported to the reinsurer—derived from loss development factors is multiplied by the initial expected losses (column 4) to yield expected IBNR reserves (column 6).

EXHIBIT 15-10
Bornhuetter-Ferguson Method—Casualty Excess of Loss Treaty

(1) Accident Year	(2) Ultimate Earned Premiums ($000)	(3) Initial Expected Loss Ratio	(4) Initial Expected Losses ($000)	(5) Expected Percentage of Unreported Losses (%)	(6) IBNR Reserves ($000)
X0	13,940	0.70	9,758	14.5	1,415
X1	13,940	0.75	10,455	17.8	1,861
X2	13,940	0.85	11,849	22.5	2,666
X3	19,110	0.95	18,155	30.8	5,592
X4	15,870	1.10	17,457	42.3	7,384
X5	15,870	1.15	18,251	56.3	10,275
X6	19,110	0.85	16,244	72.7	11,809
X7	31,310	0.80	25,048	82.5	20,665
Total	$143,090		$127,217		$61,667

Column 2 is obtained by applying the loss triangle method to earned premiums.

The expected loss ratios in column 3 are adjusted for the premium adequacy level for each year relative to the current year.

Column 5 is derived from loss development factors.

Data provided by Jerome E. Tuttle, FCAS, FCIA, CPCU, ARM, ARe, AIM, Senior Vice President & Senior Pricing Actuary, Platinum Underwriters Reinsurance, Inc.

For example, in Exhibit 15-10, in the year X5, the ultimate earned premium is estimated to be $15,870,000. Because of inadequate pricing in X5, the initial expected loss ratio (column 3) is 1.15. Multiplying the two figures yields initial expected losses (column 4) of $18,250,500. The $18,250,500 is multiplied by 56.3 percent (column 5), which is the projected percentage of losses that have been incurred but not yet reported to the reinsurer under the treaty, to yield the indicated IBNR reserves for X5 under the treaty of $10,275,032 (column 6).

Three-Part Combination Method

The three-part combination method combines the loss ratio method, the loss triangle method, and case loss reserves. This combination therefore requires three sets of weights. The weights are set so that they place most or all of the emphasis on the loss ratio method in the first year. Thereafter, the loss ratio method is phased out, and the loss triangle method is phased in. Subsequently, the loss triangle method is phased out, and more weight is placed on case loss reserves. Finally, when all losses have been reported and only a few remain open, the reserve is based entirely on case loss reserves.

This emphasis on case loss reserves is based on the belief that in the final stages of development, case reserves are likely to be more accurate than bulk reserves. Exhibit 15-11 shows a set of weights that may be used for a three-part combination. The weights are based on judgment.

EXHIBIT 15-11
Sample Weights for the Three-Part Combination Method

Months of Development	Loss Ratio Method (%)	Loss Triangle Method (%)	Case Reserves (%)
12	100	0	0
24	50	50	0
36	25	75	0
48	0	100	0
60	0	100	0
72	0	100	0
84	0	100	0
96	0	100	0
108	0	90	10
120	0	75	25
132	0	50	50
144	0	25	75
156 or more	0%	0%	100%

SALVAGE AND SUBROGATION

Insurers try to recover a portion of the losses that they have paid through salvage and subrogation. Schedule P of the NAIC Annual Statement combines these recoveries into one category because both serve to reduce paid and reserved losses.

Salvage refers to property that is transferred to an insurer and then sold to partially offset the insurer's loss payment. For example, a primary insurer pays an insured for a stolen car's value. If the car is later recovered, the primary insurer can take possession of the car and sell it to offset the loss. The amount of paid losses is reduced by the amount of salvage in the year in which salvage is received, even though the salvage might have resulted from a loss incurred in a previous year. Anticipated salvage is a reduction to loss reserves, so it reduces the liability that the insurer reports on its balance sheet.

Subrogation refers to the insurer's right to recover the amount of its loss payment from the third party who is legally responsible for the loss. Subrogation often applies to claims involving auto accidents. For example, once the

Salvage
The property that is transferred to an insurer and then sold to partially offset the insurer's loss payment.

Subrogation
An insurer's right to recover the amount of its loss payment from the third party who is legally responsible for the loss.

insurer pays the insured for the repair or replacement of the damaged auto, the insurance policy provides that any rights to collect from the third party responsible for the damage to the auto belong to the insurer (up to the amount the insurer paid the insured for the claim). Subrogation recoveries are also possible with other types of insurance in which the party responsible for the loss is someone other than the insured. Subrogation prevents an insured from collecting from both the insurer and the third party at fault for the same loss. As with salvage recoveries, insurers reduce the amount of paid losses in the year the subrogated loss payment is received by the amount of the subrogation recovery. Anticipated subrogation recoveries serve to offset loss reserves.

RESERVING METHODS FOR EXCESS OF LOSS REINSURERS

Reinsurers use essentially the same reserving techniques as primary insurers, and the reserving problems of pro rata reinsurers do not differ significantly from those of primary insurers. However, with excess of loss reinsurance, the problems in estimating loss reserves are much greater for the reinsurer, and special considerations are involved. Data from the Reinsurance Association of America (RAA) show that excess of loss reinsurers typically experience much longer loss development patterns than primary insurers do. Exhibit 15-12 shows a comparison of primary insurer and reinsurer historical loss development for workers' compensation.

Factors That Affect an Excess of Loss Reinsurer's Reserves

Several factors disproportionately affect an excess of loss reinsurer's ability to estimate reserves. The usual loss development techniques are also more difficult for excess of loss reinsurers to apply. Excess of loss reinsurers have significantly greater problems than primary insurers when estimating reserves because of the effects of the following:

- Monetary inflation
- Social inflation
- Long loss development period

Monetary Inflation

An excess of loss reinsurer's losses are affected by monetary inflation to a greater extent than are the losses of the primary insurer. For example, inflation may increase the value of property insured from an amount that is below the primary insurer's retention to an amount in excess of the retention. This would increase the number of claims to which the excess of loss reinsurer must contribute. These inflationary pressures are increased by the long loss development period for liability losses. If the primary insurer's retention is not increased to take account of inflation, then inflation has a disproportionate effect on the excess of loss reinsurer.

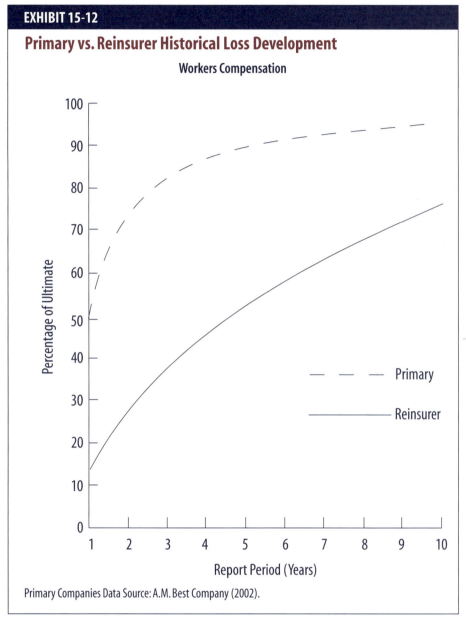

EXHIBIT 15-12

Primary vs. Reinsurer Historical Loss Development

Workers Compensation

Primary Companies Data Source: A.M. Best Company (2002).

Source: Reinsurance Association of America, *Historical Loss Development Study 2003 Edition* (Washington, D.C.: Reinsurance Association of America, 2003), p. 24.

Social Inflation

Certain trends in the U.S. legal system have resulted in higher costs for insurers. For example, judgment amounts have increased at a rate greater than inflation. There have also been legislative changes that benefit claimants. These trends are sometimes referred to as social inflation. As with monetary inflation, social inflation increases the value of claims that exceed the attachment point and increases the number of claims to which the reinsurer must contribute.

Long Loss Development Period

The long loss development period in excess of loss reinsurance results from the nature of the contract. The reinsurer is not obligated to pay anything unless the amount of loss exceeds the retention of the primary insurer. Consequently, the primary insurer is required to report only those claims that it expects to exceed some agreed amount, typically ranging from 50 percent to 100 percent of its retention, depending on the terms of the contract. However, some claims that eventually exceed the agreed amount may not initially be perceived as being that large. Consequently, the primary insurer may not initially report them to the reinsurer.

Because of the long loss development period, many reinsurers do not have sufficient data on losses that have developed to their ultimate value. Therefore, actuaries must carefully consider how long it will take for losses to develop to their ultimate value and apply mathematical techniques to develop the additional loss development factors.

The Bornhuetter-Ferguson method is often used by excess of loss reinsurers because of its ability to estimate IBNR reserves when little mature data is available.

Difficulties When Applying Reserving Techniques

Although reinsurers use the same reserving techniques as primary insurers, some of the techniques are more difficult for an excess of loss reinsurer to apply. For example, the loss triangle method for an excess of loss reinsurer often shows a wide range of values for the loss development factors for each historical accident year, and selecting a suitable factor is difficult. In addition, reinsured losses arise from a large number of primary insurers. The losses are not homogeneous, and primary insurer reserving and claim settlement practices vary widely. Constructing loss triangles using the historical claim count and average claim amounts also creates problems for setting excess of loss reinsurance reserves.

Problems arising from the lack of homogeneity can be overcome by dividing the data into homogeneous categories and constructing a separate triangle for each category. This technique may mean that actuaries responsible for generating reserves for reinsurers must divide their data not only by type of insurance, but also into other categories such as by treaty layer.

Because each excess of loss treaty is individually negotiated with the primary insurer, some treaties have special terms and conditions, such as aggregate limits whereby the reinsurer's losses will not develop beyond the specified aggregate. Other treaties cover types of insurance with unusual loss development patterns that require special consideration by both the primary insurer and the reinsurer. Although combining the results from individual treaties may enhance the statistical credibility of the loss data, addressing the special features of an individual treaty separately from the larger portfolio of in-force policies may be more useful.

SUMMARY

Reserves consist of loss reserves and loss adjustment expense reserves. Reserves represent the difference between paid losses and incurred losses. Over time, paid losses increase and reserves decrease until the entire incurred loss has been paid.

Reserves are reported as a liability on the balance sheet. If reserves are initially understated and later increase, policyholders' surplus will decrease when the understatement is recognized. Therefore, the primary insurer may not have the funds necessary to pay claims. Similarly, if a reinsurer establishes its reserves on the reserve data recorded by the primary insurer, then if the primary insurer's reserves are understated, the reinsurer's reserves also will be understated. Additionally reinsurers may be adversely affected by the delay in loss reporting.

Two general methods of establishing reserves for both losses and loss adjustment expenses are:

1. Case reserves
2. Bulk reserves

Case reserves are reserves established for the settlement of an individual claim. Bulk reserves are reserves established for the settlement of an entire group of claims. The three general methods of establishing case loss reserves when the amount of payment is uncertain are:

1. The judgment method—the claim representative estimates reserves based on experience with similar claims.
2. The average or factor method—reserves for specific categories of claims are set at an average amount.
3. The tabular method—reserves are based on data from actuarial tables.

The three basic methods of establishing IBNR reserves are:

1. The loss ratio method—reserves are calculated assuming that the loss ratio is an accurate estimate of total ultimate losses.
2. The percentage method—reserves are calculated based on the historical relationship between IBNR reserves and reported losses.
3. The loss triangle method—reserves are calculated using developments factors derived from historical loss data.

Methods of reserving can be combined. Combination methods include:

- The two-part combination method—combines the loss ratio method and the loss triangle method
- The Bornhuetter-Ferguson method—estimates IBNR reserves using expected losses and an IBNR factor
- The three-part combination method—combines the loss ratio method, the loss triangle method, and case loss reserves

Insurers use salvage and subrogation to recover a portion of the losses they have paid. Salvage refers to property that is transferred to an insurer and then sold to partially offset the insurer's loss payment. Subrogation refers to the insurer's right to recover the amount of its loss payment from the third party who is legally responsible for the loss.

Reinsurers use essentially the same loss reserving techniques as primary insurers and experience similar issues with reserving. However, excess of loss reinsurers experience significantly greater problems than primary insurers when reserving because of:

- Monetary inflation
- Social inflation
- Long loss development period

In addition, some of the loss reserving techniques used by primary insurers are more difficult for excess of loss reinsurers to apply.

CHAPTER NOTES

1. The remarriage table is used only if the provisions of the insurance policy state that the benefits are terminated by remarriage.
2. Because of the abbreviated nature of this exhibit, the average of all years and the average for five years are the same except for the first column. This would not usually be the case in practice.
3. R. L. Bornhuetter and R. E. Ferguson, "The Actuary and IBNR," *Proceedings of the Casualty Actuarial Society*, vol. 59, 1972, p. 181.

Index

Page numbers in boldface refer to definitions of Key Words and Phrases.

A

Access to records clause, **4.8**–4.9, 12.4
Accredited reinsurer, **13.4**
Admitted asset, **14.4**
Adverse selection, **1.11**
Affiliated companies clause, **4.4**–4.5
Aggregate excess of loss reinsurance, **2.19**–2.20
Aggregate excess of loss treaty
    function of, 11.5
    as part of a reinsurance program, 11.5–11.6
    pricing, 11.11–11.13
    retention and limits clause adapted for, 11.6–11.11
Alien insurer, **13.4**
Allocated loss adjustment expenses (ALAE), **15.4**
Amortized value, **14.6**
Ancillary agreements, 5.16–5.20
Annual aggregate deductible, **8.8**
Arbitration clause, **4.18**–4.21
Assets, 14.4–14.8
At-risk audit, **12.4**
Attachment point, **2.10**, 10.24
Authority to conduct audits, 12.4
Authorization, **3.11**, 3.19
Authorized insurer or admitted insurer, **13.4**
Authorized reinsurer, **13.4**
Automatic reinstatement of the per occurrence limit, 9.13
Average annual loss (AAL), **10.19**
Average method, **15.10**

B

Balance sheet, 14.3–14.10
    effect of reinsurance on, 13.11–13.13
Basis of attachment for policies, 4.7–4.8
Binder, **3.12**
Bonds, 14.6
Bordereau, **2.9**
Bornhuetter-Ferguson method, **15.21**–15.22
Broker marketing system, **3.3**–3.4
    treaty reinsurance through, 3.13–3.19
Brokerage, **3.4**
Brokers & Reinsurance Markets Association (BRMA), 1.15
Bulk reserves, **15.8**, 15.12–15.20

C

Cancellation circumstances, 5.6–5.10
Capacity ratio, **1.6**–1.8
Capital and surplus, 14.10
Captive insurer, **6.10**
Case loss reserves, three methods of determining, 15.9–15.11
Case reserves, **15.8**–15.12
    allocated loss adjustment expenses, 15.11
    calculating by using the tabular method, 15.10–15.11
    correcting, 15.11–15.12
    reported losses, payment certain, 15.8–15.9
        payment uncertain, 15.9–15.11
Cash call, **6.14**–6.15
Casualty excess of loss reinsurance, **9.3**
Casualty excess of loss treaty, clauses designed or adapted for, 9.10–9.19
    common clauses modified for use in, 9.5–9.10
    functions of, 9.4
    as part of a reinsurance program, 9.4–9.5
Casualty facultative reinsurance worksheet, 3.22–3.23
Catastrophe bond, **10.30**
Catastrophe excess of loss reinsurance, **2.13**–2.16
Catastrophe modeling, 10.15–10.23
    engineering component, **10.17**
    example of, 10.19–10.22
    insurance component, **10.17**
    issues, 10.23
    operation of, 10.16–10.17
    science component, **10.16**
Catastrophe models, **10.15**
Catastrophe option, **10.31**
Catastrophe protection, 1.5, 6.8, 9.4
Catastrophe reinsurance
    alternatives to, 10.30–10.31
    function of, 10.5–10.6
    as part of a reinsurance program, 10.6–10.7
Catastrophe risk exchange, **10.31**
Catastrophe treaty
    clauses designed or adapted for, 10.7–10.12
    pricing, 10.23–10.30
Ceding commission, **1.8**
Claim audit, **12.8**, 12.14–12.15
Claims and loss adjustment expense clause, **9.14**–9.16
Clash cover, **2.16**–2.18
Clearance and underwriting, 3.9–3.11, 3.18
Commencement and termination clause, **5.3**–5.4, 6.12–6.13
Commercial property line guide, 7.24–7.26
Common stocks, 14.6–14.7
Commutation agreement, **13.15**
Commutation clause, **9.18**–9.19
Confirmation, **3.12**
Continuous contract, **5.4**
Contract year limit, **9.13**
Co-participation provision, **2.12**
Currency clause, **4.12**
Cut-off basis, **5.5**
Cut-through endorsement, **5.17**–5.18

D

Declaratory judgment action, **9.16**
Declaratory judgment expense clause, 9.16–**9.17**
Definitions clause, **4.8**, 6.12, 7.13–7.15, 9.7–9.10
Deposit premium, **8.10**
Direct writing marketing system, **3.3**, 3.8–3.13
Direct writing reinsurer, **1.13**
Domestic insurer, **13.4**

E

Errors and omissions (E&O) clause, **4.27**
Excess of loss reinsurance, **2.10**–2.20
Excess of policy limits (XPL) clause, **5.11**–5.12
Excess of policy limits loss, **2.19**
Exclusion clauses, 4.13–4.18
Exclusions clause, 7.15–7.17
Experience rating, **8.16**, 8.22–8.28, 9.24–9.29
Exposure rating, **8.16**, 8.17–8.21, 9.19–9.24
Extended reporting period, **9.6**
Extra-contractual damages, **2.19**
Extra-contractual obligations (ECO) clause, **5.13**–5.14

F

Facultative certificate of reinsurance, **1.11**–1.12
Facultative reinsurance, **1.10**, 1.11–1.12, 3.8–3.13
    hybrids of, 1.12
Facultative reinsurance authorization, 3.26
Facultative reinsurance binder, 3.27
Facultative reinsurance certificate, 3.12–3.13, 3.28–3.30
Federal excise tax clause, **4.11**–4.12
Financial examination, **13.6**
Finite risk reinsurance, **2.20**–2.21
First loss scale, 8.17–8.21
Flat commission, **2.4**
Flat rate, **8.30**
Flat rated covers, 8.30
Following reinsurers, **3.19**
Foreign insurer, **13.4**
Fronting company, **6.10**

G

Geocoding, **10.20**
Governing law clause, **4.13**
Gross account basis, **6.10**
Guarantee endorsement, **5.19**

H

Homeowners line guide, 7.27
Hybrids of treaty and facultative reinsurance, 3.12

I

IBNR reserves, 15.12–15.19
    loss ratio method of estimating, 15.13
    loss triangle method of estimating, 15.15–15.19
    percentage method of estimating, 15.14
Increased limit factors, 9.20
Incurred losses, **15.4**
    life cycle of, 15.4–15.6
Indemnity agreement, **5.19**–5.20
In-force policies basis, **4.7**–4.8
Input controls, **12.6**
Insolvency clause, **4.21**–4.23
Insolvency fund exclusion clause, **4.18**
Insurance Regulatory Information System (IRIS), **13.9**
Insurance risk, **1.3**
Interests and liabilities agreement, **4.27**–4.29
Intermediaries and Reinsurance Underwriters Association (IRU), 1.15
Intermediary clause, **4.24**–4.25
Internal retentions and limits, 11.7–11.9
Inuring reinsurance, 10.28
Investments, short-term, 14.7

J

Joint liability, **4.27**–4.28
Judgment method, **15.10**

L

Large line capacity, **1.5**, 6.8, 7.8, 8.4, 9.4
Layers and limits, 10.24–10.25
Lead reinsurer, **3.19**
Liabilities, surplus, and other funds, 14.8–14.10
Liability for unearned premiums, 14.10
Liability of the reinsurer clause, 7.13
Licensing, 13.4–13.5
Limits, setting, 8.16–8.17, 11.12
Limits profile, 7.23–7.24
Line, **1.5**
Line of credit, **10.30**
Line guide, **2.9**, 7.24–7.27
Liquidity, **14.6**
Lloyd's property first loss scale, **3.11**

Loss adjustment expense reserves, 14.8, **15.3**
Loss adjustment expenses, **2.3**, 15.19–15.20
Loss cost rate, **8.28**
Loss development, **15.6**
Loss development factors
    selecting twelve month, 15.17
    twelve month, 15.16–15.17
    ultimate, 15.18–15.19
Loss experience, stabilization of, 1.6, 7.9–7.10, 8.4–8.5, 9.4
Loss exposures, geographic spread of, 2.23, 10.26
Loss notices and settlements clause, **8.8**–8.9
Loss occurrence clause, **2.14**–2.15, 10.10–10.12
Loss rate, **8.30**
Loss rated covers, 8.30–8.31
Loss ratio, **2.5**
Loss ratio method, **15.13**
Loss reserves, 14.8, **15.4**
Loss triangle method, **15.15**–15.19
Losses, loss adjustment expenses, and salvages clause, **6.19**–6.20
Losses incurred basis, 11.10–11.11
Losses occurring basis, **4.7**, 11.8–11.10
Losses paid and incurred, 14.13

M

Managing general agent (MGA), **12.15**
Managing general agent audits, 12.15–12.17
Market conduct examination, **13.6**
Medical Malpractice Insurance Company case study, 2.30
Method of cession clause, **7.21**–7.22
Monetary inflation, 15.24

N

NAIC accreditation program, **13.8**
NAIC Annual Statement, **13.7**
NAIC association examination, **13.8**–13.9
NAIC Credit for Reinsurance Model Act, 13.11
NAIC model law, **13.7**
NAIC Reinsurance Intermediary Model Act, 13.18–13.19
NAIC risk-based capital system, **13.10**

National Association of Insurance Commissioners (NAIC), **13.6**
Net of all reinsurance basis, **6.10**
Net of pro rata basis, **6.10**
Net retained lines clause, **8.10**–8.11
Net retention clause, **7.19**–7.20
Net written premiums, **1.6**
New York Regulation 98, 13.17–13.18
Nonadmitted asset, **14.4**
Novation, **1.9**
Nuclear incident exclusion clause, **4.14**

O

Occurrence definition for occupational disease coverage, 9.9
Occurrence definition for other losses coverage, 9.10
Occurrence definition for products and completed operations coverage, 9.7–9.9
Offset clause, **4.23**–4.24
Original conditions clause, **6.21**
Other reinsurance clause, **10.12**
Output controls, **12.7**
Outside reinsurance clause, **6.20**
Outside retentions and limits, 11.7–11.9

P

Paid losses, **15.4**
Payback period, **10.28**
Payback of prior losses, 10.28–10.29
Per occurrence excess of loss reinsurance, **2.16**
Per policy excess of loss reinsurance, **2.16**
Per risk excess of loss reinsurance, **2.13**
Percentage method, **15.14**
Policies issued basis, **4.7**
Policy documentation, 3.12
Policyholders' surplus, **1.6**
Pollution exclusion clause, **4.15**
Pools, associations, and syndicates exclusion clause, **8.13**–8.14
Portfolio reinsurance, **1.8**–1.9
Portfolio transfer clause, **6.19**
Preamble, **4.4**
Premiums earned, 14.11
Premiums written, 14.13
Pre-quote audit, **12.4**
Primary insurer, **1.3**

Primary insurer reserves, significance of for the reinsurer, 15.7–15.8
Prior acts coverage, **9.6**
Pritchard & Baird Case, 13.15–13.17
Pro rata reinsurance, **2.3**–2.9
Probable maximum loss (PML), **10.18**–10.19
Processing controls, **12.6**
Professional reinsurer, **1.13**
Profit-sharing commission, **2.4**, 6.28
Property per risk excess of loss treaties
   clauses designed or adapted for, 8.6–8.15
   functions of, 8.4–8.5
   as part of a reinsurance program, 8.5–8.6
Property per risk excess of loss treaty pricing, 8.16
Property residual market facility participation, 10.27
Proposal, 3.9, 3.13–3.18

Q

Quota share profit-sharing ceding commission determination, 6.24–6.28
Quota share reinsurance, **2.5**–2.7
Quota share treaties
   clauses designed or adapted for, 6.16–6.21
   common clauses modified for use in, 6.11–6.15
   functions of, 6.8–6.9
   as part of a reinsurance program, 6.9–6.11
Quota share treaty evaluation, 6.29–6.31
   current evaluation, 6.29–6.30
   historical evaluation, 6.30–6.31
Quota share treaty pricing, 6.22–6.24

R

Rate on line (ROL), **10.29**
Rates and forms, 13.5
Reinstatement clause, **9.12**–9.14, 10.12–10.15
Reinstatement premium, 9.14
Reinsurance, **1.3**
   regulatory concerns, 13.10–13.19
   types of, 2.4
Reinsurance agreement proposal, 3.5–3.7

Reinsurance Association of America (RAA), 1.16
Reinsurance audit, **12.3**
Reinsurance audit process, 12.4–12.8
Reinsurance audits
   overview of, 12.3–12.4
   types of, 12.8–12.15
Reinsurance binder, 3.12
Reinsurance departments of primary insurers, 1.14
Reinsurance functions, 1.4–1.9
Reinsurance intermediaries, credit-worthiness of, 13.15
Reinsurance intermediary, **1.13**
Reinsurance limit, 10.29–10.30
Reinsurance limit selection, factors affecting, 2.27–2.28
Reinsurance marketing system, selecting, 3.4–3.5
Reinsurance marketing systems, 3.3–3.4
Reinsurance needs, factors affecting, 2.21–2.25
Reinsurance placement illustrations, 3.8–3.19
Reinsurance placement process, 3.4–3.8
   complete agreement documentation, 3.7–3.8
   develop a reinsurance agreement proposal, 3.5–3.7
   select a reinsurance marketing system, 3.4–3.5
Reinsurance pools, syndicates, and associations, **1.14**,–1.15
Reinsurance premium, **1.3**
Reinsurance premium clause, **6.17**, 8.9–8.10
Reinsurance program, **2.21**
Reinsurance program design, 2.21–2.30
Reinsurance rate, 8.28–8.29
Reinsurance rate evaluation and selection, 9.29–9.31
Reinsurance sources, 1.13–1.15
Reinsurance transaction, credit for, 13.10–13.14
Reinsurance transactions, 1.9–1.12
Reinsurance-related assets, 14.7–14.8
Reinsurer, **1.3**
Reinsurers, creditworthiness of, 13.14–13.15
Reinsuring clause, **4.5**–4.8, 6.11–6.12, 7.11–7.13, 9.5–9.7
Reports and remittances clause, **5.10**–5.11, 6.13–6.15, 7.17–7.18
Reserves, breakdown of, 15.9
Reserves, methods for establishing, 15.8–15.23

Reserving, combined methods of, 15.20–15.23
Reserving methods, excess of loss reinsurers, 15.24–15.26
    difficulties when applying techniques, 15.26
    factors affecting, 15.24–15.26
Retention, **1.3**
Retention and limits clause, **6.16**, 7.20–7.21, 8.6–8.8, 9.11, 10.8–10.9, 11.6–11.11
Retention selection, factors affecting, 2.25–2.27
Retentions, setting, 8.16, 11.11–11.12
Retroactive date, **9.6**
Retrocedent, **1.4**
Retrocession, **1.4**
Retrocessionaire, **1.4**
Risk, 1.4
Risks attaching basis, **4.7**
Run-off basis, **5.4**

S

Salvage, **15.23**
Schedule F, **14.18**–14.31
Schedule P, **14.32**–14.35
Self-insured obligations clause, **5.15**–5.16
Service of suit clause, **4.10**–4.11
Several liability, **4.27**
Sliding scale commission, **2.4**
Sliding scale commission clause, **6.17**–6.18
Social inflation, 15.25
Special acceptance, **5.16**–5.17
Special termination clause, 5.9
State guaranty funds, **4.18**
Statement of income, 14.11
Statutory accounting principles (SAP), **13.7**

Subject premium, **2.11**, 10.26
Subrogation, **15.23**–15.24
Sudden death provision, 5.8
Sunrise clause, **9.17**–9.18
Sunset clause, **9.17**
Surplus liability clause, **7.18**–7.19
Surplus relief, 1.6–**1.8**, 6.9, 7.10
Surplus relief effect, 6.30
Surplus share reinsurance, **2.7**–2.9
Surplus share treaties
    clauses designed or adapted for, 7.18–7.22
    common clauses modified for use in, 7.11–7.18
    functions of, 7.8–7.10
    as part of a reinsurance program, 7.10–7.11
Surplus share treaty pricing, 7.22–7.27

T

Tabular method, **15.10**–15.11
Tail factors, 9.28
Term clause, **10.7**–10.8
Term contract, **5.4**
Territory clause, **5.14**
Terrorism exclusion clause, **4.16**–4.18
Three-part combination method, 15.22–15.23
Total insured value exclusion clause, **8.15**
Trade associations, 1.15–1.16
Transactional audit, **12.8**, 12.11–12.14
Treaty confirmation letter and confirmation signing page, 3.31–3.32
Treaty documentation, 3.19
Treaty reinsurance, **1.9**–1.10, 3.13–3.19
Two-part combination method, 15.20–15.21

U

Ultimate loss, **15.5**
Ultimate loss development factor, **15.18**
Ultimate net loss clause, **8.11**–8.12, 10.9–10.10
Unallocated loss adjustment expenses (ULAE), **15.4**
Unauthorized reinsurance clause, **4.25**–4.26
Unauthorized reinsurer, **13.4**
Underlying insurance analysis, 10.25–10.27
Underwriting audit, **12.8**–12.11
Underwriting guidance, 1.9, 6.9
Underwriting and Investment Exhibit, 14.10–14.18
Underwriting profit margin, 6.31
Underwriting record, 3.24–3.25
Underwriting risk, **2.23**
Unearned premium reserve, **13.11**
Unpaid losses and loss adjustment expenses, 14.18
Upper layers pricing, 9.31

V

Variable quota share treaty, **2.7**

W

War risk exclusion clause, **4.16**
Warranties clause, **6.21**
Withdrawal, facilitating from a market segment, 1.8–1.9, 6.9
Working cover, **2.11**